Defenders of the Faith

Defenders

o f   t h e

Faith

Inside Ultra-Orthodox Jewry

With a New Afterword

SAMUEL HEILMAN

University of California Press
Berkeley · Los Angeles · London

University of California Press
Berkeley and Los Angeles, California

University of California Press, Ltd.
London, England

First California Paperback Printing, 2000

First published 1992 by Schocken Books, Inc., New York.

The two poems on pages 68 and 69 are reprinted by permission of
Ha-Machaneh Ha-Haredi.

The photographs that appear between pages 202 and 203 are by
the author unless otherwise indicated in the captions.

Library of Congress Cataloging-in-Publication Data
Heilman, Samuel C.
Defenders of the faith : inside ultra-Orthodox Jewry /
Samuel Heilman.
p.   cm.
"First California printing"—T.p. verso.
Originally published: New York, Schocken Books, 1992.
"With a new afterword."
Includes bibliographical references and index.
ISBN 0-520-22112-5 (alk. paper)
1. Orthodox Judaism—Jerusalem.   2. Hasidism—Jerusalem.
3. Jews—Jerusalem—Social life and customs.   I. Title.
BM392.J4H43   2000
296.8'32'09049—dc21   99-35112
                                        CIP

Printed in the United States of America

08   07   06   05   04   03   02   01   00   99
    10   9   8   7   6   5   4   3   2   1

The paper used in this publication meets the minimum requirements of
ANSI/NISO Z39.48-1992. (R 1997) (Permanence of Paper). ∞

In memory of my teacher,
Erving Goffman,
who taught me how to observe.

Contents

(Illustrations between pages 202–203)

Acknowledgments

A s always, with this book as with all my others, there are many people who have been helpful to me in the effort. First, there are the people who let me observe them and whose lives and ideas form the heart of my work. While some were suspicious of me and others looked upon me as the incarnation of all they considered wrong about contemporary civilization—being a "professor" is not an honorable station in many of these circles—for the most part, people were wonderfully open, and that of course is part of my story. Wherever possible, I have tried to protect their privacy. In many cases I use pseudonyms, always indicating where this is the case. Where certain details might nevertheless allow those who wanted anonymity to be identified—if only by other insiders—I have tried to alter those details without undermining accuracy. I especially thank Avraham Schvartz for his help in understanding the world of the Reb Arelach.

I also want to thank the Hebrew University, and especially the Department of Sociology and Social Anthropology, where I was serving as Scheinbrun Visiting Professor, the Melton Centre for Jewish Education, and the Jerusalem Fellows Program, where I also served as a visitor. Without these three addresses and the help of many of the people at them, I could never have spent the time I needed in Jerusalem.

Next come my first readers. A number of people read various parts of the manuscript and offered comments and guidance. Among them were Menachem Friedman, Adam Heilman, Henry Heilman, Barry Holtz, Moshe Kahan, Philip Rieff, Michael Rosenak, Charles Selengut, Moshe Shokeid, Eliezer Witztum, and the students in a course I offered at the Hebrew University on the topic "Ethnography and Jewish Education." I owe thanks to Rabbi Reuven Fink for helping with many Jewish bibliographic references. I thank my editor, Bonny Fetterman, for her patience and encouragement. My most important first reader, and constant inspiration, is my wife Ellin. Without her, I would have long ago stopped even trying to write.

Finally, as Augustine wrote at the close of *The City of God*, speaking for everyone who ever wrote a book that was on too large a topic, "Let those who think I have said too little, or those who think I have said too much, forgive me; and let those who think I have said just enough join me in giving thanks to God."

Prologue

In the contemporary world of living color, its complexion a blur of activity moving relentlessly forward, our eyes occasionally pick out a sight that seems to be held still in the black and white of yesterday. And though we are part of the moving mass of the present, this vision of the past manages to hold us in its grasp. For no matter how compelling the present may seem, how swift its currents, the spectacle of the past retains a curious charm. Perhaps that is what strikes so many of us when in the midst of the modern city, we encounter earlocked and bearded Jews dressed in black and white, and apparently framed in tradition, relics of another time. How can they still be here, we wonder? And what does their presence tell us about where we are going?

A number of years ago a freshly minted graduate student came to my office with a question that emerged out of such an experience. Coming very recently from Omaha, Nebraska, he was new to New York and, while exploring the countryside upstate, had found himself in Rockland County, about an hour's drive north of the city. Taking a right turn instead of a left off the interstate, he had suddenly stumbled into what looked to him like a scene out of the past. Everywhere there were men in caftans and black hats, their faces framed by untrimmed beards, little children with curly locks of hair around their ears and closely shaved heads under velvet skullcaps, people speaking Yiddish. Who were these people, he wondered? Had he wandered into a *shtetl* like those he'd read about in Mark Zborowski and Elizabeth Herzog's account of Jewish life in a past generation, *Life Is with People?* "Have I stumbled into yesterday?" he asked incredulously, and would a study of this group provide him with a living model of how life was lived generations ago in the Jewish communities of eastern Europe? Where did these people come from, he wanted to know, and how had they managed to stave off the changes and modernization that all other Jews seemed to have experienced? I cannot now remember exactly what I told him then; the query turned out to be moot, for he subsequently went on to study other things. Yet the question he raised is at the center of my concern here. Who are these people who appear to belong more to yesterday than to today, and why are they still around?

My graduate student was not the first to ask me this question. I had asked it of myself as well. In 1968, just after I had been graduated from college, I took my first trip to Jerusalem. It was a revelation. Face to face with what appeared to be countless layers of the Jewish past, I literally ran from place to place, looking, photographing, and trying to absorb as much as I could. Perhaps nothing fascinated me more than the people I encountered in Mea Shearim, one of the oldest Jewish neighborhoods outside the Old City's walls. Here, I thought, in a series of narrow alleys teeming with people in black and white, bearded men in caftans, children with earlocks, and women in long dresses, black kerchiefs and stockings, was the old ghetto, the living incarnation of the past, where people still held fast to every tradition and where nothing of substance from the outside contemporary world could penetrate.

As it happened, my parents were also visiting Israel at the time and we arranged to meet in Jerusalem. Although we had been living in Brookline, a suburb of Boston, for eighteen years, my parents still very much remembered Jewish life in the Poland of their birth, a memory shrouded in nostalgia by their Holocaust experience, which had cruelly destroyed that world and torn them from it. Confirming my perceptions, my mother told me that her parents, whom I had never seen, lived in a place like this and looked like these people in Mea Shearim.

This was not the first time I heard about my forebears. Throughout my youth my head had been filled with shared memories, built of stories my mother told me about her family and the destroyed world

of her European Jewish past. Permeated with scenes of deeply pious
Jews, enfolded in ritual and wrapped in tradition, the tales were of
rabbis who effected miracle cures, and they were accompanied by
melodies that evoked bittersweet recollections of the twilight hours of
a bygone Sabbath or Passover seder, and descriptions of rich religious
customs. Although shrouded in idealization, this paradise lost, depicted as perfect in its faith and constant in its attachment to Jewish
heritage, seemed real enough to my imagination.

For years I nourished a desire—a compulsion, psychoanalysts
might suggest—somehow to witness this past and to experience the
world destroyed before my birth but from which I knew I came. But
Brookline was not Brooklyn. Although we lived as Orthodox Jews—
the modern kind that accommodated to American lifestyles and cultural patterns—the Jews around us looked and acted very American.
Now, in Jerusalem, my mother told me, was my chance to see at last
all she had been telling me about. My father, always guided by reason,
nodded his agreement. This did indeed remind him of Jewish Poland
as he remembered it. Somehow, I was led to believe, the past had been
miraculously preserved here where the Nazis had not reached.

With zeal my mother began to search for incarnations of her past.
I followed her. At last she found an elderly man, his gray-bearded
visage the face of faith, with whom she made a connection. He was, he
told her, urged on by midnight visions and inspired dreams, to make
it his sacred duty to collect alms for the poor. Would he, she asked,
after giving him a large enough donation to gain his undivided attention, be willing to host her son for a Sabbath so that he would have an
opportunity to see a way of life like the one she had lived before the
Holocaust? The man agreed, and I was soon on my way to his tiny
apartment in the "Hungarian Houses," a neighborhood within Mea
Shearim that my mother swore looked like the one she had grown up
in, where I would spend the Sabbath with him and his wife.

It was an extraordinary twenty-five hours. I seemed to move into
the stories my mother told me. After a rush to the ritual bath for a
quick dip in its purifying (although not terribly clear) waters before
Sabbath, I went to the evening prayers in a small one-room synagogue.
Then there was a traditional dinner, a look out onto the street closed
to car traffic on which I saw a parade of people looking like pictures of
the past, and a visit from my hosts' children and grandchildren. Each
young boy was asked in Yiddish to recite aloud what he had learned
about the passage that would be read from the Torah scroll—just as
my mother had told me her father used to review these same texts with
my young uncles. And then at the crack of dawn my host took me to

morning prayers in a synagogue where in my plain white shirt I stood out like a dove among penguins. Afterward there was study, singing and eating at the Sabbath table, a nap, a final visit to the synagogue, and at last the Sabbath was over and I was once again back on the street and part of the twentieth century. But the memory of that day remained with me.

Over the years since that day I came to realize that much in the tales my mother told me was a mixture of fact and fiction. No culture was quite as static or insulated as the one her memories protected. The Jewish world of Poland had been far more variegated than was implied in the haze of my mother's remembrance. Jewry in Poland had already begun to change and traditions to disintegrate long before the ravages of the Holocaust shredded what was left. Even among its most Orthodox practitioners the impact of modernization, mass migration, urbanization, and social change had been felt. The walls of the Jewish ghettos were fast crumbling and contemporary Europe was rushing in, sweeping old customs and folkways out. Jews were streaming toward a new life. Acculturation and its more extreme form, assimilation into the larger, dominant host cultures, was the rule and Orthodox reactions against religious reform and acculturation were rather the exception.[1] Nevertheless, the belief that the ultra-Orthodox were untouched relics of the past remained with me.

More than twenty years have passed since that Sabbath in Mea Shearim. The boy of that time turned into a university professor of social anthropology. Nevertheless, I still had the questions, which my graduate student once again aroused. In a world rushing headlong into tomorrow, why are there people who appear to cling tenaciously to yesterday? Is it really yesterday in which they live? Can a fortress of timeless tradition stand inviolate and unimpaired through the barrage of today's demands? Or is it an illusion to believe in today's shrinking world that one culture can remain untouched by another on its doorstep? If not in Brooklyn or Rockland County, New York, so close to the nerve centers of western modernity, then in Mea Shearim in Jerusalem, has time stood still? For twenty years I've had no satisfactory answers to these questions—until now.

That answer would come via my role as anthropologist and ethnographer. Ethnography is a tool for coherently describing culture, a way to allow readers to share in the anthropological experience, to put what has been seen into a meaningful context. If anthropologists and ethnographers succeed in their enterprise, if they give their readers a view of a world that would otherwise remain opaque or altogether invisible and convince them that had they been the ethnographers they "should have seen what they saw, felt what they felt, concluded what they concluded," they succeed not only in conquering the ephemerality of these experiences but also tacitly contribute to the preservation of a culture.[2]

My anthropological approach—suited both to my personal needs and my disciplinary strengths—has always been participant observation, learning by watching and feeling while doing. I would leave my own world and enter into the one peopled by the ultra-Orthodox. Since it was in Jerusalem that I imagined that I had glimpsed those most insulated from contemporary civilization and attached to the past— the ones I saw in New York somehow seemed too close simply to being another ethnic group in the city, savvy and up-to-date—it was to Jerusalem I would go in search of answers.

At one time I might simply have continued here by telling readers that since 1968 I have returned to Israel many times. I would have added that I have for many years lived among and studied contemporary Orthodox Jews, out of which have come a number of books and articles. And I would have closed by reporting that over those years I developed many contacts in Israel among this group, that I gained fluency in Hebrew and Yiddish, and for the last year and a half in Israel and the United States engaged in intensive observation of those commonly called the ultra-Orthodox, work that resulted in the account that follows. These days, however, such introductions are considered insufficient.[3]

Participant observation demands a delicate balance of subjectivity and objectivity. The era when the ethnographer was allowed to remain invisible, standing somewhere beyond the margins of the text, is over. As is now recognized, those whose observation is, like mine, mixed with actual participation in the culture observed are deeply implicated in the world they describe. They are not neutral instruments whose preconceptions and approach to their work can be ignored. One cannot separate the observer from the observations. Even though he restrains himself by "objectivity," his personal experiences, participation, and empathy are crucial to what he sees.[4]

Where once the great risk was that the observer might get too close to his material, the issue now is not "one of going native, but of understanding the native in oneself."[5] And so because we realize now that there are no free-floating descriptions of reality and that the agent of observation and description must himself be understood, I need to add one more bit of information about myself before I begin my account.

My interest in these Jews was, as I reflect upon it now, affected not only by my search for roots and my experiences in Jerusalem. It was also influenced by the fact that I had been raised and still am an Orthodox Jew. But mine was not the traditionalism associated with these people I wished to examine as an anthropologist. My own version of Orthodoxy was a more modern one, a way of living that allowed for a fidelity to the standards and practices of Orthodox Judaism without a remoteness from the contemporary world. This modern Orthodoxy looked with ambivalence at the people I was proposing to study. While respecting their attachments to observance and Jewish tradition, modern Orthodox Jews also disdained their traditionalist counterparts' public rejection of contemporary culture. "Orthodox Judaism is not to be identified with ghetto conditions," wrote Rabbi Leo Jung, echoing a common sentiment in the community in which I grew up.[6] For moderns like me, secular culture and contemporary civilization had a great deal to offer and need not be scorned and rejected. Coming out of that background surely must have played a role in my observations. So my nostalgia framed the ultra-Orthodox in the rosy light of the past while the patterns of my life saw them as hopelessly anachronistic. This certainly colors everything I have written, no matter how disciplined I have tried to be in both my observations and writing.

Thus, while I aim to focus most of my attention on the people with whom I spent time, who talked to me and shared their lives and opinions with me, I am not so naive as to believe that my account is "a neutral, tropeless discourse that would render realities 'exactly as they are,' not filtered through [my] own values and interpretive schema."[7] Nor do I believe that I can remain invisible in this account. In most such accounts, whether explicitly or implicitly, "the ethnographer, a character in a fiction, is at center stage."[8] If I seem too often to insert myself, my impressions, or my person into the account of the other people's lives, it is because I admit that "all ethnography," as Clifford Geertz argues, "is part philosophy, and a good deal of the rest is confession."[9]

What was I looking for? Most simply, I was looking for the Jew who remained part of the past but who could be found in the present. If I found him or her, I could, I believed, also find answers to my other questions of how this was possible and what it entailed. But of course the fundamental question was whether or not such people actually existed. As I have already indicated, I quickly gave up the idea that the Jews I had seen in America were the genuine article. While their Orthodoxy and observance were not in question, they seemed too much a part of the modern city to make me think they were part of a perfectly sealed community and an unchanged past. There were lots of gates into and out of their ghettos. They knew very well how to take full advantage of contemporary life: they were successful entrepreneurs, from the diamond trade to the electronics industry; they dealt easily with people of all stripes, far beyond the boundaries of their own neighborhoods; they played active roles in local, state, and national ethnic politics; they had made it in America. They were even the subjects of a *New Yorker* profile. How could I take them as embodiments of a wholly other world? Looks were deceiving. These people were moderns who only looked like "ancients." To find the real thing, if it existed at all, one had to reach deeper: I went back to Jerusalem to where I thought I had glimpsed it twenty years earlier.

In Claude Lévi-Strauss's landmark book on tribal life in Brazil, *Tristes Tropiques,* he describes his long search for the true primitives whom he hoped to discover upriver in the jungle and whose lives he intended to document, understand, and thus preserve in some way. His sort of anthropologist-as-seeker approach seemed to me the ideal model for what I wanted to do in Jerusalem. Many of the city's ultra-Orthodox were for me, no less than the Brazilian natives were for Lévi-Strauss, a departure from the familiar, inhabitants of another world. This was a world filled with miracle rabbis, sectarian groups, committees for purity, students of obscure texts, secrets, and an animosity to the way of life I represented. In places like Mea Shearim, where the signs and the attitudes of many locals made it clear outsiders were not welcomed, I expected to find the absolute other, sequestered and opaque, whom modern, secular culture had somehow left untouched. So what Lévi-Strauss tried to do in the jungles of Brazil, I decided to do in the streets, alleys, and neighborhoods of the Jerusalem ultra-Orthodox— *haredim,* as they are called today in Israel.

"The search for the primitive is," wrote Stanley Diamond, one of my first anthropology professors, "as old as civilization. It is the search for the utopia of the past. . . ." [10] For me the search for the haredim began indeed as a search for the utopia of the past in which my grandparents lived. But at another level this was an exploration of civilization: I was trying specifically to discover to what extent the ultra-Orthodox were in fact "Jewish primitives," people who had successfully insulated themselves from the trends and realities of contemporary culture. Like Lévi-Strauss, I would go as far into the unknown as I could to find the extremes.

I did not go simply in search of "experiences." The yeshivas of Jerusalem and its holy places are filled with such adventurers and seekers. Rather, I was on a research adventure whose aim was to understand, document, explain, and thereby preserve what, if I found it, was surely the last vestige of the Jewish past. Lévi-Strauss had hoped in his account to take himself and his readers to remote places of the past that would otherwise remain beyond reach of the present. So do I.

Lévi-Strauss's trip into the jungle offered not only a paradigm for my quest; it also offered the warning of what might await me once I found "the absolute other." The deeper into the jungle Lévi-Strauss went, and the more he deciphered the character and life of the people with whom he came into contact, the more he discovered how much of that primitive world had already been touched and transformed by the modern one from which he came. He found "shreds of Voltaire and Anatole France which impregnated the national culture even in the depths of the bush." [11] Instead of the civilizations radically different from his own that he expected to find, he came upon "impoverished imitations of his own." In the tropics, which were "not so much exotic as out of date," he found "former savages." [12] Was this end awaiting me as well—to penetrate at last the most insular precincts of the ultra-Orthodox world only to find people already absorbed by the situation of modernity, like those I saw in America?

I have always agreed with the proposition that in anthropology, understanding a life pattern different from one's own "is more like grasping a proverb, catching an allusion, seeing a joke," or even "reading a poem" than it is like doing systematic science. [13] That is why I have used an approach that Lévi-Strauss, in his exploration of "the science of the concrete," calls "intellectual bricolage." Although once thought to be the tool of the savage or primitive mind, bricolage turns out to be a most effective way of allowing a member of one culture to encounter another. In this technique one makes sense of reality— which is often inconsistent and constantly changing, and not nearly as ordered as sociologists and anthropologists would have us believe—by improvising ideas, making "do with 'whatever is at hand,' " moving freely from one insight to another as the need arises. [14] Hovering between perception and conception, the intellectual bricoleur is not trapped inside a formal system of thought or a single conceptual category that binds him when he encounters something that does not fit neatly into that framework. He may begin with concepts, but as a bricoleur he must be prepared to bounce away from them, to be intellectually opportunistic in the best sense of the term. As long as an explanation works, he uses it. Like the whittler who finds that whatever he may have set out to carve he must also be ready to improvise according to the real characteristics of the wood in his hand, the intellectual bricoleur must also be prepared to see not only what he sets out to discover but what the people he watches show him.

For those who yearn for final explanatory frameworks and who cannot tolerate inconsistency or provisionalism, bricolage may be unsatisfactory. But bricolage allows the observer to be more of a participant than he could be were he to be rigorously scientific—to be at times more like an insider than like a stranger. As a bricoleur, I sometimes allowed myself to be caught up in the experience of a pilgrimage, a wedding, or a funeral even as I at other times remained distant and objective. Of course, bricoleurs can get carried away; distortions do occur. And it was the ethnographer in me who wanted to describe things as realistically as possible that acted to counterbalance the bricoleur.

What of the people I describe, would they not be the best judges of the accuracy of my interpretations? Perhaps. To some extent I have indeed tried out my understandings on them. But I do not make those I observe the final arbiters of meaning in interpreting their actions and ceremonies. As Emile Durkheim responded to the challenge of the authority of interpretation: "Which of us knows all the words of the language he speaks and the entire signification of each?"[15] The participant observer can sometimes know more than the pure participant.

People were tremendously open to me, accepting my presence, my probing questions, and my involvement. They knew I was not coming to convert or to be converted. I got as close as I could; but except for one fleeting moment during a pilgrimage, about which I write in the pages ahead, I never really felt like the people I observed. I did not "go native." But that turned out to be helpful at times, as I demonstrate in my discussion of their sex lives. Like William F. Whyte in his now classic study of the Italian working class, *Street Corner Society*, I found that "people did not expect me to be just like them; in fact, they were interested and pleased to find me different, just so long as I took a friendly interest in them."[16] Not that there were no problems. After months in their schools, from kindergarten to the yeshiva, I was asked to leave because the principal believed my presence was beginning to affect his students. Just as their absolute otherness was evaporating under my observations of them, so was mine under their mutual observations of me. In the closed atmosphere of the world I was observing, the head of the school saw that as dangerous. To be fair, no one else in the school felt this way. And after I had spent time talking about sex and the intimate details of married life, a broadside was posted by the "Modesty Patrol" on the walls of Mea Shearim warning people that there were "strangers in the vicinity asking disgusting and improper questions," and if such a person should approach them they were to walk away immediately or if called, "hang up the phone." I was not mentioned by name, and it's possible there were others to whom the poster referred, but in any event, I stopped my inquiries—though by then I had gathered enough information on the subject for my purposes.

What I discovered turned out to be very different from the impressionistic scenes of twenty years ago or what was embedded in me as a Jewish son and grandson. I did not find the incarnation of my imagination. But perhaps that is the price one pays for being (and choosing to remain) an anthropolgist and an outsider. I have given up looking for living incarnations of the past; I no longer expect to find my grandparents.

A word or two about organization. While bricolage is my technique and ethnography my aim, this does not mean I have altogether given up conceptual frameworks. There is an organization to all of this. This is the way my account of life among the ultra-Orthodox, the *haredim*, is ordered: Following a first quick dip into the haredi world, I offer some social history and definitions to allow the reader, particularly one new to the subject of Orthodox Jewry, to know where these people came from and who they are. Then the book is divided into three general motifs: community, education, and passages. First comes the community, with a particular focus on the Belz hasidim, as a case in point. I follow them to their celebrations and gatherings to find out what is important to them and how they bond together. Their creed is then expressed through the words of one of their popular writers and spokesmen. He tells who they are, while street celebrations on the holiday of Purim demonstrate who they are not. The next two chapters offer an opportunity to pierce the inner circles of haredi community life. The first takes the reader on a religious pilgrimage and the second brings him around the table of a small and extraordinarily insular sect of hasidim, the Reb Arelach, at the mystical third meal of the Sabbath.

In the section on education, the purpose is to show how these people are molded and made, how they transmit their culture and values from generation to generation. These chapters offer a chance to sit in on classes, hear stories, and get a talking to by the rabbis, scholars, and guides who transmit that culture. The idea is to put the reader next to me as I went to school.

In its last third, the book offers a panorama of passages: matchmaking, betrothal, wedding, and death. The aim here is to tell what haredim are by watching how they handle the transitions in their lives.

These benchmarks of life are chances to get an idea of the essentials of haredi identity. We look at the public face of haredim through their ubiquitous wall posters. Then, finally, we get a glimpse of the most private of faces, the sex life and the intimacies of the bedroom. All this leads to my conclusions, which come in the framework of a visit to a scribe.

Throughout, I have tried to trace a journey from the outer fringes of the world of the ultra-Orthodox, to its furthest extremes. Always my compass has been set by the quest for the essential elements of who these people are and what makes them so. In this quest, I have tried wherever possible to look first for simple explanations, those based on what Marvin Harris has called, "ordinary, banal . . . needs and activities." [17] For me simple answers always seem to be the best ones; they assume a certain basic logic to human activity, an assumption that is at the base of the dual disciplines of sociology and anthropology that inform my vision. And yet, as intellectual bricoleur and participant observer, I have also remained open to the spiritual, mystical, and complex, the explanations that the people themselves sometimes offer for their way of life. Finally, I come not to judge these people or to praise them. I come only in search of understanding.

Some have argued that anthropologists are always coming in to a culture in progress, trying to catch up with a story already being lived and therefore never seeing the whole picture. I do not deny this possibility—that I have seen only a piece of the large picture. Accepting the limitations of my discipline, recognizing the drawbacks of my methods, admitting the prejudices ingrained in me, and agreeing that a short stay cannot equal a lifetime of an experience, I nevertheless offer my interpretation of a culture. To those who ask if all I say is the truth, I can only reply in words that echo what the Cree hunter, brought to court to testify under oath about the Indian way of life, replied to the ancient question about telling the whole truth and nothing but the truth: "I'm not sure I can tell the truth. . . . I can only tell what I know"—and what I learned. [18]

Defenders of the Faith

1

Mikveh:
Taking the Plunge

On the afternoon before Yom Kippur, the holiest day of the Jewish year, the door to the *mikveh*, the ritual bath in this Jerusalem neighborhood, was wide open. Someone had jammed a doorstop under the door to keep it from swinging back and forth as dozens of bearded men and earlocked boys dashed inside to immerse and purify themselves in preparation for their atonement. Only a few weeks earlier, I had come back to Jerusalem to take up the task of learning about the ultra-Orthodox Jews who were now lining up for a dip. Somehow this place where they stripped off all their outer clothing and got down to the bare essentials felt like the right place for me to start. To follow them I would have to plunge in to their world. Although I had been to a mikveh before, the places I went to were more like health clubs than what I imagined a mikveh in this neighborhood might be. I hesitated at the door.

Any collection of water is suitable for a mikveh, according to Jewish law, as long as it contains enough volume for a person to immerse himself completely. The rabbis, keepers of the revered oral tradition, however, stipulated that according to the law, only water which has not already been drawn—that is, has not been in a vessel or other receptacle—may be used. And thus rain—"living waters," the rabbis call it—often collected through a complex system of pipes, makes a pool into a mikveh. As for size, the rabbis further established that the minimum quantity for immersion is what may be contained in the space of a square cubit to the height of three cubits—somewhere between 60 and 250 gallons, according to various students who later immersed themselves in more exact calculations. After such a minimum of "living waters" are gathered, additional drawn waters may be added. And thus one set of living waters may give life to others, expanding almost limitlessly the number of mikvehs that may be constructed in the precincts of tradition.

"Go in," a voice behind me said. "I guarantee it's clean." A short man, almost as round as he was tall, stood there, a satchel in his hand, a round, wide-brimmed black hat on his head and a threadbare caftan wrapped tightly about his waist. The points of his curled-up shirt collar looked as if they were connected to his wiry white beard. I was not sure that what he would call "clean" exactly matched my own definition of the term. By Jewish law the waters of the mikveh had to be "natural"; no chemicals, no artificial disinfectants. Still, he obviously knew what people who looked like me cared about when we went into a mikveh—so maybe it really was clean.

"*Nu?*" he urged me forward. "What are you waiting for?" He was in a hurry to get going, to have time to sit down to the last meal before the onset of the great fast day which would begin in just a few hours at sunset. If I were going to take the plunge, now was the time.

"You need a towel? Here, take one of mine. You can get soap at the door." His attitude completely disarmed me; if people were going to be this open to me, I was going to go ahead no matter what the water looked like.

I wanted to ask him if I would be stared out of the place, with my clean-shaven face and contemporary clothing. I wanted to ask him whether my presence would contaminate everyone there, or at least if I was likely to feel that way. But instead I smiled, took the towel, thanked him, and followed him down the narrow stairs inside. He moved ahead of me without another word.

At the next level down, in front of the door to the actual baths, some young boys sat at a table covered with receipt books. They were collecting for a variety of Jewish charitable institutions and had chosen this location as an auspicious one for their efforts. Behind them was a poster with an image of the Western Wall, this last remaining relic of the Holy Temple, and across it emblazoned in large black letters was God's biblical injunction to those who came up to the Sanctuary: "Thou shalt not appear before me empty-handed." A Jew on the way to the mikveh and carrying out one commandment would, these boys apparently reasoned, certainly be inclined to couple it with another for good measure. From the looks of the receipt books, their decision had been a good one. I handed them a few bills. Carefully, they wrote out my name and address on the stub of the receipt book. Although I did not realize it, my name now was being added to a master list, and in the days to come someone would appear at my door asking for more money for some other worthy institution of Jewish learning or maybe for money for an impoverished bride and groom who needed support to start their new family.

I descended another narrow flight of stairs, past a small group of men who stood reading some notices on the bulletin board. One of them pointed at a particular poster and the others laughed. I read it too, but I did not get the joke. You had to be an insider, I suppose, to understand it. The mikveh was obviously more than a bathhouse; it was also a place to gather information about local matters.

"How many?" asked a young boy who sat behind the cash register on the lowest landing. His chin barely made it up to the drawer of the register, and his blond earlocks brushed the tabletop. He could not have been older than eight.

"One."

"Four shekels," he said. That's about two dollars at the current exchange rate.

"Soap?" I said, taking a little hotel-size bar from the box on the table.

"Another half shekel."

I handed him a five-shekel coin, and he gave me change along with a receipt. Maybe it was true, as I had heard, that the schools in these neighborhoods only grudgingly gave time to nonreligious studies, but when it came to arithmetic, this youngster knew all the numbers he needed.

Near him, taking a break from running the cash register and apparently immersed in the study of the tractate of Talmud dealing with the laws of the day, sat another, older boy. He swayed back and forth as he hummed the words of the book in the characteristic singsong of yeshiva learning.

Coming from around the corner, I heard loud cries of what sounded like children at play. There was something frenzied about the laughter that startled me, and, having second thoughts about continuing inside, I slowed my pace just a bit. But behind me there were already three other men coming down the narrow stairs; and the man whose towel I now held had already gone inside. I kept going.

Once inside, I found myself in a steamy maze of rooms around what must have been half a dozen small cloudy blue pools, inside of which were ghostly white bodies, bobbing up and down. "The sign of a scholar," I once read, "is the whiteness of his hands, the softness of his skin. For he spends his days not outdoors in the sun but inside over the pages of the sacred scriptures, his fingers tracing a line down the columns of holy words."

Here, in the mikveh, where men wander about without their clothes, a new perspective on the body of Orthodoxy is to be gained. The distinctions among the members of different groups visually disappear. Gone are the high socks and knickers of the followers of the rebbe of Ger or the golden coats of the Bratslaver hasidim. The neat frock coats of the head of a yeshiva and the baggy trousers of a fundraiser are put on a hook. Instead, the place is filled with young bodies and old ones, tall and short, fat and thin, dark and light skins, redheads, brunets, and graybeards. A man, towel and soap in hand, sprints on tiptoes to the shower, to cleanse himself of even the smallest speck of dirt that would separate him from the purifying waters of the mikveh. He moves as if he does not want to defile himself by stepping in the wrong place; his long brown earlocks wave wildly as he skirts along the skids on the floor. There is also the hint of embarrassment, of being seen in one's nakedness in public; out of the shower the man rushes to slide under the cover of the cloudy and lukewarm waters of the mikveh.

Indeed, between the moment of nakedness and the immersion, there seems to be only rushing. Behind him, two boys, about ten or eleven years old, likewise rush toward the water to join three or four of their friends who instead of dipping three or at most seven times and leaving like the older men, are splashing and playing in the bath. Unlike most of the adults, they do not bother showering beforehand. But just as they are about to step down into the water, a voice calls them: "Anschel, Meyer'l."

An older man motions them back with a curled finger and then points toward the shower. "Quickly, quickly," he tells them.

"But, Tateh, we're clean enough."

"Take the soap." The father ignores their protests and sees to it that they are covered with suds before he lets them rinse off and enter the mikveh. This father may look very different from me, as do his sons from mine, but there is something very familiar about this interchange, a familiarity that makes me feel suddenly that learning about these people may not really demand a journey to altogether foreign provinces.

And what do the people, supposedly steeped in religion, who are about to purify themselves for the great and awesome day talk about as they prepare themselves for their immersion? Is this a time of soul-searching too? Does the fear of Heaven enter them as they prepare themselves for the Day of Atonement?

"*Nu*, Yankel, did you hear that the revenue men came into Itsche Meyer's shop to check his tax receipts, but he ran out through the back door and hid in the yeshiva until finally they gave up waiting for him."

"Again?"

"He was white with fear when he came out."

"They killed his brother with nuisance audits; he got a heart attack from worry. If I would be him, I would be afraid too."

"Thank God, he's alright now. They never go into the yeshiva. But look, they hate us; they'll always try to get us."

I hung my clothes on an empty hook and waited for an empty shower, my towel wrapped around me to hide my nakedness, as the others did. My turn came at last. I moved quickly. This was no place for long ablutions. Rinsing off my suds, I made my way toward one of the pools. No one seemed to look at me. My fears of being stared at were unfounded. They let me inside, but then they erased my presence with inattention. It was as if I did not exist. Only community insiders got attention; in this place I was nobody.

And why? Looking around me, I discerned that for them to see me was also to admit that I, the outsider, saw them, exposed in all their nakedness. To the members of this insular community that was inconceivable. But for an observer like me, this kind of invisibility could be a blessing. To see without being seen, to be inside without losing my outsider status, was precisely what I hoped I could do.

Not all the pools were equally popular. None was especially inviting. Of the two side-by-side baths in the alcove closest to me, one was filled with young boys splashing about and the other looked empty. I turned toward the empty one. As I stepped down the slippery tile stairs, the crew-cut head of a man suddenly rose up out of the blue, and then his eyes, milky white forehead, dripping black beard, and pale chest. Step-by-step, without a word or even a nod toward me, he walked up and out of the water. Those going in took care not to walk on the same side as those going out for the entering are impure while the exiting are, according to the ritual, reborn in purity. I was still among the impure.

Only the children at play seemed to break this strict protocol. But they made up for that with their enthusiasm. Their voices injected life into this place. Their faces shone with excitement.

I dipped down three times and, like the others around me, spread my fingers and toes to let the water flow to every part of my body. And as I came up for the third time, I found myself at last being stared at. A man who looked to be in his seventies stood at the top of the few steps and squinted down at me. His puzzled expression said everything: I was taking too much time and space. The locals do their dip faster and with apparently less self-consciousness. The mark of an outsider is always that self-consciousness, the effort to be overly punctilious. Suddenly, aware of my nakedness, I walked quickly up the stairs and toward my towel. Finding my clothes, I began to dress quickly.

From a hook on the wall, the man who passed by me took his pink towel and glided back along the wooden skids to where his clothes hung. Layer by layer, as he dressed himself, he took on more of that identity which was framed by his clothes. First came the large *gatges*—baggy, loose-hanging, yellowish-white underpants that reached down to the knees. Like the rest of his garments, these appeared to be relics of another century in eastern Europe. His undershirt was a perfect match, loose and held together with white buttons. On his cropped hair, so quickly dried, he placed a white crocheted skullcap with a peaked tassel top. Next came the white but rather rumpled shirt, his black baggy trousers and at last a black striped *arba kanfos*, the four-cornered tunic on which the *tzitzit*, ritual fringes, are knotted. The fringes are there to remind him of his religious obligations, the black stripe on the tunic a sign that he still mourns for the destroyed Holy Temple and awaits a messianic redemption in the days ahead.

Around me a few men put on special white caftans for Yom Kippur, but most got back into their black ones; for them there were still things to be done before the final preparations for atonement. How different was it when the high priest bathed and dressed, as the Talmud recounts, in his special garments of the day? Pasts become superimposed upon the present here and one cannot think about now without being caught up in then.

Standing in my underwear, I searched in my pants' pocket for my knitted skullcap. Finding it, I slipped it on and then took my tzitzit, and with an audible recitation of the blessing that one said when donning these fringes, I put them on.

"Only in the morning," said the man next to me.

"Pardon me?"

"No need to say another blessing on your arba kanfos now, if you said one this morning," he explained.

My religious display had backfired. Rather than marking me as an insider, one at home in the world of Jewish ritual and tradition, it revealed my ignorance. Clearly, there was much for me to learn if I wanted to find out about these people. Still, I was not altogether an outsider, as they could see. Maybe that was why I had been corrected.

Briskly, I slipped on the rest of my clothes and moved up the stairs in the flow of men and boys leaving the bathhouse. Outside, the street seemed far quieter now. Sundown was coming. The man whose towel I had taken was standing at the door. "Leave the towel in the basket," he said. "It belongs to the mikveh."

I thanked him.

"Gmar hasima tovah," he said, offering the traditional wish that I might be inscribed in the Book of Life for the new year. And then he was gone, walking through one of the many gateways that led off to a courtyard and another life.

Around me, many of the people on the street looked ready for the holy day. Quite a few had by now exchanged their black hats for their *shtreimels,* the fur hats by which they mark Sabbaths and festivals. Quite a few were dressed in pure white, a change from their normal coats. In place of their black shoes, they wore canvas sneakers. On Yom Kippur the wearing of leather, a reminder of the animal slaughtered for its hide, is prohibited. But these sporty sneakers looked so oddly out of place. A few men wore straw slippers; to me they seemed far more authentic-looking. But they were among the minority. I had a lot to learn about what was authentic.

The women were now all out of sight. Inside, they were putting the final preparations on the meal with which every Jew here would separate his Day of Atonement from the rest of the year. From quite a few windows I could already smell the soups or the fish. The full glory of the woman is inside, the people here often say. Is this what they mean?

On the corner, in an open lot, a couple of Arabs stood near a pile of palm fronds they had brought from the oasis at Jericho. This is the time of year when the Orthodox begin to build their *sukkot,* the little booths in which they will symbolically dwell during the holy day a few days after Yom Kippur. The palm fronds are a preferred thatch for the roof, which, according to Jewish law, must be temporary, allowing both shade and heavenly light to enter. But the Arabs do not understand that they are too early, or perhaps too late, for any sales today.

"Look at the dumb Arabs," I hear one of the purified say to another as they leave the mikveh; "they think they're going to find customers today." Whatever purifications they have undergone, it has not washed away their contempt for these outsiders.

But if they have contempt for Arabs and revenue men from the

Israeli government, many of those I see display an altogether different attitude toward one another. Everyone seems to be either offering a blessing to his fellow for the new year or reciting the ritualized formula by which a Jew must beg his friend's forgiveness; what one's comrade does not forgive, the rabbis asserted, Heaven can never forgive. But comrades are apparently only a select few. Excluded are Arabs and strangers.

More and more, the entire city grows silent as people sit down for their last supper. From the windows comes the sound of forks and knives striking dishes. Inside some of the countless synagogues here, there was a hum. Cloaked in their prayer shawls, some of the men who arrived early for the evening services began to murmur *tefillat zaka*, the private enumeration of sins and plea for forgiveness:

> "Master of the Universe, Father of mercy and pardon whose right hand is stretched forth to receive those who return to Him, Thou who hath formed human beings for a superior end and created two inclinations, the good and the evil, so that the choice would be ours to select good or evil . . ."

A few of the voices break, especially when they come to the words:

> "And now, my Lord, I did not hearken to your voice, and I walked in the direction of my evil inclinations, swayed by my heart, scorning good while choosing evil. Nor was it enough that I did not purify my body, but, even worse, I defiled it."

The litany of defilements is long: impure thoughts, lusty desires, the spilling of semen, sometimes by accident but other times on purpose. These were people overcome by an anxiety about their faith, even as they defended it: people who had just purified themselves stood there reminding their Maker of their impurity.

And then the holy service began: "In accord with the Divine Presence and in accord with the congregation, in the assembly on high and the assembly below, we permit ourselves today to pray with sinners." It was hard to tell who were the sinners and who were the righteous, or even what the dimensions of sin were. Did these people really believe they were sinners or was this just part of the ritual of the day?

At last, the haunting melody of the Kol Nidre, the absolution of vows made and not kept, inaugurates the service. From block after block, in large synagogue and small, the familiar melody of this prayer echoed and reechoed. Time seemed stopped as I listened to the tunes that have been sung for generations. And yet while the past was very much alive, I could not help but sense the present too.

2

Who Are the Haredim?

When English speakers refer to the approximately 12 percent of Jews who, out of a world population of 12 million, are attached to tradition and ancient principles of faith, scrupulous in religious observance and ritual, they commonly call them "Orthodox." There were times when the Orthodox Jews positioned themselves outside the mainstreams of contemporary culture, but in the last fifty years, most of them have increasingly demonstrated their capacity to find their place in the stream, albeit on its right banks. These days many Orthodox Jews pass nearly indistinguishably among other contemporaries, preserving their religion in compartments of their lives that remain largely out of view to outsiders. What they do not camouflage, a skullcap or a kosher meal, they have learned to transform so that it is as umremarkable as an Afro hairstyle and as acceptable as bagels and lox. Presumably, they have accomplished this at least in part by making compromises.[1]

But there are other Orthodox Jews who have not merged as easily into the mainstream. These are the ones to whom I turn my attention here. Many call them not simply *Orthodox* Jews—which they are— but *"ultra*-Orthodox," assuming that they maintain stricter standards of faith and observance. While the term still has currency in America, many Jews have replaced "ultra-Orthodox" with "haredi" or in the plural "haredim," a Hebrew term that is current in Israel, where slightly over half of the approximately 550,000 Jews who probably fall into this category live. Why? What does the term really mean; and who really are these people?

In biblical Hebrew, the linguistic point of origin for Jewish experience, the term "haredim" appears in the book of Isaiah (66:5) when the prophet admonishes his people with the words "Hear the word of the Lord, you who tremble [haredim] at His word." This text, still recited aloud in the synagogue by the devout on several Sabbaths during the year, depicts haredim as those singular people—along with the poor and contrite of spirit—who defend the faith and keep the law, are neither apostates nor heretics, and therefore share a special, exquisitely mutual relationship with God.

In modern Hebrew, "haredim" was first used to denote all Jews who were religious, observant, and pious. Later, as the distinctions among the observant became clearer, evolving modern Hebrew began to use *dati* as a generic term for the "religious," though in common usage it became associated with those observant Jews who by and large had accommodated to modern lifestyles. "Haredim" became reserved for those religious people who had not made such accommodations and compromises. This terminological distinction has begun to gain currency even among English speakers. Why?

Perhaps the simplest explanation for the usage is that it helps denote an obvious difference between types of observant Jews; and unlike "ultra-Orthodox," it does not immediately imply any aspersions of others' religious status. There may be another reason that has to do with Jewish ethnic pride. At a time when Jews have returned to their biblical homeland and resurrected their ancient tongue, they no longer need foreign labels. Both "Orthodox" and "ultra-Orthodox" come from a language foreign to Jewish experience. Unlike them, "haredi" resonates with Jewish meaning. Language, after all, is also an expression of nationhood. For today's ethnically more secure Jews, "Orthodox" becomes "dati" and "ultra-Orthodox" becomes "haredi," just as "Isaac" becomes "Yitzhak."

Yet while other Jews increasingly use the designation, ironically haredim generally do not use it to refer to themselves. Rather, in their vernacular Yiddish, they commonly call themselves *Yidn*, Jews, or more specifically *erlicher Yidn*, virtuous Jews. This insider name implies their conviction that, contrary to what others may suggest, they are *not* a separate sect called "haredim" nor a subgroup in a new homeland for Hebrews but very simply the true Jews. If these "Yidn" are indeed haredim, then this must mean that to them there is something essentially Jewish about being haredi and something essentially haredi about being Jewish.

To haredim, this essential, exhibited in their words and deeds, is firstly an emphasis on *traditionalism*. To maintain tradition when all about you others do not, to define a world of sacred order when the profane is the order of the day, to assert that change need not occur when all around you everything has undeniably changed, is a fundamental transformation of the meaning of tradition, the sacred, and the past. Unlike people in the traditional world of the past who, conceiving of no other way to live, generation after generation passed on unchanged what was handed down to them (that, after all, is what "tradition" means), *traditionalists* live in a situation of modernity, surrounded by competing alternatives in life. Among these alternatives they knowingly choose a way of life that ideologically champions the past over every other time. They steadfastly see the day before yesterday as superior to today and tomorrow only meaningful if it returns one to the glories of an earlier time. But as traditionalists they do this at a time when these ways of life are essentially out of place and out of sequence. While their nonharedi contemporaries look forward to the newest model, haredim like the old better and believe that "the generations of Jews are in constant descent."[2] In traditionalist thinking, the new is never improved, only corrupted; our forebears were always greater than us and what they did must serve as the model for us today, tomorrow, and forever.

Again and again as I spoke to these Jews about their notion of the ideal patterns of life, I heard the phrase *yisrael sabbah*. It meant the paradigmatic way of the "Jewish grandfather."[3] These Jews were part of what Margaret Mead once called a "postfigurative culture," agents of the ancients, preserving and restoring the past in the present in what they believed to be an "unchanging continuity."[4] As one rabbi, head of a small yeshiva in Jerusalem, put it, "We don't originate anything here." Such an aggressive assertion of the superiority of the past becomes a way to express distance from contemporary culture and ways of life.

Beyond this traditionalism there is a second essential of haredi life: to be one of those who "tremble at His word" means to share an existential angst about the continuing survival of Judaism and Jewish ways of life (the two are one as captured in a single term: *Yiddishkeit*) and about its capacity to withstand the cultural onslaughts of modern secular society. As one man said to me, "In today's world, Yiddishkeit is under attack." They see themselves "as a force endlessly combating obstacles," convinced that "catastrophes of existence come as the inevitable culmination of past choices and experiences," which most contemporary members of secular society have made and had.[5] But what are the roots of this traditionalism and existential anxiety about Jewish survival?

Origins

To trace the social and psychological origins of haredi angst and traditionalism, one must go back at least two hundred years to Europe, where most Jews then lived. As an organized and identifiable movement, Orthodoxy, from which the haredim emerged, originated there and then in opposition to the rapid change and religious reform that was beginning to sweep Jewish life. This began with three intertwined forces that shook the world in the eighteenth century: industrialization, urbanization, and mobility.

During the industrial age, with the accompanying movement of populations that served it, in the burgeoning, anonymous city, traditions were quickly outdated and faith was expected to give way to reason. This was a time and place where "nothing remained unchanged but the clouds."[6]

For industrial society what one did was far more important than who had been one's ancestors. Now "the free agreement of individuals," often based on contracts or economic arrangements, was the order of the day.[7] Consequently, governmental edicts of tolerance, political upheavals, and social revolutions spread like a wave eastward across late-eighteenth- and nineteenth-century Europe. Old authorities of all sorts found their control crumbling. Universalism began to eclipse provincialism. People began to look beyond the horizon of their family, tribe, village, and traditions, thinking of themselves increasingly as individuals in unmediated contact with life.

Dispersed among those undergoing these transformations, Jews discovered that—even in their ethnic enclaves and despite the fact that many still considered them a pariah people—they too experienced these effects. In some places more than others, but everywhere to some degree, the ramparts of tradition which enclosed them in ghettos and a world ruled by the eternal yesterday of Judaism began to collapse.[8] Precisely because they had no place of their own and were not part of a landed aristocracy or Christian nobility, these wandering Jews had more to gain by the changes than many others. And they did gain.

This process was referred to both by historians and contemporaries of the time by a variety of terms, most commonly "emancipation."[9]

After emancipation, life changed. Whereas in preemancipation Jewish society "the observance of the Jewish tradition could and would be enforced by the organs of the Jewish community," a kind of tribal, almost familial order, the *new* Jewish community that emerged *after* emancipation "was denied the right to impose its will concerning thought and action on the individual."[10] Freed from formal community controls, being Jewish became increasingly voluntary. "Everywhere," historian Jacob Katz concludes, "the individual gained a certain amount of freedom in evolving or absorbing the ideas and determining his conduct accordingly. Jews also gained this leeway in their relation to the community and the traditional values represented in it."[11] The new Jewish community exercised its authority informally, through generally accepted social norms, or folkways. Once being Jewish became a matter of choice and not destiny, it had to make itself attractive in the marketplace of possibilities available to the individual.

As the Jews swiftly discovered, there was a moral cost for leaving the limiting world of tradition. In order to enter the mainstream of the host non-Jewish societies, to be truly emancipated, they had to diminish their Jewish identity or at least make it at best secondary. Given the chance to cease being a stranger or a pariah, many Jews quickly threw off what Voltaire had called their "superstitions and prejudices," and chose assimilation and the new social opportunities it engendered.[12] While a complex process, assimilation may be defined basically as a process in which strangers or newcomers so thoroughly learn the ways of the host society (which accepts them) that they become for the most practical purposes indistinguishable from it. In the most extreme cases, the assimilated—who commonly constituted a minority—abandoned their original identity and patterns of culture for ways that were new.[13] Jews became ex-Jews.

Others, faced with these new cultural opportunities, tried to find some middle ground that would enable them to be both loyal citizens of the new civil societies while also maintaining old religious ties. They advocated acculturation, a process by which "an individual achieves continuing competence in his [host] culture," but stops short of complete assimilation.[14] This was the option selected by *maskilim*, so-called enlightened Jews. Early maskilim promoted culture contact with the world outside the Jewish one but spurned complete absorption. In practice, they became literate in the language of the host society, not just a Jewish vernacular or the holy tongue of Jewish texts. They moved beyond exclusive attachment to the local Jewish community (for example, having friends or political loyalties that were not only Jewish) and left the ghetto, got a university education, and pursued professions not, strictly speaking, bound up with Jewish concerns. They shared in the values and ethos of an emerging secular society, not only tolerating other points of view but perceiving them to be legitimate and even attractive. They became pluralistic in attitude at the very least and often in practice as well.

For them the ideal was, in the words of one, to "comply with the customs and civil constitutions of the countries in which you are transplanted, but at the same time, be constant to the faith of your forefathers." [15] Translated into a popular aphorism of the day, this became: "Be a person when you go out in the street and a Jew in your home." [16]

The street took over; many maskilim were drawn increasingly into the orbit of general culture and discovered growing difficulty in holding fast to their Jewish ties. Many of their children slipped toward the most extreme forms of assimilation: they stopped being Jews. (One of the early maskilim, Moses Mendelssohn, had six children: "Two turned Catholic, two Protestant. Two remained Jews—but last-generation Jews.") [17]

Yet while many maskilim may have assimilated, their ideal of cultural pluralism did not disappear. It influenced a variety of other Jewish movements that sought to make their peace with modern society. And its basic premise that contact with the world beyond the Jewish one could be inherently legitimate and beneficial without being culturally destructive for the Jews remained influential, affecting diverse elements of Jewish life. In the humanities it set the stage for the rebirth of modern Hebrew and the development of secular Yiddish literature. By writing about contemporary matters in these ancient and time-honored Jewish languages, one could remain bonded to Jewish culture while also fostering links to contemporary society. In political life, cultural pluralism fed into the idea of a modern, secular Zionism—a political ideology that merged with Jewish nationalist aspirations with the modern secular notions of liberalism, socialism, and the nation state. Thus a Jewish state could become like all other states without losing its specific Jewish character.

In the domain of Jewish images, aesthetic standards and refinements derived from the host culture were applied to synagogue architecture, liturgy, education, and personal style or appearance. Functionally, this meant shaving off earlocks and beards, donning contemporary and fashionable clothes, remaking the synagogue so that it was more in line with the dominant Gentile places of worship, exchanging Jewish learning for the scholarship of university, and generally omitting parts of the traditional way of Jewish life that appeared irreconcilable with the new position of Jews.

The *Haskalah* (Jewish enlightenment) also affected religion. To accommodate to the host society with compromises that minimized the strains of practicing Judaism in a Gentile world, some Jews sought merely to *re*-form Judaism, to make it fit in with the times. To many "reform" Jews, no part of Jewish life seemed more irreconcilable with emancipation, enlightenment, and the acculturation they aspired to than traditional ritual practice and prevailing Jewish images. Hence, Judaism became for many early reformers a fundamental break from ritual praxis and tradition and primarily a matter of morals and ethics. Others, more conservative in approach, sought limited acculturative "changes that were not in conflict with the spirit of historical Judaism," but which "could be made validly in the light of biblical and rabbinic precedent."[18]

In sharp contrast to maskilim or reformers who opted for acculturation in one way or another were traditionalist Jews who were repelled by the values and ways of the world outside their own and wished on the contrary "to stress the values in aboriginal ways of life, and to move aggressively . . . toward the restoration of those ways."[19] These Jews "brought into consciousness and into confrontation with one another two opposite things: the spiritually negative character of the contemporary world and the spiritually positive character of the past tradition."[20] Many called them "Orthodox Jews."[21]

While they did not all share the same view of the world or even necessarily agree on what the tradition demanded of them, they rejected the dualistic model implied in the "be a person in the street and a Jew in the home" formula; on the contrary, the Orthodox asserted that one had to everywhere and always remain fully a Jew. To many of them Haskalah became nothing less than a recipe for full-fledged assimilationism and "maskil" became an ignominious identification. In their thinking, dual identities inescapably steered Jews to the ultimate evil: absorption into non-Jewish culture. Implicit in this position was the conviction that in the competition between the Jewish and the Gentile street, the world of the street would ultimately overtake all who were less than total in their Jewish involvement. That was why in the book of Leviticus God had warned their Israelite ancestors that those who strayed from the ancient ways "shall be lost among the *goyim*, and the land of your enemies shall eat you up" (26:38). Haskalah, and even more so reform, would lead to the speedy fulfillment of that curse.

They believed that only those who remained punctiliously loyal to

Jewish ways—even in the smallest details—could survive as Jews. While they were called Orthodox, they did not emphasize *doxa,* belief, but praxis. For these Jews, the particulars of Jewish practice, ritual, and custom were anchoring lifelines in a rapidly changing world. Recalling talmudic assertions that at a time when the Jewish way of life is under attack "even changing the color of one's shoelaces is prohibited," these Jews resisted any alteration of their patterns of practice, image, and culture.[22] This then was their fundamental belief: to preserve themselves as Jews they would have to preserve their traditional practices. Ritual, study of Jewish texts, observance of ceremonial, custom, even certain folkways were not dispensable husk but rather the vital kernel of Jewish life.

All this had another consequence: it kept one from becoming fully comfortable with the surrounding culture. It maintained the Jew as outsider. Unlike either the assimilationists or the acculturating Jews, many of these Jews tried purposefully to remain strangers and sojourners in the contemporary secular world. That was the essential message they read in the promise by God in Leviticus 20:26: "And I will separate you from the nations to be for Me." One should not try to be a Frenchman, a German, an American, or even a secular Israeli or any other kind of citizen, but always a Jew. The world beyond the Jewish one was essentially evil and one must "distance oneself from it . . . so as to not learn its ways."[23] Jews could never forget that they were in exile.

Still attached to the tribal idea of a "Chosen People," many of these Jews repudiated cultural pluralism and turned their backs on the world outside their four cubits of Jewish existence. In the nineteenth century when most of this was happening, this was more the case in eastern than in central and western Europe. There were of course exceptions in the east. Cities like Odessa or Warsaw with their high culture and cosmopolitan atmosphere became places where assimilation flourished. But Orthodoxy generally bloomed in the east and reform in the west while places in the middle like Austria-Hungary were divided between both extremes.

From the very outset, even the Orthodox Jews were not all alike. At one pole were those who sought some sort of accommodation. Known as the neo-Orthodox—most of whom lived in German-speaking societies—they sought to retard the movement by opposing reform without denying some of its acculturative goals. They evolved a modified cultural pluralism that demonstrated the capacity of historic Judaism to harmonize its teachings with modern culture. *"Torah* with *Derech Eretz,"* was their slogan: the traditional Jewish way inserted into the design of local culture. Although they accepted the legitimacy and value of other ways of life, they viewed their Judaism as first among equals. As Rabbi Samson Raphael Hirsch, one of the early and most eloquent voices of neo-Orthodoxy, pointed out: "For us, progress is valid only to the extent that it does not interfere with religion."[24] Progress, yes; reform, no.

At the other extreme of Orthodoxy were those who rejected as much as possible the attractions of the host cultures to which many Jews flocked. As one editorialist later put it, "It is a commandment to hate them, and that is one of the commandments of the holy Torah, to hate those who pervert others from the way of *Yisrael Sabbah*."[25] They rejected *chukos ha goyim*, ways associated with Gentiles.[26] Refusing to grant non-Jewish culture and its values legitimacy, they discouraged their children from becoming literate in the local vernacular, dressing in the fashion of the times, moving out of the ghetto, going to the university, or in any way openly acculturating. To them cultural compromise was unthinkable and neo-Orthodoxy weakness. Precursors of today's haredim, from the outset they struggled against almost every capitulation to the cultural and social demands of the non-Jewish world surrounding them. Thus, for example, Rabbi Naftali Zvi Yehuda Berlin (1817–1893) refused to allow into the Volozhin Yeshiva in Lithuania "any secular learning, and for this reason the yeshiva was closed [by the government]." The grounds for this refusal, as he explained in his will, were that it was "necessary to separate between the sacred and the profane, for it is the case that not only do all profane [i.e., secular] matters which become mingled with the sacred not become sanctified but they also cause the sacred to become profaned."[27]

"Jacob and Esau are two opposites," as Rabbi Shlomo Halberstam (1848–1906) of Bobov, Poland, put it in commonly heard terms that saw Jews and Gentiles symbolized by the two biblical brothers, "and it is unthinkable that there should be any connection between them in any way."[28] If much of the two thousand years of the diaspora had led to Jewish persecution and degradation, these Jews responded by categorizing everyone who was not a Jew as some inferior being. Jacob and Esau, said the great Maharal, Rabbi Loew of Prague, "are two fundamental opposites in practice, like fire and water, which cannot coexist in the same basket."[29] Esau included not just those who were formally non-Jews; Jews who lived like the goyim were also goyim.

Ironically, at the outset many Jews who took these stands were themselves already somewhat more acculturated than they were prepared to let the next generation become. Many could speak in the vernacular, often wore clothes that, if not altogether stylish, were undeniably European, had cut or at least trimmed their beards and ear-locks and had innocently accepted some of the elements of the host culture. However, the more successful reformers became in attracting members and the louder their voice became in the organized Jewish community, the more sharply did the Orthodox oppose them and the more aggressively traditionalist they became. *"He chodosh osur min ha torah,"* the phrase Rabbi Moses Sofer (1762–1839) used to decree that "the new is prohibited by the Torah," became the motto of many in this movement that rejected reform by championing the past. Yet instead of leading to stasis, this attitude evolved into a dynamic wherein children would become more haredi than their parents. How?

In the wholly traditional world, people knew what Judaism de-manded of them. They did not have to check code books and texts to know what was right and wrong. Instead, they relied on cultural com-petence that came from their living in an environment governed by a relatively stable tradition over which there was little or no debate. But the modern world was increasingly undermining stability and severing continuity with the past. With the break-up of the ghetto and the seemingly ceaseless change that accompanied it, people felt increas-ingly removed from the norms of the Jewish street. How could one know what exactly to do? What was insignificant custom and what unalterable law?

In this new atmosphere those who wanted to remain true to the tradition had either to improvise or go "by the book." Since improvi-sation runs counter to the ethos of traditionalism, this meant that books—especially codes of conduct—took on a greater importance than ever before, and studying them became a crucial feature of main-taining continuity. For many of those who came from the yeshiva world, the quintessential people of the book, this decision to go by the book was an easy one. They were already absorbed in unpacking an-cient texts and rabbinic commentaries. Protected by the walls of their institutions, they also did not have to make the same compromises with the books' demands as did those who lived in the real world. But when the real world changed, the book became an anchor of authority for everyone, "a refuge" and "a sanctuary from the onslaught of con-temporary society"; the yeshiva students were its guardians.[30]

Code books were always important in the life of Jews, particularly in times of cultural transition. Now, when mass production made them widely available, they filled the social and cultural vacuum left by the demise of traditional norms. Studying these books that articulated every jot and tittle of law and custom became the absolute prerequisite for religious behavior throughout the traditionalist world.

All "this opened the way for individuals and groups to compete, as it were, among themselves on the degree of stringency and intransigency, within the range of alternatives found" in the code books.[31] But many of these stringencies were paradoxically new, representing radical continuity and radical change at one and the same time.

Hasidim and Misnagdim

The competition for the role of guardians of the heritage was not new. Already at the end of the eighteenth century, within the Jewish world of eastern Europe, there had been ferment and change. Jews were swept up by Hasidism, a spiritualistic, pietistic, and charismatic movement that began in Podolia and Volhynia and spread into Galicia, Poland, Russia, the Ukraine, the Austro-Hungarian Empire, Moldavia, and even Lithuania. In several generations it absorbed huge numbers—perhaps a majority—of the region's Jews.

Based on a way of life exemplified in the early eighteenth century by its founder Israel ben Eliezer, the Baal Shem Tov, of Podolia and elaborated by his disciple and successor, Dov Baer, the Maggid of Mezerich in nearby Volhynia, and their followers, Hasidism emphasized that true piety and "the love of God is not to be attained by intellectual power or learning, but by the outpouring of the soul in prayer."[32] Closely tied to principles of mysticism as elaborated in Lurianic Kabbalah, Hasidism seemed to tap hopes for a spiritual repair (*tikkun olam*, the mystics called it) that many Jews living under the double strain of persecution and enforced poverty nourished. This was, many have argued, an iconoclastic folk-religious reaction to the strict legalism of elite rabbinic Judaism as it had developed in the world of the yeshiva, the academies of higher Jewish learning that were most prominent in Lithuania but which were a part of all traditional Jewish life.

Even as they reveled in old traditions, accepting "the whole of Jewish teaching," hasidim also established radical new patterns of Jewish life.[33] They marked themselves with distinctive dress and customs, delved into mysticism, differed with established rabbinic norms of how and exactly when to pray or what was the proper way of ritually slaughtering meat, whether scholarship or piety was paramount, and in general began a struggle over various religious choices. Yet the hallmark of their existence was their relationship with their *rebbe*, who was considered a *zaddik*, a perfectly righteous man. They believed in the extraordinary power of his individual spiritual contemplation of and encounter with God.

The rebbe was not just a model of the redeemed, spiritually repaired Jew; he was also a charismatic and mystical intermediary to God. As Rabbi Mendel of Rymanov, one of the early leaders put it, "Zaddikim are the chariot of God."[34] They were a "pipeline" to Heaven, part of the great chain of being that went from Moses, through the prophets and to the zaddik.[35] Insofar as the zaddik's followers were bonded to him, they too could share in his charisma and become part of this chain. While there were some rebbes who disavowed the extraordinary claims made on their behalf by their hasidim, in every case the rebbe played a crucial role in defining the nature of his brand of Hasidism.

The emergence of a rebbe who by virtue of his capacity for spiritual repair was beyond the rational and thus somehow beyond the law, a messianic redeemer, marked not only a kind of return to the extraordinary era of the prophet; it was also a revolutionary breakthrough to a new kind of Judaism. In its rebbes, its outlook and practice, Hasidism fostered an "almost complete transformation of all the spheres comprising the world of Judaism."[36] To the accusations that they were radically breaking from the norm, the hasidim offered a variety of replies. Thus, for example, Rabbi Nachman of Kosow, justified his Jewish modifications with the rhetorical question: "Did our fathers [succeed] in bringing the Messiah?!"[37] New, competing approaches were offered.

Hasidim were not all alike by any means. Almost from their beginnings they were divided into courts, each of which followed its own rebbe, who took his title from the community in which he asserted authority: Ger in Poland, Lubavitch in Russia, Belz in Galicia, Satmar in Hungary, and so on. As each disciple of the Baal Shem Tov and the Maggid of Mezerich found a following, he set up his own hasidic court. Hasidim differed about the gifts and abilities, the charisma, of their respective rebbes; they also disagreed about the best ways of effecting salvation and repairing the spirit. They were divided over the benefits of studying mysticism versus studying hasidic lore or even Talmud. Each new rebbe and his followers shaped Hasidism in their own image, and in time asserted that their version of what being a hasid meant was the correct one. The best way to prove this was, of course, to show that their rebbe was able to effect more miracles and attract more followers.

The rebbe became "the unifying agent binding his adherents together into a single, close-knit society, the redeemer of his own little circle of disciples."[38] He acted as a model, a spiritual guide, for his followers. If he stressed long earlocks and beard, in strict adherence to the biblical injunction not to cut off the "hair on the sides of your head or the edges of your beard" (Leviticus 19:27), or wore a sash around his waist during prayer to separate the higher and lower parts of his body; if he took to wearing knickers or a fur hat, his hasidim would do this too, in the belief that this would perfect their spiritual repair and make them better Jews. The idea of special practices beyond the normative expectations of Jewish law became a fundamental aspect of hasidic life.

Dynasties arose in which the charisma of one rebbe was passed on to his chosen successor, commonly a son or a son-in-law. But only followers of the new rebbe could affirm his chosenness. Not infrequently, successions were the subject of controversies and schisms, one clique going with a son and another with a son-in-law or other outstanding disciple who they believed should carry on the traditions of the deceased rebbe. And thus, through a kind of cultural mitosis, Hasidism grew more complex and far-ranging.

Hasidim shared with the rebbe their hopes and dreams, tragedies and celebrations, and often asked him to make crucial life decisions for them. They also drew close physically, sitting at his Sabbath table, crowding around him, and eating his *sherayim*, the leftovers of his meal. They saw to his physical and financial needs. All this became part of a Hasid's way of serving God and Judaism. It also became a means for each rebbe's hasidim to bond with one another. If nothing else, Hasidism fostered collective intimacy. As a secondary consequence this led to a "tendency of the hasidim to segregate themselves from the rest of the community."[39] In time, this secondary consequence became an end in itself. Hasidim attracted "young men [who] would leave their parents, wives, and small children and travel in groups to visit these great 'Rebbes' and to receive instruction from them in the new doctrine," while sitting at the rebbe's table.[40]

Opposing Hasidism were other Jews, many of Lithuanian origin, who remained convinced that only a rigorous and unyielding attachment to the Talmudists' reading of the law constituted true Judaism. Known as *misnagdim* (literally, "opponents" [of hasidim]), they objected to the idea of a zaddik who was somehow beyond the law. For them authority came from scholarship not piety, family ties, or mystical spiritual sources. Misnagdim looked to the *rosh yeshiva*, the head of the talmudic academy, whose scholarship was supreme, as the true rabbi. To them, hasidim emphasized all the wrong things and "discouraged the study of the Talmud and thereby had an adverse effect on Lithuanian talmudic scholarship."[41] They were perverters of Judaism who made their own emendations and deletions to a tradition that misnagdim believed was subject only to rabbinic interpretations.

(This attitude toward unschooled Jews was not new in Judaism. During talmudic times, rabbis distinguished between *haverim*, those who properly understood the law, and the *am ha'aretz*, the simple folk who based their practices and beliefs on custom and everyday wisdom rather than scholarship. The misnagdim were simply the latest version of the haverim who in turn looked upon hasidim as am ha'aretz).

Conflicts were heated and intense. Thus, for example, a native of Amdur, a village in Lithuania where the dissension was especially sharp, writes in his memoirs that he recalled that misnagdim "were traditionally believed to go into mourning and sit *shiva* when a member of the family became a hasid." [42] To the misnagdim, hasidim were heretics. If the differences of custom and tradition that separated the two groups seem in retrospect minor, they did not seem so to the opponents.

Yet the influence of Hasidism was felt even among misnagdim. The relationship with the rosh yeshiva began to parallel the relationship hasidim had with their masters. The idea of devotedly following a *gadol*, a great eminence, became firmly established among both these groups. It was an idea that would remain embedded in the character of Jewish life and play a growing role in the years to come, particularly among haredim. If a hasidic rebbe commonly passed his charismatic office on to his son, son-in-law, brother, or star disciple, the rosh yeshiva often did the same with his office.

In another parallel misnagdim created separate societies of followers. Instead of the rebbe's court, there was the yeshiva. Etz Hayim in Volozhin (1802), and later Knesset Yisrael in Slobodka (1882), Knesset Beit Yitzhak in Kaminetz (1897) and others created a new kind of student society, dedicated to a totalistic involvement in Judaism. Unlike the old-style yeshiva—which was little more than a study hall and library in a local house of prayer—these new institutions attracted and took in young men in their early teens or younger from outside their immediate vicinities, separated them from their families, socialized them into a way of life dedicated to Jewish learning and subordinated to the views of the rosh yeshiva, who in every respect was *in loco parentis*. Remade inside the walls of the institution into an image of the rosh yeshiva, the yeshiva students, like the hasidim at the rebbe's court, became reflections of their master.

Da'as Torah

There was another way that hasidim and misnagdim began to resemble each other. Both believed in *da'as Torah*. Originally, da'as Torah was something *hachamim*, rabbinic scholars, had. It was their ability "to interpret day-to-day events in a proper Torah light," discern what the tradition had in mind, and thereby extrapolate from it, thus being able "to anticipate the ramifications of events . . . in the future."[43] With da'as Torah rabbis could deliver guidance beyond the judicial. The rebbe had a mystical power. But in time, it too evolved into da'as Torah.

As modern life threw all sorts of apparently unprecedented new realities that seemed to go beyond the boundaries of the Torah into the basket of human experience, traditionalists turned to the concept and bearers of da'as Torah to fill the vacuum created by the seeming silence of the time-honored texts on many of these matters. "For the *talmid chacham* [Torah scholar] is like the Torah itself and he is in its image, and therefore it is certain that for this reason the Torah also commanded us to 'not depart from all he will instruct you,' for the *hachamim* are the Torah itself, and as the Holy One, may He be blessed, decreed and gave the Torah to all of Israel, so he gave us the *hachamim* and they are also the essence of the Torah."[44] "My will," as hasidic Rabbi Avraham Mordecai Alter of Ger put it even more starkly in a 1922 letter to his followers, "is the will of Heaven."[45] In return, the attitude of the simple Jew toward these rabbis was: "We reinforce them, totally discounting our own ability to interpret events for ourselves!"[46]

The Differences Evaporate

Although in their origins hasidim and misnagdim opposed each other, both were engrossed in building institutions and articulating practices that stressed a high level of involvement in Judaism and Jewish life. For a time they may have remained blind to the similarities between them. But by the late nineteenth and early twentieth centuries, when they began comparing each other to the reform Jews and the acculturating masses who were attracting far greater Jewish numbers, the differences between them suddenly seemed quite small indeed. For while hasidim and misnagdim argued over how to practice Judaism and which rituals or customs to emphasize, over whether the rebbe or the rosh yeshiva was correct, other Jews were ceasing to practice rituals altogether and had abandoned all sorts of religious masters. Against that background, misnagdim and hasidim looked alike and ineluctably became allies in a campaign that sought to reverse what they saw as the demise of Judaism. By the twentieth century, hasidim and misnagdim, once fierce rivals for control over the soul and mind of Judaism, found themselves thrown together in the cause of traditionalism. "Even in Lithuania," where misnagdim and hasidim had clashed most furiously, "both sides—the yeshiva Rav and hasidic Zaddik—came to realize that in the light of the trends toward assimilation there was no place for disputes between them in religious matters, despite great differences in their respective interpretations of Jewish teaching."[47] Both became Orthodox Jews, and often most vigorously and radically Orthodox: haredim.

Hasidic rebbes and their followers were beginning to act more like misnagdim, emphasizing Torah study and yeshiva learning. By 1922 hasidic Rabbi Moshe of Stolin-Karlin founded a yeshiva that merged elements of both misnagdic and hasidic approaches to Judaism. "The yeshiva was called Beth Israel and the main subject taught was Gemara [Talmud], the aim being to achieve a synthesis of Lithuanian talmudic scholarship with the spirit of Karlin Hasidism."[48] By the eve of World War II, one could find "the difference between the misnagdim and the hasidim [had] become less pronounced, there were hasidim that prayed and studied in misnagid synagogues and batei midrash [houses of study]."[49] Eschewing radical mysticism, so much a part of early Hasidism, for the more sedate study of Talmud, one of the later more conservative hasidic leaders explained that while Kabbalah might be " 'a strong drink that strengthens the heart' its influence lasts but a short time, while 'the study of Talmud' is like a piece of bread which even though at the moment of its eating does not taste as pleasing 'as the drink,' the plain bread nevertheless works for a far longer time 'and strengthens the entire body of a man and not simply his heart.' "[50] And, misnagdim adopted some of the spirituality of Hasidism and the charismatic elements of leadership.

If the differences between hasidim and misnagdim seemed to wane in the light of these developments, they did not disappear. They were simply neutralized by the overwhelming problems of contending with the rapid pace of assimilation and cultural change. Two or three generations later, in the days that the pages ahead will detail, these differences would wax again. Asked in 1989 what he believed to be the closest religion to Judaism, one contemporary head of a yeshiva which was a bastion of misnagdim is reputed to have replied, "Chabad," an acronym for the Lubavitch brand of Hasidism.

Agudat Israel

In the evolution of haredi Judaism another important benchmark is the formation of Agudat Israel. Responding to what they considered the deterioration of traditional Judaism as represented by reform as well as secular Zionism, some Jews submerged their differences in an effort to resist this sort of change. As part of the effort, they joined together in 1912 in Kattowitz, Upper Silesia (in East Prussia), and founded a political union of Orthodox Jews that they called Agudat Israel. The organization became a major voice of traditionalist Orthodoxy.

"Agudat Israel was founded to help construct a thousand-foot *mechitzah* [separation] between us and them. There must be absolutely no connection between authentic Judaism and diluted Judaism. Absolutely none!" [51]

The Agudat Israel union, which brought together hasidim, misnagdim, western and eastern European Jews, was a fragile one. Ironically, while the coming together in Agudat Israel—a radical organizational and tactical departure from the localism that characterized Orthodoxy beforehand—was meant to point out to members their common feelings and aims, it also highlighted their differences. Not only were there hasidic-misnagdic splits whose residues were still felt in certain quarters, but there were also the fundamental differences between the easterners, who believed that "the only plausible basis for unity was the maintenance of the status quo [which demanded that] each group should retain its way of life without change," and the westerners, who believed that there was an advantage to absorbing some of the outside culture and in particular its educational opportunities and intellectual wealth. [52]

To overcome those differences, or at least to unite themselves, Agudists tried to find what they all shared in common. In addition to their obvious animosity to reform and the rising tide of secularity, they all accepted traditionalist rabbis as the supreme authority of Jewry. Agudat Israel accordingly organized the Moetzet G'dolay Ha-Torah, the Council of Torah Sages. This board of rabbis, whose sagacity no one could challenge and still call himself Orthodox, was both a symbol and an instrument for guidance to the Agudah as to what it stood for and what was acceptable. These rabbinic eminences with their da'as Torah gave a sorely needed legitimacy to the organization and countered the weaknesses of its newness, helping counteract the Agudah's inherent tendencies toward splintering.

Membership on the council, which included misnagdim and hasi-

dim, confirmed an enhanced status for these rabbis; they were no
longer relatively local heroes but were instead becoming universally
recognized Orthodox Jewish leaders. Figures like Rabbi Israel Meir
Ha-Cohen (Kagan), better known as the Hafetz Hayim, Rabbi Chaim
Soloveitchik of Brisk (Brest-Litovsk), Rabbi Chaim Ozer Grodzenski
of Vilna, and Rabbi Avraham Mordecai Alter of Ger (Gora Kalwaria)
became recognized authorities far beyond their immediate communities. It was not unusual to hear them referred to, as for example Kagan
was, as "both the *zaddik hador* [the righteous man of the generation]
and *gaon hador* [genius of the generation]."[53] As gadolim, great sages,
the differences among them became blurred. To be sure, in the age of
"going-by-the-book," their writings had already played a role in this
process.

To remain beyond challenge, these leading rabbis and others like
them held to the most demanding requirements of Judaism. To do less
would have opened them to the accusation that they were making
compromises and following the nefarious path of reform.[54] That they
sometimes set a higher standard than most people could be expected
to follow is illustrated by the following story:

> The late Ephraim Kaplan, an American Jewish journalist, on
> visiting the sage [Israel Meir Ha-Cohen (Kagan)] in Radun, asked
> him what one must observe in order to be a good Jew.
>
> "Observe the *Shulkhan Arukh* [Code of Law], and that means all
> the mitsvoth [commandments] expounded therein," was the rejoin-
> der.
>
> "If so, you exclude ninety percent of the people from that privi-
> lege," argued Mr. Kaplan.
>
> "True," retorted the Hafetz Hayim [Kagan], "but if you buy a
> bottle of pure alcohol and reduce its strength and adulterate it, the
> shopkeeper who sold it to you is not to be blamed for the changed
> strength. You asked me to define pure, unadulterated Jewishness,
> which I did."[55]

Building ever higher "fences around the Torah," (a phrase the
rabbis used) and turning away from the false charms of the outside
world became for many essential to the preservation and enhancement
of their tradition. Gradually, all of Agudat Israel became haredi, aim-
ing for the "pure and unadulterated."

Mass Migration, the Holocaust, and Zionism

Even in the absence of any other events, all of this might well have
been enough to lead to the evolution of haredim. But three other

crucial not altogether unrelated, historical developments virtually guaranteed their emergence and growth: mass migration, modern secular Zionism, and the Holocaust.

Made possible by improved means of transportation, Jewish emancipation, and the shifting of political boundaries, mass migration affected Jews by separating them from where they had lived for generations. The integrity of communities and custom was eroded by these mass migrations. Between 1881 and 1930 about two and a quarter million Jews came to America from southern and eastern Europe. At the same time approximately 182,000 Jews, most of them from Europe, immigrated to the Land of Israel, the ancient Jewish homeland.[56] Both America and Israel were new worlds where Jewish tradition had to be transplanted onto a not-always-hospitable soil. To the religiously observant, America was a *trefe medina*, an unkosher state where there was no Jewish past to build upon and traditional Judaism was under siege. America, where "the important thing is to keep going," abhorred tradition.[57]

If America was a problem, Zionism—particularly its secular form —was anathema.[58] There were several reasons for this. First was the theological argument, perhaps encapsulated in the Psalmist's assertion (127:1): "If the Lord will not build the house, they labor in vain that build it" and affirmed in the talmudic assertion by, among others, Rabbi Judah who declared: "Whoever comes up to [prematurely settle] the land of Israel transgresses the positive commandment which says (Jeremiah 22:2), 'Unto Babylon shall they be carried and there should remain until the day I think of them, says the Lord.' " The secular Zionist enterprise in the Holy Land was a heretical "rebellion against the kingdom of Heaven," which sought to illegitimately hasten the end of exile through the actions of sinners rather than waiting for messianic intervention.[59]

Second was the objection to the religiously unacceptable notion of a Zionism that suggested the Jews could become a "people like all other people." This concept of "normalization" for a wandering and stateless people ran against the Orthodox notion of Jewish uniqueness.[60] The Orthodox did not want a "normal Jewish state," but one that was altogether different. "It was not worthwhile," the Hafetz Hayim was quoted as saying, "to become another Albania or even another Belgium after nineteen centuries of suffering. A state must be established on Torah foundations."[61]

Third, the idea of cooperating with the unbelievers and heretics at the forefront of the secular Zionist movement was, many Orthodox believed, tantamount to giving legitimacy to the idea that one could properly express Jewish identity in ways other than the religious. And there was the theological problem of heretics and sinners having a role in the ultimate redemption of the Jews from the punishment of their exile.[62] "Fortunate is the man who walks not in the counsel of the wicked, nor stands on the pathway of sinners nor sits in the seat of the scornful," the Psalmist declared (1:1). This meant, explained Isaiah Margolis, a haredi thinker, "Any of we the [God-] fearing . . . who associated with them [the Zionists] will be caught in their sins."[63]

Fourth was the cultural character of Israel. It was "a society deeply absorbed in its own transformation and renewal, one that inherently values the new over the ancient, the young over the old, the future over the past."[64] As such, it seemed the wrong place to stress old ways, traditions often associated with eastern European Jewish ghetto life.

Finally, there were political and strategic resistances to the idea of Zionism. Those western neo-Orthodox who wanted to stress the capacity of Judaism to be in harmony with local conditions did not want to emphasize the idea of a separate Jewish homeland where Jews were more at home, particularly when they were not convinced that political conditions would allow for the fruition of hopes for a return to Zion. And the east European Orthodox could not see abandoning their institutions and core communities for the weaker periphery in the Holy Land. Both groups kept the wish for a return as an article of faith, to be repeated in prayer, but not to be turned into a program of action. In fact, many of the traditionalist orthodox were certain that any activity to bring about Zionist aspirations was not only heresy but something that would only aggravate the authorities who needed only the slightest excuse to persecute Jewry. In the end, they presumed, Zionism would cause trouble for those who wanted to live their lives and practice their religion undisturbed. So deeply rooted was this conviction that in time some haredim would aver that the sinful and strategically mistaken actions taken to hurry the end of the exile and create a Jewish state had led to the explosive and injurious results of the Holocaust.[65]

Most reluctant to leave the ghettos and be set adrift in a world hostile to their religious practices, the traditionalist Orthodox were among the last immigrants to arrive in large numbers in Israel and America. Most might have remained even longer in their European Jewish surroundings had not the even greater cataclysm of the Holocaust occurred. Decimating their numbers, obliterating the communities from which they had come, murdering many of their leaders, and testing their faith in the possibilities of spiritual repair and God, this catastrophe forced even the most insular and Orthodox of Jews to flee the communities in which they had been forged.

After the Holocaust nothing was exactly as it had been. "Paradoxically, it was the destruction of Eastern European Jewry in the twentieth century that created the conditions which enabled the spread of ultra-orthodoxy."[66] This trauma intensified the sense of breach that mass migration and the social changes that accompanied it had already aroused in Jewish consciousness. After the Holocaust there was no going back. Now even the most traditionally oriented of Jews were forced to reincarnate the past. A new religious framework was created by the survivors.

The circumstances of their new incarnation was, however, significantly different from their previous one. Not only were they in new and very different sorts of places, they were carrying on their struggle to maintain their traditions and their opposition to modern western culture in the capitals of this very culture, becoming most concentrated in New York City, the quintessential modern megalopolis, and in the two largest metropolitan areas of Israel, the exemplar of a modern state.[67]

To be sure, they were not rooting themselves on a totally barren soil. Before the Second World War there had been an Orthodoxy in America, but it seemed to be demographically undernourished and waning, institutionally weak, and encircled by an undermining American secular culture. In the Land of Israel and particularly in Jerusalem, there had long been a settlement of Orthodox Jews who, immersed in the world of ritual learning and sacred service, awaited the coming of the Messiah. But as the days of the state approached, it too found itself surrounded more and more by a dominant secular Zionism. In both places, in addition to the energy they had to invest in building a positive culture, the traditionalist Orthodox immigrants also had to absorb themselves with what they must avoid and how to maintain their separatism. In short, in this sort of world one had to be on guard, anxious, worried, "haredi" about one's Orthodoxy.

This was just the sort of anxious Judaism suited to people who saw themselves as survivors. Being survivors was an important element of the haredi world. With only a fraction of their leadership surviving the war, many of whom were still reeling from the shock of the destruction, post-Holocaust, New World haredim had a special sense of mission. They felt that they should and could resurrect the world they remembered. This tendency was intensified by feelings of having to live up to the idealized memories of their forebears who had perished in Europe or who were located in some mythic past beyond the great abyss of the Holocaust. So they enshrined the way their forebears dressed in that world of Europe, spoke its Yiddish, recited Hebrew in

its European inflections, even identified themselves in European Jewish terms: they were from Belz, Lithuanians, Bobovers. But of course
to be Belz in Jerusalem or Bobover in New York or a student at a
Lithuanian yeshiva in Lakewood, New Jersey, or B'nai B'rak, Israel,
is not the same as being Belz in the original Galician village of Belz, or
Bobover in Poland, a student in Slobodka, Lithuania. These became
ideal—rather, idealized—types. They were framed in a halo of nostalgia and survivor guilt.

"Our thoughts and attitudes must be informed by a constant awareness of our place as the successor generation to the glorious one that
was destroyed in World War II."[68] The dead Jewish world was resurrected and given a life even more potent than before. This was a
revolutionary idea, dressed in the garments of putative continuity.
Looking like their forebears, continuing to dip into the Talmud the
way they had done for generations, trying to maintain hasidic dynasties
and customs of the past, these Orthodox Jews were by their very
existence demonstrably withstanding even the fire of the Holocaust
and the winds of change that surrounded it.

In addition to the sense of irrevocable break from the past and the
survivor ramifications, the Holocaust proved to them that all efforts at
making it into the non-Jewish world were destined to failure. "Fourth
generation descendants of assimilated Jews who had abandoned their
faith were sought out by oppressors and expelled, or murdered," and
thus there was no point in trying to end existential exile by some
independent act of acculturation.[69]

Yet the Holocaust forced these Jews to find sanctuary where the
very same non-Orthodox Jews they had once shunned and opposed
were in control. No longer even close to being one of the most popular
Jewish movements, in places not their own, these Orthodox Jews became part of a beleaguered minority. This created a mix of feelings.
There was the resentment that came from being foreigners and outsiders in every sense; and there was the empathy that came from a
postwar realization of the common fate that befell all Jews. Resentment led to an estrangement that sharpened the edge of haredi Judaism, while empathy fostered the conditions that enabled Orthodox
Jews, at least in the early years, to receive support from their erstwhile
opponents. Thus, the Belzer rebbe, a refugee from the Nazis whose
family and a majority of whose supporters had been murdered, lived
in Tel Aviv, where some of his financial support came from socialists
and unbelievers.

For a time many of these Jews were overcome by a sense that their
rigid Orthodoxy and reluctance to change may have contributed to

their victimization in the Holocaust. Had they been more willing to leave their enclosed Jewish communities in Europe, they might have gone to America or Israel sooner and saved themselves. Had they mitigated their opposition to America and the Zionist idea, more might have escaped the horror.

"And now who will assume responsibility for the holy blood which is being spilled?" asked Rabbi Issachar Teichtal, an Orthodox opponent of Zionism before the war, writing in 1943. And he answered: "It seems to me that all those leaders who prevented the Jewish people from going to join the builders [of the new Zionist state] cannot wash their hands and say, 'Our hands did not shed this blood.' "[70] Similar arguments could have been made about those who discouraged Orthodox Jews from going to America before the war.

Moreover, had they been willing to integrate linguistically into the societies in which they found themselves instead of continuing to speak only their Yiddish, had they been more robust instead of the pale yeshiva boys who sat over books, had they been willing to change their appearance and style to be more in line with general European culture, they might have been able to hide more easily among the Gentile population and perhaps survive in greater numbers. In their refusal to make these adjustments that gave advantage to the non-Orthodox who had made them, these Jews suffered disproportionately in the Holocaust.

"The Jews in Slovakia, who were for the most part organized in Haredi communities and excelled in piousness and in the pure belief in the sages . . . were also nearly all wiped out. And in Rumania it was still more forcefully apparent that the Holocaust had singled out Haredi Jewry in particular. One hundred and forty thousand Jews from Carpathian Russia, all of them followers of popular Hasidism, were deported to the crematoria in Poland. . . . Romanian Jewry consisted of . . . the Jews of Transylvania [who] were Haredim in the Hungarian fashion, the Jews of Bukovina [who] were Hasidim in the style of Rozhin and Vizhnitz, the Jews of Bessarabia [who] practised an original form of Judaism. And finally, there were the Jews of Old Romany, assimilated and detached from the traditional tenets. Yet of all the Jewry of Rumania, only the Jews of Old Romany survived. . . . In short, whoever was more pious was utterly destroyed."[71] But haredi Judaism was not utterly destroyed.

"A social structure shakes," Philip Rieff tells us, "when its members must stimulate themselves to feverish activity in order to demonstrate how alive they are."[72] The cognitive dissonance between the reality of their physical destruction and their attachments to the way of life that seemed to abet that destruction forced haredim to work even harder to "protect their convictions, managing to keep them unscathed through the most devastating attacks." Like many whose deeply held beliefs and way of life are challenged by new realities, the haredi Jew did not give up those beliefs and way of life. On the contrary, "presented with evidence, unequivocal and undeniable evidence, that his belief is wrong: what will happen? The individual will frequently emerge, not only unshaken, but even more convinced of the truth of his beliefs than ever before. Indeed, he may even show a new fervor about convincing and converting other people to his view." [73] That was precisely what happened to haredim. After the initial shock, by mid-century they intensified their religious ardor and reconstructions of their Jewish reality. For many the struggle—more precisely, the culture war—against Zionism acted as a framework within which their new traditionalism would become sharpened and shaped. Israel, the Jewish state reborn after the Holocaust, would be the place where one could be more haredi than anywhere else. Only a concerted effort to remain apart from these forces of evil that were Zionism and the secular Jewish state could save Judaism and the Jews who practiced it faithfully. Active struggle and confrontation would hone haredi Judaism.

The competition for a definition of what a Jew is and in time even who a Jew is was obviously most vigorous in a Jewish state. In the diaspora, where they were a beleaguered minority, the safest way for traditionalist Jews to preserve their way of life was simply to keep to themselves. This attitude would be found among many American ultra-Orthodox. But in Israel keeping separate was insufficient since others were then controlling the basic definitions of Judaism and of being a Jew. What meaning did it have for being Jewish if, for example, there was civil divorce or women's suffrage in America? But these same particulars in a Jewish state had an altogether different significance, for they became defined as Jewishly legitimate and as such potentially undermined established theological or ritual sacred order. Here in the hothouse of Jewish resurgence, the haredim had to demonstrate there was another way.

By the mid twentieth century haredi life, especially in Israel, was in a decisive face-off with its antithesis: the Jewish secularists, the *chiloinim*. Many were brothers and neighbors. More than that, the chiloinim were the authorities. In Israel they were the government and in America they were the Jewish establishment. The very people who had abandoned what was viewed as the right path, the *halacha*, were pulling all the strings. They allowed the haredim their existence but only as marginals. The secular supporters of the Belzer rebbe in Tel Aviv imagined he would be the last of his ilk. Premier Ben Gurion released what was then a few hundred yeshiva boys from the Israeli universal military draft for he assumed there would be few more like them in the future. With noblesse oblige, American Jews could give money to yeshivas so that a few boys could study ancient sacred texts because these few kept a small memorial lamp of Jewish life burning. They were the kaddish for the past. But the lamp was not extinguished.

To Be Haredi Today

Taking advantage of the free market in ideas, they asserted, in the words of a Yiddish proverb popular among the Orthodox: *"De Toyreh ist de beste schoyreh"* (The Torah is the best merchandise). Where the normative values were freedom and permissiveness and the proclivity for the novel, they pushed discipline and authority along with the superiority of the old over the new. When secular education seemed inevitable, they founded yeshivas and pressed their young into them. There they nurtured a counterlife.

The yeshiva, bastion of the book and palace of the rabbis, became the embodiment of haredi life. It provided isolation and protection from the evils outside. The traditional Jewish concern with ritual learning was reconstructed as a defense mechanism, an inoculation against the dangers inherent in the encounter with the virus of modernity. From early childhood until after marriage—and in Israel even longer—the young would be kept in school. Originally, the institution was meant only for the males—and it largely remains still a boys' and mens' preserve, but today the idea that females must also be given some sort of education and socialization (although with different subjects) has become an accepted feature of haredi life.[74] And when the women stopped going to school, they were taught that only a yeshiva boy was the ideal mate. To the people of the haredi yeshiva, secular educational achievements were *goyim nachas*, pleasures only for the Gentiles, of a wholly inferior order.

Economic realities, however, were not easily ignored. One could not as easily neglect the necessities of making money. This forced many out of the yeshivas and into the workplace. With a limited secular education, most haredim could only work in retail trade or manual labor. In such circumstances the need to interact with the non-Jewish and nonharedi world in order to make a living inevitably forced many haredim to downplay their culture war. Culture wars go into the back room when the customer is around; religion is religion and business is business. That had happened in America.

While they did not give spiritual meaning to their business (except insofar as the money allowed one to support haredi institutions), many of these Jews did give their time to it. That left less time, energy, and sense of self for being haredi. In America many ultra-Orthodox Jews tried to limit the impact of this reality. They tried wherever possible to work in those industries where others like them work, as if there were safety in numbers. Diamonds, more recently electronics merchandising, jobbing, retail sales in their own neighborhoods, and of course work in education and the supply of Jewish religious needs— everything from doing circumcision and ritual slaughter to the preparation of Torah scrolls and the selling of holy books—became their occupational domains.

To remain haredi, however, requires more than proximity to like-minded people or jobs that could be flexed around religious and communal needs. It requires separation from and antagonism to the outside world. The yeshiva was the best place for this. Haredim poured community resources into building schools. Parents struggled and saved to send their sons or sons-in-law to the yeshiva in order to give *them* a chance for a religious meaningful life. The longer the stay in the yeshiva, the better the protection.

With their early marriages and many children, mandated by custom and religious practice, even traditionalist Orthodox Jews were limited in the number of years they could stay in the protection of the yeshiva. Commonly, in the diaspora, especially America, after several years of married life, usually after the birth of the first or second child, the young man left the yeshiva and went out to work, with all the attendant ramifications of this change in his status and situation.

But in Israel things were different. Although they saw the same significance in yeshiva life and commonly had even less money and greater need, which put pressure on them to leave the shelter of the school, young Israeli haredim who did so were subject to the universal draft. Entry into the army is a great risk. First, it places the haredi in a secular world where he must conform completely. Moreover, because in Israel the army is a central institution of the society, one of the major mechanisms of socialization by which Jews are made into Israelis (that new version of the Jew that the haredim abhor), involvement in it (both as a draftee and until the age of fifty as an annually mobilized reservist) is a route to becoming like all other Israelis. If young men and women serve during the formative years of their lives with nonreligious Jews, share the intense experience of combat or even basic training, they might emerge from this experience with their faith and way of life undermined. Even more than many other militaries, the Israeli army makes deep impressions on the adolescents it transforms into soldiers. The haredim know that, and they therefore avoid the draft as if their very life depended on it—which it does. How haredi can one be when one must take orders from an officer who is not only not a sage but is probably a sinner and who demands that one act and look like a Gentile? So Israeli haredim continue to encourage their men to stay away from army service as long as possible, no matter what the cost.

Because of those deferments Ben Gurion offered and the coalition politics in modern Israel that give haredi political parties like Agudat Israel funds in return for political support, the yeshivas are supported by government funds, allowing people to remain inside for years. Israeli haredim stay in the yeshiva until well past adolescence and soldiering age, until they have been hammered out in the crucible of the Torah academy into a purebred haredi. This does not, however, necessarily mean they are scholars; often they are not. But they are defenders of the faith, cultural warriors in the battle against secularity.

Ultra-Orthodox Jews outside of Israel try to approximate this haredi existence. They send their young men to yeshivas and then to postgraduate *kollels* where study continues and their only obligation is to be set apart from mainstream culture and remain steeped in Jewish texts and ways. But their successes are limited by a structured situation beyond their control. Their Israeli counterparts, on the other hand, are supported in their ways of life by the government. With the monthly stipends they get from the yeshivas, and the other money they can make under cover of their deferments, the Israeli haredim are far more able than their American counterparts to maintain their life apart from countervalues and alternative visions, unsullied by compromise. When a diaspora Jew wants to express the haredi aspects of his character, he can either engage in a confrontation with other kinds of Jews—reform bashing, for example—or better yet, he can go to or at the very least focus his attention on Israel, where he engages in opposition to Zionism, Jewish secularity, and all that constitutes the modern Jewish condition.

Culture War

If it is clear by now that haredim are involved in the creation of a cultural alternative to the secular and profane order of contemporary existence, that they are opposed to deliberate compromise with ways of life different from what they imagine the Jewish sacred past to be; and they negate anything that seems to them to resonate with Gentile ways; if to be haredi means being continually anxious about the capacity to accomplish this in the threatening situation of post-Holocaust modernity, particularly in Israel, this still does not give concrete content to the term. To do that one needs to know precisely what the values are that haredim promote and what they scorn.

In part, an answer to this question comes in the pages ahead, emerging out of my observations. As I discovered, the aspects of life that they seem to emphasize and defend are determined in some measure by the world they perceive as opposing them. Haredim are inextricably linked to the ways of life they oppose. And those are always changing. To succeed in being haredi, their opposition must be dynamic and flexible, ready to shape itself to the ever-changing realities against which it has set itself. Before all else, they must always know what they are not.

If in these days contemporary society chooses to emphasize open and unencumbered encounters between males and females, with individuals themselves choosing whom they will marry, haredim stress the separation of the sexes, with the community acting as the agent for marriage. If the contemporary world encourages humans to take their destiny in their hands, haredim demonstrate how the future is totally in the hands of Heaven. If contemporary people dress in bright colors, the haredim show that true life is in black and white. There is a sense among haredim of their living in an alternative world from the one shared by those who do not live by the same rules and proscriptions.

The haredi essence is to offer extreme and opposing alternative Jewish values and perspectives. "He who champions a middle course and scorns extremism, has a place among counterfeiters, with those lacking wisdom. If there is no extremism, there is no completeness," wrote Rabbi Avraham Karelitz, the Hazon Ish, voice of a new haredi Judaism. "Those who testify that they have not tasted the sweetness of extremism testify thereby that they are bereft of faith in the essentials of the religion. . . ."[75]

Whatever the others do is what the haredim must not do; whatever they value or believe is what haredim disdain and doubt; what is normal to them is abnormal for haredim. If it does not thus contest the other realities, haredi society risks tacitly conceding the attractions of the contemporary world. And if *that* is possible, it is also possible to be morally enticed by those attractions. Ironically, and in spite of themselves, haredim have become increasingly concerned with tracing every new fall from grace that occurs in Jewish life and which they must counter. "We know much more about you than you know about us," a Jerusalem haredi once explained with evident pride and perhaps no less accuracy.

But are they successful in protecting the traditionalist way of life? And how precisely do they do it? How do they keep themselves vital? To answer these questions, we must move from history back to ethnography, to look at the blood and tissue of haredi life. To do that one needs to go into the community.

3

Community

To speak of the haredi community as if it were one indivisible entity is obviously impossible. In spite of the social forces and historical developments that have pressed various of these Jews into common cause and physical propinquity, the divisions among them remain very real. These are distinctions based upon the competing alternatives within Hasidism or between hasidim and the Jews who associate themselves with the Lithuanian yeshiva world. A walk through the various neighborhoods where haredim concentrate cannot help but make one aware of these differences and boundaries.

There are in general four ways in which these distinctions are displayed: the physical, the institutional, the political, and the social. The physical is perhaps the most obvious. The observer's wandering eye beholds ubiquitous signs atop buildings and outside doorways that identify them as the center of one or another community: here is the yeshiva of Karlin-Stolin, there the home of Kaminetz, here the center of Satmar, there the Bucharian Synagogue; in this direction one gets to Kiryat Belz, while going the other way leads to the Spinka hasidim of Jerusalem; here is Kollel America, and there is Zvil. As one reads the signs in passing, it almost seems as if one is traveling the world.

But this is the *Jewish world*, where all the sites are places of Jewish significance. Many, if not most, of the towns and villages whose names mark these places are in these times simply distant memories, shadows, mythic places. Yet the communities and institutions they represent are very much alive, and these buildings (and signs) are in many ways physical symbols of a group's existence and vitality. Indeed, the larger and more impressive the headquarters, commonly a yeshiva (school) and synagogue, the larger and more impressive is the group that calls this place home. For hasidim, this extends as well to the rebbe's accommodations: the more splendid these are, the greater the glory of the group.

In the symbolic effort to express and affirm their survival, even after the triple onslaught of the spiritual challenge of modern secular society, the dislocations of migration, and the destruction of the Holocaust, and as a sign of their continuing endurance, haredi groups have increasingly begun enlarging in size or number (or both) the buildings they inhabit. Thus, for example, numerous hasidic sects—the followers of the Zviler rebbe, the Belzer, the Karliner—to name three—have marked their recent growth by building a bigger yeshiva. Lubavitch (Chabad) hasidim—one of the groups most successful in recruiting members—go even further, erecting an exact replica of their rebbe's Brooklyn headquarters in their Israeli village of Kfar Chabad. Dozens of yeshivas seek to expand their quarters; groups find new places to stake a claim. Haredim fill one neighborhood after another—moving into existing buildings or constructing new ones—and expand the number of neighborhoods they call their own.[1]

While the numerical growth of these Jews—largely the result of high birth and low dropout rates—undoubtedly accounts for some of this expansion, particularly the increase in the number of residences and the explosion in the number of haredi neighborhoods, some of the building of new and enlarged yeshivas and headquarters is in some measure stimulated by the internal competition for followers. For among haredim, as among others, nothing succeeds like success. Those groups who are not obviously growing will have a harder time holding on to their own.

Where there is no growth, there is shrinkage. In the contemporary pluralist world, where different groups brush shoulders with one another in sometimes uncomfortable ways, no group can be certain that it will not lose its adherents to another. And while the haredi world now seems to be able to hold on to most of its own, this does not mean that each sector of that world will be equally successful. Indeed, given that haredim sense themselves to be a minority in a sea of often

unsympathetic others, they are often attracted toward the largest of
the groups among their own. In their relatively closed world, the desire
to be part of something really big is a means of individual empower-
ment. Nothing so much gives members of a minority a way of disre-
garding their numerical weakness than to find themselves in a large
assembly. To stand in a grand building with hundreds or thousands of
one's fellow members, to feel oneself swallowed up in the crowd, or to
encounter one's group's outposts and fellow members in many places
confers upon the insider a sense of belonging to something larger than
life and larger than himself, a sense that he is not isolated.

Not only buildings have the capacity to nourish this feeling. Institutional growth does so as well. To have built and to sustain many
associated institutions—for example, a network of well-attended
schools, a highly utilized religious court system to which Jews come
for adjudication, or whose imprimatur of *kashrut* many people who
observe Jewish dietary laws respect, a successful alms-gathering organization, or a political party that garners many votes—can also be the
mark of a group's vitality. To be sure, institutional strength also trans-
lates into increased income, although when badly managed it can also
lead to increased costs (as has been the case with several hasidic
groups). But the symbolic importance of the institutional growth goes
far beyond the instrumental enhancement it provides. It is a sign
of life.

And then there is politics; it too can be used to point to growth and
life. Since at least the formation of Agudat Israel, Orthodox Jews have
formed themselves into political parties. In the State of Israel, this has
flourished, abetted by a parliamentary system that gives enormous
power to small parties. While the Orthodox have never been sufficiently numerous to dominate the large parties, most notably the
Labor and Likud blocs, they have always constituted a group large
enought to combine with a leading party and thereby form a majority
coalition in the 120-seat Knesset.

For a long time Orthodox Jews were generally divided into two
major religious political groupings that mirrored ideological differences among them. All Orthodox parties were focused around a concern with religious matters and legislation that guaranteed that, in
the Jewish state, Jewish law would not be desecrated. However, they
differed over Zionism. One political cluster, foremost among which
was the Mizrachi which later evolved into the National Religious
Party, supported the legitimacy of political Zionism. Haredim
shunned these parties. They at best tolerated the Zionist state or at
worst repudiated it.

Epitomizing the most extreme rejectionists of Zionism were the Eda Haredis and Neturei Karta, haredi groups that considered the only legitimate activities in the Holy Land to be religious. Unconditionally opposed to the idea of a secular Jewish state, they saw its creation as conceived in sin and doomed to failure. They would brook no accommodations with it, even prohibiting their members from voting in state elections or accepting state funds for their private school systems. As the state became an undeniable and dominant reality, their numbers gradually diminished. Other haredim, by far the larger group, gradually and sometimes grudgingly, made their peace with the reality of a Jewish State of Israel. As they had come to terms with other secular temporal powers, they accommodated to the State of Israel while scorning its Zionist ideology. This was the approach of Agudat Israel.[2]

Agudat Israel was a diverse party, embracing all voting haredim— hasidim, Lithuanian yeshiva-types, and even Sephardic Jews from Muslim countries, some of whom became absorbed by the haredi world when they immigrated to Israel. Until 1984 haredim essentially had two choices in every election—either to vote for Agudat Israel (or its junior partner, Poaley [the Workers of] Agudat Israel) or not to vote at all. But that year the haredi political world began to splinter.

Courted more and more by the major parties, Agudat Israel had over the years entered the corridors of power, at its height having its people serve as chairs of the all-powerful Knesset Finance Committee. Money flowed quickly from the government to religious parties like Agudat Israel that were key to forming a ruling coalition. Ironically, this more powerful party now began to split along the old lines that had gone into making it as well as some new ones. Lithuanians worried that the hasidim were gaining too much influence, patronage, and funds. Hasidim tried to turn the party into a vehicle for their different needs and concerns. And then there were the Sephardim, most of whom were Moroccan Jews, who had always voted for Agudat Israel.

These Sephardim were neither hasidim nor misnagdim. Torn from a cultural milieu and social reality in which tradition, Jewish observance, and folkways were concentric and simultaneous, many of them suffered a culture shock when, during the 1950s, they came in mass immigrations to Israel. Most evolved into secular Israelis with ties to a folk tradition that was also a Jewish tradition. A small minority among them were, however, absorbed into the Lithuanian-style yeshivas. They learned Yiddish, dressed in the black of the haredi world, and began to assimilate some of the haredi worldview. Even after they formed their own separate system of Sephardic yeshivas, many of the most religious among them continued to look upon the heads of the Lithuanian yeshivas as their moral and political leaders. In 1984 they formed their own political party, the Shas Torah Guardians.

Present at the birth of the Shas party were Rabbis Eliezer Schach, aged head of the Lithuanian-style Ponovezh Yeshiva of B'nai B'rak, and Ovadia Yosef, former Israeli Sephardic chief rabbi and outstanding sage. Rabbis Yosef and Schach each had their own reasons for forming this party. Yosef felt betrayed by the powers of Agudat Israel which had not supported his bid for another term as chief rabbi. His ouster, moreover, could be portrayed as an affront to all those who looked upon him as a holy man. It was another case of Ashkenazim dominating and humbling Sephardim, a pattern that had characterized most of the first twenty years of the state. Schach, on the other hand, was concerned that Sephardic Jewry was becoming too much under the sway of the hasidic trends within Agudat Israel and wanted an ally who would help pry funds loose from the burgeoning hasidic institutions. Encouraging the formation of a separate party for the Sephardim was one way to demonstrate to the leaders of Agudat Israel that they needed to pay more attention to the nonhasidic elements in the party or risk losing ground.

There was also another reason for creating Shas. Sephardim, who by the late 1970s found themselves to be a majority of Israeli Jews, were no longer content to be last in line. Just as the secular among them had played a role in the rise of the Likud party to power in the previous decade, so now the religious among them saw an opportunity for their own political coming of age. In the past Agudat Israel, with its European Ashkenazic Jewish roots, had always given support first to Lithuanian yeshivas and hasidic institutions and only last to the new Sephardic ones. A Sephardic party would guarantee more support from the powers that be.

Shas victories in the vote for the Eleventh Knesset were dramatic —the haredi echo of the Likud displacement of Labor. The two seats they gained in 1984 were equal to the number lost by Agudat Israel. And their two political godfathers, Rabbis Schach and Yosef, emerged as important political powers. This meant in turn that Lithuanian and Sephardic power was enhanced in the haredi world.

Four years later the strains within the haredi political fabric became even sharper. Having seen the successes of Shas, Lithuanians, again with the encouragement of Rabbi Schach, formed yet another haredi party, an expression of a deepening split between hasidim and misnagdim in the Agudah. The new party was called Degel Ha-Torah, Torah Flag. Three haredi-headed parties (four, if one counts the old Poaley

Agudat Israel) now vied for votes. Agudat Israel became the party of the hasidim, primarily lead by the large Ger group and Chabad Lubavitch hasidim, whose rebbe from Brooklyn urged his supporters to vote for this organization, which he believed would unite all haredim under one banner. Shas was the party of the religious Sephardim, all of whose candidates were rabbis but many of whose voters were ethnics who supported holy men even if they did not live like them. And Degel Ha-Torah was the party of the Lithuanian Yeshiva people, along with Belzer hasidim, who had hitched their fortunes to this new party in an effort to forge a separate political identity in haredi politics. The result was a more than doubling of haredi representation in the Knesset, from two seats for Agudat Israel in 1984 to five in 1988, for Shas a jump from four to six seats, and for the newly formed Degel Ha-Torah two seats. The political process demonstrated to themselves and others: "We have ceased being a black bloc; now we are equals."[3] The internal competition was, however, not only to see who could garner the most ballots for the Knesset; it was also to see which group was most popular among haredim.[4]

Finally, there is the most significant expression of distinctiveness of all: social growth. The larger the number of adherents a group has, the more social institutions it will be able to sustain and the greater its economic power (both as consumers and as providers of particular services). And of course large groups have many such institutions as well as large buildings and political power.

There are many occasions during which a group will have a chance to display its social proportions. Among the most common for hasidim are gatherings at the traditional Sabbath or holy day meal with the rebbe; for the misnagdim these are gatherings for lectures that the rosh yeshiva offers. And for all groups there are political rallies and protests, funerals (particularly of dignitaries), weddings, and sometimes even a bar mitzvah. These important benchmarks of life (which occur frequently), although manifestly celebrated for religious reasons, have become for most groups social opportunities. They provide a pretext for them to assemble publicly and show how many they are. Indeed, within the haredi community, hardly a week goes by (except during those traditional mourning periods of the year, the seven weeks between Passover and Shavuot and the three weeks preceding the Ninth of [the Hebrew month of] Av) without some such celebration. And funerals can go on all the time. A wedding, often an alliance across groups, allows each of the clans in question to display their size before the other and before the eyes of the world. Ironically, even the deaths, particularly of some important leader or rabbi, become occasions for a celebration of group life. One of the best occasions to demonstrate that the group which revered and followed him has itself *not* died is in the size and majesty of the funeral that they assemble on behalf of the dead.

In a sense, haredim, like all groups, need opportunities to perform their culture, to enact, materialize, and realize who and how many they are. To reflect, communicate, perpetuate, and develop what they are for the benefit of others and themselves is at the heart of many of these community assemblies.[5] In these moments people affirm their membership even as they display it.

How is one to see all this? One must go into the community and participate in them while observing the assemblies. And then, with the perspective of distance, cultural performances become narrative accounts, descriptions thick with cultural meaning. A thousand words become a picture. This, in short, is the ethnographic task. Through a series of such ethnographic interpretations of cultural performances, the result of my repeated forays into haredi communities, I tried to see the weave of the haredi community.

Admittedly, to draw general inferences about the entire haredi world from any particular address is hazardous, for—to the haredim —specifics count for a great deal. To insiders even small matters are distinguishing features of crucial significance and differentiation. And yet, seen from a certain anthropological distance, there is enough similarity to allow for comparative generalization. It is from this distance that I describe what I saw.

4

A Bar Mitzvah in Belz

For months the large Belz hasidic community in Jerusalem had been looking forward to the bar mitzvah celebration of their rebbe's only child, Aaron Mordecai. But this was more than the thirteenth birthday and the ritual coming of age of the "crown prince"; it was also the culmination of the Belz celebration of fifty years of existence in Israel. As one Belzer hasid put it: "We only had seven days to prepare for the *bris* (circumcision), but we've been waiting for this thirteen years." He might have said fifty. This jubilee of Belz hasidim in the Land of Israel commemorated their cultural survival and social renewal in spite of the turmoil of those years. To observe it would be a chance to see and feel something of the Belz community.

Who Is Belz?

The Belz dynasty traces its origins to nineteenth-century Galicia, a territory that straddles southeastern Poland and the region around Cracow and the western Ukraine and the region around Lvov (Lemberg). Belz, a small town forty miles north of Lvov, was the first court of this group of hasidim. The founder or first rebbe, Shalom Rokach [1] (1779–1856), was a descendant of great rabbinic scholars on both his father's and mother's side. After his father died at the age of thirty-two, the young Shalom was brought up and instructed by his uncle, Rabbi Issachar Baer of Sokhol, whose daughter he married. Although influenced by a variety of hasidic masters of the time, Shalom became most attached to the "Seer of Lublin," Jacob Isaac Horowitz, one of the most prominent disciples of the Maggid of Mezerich. Horowitz (1745–1815), the guiding light and founding spirit of large numbers of Polish hasidim, returned the devotion of his disciple and ultimately recommended Rokach for the post of rabbi in Belz. Here, early in the nineteenth century, Shalom established his independent reputation as a zaddik and stimulated a following.

When the word went out that the new rebbe could perform miracles, thousands began to make the pilgrimage to Belz. Increasingly, this little town, with its proud history of renowned rabbis, and which at its peak in 1921 was populated by barely four thousand people (half of whom at the time were Jews), became one of the most important centers of Galician Hasidism. In time, as his following grew, Shalom "built a splendid *Beit Midrash* in Belz," a mark of the growth and importance of his branch of hasidim. [2]

Meanwhile, the Haskalah was making inroads in the region. A contemporary Galician maskil, Joseph Perl (1774–1839), satirized and attacked hasidism, describing the zaddikim in unflattering terms. Other maskilim accused the hasidim of evading state taxes and informed on them to the authorities. In 1836 the government decreed "that no rabbi should be appointed who had not taken an academic course," forcing these Jewish scholars to enter into general culture and busy themselves with secular learning. [3] These and other such developments moved Shalom to become a vocal opponent of Jewish acculturation and Haskalah.

Shalom was succeeded by his fifth and youngest son Joshua (1825–1894). Concentrating on the development of an organization and institutionalization of Belz influence, Joshua became politically active. In 1882, thirty years before the founding of Agudat Israel, Rabbi Joshua convened a thousand rabbis and lay Orthodox leaders in the framework of the recently founded Machazikey Ha-Dat organization, which struggled to maintain the influence and standards of Orthodox Judaism in the face of the secular tendencies of the Haskalah. The organization published its own newsletter, *Kol Machazikey Ha-Dat*, an organ by which Belzers sought to spread their point of view and enhance their influence over Orthodoxy in eastern Europe. It published a list of acceptable Orthodox candidates for the election to the parliament in 1879. Rabbi Simon Sofer (1821–1883), son of the Hatam Sofer, the great champion of traditionalism, was one of the successful candidates that Belz supported. Under Joshua's leadership, Belz hasidim became associated with extreme counteracculturationist views, rejecting all compromises with secularity. "In Belz they were scrupulous about embellishing their ritual observance . . . in accordance with the customs of Hasidism—in dress, behavior, and especially in a way of life that would betray not even a scintilla of flexibility or compromise. Even the smallest deviation from custom was treated as an infraction of the Hatam Sofer's principle that 'the new is prohibited by the Torah.' "[4] In the Belzer rebbe's words: "We have 613 commandments. Every one is holy and dear to us. We cannot forget even one of them."[5]

The number of Belz hasidim grew. Like his father, Rabbi Joshua continued the building and extensions of the Beit Midrash of Belz, and it became one of the traditions of every rebbe of Belz to enhance the structure of the Beit Midrash.

Upon Joshua's death, Issachar Dov (1854–1927), the youngest of his sons, became rebbe. He now headed a court that could count among its followers the bulk of the Jews in places like Lvov, Drohobycz, Tarnopol, Jaroslaw, Przemysl, and other major centers of Galician Jewry. Even more aggressive in his battle against what he viewed as the corrosive influences of contemporary society, he used the Machazikey Ha-Dat organization to oppose even the newly formed Agudat Israel, which he considered to have endorsed too many innovations and compromises. A strict adherent to the notion of the status quo, Issachar Dov, according to his son and successor Aaron Rokach (1886–1957), refused even to eat a vegetable cultivated in a hothouse as part of the Passover seder on the grounds that his forefathers had not eaten such vegetables and therefore neither could he. "We must behave in exactly the way our holy forefathers and teachers did."[6]

Aaron Rokach continued his father's ways. Like his great-grandfather, he also became part of the Sokhol family, marrying his cousin, the daughter of Rabbi Shmuel of Sokhol. Aaron lived an ascetic life, acting as a model Jew for thousands of his followers. But the events of history overtook his life. The Nazi conquest of Poland led to his flight, first to Sokhol and then to Przemysl, where thirty-three members of his family were murdered. Confined to the ghettos in Vizhnitz, Cracow, and Bochnia, he finally escaped and in 1944 reached Tel Aviv with his brother Rabbi Mordecai of Bilgoray and his *shammes* (aide), David Shapira.

A broken man, shorn of his beard, Aaron Rokach was for a time a shadow of his former self. Not only had he lost his family, he had also left behind his hasidim, many of whom were consumed in the firestorm of destruction, because they did not leave for Zion or America but had chosen instead to stay close to their rebbe. In the years immediately after the war, the rebbe was supported by people who did not count themselves his hasidim but who saw in him the incarnation of and memorial to the world of east European Jewry so cruelly destroyed. Undoubtedly, the rebbe, like many other Holocaust survivors, was burdened with remorse and a sense of survivor guilt. The grandeur that was Belz seemed relegated to the past.

But in time the rebbe recovered his bearings and began again to build a following on the new soil of Israel. The seeds of this rebuilding in the Holy Land had already been sown with the establishment of a first Belz *shtibbel*, or one-room synagogue/study hall, in 1939. At that time, on the eve of the war, some had already recognized that change was coming and had made the move to resituate; but they had been few in number.

Upon arrival, the rebbe divided his time between secular Tel Aviv and Jerusalem. As its strength returned, the court of Belz moved to Jerusalem, a city dominated by religion.

When Rabbi Aaron died, seven years after the death of his younger brother, Rabbi Mordecai of Bilgoray, the single possible successor to the crown of Belz was Mordecai's only son, Issachar Dov (Beril), then nine years old. While the young boy—called the Yanuka (Child)[7]— matured, Belz experienced all the tribulations of an interregnum period. Managing to survive as an influential court in the new environment was no easy matter.

With fewer people attracted to Hasidism in 1950s Israel than had been the case in the heyday of pre-Holocaust Poland, and in an atmosphere of growing competition for turf and influence, Belz stood on the verge of disintegration. There was no rebbe around whom the faithful could flock, no person to embody and symbolize their aspirations and spirit, no one to intercede on their behalf before the heavenly court or (some might cynically suggest, even more importantly) no one to intercede with the earthly powers that be on the hasidim's behalf. To survive Belz would have to recreate itself, its institutions, influence, and membership. Indeed, with a little boy at its head, it would even have to recreate its rebbe.

An important step in this process was the arranged marriage between the eighteen-year-old rebbe and Sarah Hager, the daughter of Rabbi Moshe Yehoshua (b. 1916), the rebbe of Vizhnitz, a major hasidic leader of his generation, with a large group of followers, and a prominent member of the Moetzet G'dolay Ha-Torah (Council of Torah Sages) of Agudat Israel. With this wedding a new chapter began in Belz history. The young rebbe, taking his new wife from the Vizhnitz court in B'nai B'rak near Tel Aviv, moved to Jerusalem full time and began to exercise the leadership for which he had been groomed. This leadership meant, above all else, attracting more members to Belz. Many of these were young men, like the rebbe himself, who were either from other hasidic courts or else part of the unaffiliated portion of the haredi world. A number were young immigrants from Rumania. Others were children of Holocaust survivors. In short, Belz after 1966 became a collection of followers who were first-generation adherents to the Belz way.

Rabbi Issachar Dov carefully navigated among the various competing hasidic powers in Israel. These included not only Vizhnitz, to whom he was bound through his wife, but also Ger, the single most powerful and largest hasidic group with headquarters in Jerusalem. Because he was young and untested, the Belzer rebbe did not have the reputation and associated admiration that would make him a universal haredi leader. He was not automatically put on the Moetzet G'dolay Ha-Torah, and indeed his relations—as traditionally had been the case in Belz—with Agudat Israel were ambivalent at best. Because the party had become a major voice of haredi Judaism in Israel, he could, however, not divorce himself from it completely. Nevertheless, he had no real base of support in Agudat Israel. Much later, in the late 1980s (just before the bar mitzvah) he would join with Rabbi Eliezer Schach and the Lithuanian yeshiva world in forming the Degel Ha-Torah party, which ran its own candidates in competition with Agudat Israel for a place in the Knesset. But in the late 1960s and early 1970s the young rebbe and his aides were building the organization. This meant building *mosdos,* institutions.

The larger the Belz group became, the more institutions it created. Not only did the yeshiva in Jerusalem's Machaneh Yehuda neighborhood grow, but Belz attracted followers in America, in the few places in Europe where hasidim remained after the World War II, and throughout the Jewish world. Belz schools were established in Jerusalem, B'nai B'rak, Haifa, and Ashdod in Israel; in London and Manchester, England; Montreal and Toronto, Canada; Antwerp, Belgium; Lugano, Switzerland; Monsey, in New York's suburban Rockland County, and Brooklyn. In Israel, searching for fiscal support for a student body that outstripped its membership's capacity to support it financially, Belz—unlike many of the haredi groups, accepted funds for education from the Zionist state. This decision, castigated by many of those who vehemently opposed any and all compromises or tacit recognition of the legitimacy of Zionism and who wanted nothing of the state in the schools—primarily hasidim of Hungarian extraction, most prominently the Satmar—lead to Belz establishing a far more distinct identity in the bubbling caldron of Israeli haredi life. According to many, they were renegades. Yet, with the financial subsidies they received, their network of schools grew even more, and with them the numbers of their adherents continued to swell. Young parents, as many of the new Belzer hasidim were, needed schools for their large families, and Belz was supplying their needs.

As their numbers grew, so too did their economic clout. Conspicuous in this was the Belz decision to involve itself in the certification of kosher meat, an important source of income. This decision aroused competitive conflict with other established haredi certifiers, most prominently the Eda Haredis and the Hungarian hasidim. While Belz claimed only to want to certify foods for its own people, this entry into the lucrative business of kosher certification was seen in many quarters as an attempt to compete for precious funds. Bitter turf fights broke out, some of which led to street battles in Jerusalem and even in New York during one of the rebbe's visits to his hasidim. But Belz did not abandon its decision to certify foods as kosher.

The rebbe's activities and successes, especially but not only the controversial ones, enhanced his position and charisma among his followers. Old Belz traditions were revitalized. A newsletter, *Ha-Machaneh Ha-Haredi*, was being published. With the funds coming in, the yeshiva was being enlarged; a new massive headquarters was being constructed in the new Kiryat Belz, a Jerusalem neighborhood filled with new Belz families. In well-appointed apartments, no longer in the squalid streets surrounding the markets of Machaneh Yehuda, Belz was rising like a phoenix. One hasid quoted the book of Job (8:7) to capture Belz's rebirth from the catastrophe of the Holocaust: "Though thy beginning was small, yet shall thy end be greatly increased."

Once again, Belz had a powerful and influential leader who, as one of his hasidim explained in *Ha-Machaneh Ha-Haredi*, caused Belz to "develop and extend the boundaries of its holiness in numbers and quality."[8] That their rebbe's charisma was not universally recognized in the haredi world was secondary to his disciples. They knew that Belz was looking toward a grander future that would once again recall the majesty of its past, a past that the followers, although new to the fold, embraced as their own. It was against this history that on the seventh of Cheshvan, October 18, 1988, and the days preceding it,

Belz celebrated the bar mitzvah of the rebbe's only son as well as their jubilee year in the Land of Israel.

Bar Mitzvah

In the weeks and months preceding the celebration, much of the information about the events was passed by word of mouth. Members of the Belz community, of course, knew exactly what would happen, when and where. This was their *simcha,* their joyous occasion. The hasidim shared in all the family celebrations and benchmarks of their rebbe's life. The line between personal and public life was a blurred one, for the personal life of the rebbe was intertwined with his public persona. His son's bar mitzvah was a Belz festival.

Earlier in the week, at the opening gathering of the jubilee celebrations, Belzer hasidim and those commemorating the occasion with them had filled Binyanei Ha-Uma, Jerusalem's convention center, to overflowing. The festivities had opened with a presentation of awards to school youngsters from all the Belz institutions who had excelled in examinations in Talmud, Mishnah, Jewish law, Torah, and commentaries. Each of the children who were called by name toasted the rebbe and passed before him. Afterward came speeches that recounted the Belz saga. It was a story not only of an organization but of a family, the narrative account of Aaron Rokach, his brother Mordecai, Issachar Dov, the current rebbe, and his son, the bar mitzvah boy, Aaron Mordecai, the namesake of his grandfather and of his great-uncle and the palpable sign of "the triumph of Israel." [9] Israel, the Jews, Belz—they were all one.

Although the Belz community numbers in the thousands, insiders share a sense of intimacy, almost like a family or, more precisely, a tribe. Thus, when earlier in the month I asked a Belzer hasid on the street for the date of the bar mitzvah, he first asked who I was and who I knew. Information in this intimate community commonly serves as a boundary marker. But because Belzer hasidim had grown to be a powerful force in the haredi world, even the secular press and electronic media would cover this particular celebration. So, the hasid was not that surprised that outsiders like me would ask about it.

For Belzers this occasion marked one of the most significant developments in the postwar haredi world. These Jews, once the bare remnants of an abandoned and charred world, marginal to the present and unlikely to be part of the future, were now news. They survived and thrived. They could not be ignored. There was no mistaking the sense of triumph this fact gave the haredim. Ironically, it was the fact that outsiders could not ignore them that endowed the events with an especially enhanced importance. And yet, although they might hear the news, as Yisrael Eichler, editor of the Belz newsletter *Ha-Macha-neh Ha-Haredi,* put it in his report of the events, "No stranger could comprehend this." [10]

With a smile of triumph the Belzer hasid told me that the celebrations would start in the morning, reach their peak about 2 P.M. at the still-unfinished new Belzer yeshiva in Kiryat Belz, but that if I was not there early, I probably would not be able to get inside as all the doorways would be locked by 1:30. The Belzers had planned carefully.

Although strictly speaking there were no invitations, for, as one hasid put it in Yiddish, "A good friend comes on his own," I knew— and the gatekeepers reminded me—that without a special pass I was not likely to get inside at all. Sentinels and hired security guards were everywhere. To be sure, this fact itself was symbolically freighted, for not only did it vividly suggest a watched-over palace of the king, it also implied that the affair was something so significant that outsiders would *want* to come even though uninvited.

For the Belzers the new building, a massive structure that would be one of the largest yeshivas in the world, was a monument to their renewal—no less than the bar mitzvah itself. Once again, a Belzer rebbe was enlarging and enhancing his yeshiva. About a month before, in the rebbe's sukkah, the temporary tabernacle built outside the old yeshiva in Machaneh Yehuda and in which the hasidim celebrated the holy days with their rebbe, I had seen a remarkable poster that alerted me to the symbolic power of the new building. Surrounded by flashing lights were three drawings. On the left side was a picture of the yeshiva in Belz, in flames. In the center was a drawing of the Holy Temple in Jerusalem, also now destroyed. And on the right was a painting of the new yeshiva, resplendent and massive. Above the pictures were the words "From Belz to Belz." The message was unmistakable. Old temples might be destroyed by the enemy, but they would be rebuilt. If Belz could rebuild the grandeur the Nazis had destroyed, then all Jews would also someday rebuild the grandeur of the Holy Temple. This was an expression of death and transfiguration, of hope and messianic redemption. First the Belzer temple would be rebuilt and next would come the Holy Temple in Jerusalem. Renewal was at hand, repair was possible, salvation was around the corner.

And now at the bar mitzvah—even though the new quarters were still a shell, the inside unfinished, outside stairways and ramps quickly constructed, diesel-powered halogen lamps freshly installed, and chairs and a stage temporarily set up for the hundreds who packed the space—an important step toward the new day was being taken. Not that anyone among the faithful would have dared to say that the Belz yeshiva could take the place of the Holy Temple, nor would they, like the Zionists inflated with active but ultimately counterfeit messianism —at least from the haredi point of view—suggest that the End was at hand. That was all for God to decide. But that these local Belz events could somehow be coupled with even greater Jewish promises certainly enhanced the sense of momentous celebration and exaltation among the faithful insiders. Indeed, to many Belzers everything they did— the building of their institutions and of their structures—was to enable them, as one of their spokesmen put it, "to raise a generation with whom we shall not be ashamed to greet our virtuous messiah." [11]

On the morning of the day, Kavod Kodsho (His Holiness) Sh'lita (May He Live for Many Good Days, Amen), as young Aaron Mordecai was referred to in the pages of *Ha-Machaneh Ha-Haredi* and by many hasidim, marked his coming of age by donning his *tefillin* (phylacteries) at the morning services for the first time. Now he had this obligation like other adult males. At the yeshiva there would be a festive meal to celebrate the occasion, to hear some words of Torah from the boy and his father as well as the other dignitaries, including his grandfather, the rebbe of Vizhnitz.

Approaching the yeshiva, one could not help but be struck by the way the entire neighborhood radiated the affair. There were signs blessing all who came "in the name of God": B'RUCHIM HABA'IM BE-SHEM HASHEM.

Another huge banner proclaimed: BE-SEMAN TOV UVE-MAZAL TOV, "Under a good sign and a good star." Some signs were bilingual in Hebrew and Yiddish (although Hebrew was always the dominant [top] language of the sign), while others were bilingual in Hebrew and English (for those guests from England and America who were often more comfortable in English). In many windows signs of the Degel Ha-Torah party were also hung. Politics and religion mixed easily here.

Strings of lights stretched across the streets. On all the surrounding lanes, painted arrows pointed one toward the yeshiva. It was as if the map had been rearranged so that all roads led to Belz. Loudspeakers hung on the building, broadcasting the sounds of singing from those inside. Periodically, the singing stopped while the rebbe's words echoed throughout the neighborhood.

And if the signs, sounds, and lights were not enough, there were the people. Around the yeshiva and on the stoops of nearby houses were scores of little Belz boys wearing their festive best, most notably the black-velvet *kashketl*, a cap once worn throughout Galicia by Jews and now the distinctive headgear of Belz youngsters. Married men wore their finest caftan and the fur shtreimel atop their head. The little girls wore their most elaborate finery; their mothers wore fancy dresses and, in line with the custom of the married keeping their own hair under cover, finely coiffed wigs on their heads. Indeed, the attractive women were perhaps the most striking sight of all as I approached.

As I looked at these women, I could not help thinking to myself that if I did not know they all had husbands who looked as if they came out of an earlier century, I would suppose their spouses to look as up-to-date as the women did. If their husbands dressed in ways reminiscent of the dour Amish, their black meant to symbolize mourning for the destroyed Holy Temple and reminding them of their exile from its glories, these women seemed to have long given up mourning, and looked nothing like the Amish. They *appeared* to be women very much of this world. Perhaps if only one or two women looked fashionable I might consider it an anomaly. But every woman did. This must be significant, for the men could not be oblivious of their wives' appearance. Could it be that through these women the men had found a way vicariously to be this-worldly? A man might be forced by convention and custom to appear archaic, but he could permit (maybe even encourage) his wife to look very much up-to-date. Her appearance could serve as an emblem of his affluence and success. Indeed, it seemed that the American Belzers—more so than their poorer Israeli counterparts—were more likely to have such well-dressed wives. In a sense, the American Belz hasidim, like Americans in general, were more caught up in the conspicuous display of wealth, fashion, and position.

Although deep inside a haredi enclave, I was subtly reminded of how close the outside world was, and could not help suspecting that it had already penetrated these apparently protected precincts. I saw this too in the physical appearance of the Kiryat Belz neighborhood. This was not like the impoverished surroundings in Mea Shearim, the old haredi ghetto in Jerusalem that seemed to mirror an aesthetic of another, older time. Rather what I saw in Kiryat Belz were small freshly built apartment units of three or four floors, all with breathtaking views of the Judean Hills. From the outside they looked no different from any other of the new suburban neighborhoods ringing Jerusalem.

Many of the security personnel carried walkie-talkies. This was a well-organized and modern force whose aim was to keep order. The use of this modern force seemed to me to reinforce the subliminal message of the women's fashionable dress and the modern apartments. All were evidence that wherever ideology was silent, Belz had found a way to fill the ideological vacuum with the up-to-date. Throughout the day I would see further signs of this: the newest cars, the most modern video recorders on which to photograph the proceedings, the highest-quality recording tape, the newest high-tech microphones, up-to-date halogen lamps, and (as I would discover later in Belz homes) personal computers, modern furniture and décor, and all else that was current to support their tribal activity in the most up-to-date way.

Yet there were activities going on here that emphasized another world and time, a more traditional side of Belz life. When I got inside and managed to observe the proceedings around the festive table at which the rebbe and his son, as well as other dignitaries, sat, these would capture my attention.

Penetrating Belz

Getting inside required passing a number of barriers, both physical and social. First there were the guards. The security personnel were only the first hurdle. What did I want, one asked me. In spite of the small knit yarmulke on my head, my orange corduroys and clipped hair obviously marked me as an outsider. I explained that I had been invited (which strictly speaking I had not been; what I did have was the name of someone inside the community who was supposed to get me in).

"I don't know anything about it," he replied. But apparently reasoning that if I was interested in getting inside, I was ready to go to the next gateway, he sent me to the entrance marked RABBIS. Through here had come many a rosh yeshiva and rabbi, including the rebbe of Slonim, the rebbe of Rachmastrivka, the rebbe of Sadigora, and others.

Unsure exactly where that was, I climbed the path around the stone building. As I made my way around, I heard the singing of the hasidim. It was a Yiddish refrain I knew. *"Der rebbe zoll leben, a mazal tov, alle hasidim a mazal tov, alle Yidn a mazal, und a mazal tov"* (May the rebbe live, in good fortune, all hasidim in good fortune, all Jews in good fortune, and good fortune). The rebbe, the hasidim, the Jews, and good fortune were all one: Yidn were hasidim. And then suddenly the singing stopped, and the high-pitched Yiddish cadences of the

rebbe could be heard. He talked to the instantly silent crowd about
the important milestone of fifty years' existence in Israel that they were
celebrating today; he could be heard for blocks as he recounted the
struggle they endured—the moments of anxiety and loss of the years
during and after the Second World War and their remarkable rebirth
after the Holocaust. Then he began to list names of those who had
been Belz in generations past. He began in Galicia, and then he worked
his way forward to Jerusalem. The names were etched in Belz collective memory.

"Not by our wisdom did we merit all this," he told the assembled,
"but with the help of heaven, and by the merit of that zaddik, his
holiness, our rabbi and teacher, Rabbi Aaron, may his virtue protect
us, Amen." The rebbe invoked the use of gematria, the numerological
formula by which Hebrew letters are turned into numbers and then
translated into new letters. In *gematria*, the letters for "Aaron lives"
were equivalent to those of "Mordecai." Mordecai was the rebbe's
father, the previous rebbe's brother. And Mordecai was also the famous hero of Purim, the proud Jew who would not prostrate himself
and bow or scrape before Haman, enemy of the Jews. Those who
would not compromise their Judaism—even before Haman—like Belz
would in the end be triumphant. And what was true in the past must
continue into the future: "To build and be built up, to increase Torah,
the fear of Heaven, and Hasidism." All this was symbolized in Aaron
Mordecai, the bar mitzvah boy.

Whatever else was going on here, the essential celebration of this
hasidic group (and perhaps of all Orthodoxy) was of stubborn survival.
In spite of the ideological and physical assaults, they had managed not
only to survive but to grow. They were now as numerous as they had
ever been in their history, and perhaps even more powerful. Certainly,
the neighborhood and the new edifice they were building testified to
their economic strength. And economic strength was a sure sign of
physical and moral vitality. The last few years of the new rebbe's
leadership had led to a spectacular transformation of Belz from a small
and struggling sect to its current condition of vigor. He might be
invoking the names and memory of his uncle and father, but the
assembled were being inspired by him and his son.

Reflecting on this message and the celebrations, one hasid would
later write: "I was privileged . . . to witness the new blossoming of
the Belz world." Those assembled here were "an undeniable proof
that there is a revival for those who sleep in the dust." As he looked
around him and thought about all that Belz had accomplished since
the war, he could not help but "marvel how—from those survivors of

the sword, those 'brands plucked out of the fire,'[12] from those refugees who remained years without city and family members—did this grand structure bloom?"[13]

So that was it. This was not simply a celebration of survival; it was a triumph over the Holocaust. "There is no resurrection of the dead greater than this," said Rabbi Pinchas Friedman, head of the Belzer yeshiva, describing the gathering at the convention center.[14]

The horrible failure that had led so many to the slaughter, the refusal to abandon European centers of Jewish life for the refuge of America and Israel, a tragedy that the survivors still felt sad and perhaps guilty about, was at last being overcome. They were back to full strength and growing. It was joy mixed with tears; tears about the sacrifice of the past, joy in the second chance that this resurrection offered. Those whom the enemies had tried to destroy "were not dead but living still."[15]

A few days before at the convention center, the Belz rosh yeshiva wrapped this message in hermeneutics and midrash:

"Our rabbis were taught," he began, citing a talmudic discourse on the third chapter of the Book of Daniel: "At the same time that the Babylonian King Nebuchadnezzar threw Chananya, Mishael, and Azarya into the fiery furnace, the Holy One, blessed be He, said to Ezekiel: 'Go and restore the dead in the valley of Dura.' And those bones came and slapped Nebuchadnezzar's face."[16]

The history of the resurgence of Belz gave this talmudic account of the Bible a new gloss: "See, we are the bones of our departed come to life.

"Rabbis, teachers and friends! This holy assembly is the resurrection of those dead bones that were cremated in the Holocaust, for their holy way serves us still as a torchlight illuminating our way in the darkness of our exile. This holy assembly is the slap in the face that still rings on the faces of all the Nebuchadnezzars: You wanted, God help us, to obliterate the Jewish people, and see they still live in their holiness, purity, Hasidism, and punctilious observance as in days of yore."[17]

Again and again in haredi circles, I would encounter this theme that the rebbe now echoed. It was a desire to somehow put the Holocaust into the past. The haredim wanted and needed a way to mourn without being destroyed. They needed the present to make sense of the past for them. They needed to turn the travail into a meaningful prelude to triumph. As Rabbi Friedman suggested at the convention center celebrations, they were Isaac, survivor of a holocaust, who ultimately had redug the wells of his father Abraham, which Gentiles and enemies had stopped up. Saved from death, Isaac had assured Jewish continuity.

The words of the rebbe echoing in my ears, I reached the back entrance of the yeshiva. It was cut off by several fences and a swarm of hasidim—mostly teenagers—who stood outside or else who, with arm bands on their caftans that identified them as ushers, manned the gates.

"Where is the entrance for the rabbis?" I asked.

They looked at me; surely I was not one of *their* rabbis. Still, this was an extraordinary day; all sorts of guests were coming to the gates of Belz.

"On the other side, at the bottom," one of the youngsters pointed me toward the correct entrance.

Weaving my way through groups of little boys who ran around the building and past girls who sat in the doorways of the houses, I passed the women's entrance, where a throng of women were trying to press themselves into the relatively small space allotted them. At the convention center they had seen the proceedings on a video screen; here they were pressing to peep through the cracks in the doorways. Others were upstairs crowded into the ladies' gallery. The women could be seen from the outside but from the inside they would be invisible, screened by the dividers that separated them from the men's view.

At last, I reached the rabbis' doorway. I passed the first guard with a self-assured walk and demeanor that suggested that I belonged there. Next I passed three hasidic ushers walking the other way. I had gone only a few steps when I was called back in Hebrew by one of the three hasidic sentinels. "Excuse me," one said, "where are you going?"

"I was told to come here," I replied, invoking the name of my contact, making sure to use the Yiddish pronunciation of the name—the way insiders would refer to him.

"Did you get a ticket?" I was asked. Everyone had tickets that directed him to sit or stand.

"I got a phone call," I answered, obviously unfazed by not having a ticket. That self-assurance apparently was sufficient to get me by this second hurdle. Now, as I entered the building, I came to another sentry. This time he was a nonhasid.

"Your name?" he asked matter-of-factly.

"Heilman," I replied.

He took out a computer-prepared list and looked for the name. I knew it would not appear on the list, but the sentry did not. He searched the list carefully, expecting to find my name. There was no "Heilman." But on the Hebrew list the letter ה (H) could easily appear to be a ‫ד‬ (D) "Deilman," he said at last. "Maybe this is it. Is your first name Lewis, and are you a lawyer?" The organizers had identified the invited guests.

"Yes," I answered, knowing that he who hesitates is lost. Deilman, whoever he was, was probably already inside, and if not, he would get in anyway since his name appeared on the list. In the meantime, I would disappear in the crowd. I passed the third barrier.

Through the labyrinthine halls, I walked up and around until two flights later, I came upon a small gathering of hasidic men who wore ushers' arm bands and who nibbled sherayim of the rebbe's meal, the blessed food that all hasidim share with the rebbe and one another. One of them turned to me with a look of inquiry on his face. Still chewing on his food, he raised his eyebrows and flipped over his hand inquiringly. "Nu?"

"I'm invited," I said.

"To what, the bar mitzvah?" he asked.

"What else?" I responded, in a style meant to resonate with familiarity. Jews after all answer with questions. "Where do I go?"

"Look, I'll let you in this door," he said, pointing to a small entry next to where we stood.

All of a sudden, the ease with which I was getting in was starting to make me anxious. What if I found myself on the dais after walking through the door? What if everyone turned to look at me and realized I was crashing this affair? "I am not sure how long I can stay," I said, "and I don't want to be in a place where I won't be able to leave from easily."

"Don't worry," the hasid said, "the way I let you in you will find a way to leave when you wish." He opened the door for me.

Walking through, I found myself alongside the dais. But I was on its margins, near the head table but separated from it by a wooden barrier. The view was perfect. I found a place to stand on a bleacher among some boys. The rebbe was speaking again, but a moment or two after I had settled into my place, he stopped.

A hasid, one from the choir for which Belz was famous in the haredi world, began to sing. These were songs, many of them composed for the occasion by Yosef Tzvi Breuer, head of a Belz school in Ashdod and self-taught composer. The singing was accompanied by a band, made up of the latest synthesizers and electronic instruments. A number of hasidim holding microphones were dispersed among the crowd. They were clearly there to enhance and organize the singing.

The crowd did indeed join in, clapping and swaying as one. On my perch on the bleachers, I could feel the bounces. Pressed between two young hasidim, I found myself swaying back and forth with them and in rhythm with the song. From behind I felt a hand on my shoulder, just as I would have had we been dancing in a circle, pushing me back and forth.

No matter how large the space, hasidim needed to press against each other and toward the center, the rebbe. They needed to be *touched* by one another to feel the community. That was what I was sensing in the most palpable way. Although we were assembled inside a cavernous room, inside this huge hall was the little shtibbel, the small one-room synagogue with which Belz began. This time its walls were human and its reality was embedded in the conscious experience of all those inside. Like all the others, I too felt the crowding and intimacy, the presence of those around me. I smelled their bodies, shared their food and their space. Without this physical intimacy, this blurring of the boundary between the self and others, much would be lost. And so no matter how big a place the Belzers built, it would still require people to be crushed together shoulder-to-shoulder. That was true even in the still uncompleted new building. The crowd and the community had to implode on each other or risk being dispersed and diminished. To feel the body politic one had to be one with the tribe. That, as I would discover later at the many tishen I attended, was part of the repeated experience. It was why eating sherayim or toasting the rebbe was critical. Intimates share space, food, utensils, fortune, spirit, life.

Soon, in spite of my desire to be an observer, I heard myself becoming a participant, singing along with everyone else. It was easy at first because the singing was no different from what I might have done at any one of the countless bar mitzvah celebrations I had attended in my life. After all, Jews of all sorts had appropriated many hasidic melodies. The Vizhnitz melody, sung now, was one whose tune and words I knew well. Hasidic melodies had become part of general Jewish culture, and singing or knowing them no longer marked one as an insider.

So Belz kept writing new ones. They tried to weave a melodic boundary marker. But then they had to find ways of teaching their own the new tunes. So they put them on tapes and distributed them among insiders. Barely a week after the bar mitzvah a cassette filled with all the new songs written for the occasion and adorned with a picture of the rebbe, his son, and their hasidim seated around the festive table was on sale in the Belz community. Soon, the tapes, inevitably, reached a wider market (hawkers on Jerusalem or Brooklyn streets sold them easily), and then once again new songs had to be made up, songs that helped define the community of insiders.

The View from Inside

I looked along the dais and out into the room. The sea of black and white was overwhelming. On the long table were candles, bottles of sweet red Hebron wine, pieces of twisted challah loaves, and the staple food of all Jewish celebrations: gefilte fish, boiled carrots, chicken, and drinks such as soda, cola, wine, and grape juice. The spread on the tables was modest. The organizers claimed this was to downplay the trappings of royalty and to give the participants a homey, familiar feeling. This was to be a model for celebrations, too many of which had become overly elaborate among the rank and file—elaborate to the point of hedonistic wastefulness. Cynics whispered that there were other reasons for the modesty of the menu: too much money had already been spent on the celebration and costs had to be contained.

At the head table the rebbe, in fur hat and shiny black caftan, was sitting on a velvet-covered wooden armchair, a kind of throne, and next to him was his son in a tall mink hat, a *spodik*, his long curly earlocks held against his temples by the black-rimmed glasses he wore. On the other side of the bar mitzvah boy sat his grandfather, the Vizhnitzer rebbe, his face framed in white hair, a round and rich-looking shtreimel upon his head, resting at a slight angle. There were other dignitaries, some related by blood, others tied by pedagogy; in the scholars' society that haredi Judaism had become, a teacher was at least as important and as close as a blood relative—if not more so.

Men with cameras, still and video, circulated through the crowd, capturing every moment on film. When the rebbe danced in a three-some with his son and father-in-law, even as the hasidim pressed around them, the camera managed to capture the moment. When the head of the Ponovezh Yeshiva, Rabbi Schach made his way in, a sign of the coming together of Belzer hasidim and the Lithuanian yeshiva world—an alliance reflected in the recently formed Degel Ha-Torah political party—shutters snapped. When an elder leaned over to whisper a word of wisdom or congratulations to the bar mitzvah boy, someone took a picture. Everything had to be visually recorded for, as one after another of those present said to each other: "Words cannot capture this."

The occasion was being treated as historic in proportions, one of those moments in a community's existence by which it marks its life. For years after, Belzer hasidim would undoubtedly distinguish themselves by recalling that they had witnessed this gathering. That was why they had come from the faraway corners of Belz life to be here at this time. Their coming, in turn, had underscored and confirmed the importance of the occasion and displayed the breadth of their community. Above all else, even as they seemed to be honoring the rebbe and his son, Belzers were celebrating themselves. Picture after picture was made of the sea of bodies. In the photos these living faces stretched to the edges of the picture—in contrast to those horrible photos of the dead which had been all that remained of Holocaust-ravaged Belz. The frames were now filled with life, a life blotting out the images of death still emblazoned on a haredi consciousness.

While most of the faces in the room were young—a sign of the vigor and future of Belz—and the youngest were those piled on the high rafters, on the back benches, and along the edges, there were also elders close to the rebbe, people whose presence symbolized continuity. These were men whom everyone watched, whose tears dripped with meaning, whose sorrows and joys were metaphors for the group's. And it was their task to instruct and thus include these newcomers in Belzer collective memories. "This is the miracle of the rebirth and reestablishment of Belz Hasidism," said one, characterizing the occasion.

"Remember the wonders He performed," said one man quoting the Psalmist (105:5). "We must recall the greatness of God's kindness by which He has brought us all together here even as we remember the terrible and awful destruction that nearly befell all of us, that were it not for God's mercy, we would have all suffered. And so, 'let my tongue cleave to my cheek if I do not recall you.' "[18]

Said another man, weaving verse with expressions of veneration: "Behold how good and pleasant it is for brothers to assemble together —brothers in conviction, brothers in manner, hasidim knotted together and fastened tightly under the guidance of his Holiness, our Master, Teacher, and Rabbi, may he live for many good days, amen."

Joy was, however, tempered with abiding haredi anxiety. "We might think the trials of our fathers were only for them," but in truth "the deeds of our fathers are signposts for their sons." The past is prologue. The sons may yet have to experience "exile, hunger, hounding, persecutions, and all the rest."[19] Danger always lurked at the edges of the haredi sense of Jewish existence. "Rejoice with trembling," the Psalmist warned.[20] Haredim never forgot that.

The singing began again. The crowd swayed. At the same time, food and drink were being passed throughout the crowd, part of the continuing distribution of the rebbe's meal. Not until everyone had tasted something from the rebbe's table would the community have ritually expressed its bonding.

The singing stopped with the announcement by the gabbai, the rebbe's aide and religious valet, that we would soon be saying the grace after the meal. On the tables hasidim reached for the little cups of water to pour over their fingertips which, having become ritually impure by touching food, were now to be laved before thanking God for it. Someone brought in a basin with a large cup filled to the brim with water, and it was handed, head over head and hand over hand to the dais. Around me some of the boys who stood along the bleachers scrambled to find a way to carry out these ablutions. A few used the few droplets of soda or other liquid in the cups that some of them still held from the meal. In these ritual matters, each, according to his station, prepared himself for grace.

A microphone was placed before the bar mitzvah boy, who would lead the benediction. No hymnals were distributed; everyone was expected to know the words by heart, words said after every meal. This was Aaron Mordecai's second important activity of the meal. The first had been his brief Torah address, an exegetical exercise meant to demonstrate his intellectual and Torah skills but, in the time-honored custom, interrupted by songs throughout. The interruptions are meant to put all bar mitzvah boys in the same position. Under cover of the interruptions they can overcome their nervousness. But the interruptions are also a test to see who can focus his attention even in the face of the interference. Aaron Mordecai had passed his test; he was clearly the crown prince. Now he could lead the prayers. He began with the call in Yiddish: "Gentlemen, let us say grace." Next, as he was to intone the line when the leader normally lists those most esteemed among the assembly and begs their indulgence to lead the grace, he mumbled, seeming to me to be a bit unsure about precisely whom he was supposed to include in this list.

The grace was recited in hushed undertones, rather quickly and somewhat dispassionately. The time for singing was past. If I had expected a spirited thanks to the Lord for His bounty on these tables, I was disappointed. Displays of ecstasy in prayer, so common for hasidim, were for other occasions.

Now the sun was setting, and the time for the afternoon prayers, Mincha, was at hand. As everyone pivoted to face toward the Temple Mount in the Old City, a stillness settled across the sea of black and white. A quiet murmur filled the air, and waves of worshipers swayed back and forth, their eyes closed in devotion. Though the hasidim were pressed together, each one seemed to find sufficient room for his devotions. At the end, everyone waited for the rebbe to finish. This was the rule. No matter how intense and devoted the worshiper was, his rebbe always took longer to complete his prayers for the rebbe's perfection and devotion was always greater.

"One of the miracles at the Holy Temple," a hasid said to me later, reflecting on this moment, "was that no matter how crowded it was, everyone had room to bow and make the steps necessary to complete his prayers. This is what we felt too at the bar mitzvah." Once again, the parallels were being made. Belz were all Jews, and the yeshiva was the Holy Temple.

On the dais the rebbe stood up with his son, and several of the hasidim near them began to dance. Whenever the rebbe stood, the whole hall stood; and when he sat, they sat—or were signaled to sit by the gabbai. This is not to suggest that all went smoothly and decorously. There was shouting and pushing—but all this seemed to be part of the expected proceedings. Every so often, I would feel the pressure of the swelling crowd as someone tried to squeeze onto the bleachers or someone else pushed forward to see better. Several times I was literally pushed off my perch.

The rebbe and his entourage began to make their way out of the main hall, and the hasidim burst into song again. *"Der rebbe zoll leben, a mazal tov, alle hasidim a mazal tov, alle Yidn a mazal, und a mazal tov."* As the rebbe and his son were danced toward the exit, his armchair was picked up and passed over the heads of the crowd and toward the back. Like everything else that was his, it was endowed with a kind of sympathetic sanctity. Hands popped up from everywhere hoping to share in holding or even touching the chair. And in a flash the large chair seemed to fly through the room. For those at the edges of the throng, it must surely have looked as if it had a magic life of its own. Perhaps someday the hasidim would tell a story of how the rebbe's chair floated out of the room as soon as he left it. Surely the narrative recounting of these moments would raise them ever higher, until collective memory had transformed the events into a myth of the most sacred order. Generations of previous hasidim had done this; there was no reason to suppose that their successors would not do so too.

By about 6 P.M., after the rebbe left, the hall began slowly to clear. The band continued to play music while someone took the microphone and began to thank a series of organizations, including the city of Jerusalem and the security service that had provided assistance at this event. Like a list of closing credits, these words of thanks made it almost seem that they were formally ending a festival of some sort.

After a few minutes I slipped out the same door I had entered. The hallway was choked with hasidim, many of them smoking and chatting. They were congratulating one another.

"You know what this was like?" one of the hasidim said to me when I asked him what he thought about the day. "I'll tell you. We came in separately; but when we got together, we stopped being separate. Maybe you as an outsider might see us all together like a bowl of fruit; even in the bowl, each fruit stands out alone. But I will tell you, we're like this." He held up a bottle of wine he was taking away as a souvenir. "Each of us came in as a separate little bottle of wine, and when we came together, we each poured ourselves into a single big bottle. And inside that big bottle we were all mixed together into a new wine. And then we each took our little bottle and refilled it from the big bottle in which our separate wines were mixed together. So now we can all drink from the same source."

The image was not arbitrary. When the rebbe shared his wine with his hasidim, that was just what he did. With dozens of bottles arrayed on the table before him, he sipped from one and then all the rest were opened, mixed with the bottle from which the rebbe drank, and then they were all refilled and redistributed to the hasidim. As each man took home a bottle, a treasured keepsake and palpable reminder of the occasion, he took with him a "mix" of a wine that contained in it the rebbe's drink blended with everyone else's.

"And so?" I asked.

"And so," he answered, "the message to us is clear." He quoted a talmudic dictum: "Do not separate yourself from the congregation." He hugged the bottle close to his chest and walked off into the crowd.

Another hasid, Shalom Hayim Porush, shared his feelings about the occasion: "The Holy One, blessed be He, fashioned a cure for the plague we experienced. That small group of hasidim who established the first Belz place to pray in this land," his eyes glistened, "were preparing the cure for a plague that would only occur later." [21]

This had been a tribal celebration. For the elders, those who remembered the dry years between the previous rebbe's death and this one's ascent to majority and leadership, some of whom remembered even the plague of the Holocaust and its aftermath, this huge party was a sweet moment. It meant that they had held on. It meant that they had successfully made the transition to the modern age, had crossed over the river of fire and blood and passed through the winds of change and had come out intact. Belz was rebuilt. It might not be the same Belz from an analyst's point of view, but to the elders it was enough of a Belz to serve their needs.

Taking Leave

Outside, boys and young men thronged about the car that would take the rebbe away. These boys were the troops upon whom the tribe depended, for they were always already to throng and swarm, to crowd and give the image of teeming life. An American model, the rebbe's car was quickly ringed in black coats. Nearby a large, rented, shiny new Volvo—the car all high Israeli officials used—was being filled by some hasidim with audio and video equipment.

People began to leave. I could see new valises packed and waiting on a number of doorsteps. Taxis came and went as women and some men bargained with the drivers over rates to the airport.

Suddenly, there was a hubbub. Out of the building moved a phalanx of women. The men parted for them. At their front, dressed all in royal blue with a velvet crownlike turban atop her head, walked the rebbetzin. Daughter of the Vizhnitzer, wife of the Belzer, mother of the crown prince, she was a young woman, in her thirties, dark and good-looking. This was a moment of glory for her. A few boys called out: "*Rebbetzin, a mazel tov.*" She turned and smiled back at them and nodded thanks. Quickly, she moved away. Her appearance on the scene was not at all as dramatic as her husband's. He was, after all, the symbol of their life; she was only the receptacle from which the heir had come, an only child in a society where large families were the true glory with which a woman was to be crowned. But all that was secondary now; the future seemed secure for the moment, and everyone was happy.

Two hasidim tried to capture the occasion in epic poems they published in *Ha-Machaneh Ha-Haredi*. They began the process of raising the gathering to mythic importance. One wrote: [22]

> I'll raise thee O Jerusalem to my chief joy.
> To the court of Belz hasidim to see the boy.
> Hundreds of hasidim on my way, I see more,
> So many come, a crowd as never seen before.
>
> The young, the old, a host, all going,
> Like a rumbling river of lava, flowing
> To the holiness inside, all a'glowing,
> To join the holy assembly, a nation growing.

They stand pressed together and all sing in bliss:
Rejoice in the Lord and be happy with this.
And with them dance corners and tremble all walls,
In a blaze of their song, and the dancing in halls.

And seeing all this—I could not forget
The miracles, wonders, and kindnesses, yet
The Creator did not forsake and forget,
Saving the sprout, the branch of our fathers.

And the other concluded: [23]

> And this young man,
> Heir of bijous, [24]
> Master of Joy,
> Aaron Mordecai,
> With the light of hasid-ness
> Does shine as a witness, that
> "Israel is Alive!"

5

Binding Ties

The night on which the fifth candle of Chanukah was to be lit, the twenty-ninth of Kislev, I wanted to return to Belz, to see and feel more of the way this community binds itself together. This time I would go to the old yeshiva, the one at the end of Agrippas Street in the Machaneh Yehuda market district. Now that the jubilee celebrations were over, the center of activities returned to this old part of town. It would be more than two years, at least, before the new building would be ready for daily use.

To celebrate the annual holiday of lights, Belz hasidim gathered with their rebbe in the yeshiva to kindle the menorah and to listen to the new melodies composed for this year's celebration. An outsider who once observed the yearly event called it the "Belz Oratorio." Although surely no one at Belz would name it that—a term that had no place in Jewish tradition—what they did neatly fit the formal definition of an oratorio: an extended musical composition without action, scenery, or costume, adapted to a religious service and sung by solo voices and a chorus. And, as I would discover, it was an event wrapped in drama.

At a little before seven in the evening, when I arrived, my tape recorder tucked into my pocket, hasidim were streaming into the building. Some stood in small groups in the vestibule, another few gathered around a sign on the bulletin board. The sign announced a planned trip—some might call it a pilgrimage—to Belz in Poland, for $1,400. For many of them this would be a first opportunity to visit this town of their group's origins and, more importantly, to stand at the grave sites of some of the previous Belzer rebbes, there to pray for their intercession with the Almighty. In Jewish tradition, visits to the graves of holy men were always important, but for the last forty years or so only an intrepid few had been able to return to the tombs in what was once the heartland of European Jewry. Now that eastern Europe was becoming more open, such trips were becoming accessible to greater numbers. Among the last Jews to leave Europe, hasidim were now among the first to return. For them these east European sites, once the outposts of exile for a wandering Jewish people, had now been transformed by history and Holocaust into symbols of a Jewishly rooted past. They were sanctified.

If there seemed an irony in Jews from Jerusalem making a pilgrimage to Poland, that paradox could perhaps be explained by the fact that these were Jews who, in spite of their being in Jerusalem, still saw themselves in an existential exile. Until the arrival of a true Messiah who would bring about redemption, Jerusalem and Belz remained linked in exile. They might mourn for the Temple in Jerusalem but it was in Belz that their tears would flow most freely. The destruction of both was mourned, for both were symbols of a past to be preserved. A few of the people at the bulletin board talked about going, while all around them others prepared for the candlelighting. It was time to go inside the main sanctuary.

Already, there appeared to be almost no seats available and people were beginning the frantic search for standing room and squeezing space. Some young boys were even stretched out along the molding circling the ceiling and some sat atop the heating ducts. Quite a few had their own tape recorders. Like me, they wanted to capture the occasion; the difference was that for them the tape would become a family memento while for me it remained a cultural artifact.

A young boy with whom I struck up a conversation at the edge of the crowd told me that the ceremony would begin at half past seven, but it did not. Nothing of formal consequence could commence before the appearance of the rebbe, and that did not occur until almost forty minutes later.

When the rebbe came, the action began, and everyone was drawn together and toward him. I would see this in every encounter of hasidic congregations with their rebbe. Once at another hasidic court, an insider, warning me it was about to happen, called it "the pressure." "Careful," he cautioned me as we walked near the rebbe who was entering his sanctuary, "the pressure now will become very great." And indeed it was.

To be sure, it is not simply the rebbe who serves to tie the Hasidim together. There are customs, traditions, ideas, melodies (as I would discover especially tonight) that can serve as well. That all of these are filtered through the person of the rebbe is what gives Hasidism much of its character. But it is not the rebbe that one actually feels; it is the group that coalesces around him that one experiences and that gives Hasidism its special intimate character.

"And what exactly will happen when the rebbe comes?" I asked the boy.

"The rebbe, may he live for many good years, will come in and light candles. There will be singing. He'll say some *Toyreh* [Torah]."

"And then?"

"And then it will be over."

"About when?"

"Nine forty-five."

He was right. There was a matter-of-factness, a kind of controlled enthusiasm about the occasion. Yes, there were spiritual highs, moments of collective excitement. But they were institutionalized, almost routine. And when they were over, that was all. This was not the wild, uncontrolled Hasidism one read about in the folktales that recounted the exotic life of the Baal Shem Tov and his founders at the dawn of the hasidic movement. These were not the frenzied few whom the misnagdim once railed against for desecrating the law and overturning tradition. They were simply Jews who kept spirituality boxed into compartments of their lives. From ten past eight until nine forty-five they would be high on Hasidism, and then they would close down for the night.

That was a kind of spirituality familiar to me. It was like the prayers I had learned to live with as a modern Orthodox Jew. We put ourselves into a context of devotion, prayed—even with acute intensity and ardor—but we were not carried away by the act. When it was over, it was over. Predictable, routine, and methodical. It was piety for a modern society.

A young man approached me. He appeared to be in his early twenties. His beard was just beginning to fill out and it framed his olive-shaped face. Behind dark-rimmed glasses his coal black eyes smiled at me.

"Does his honor know someone at Belz?" he asked in a style of speech that seemed at once archaic and carefully calibrated to elicit information without putting me off. He was not trying to chase me away, just place me.

"Not exactly," I replied and went on to explain that I had come to see what I'd heard was a "one-of-a-kind" occasion, the Belz lighting of Chanukah candles. It was a reply that communicated respect, something the haredi valued from a person who looked so obviously the outsider.

The young man smiled broadly now. "You are right; it is very special."

The idea that an evident outsider would be interested in Belz was appealing. In a sense, the smile on the young man's face was one of triumph. As I would later learn, and witness many times, the interest shown by the acculturated like me in the traditions of those who openly displayed contempt for acculturation was for the haredim evidence of their cultural victory in history. "You went out there," one of them once said to me, "but in the end you were drawn back. You see that what truly matters is in here, not where you have been living."

"So what happens?" I asked, pushing the button on the small tape recorder in my pocket so that I could keep track of what he told me.

He sketched the process of the rebbe's lighting and the singing. Then he concluded, "But you'll see for yourself."

He was interested in learning more about me, trying to discover precisely whom they had snared: "Is this your first time at Belz?"

I told him I had been at the bar mitzvah celebrations and had also visited the Belz sukkah late at night, in the midst of one of the gatherings around the rebbe's table.

"So you know that Belz is not like anyplace else." The distinctiveness of the group was important to emphasize. No hasidic court could imagine itself interchangeable with any other. "You have a connection to Belz?"

"I had a grandfather who was a Polish hasid."

"Maybe Belz?"

"Maybe Belz."

"What was his name?" The family of Belz hasidim was not so big; insiders remained within its boundaries, names were known.

"Kirschenbaum."

"There is a Kirschenbaum in B'nai B'rak. A relative perhaps?"

"Could be."

"So you are 'Kirschenbaum'?"

"No, that was my mother's father. I am Heilman."

"And what does his honor do for a living?" Again the formalized show of respect camouflaging—although just barely—the pursuit of information. Identify the outsider; see if he is Esau or Jacob. Do not be blind to disguises, for Esau hates Jacob.

"I am a teacher."

"A *melamed* in a *talmud toyreh?*" he asked, using the term for an instructor in a religious school, a primary teacher. Maybe I was not really such an outsider.

"Not exactly. I teach at the university."

"Oh!" he said with a very broad smile, like someone reeling in a very big catch, "so you're not a teacher. You're a *lecturer.*" He emphasized the term that in Hebrew commonly distinguished between those who taught at the university and those who were schoolteachers of another sort.

And now, having given so much, I felt the prerogative of getting something back.

"And your name?"

He gave it to me.

"And what does his honor do?" I asked, having learned quickly how to frame requests for information.

"Of course, I learn in the yeshiva," he replied. Everyone of his age was a student in the yeshiva. Yet not all yeshiva students were alike. Some were devoted to, and good at, learning. But others, even though devoted, were less inclined to scholarship. And some made no pretense of an absorption in study, pursuing other interests, of course always under the formal cover of being in yeshiva. This fellow was one of the latter. His particular task was to be a deputy in charge of making connections with physicians. If anyone in Belz got sick—male or female—he would if necessary connect them with the proper physician.

Did people first go to the rebbe for advice and did he then send them to this young man, who in turn brokered them to a physician? I asked. He laughed.

"Of course not." They went to the physician straight away if they had problems. They knew that health care was something you get from doctors. They were not fools.

"So what do you do?"

"I tell them which doctor to see, who is good and who will help them best."

The young man was a referral service.

And did he know all the physicians according to their specialty?

"Yes, of course." He knew all the best people. He had always been interested in these matters as a boy, and he had familiarized himself with them.

"Of course, I am not a doctor, but I know all that's necessary to know about medicine."

Why did hasidim not become physicians, I asked.

"And what do we need to become physicians for?" It was a question that one did not ask. "And why don't we become fishermen? Because we don't feel the need to become fishermen or doctors. We have been put on earth for other purposes."

But he smiled a kind of agreement when I said that it was good that some Jews had become physicians.

"Do you always send your people to religious physicians?"

"You mean those like you with the knit *kippah* [skullcap]?" He was referring to the nonharedi Orthodox. These were Jews who had found a way to shrink the yoke of their Judaism to allow room in their lives for others sorts of things, like medicine.

"I suppose," I answered.

"Of course not," he replied. "I send them to the best physician. And most of them are not religious."

"How can this be?"

"Do you think," he smiled at the silliness of my question, "that there is any purpose in sending someone who has come to you for help, who wants you to advise him in medicine, about which he doesn't know every much, do you think it is right to send such a person to a doctor just because he is religious, even if he's no good?"

He was right, of course. My assumption that to be a haredi hasid was to somehow lose sight of what good health means was preposterous. He and I were both living within the contemporary city, citizens served by the same health system. Both of us wanted what worked best. He no less than I was aware of what science and technology offered, and he was not about to let his attachment to the ways of yisrael sabbah turn into an obstacle to his survival. After all, "we want to survive, no less than you," as he explained.

"But the physicians come to us too," he said, and pointed my attention to a table near the front of the room. There sat another man in a knit skullcap. I recognized him, a physician who headed one of the most important units at the Hadassah Hospital. Like the others, he was waiting for the arrival of the rebbe.

While we had been talking, a palpable excitement began to permeate the room. The crowd shifted and a new murmur passed through it. The time to switch to another level of involvement, an involvement in ritual matters was approaching. "Soon, soon, we'll begin," my guide told me, giving words to the feelings.

"Why so late?" I asked. The law required a Jew to light the Chanukah candles with the first twinkling of stars, the first moment of the next day. Now it was quite late, long after the first stars had come out on this winter night.

"The Belzer rav thinks about his hasidim like a father. He wants to let his hasidim go home and have a chance to light their candles and eat." And if that was not enough of a reason, then: "In the multitude of people is the King's glory." He quoted the verse from the fourteenth chapter of Proverbs. I would hear it many times, especially when haredim talked about the importance of mass gatherings. Only when every hasid has gone home to light candles and his family has eaten can they all come here. And everyone was expected to come to the rebbe's lighting.

"But come," my companion said, cutting short our conversation, "let me find you a chair so you can see the rebbe." To see the rebbe, to be close to him, that was the most desirable position. The higher one's social position, the closer his placement to the rebbe.

Ironically, often guests got closer than most of the regular hasidim. To the guest, perhaps this was a compliment. But in fact, to put the guest in the spotlight near the rebbe was a way of displaying to all the hasidim that the outsider had come to pay respects to them, to their way of life, to the symbol of their being, the rebbe. We were trophies of cultural battles won.

With a few whispers and waves of his hand, my host handed me over to another hasid, who led me to a place where a once-packed bench miraculously appeared to have ample space for me. A few young boys were easily dislodged. Once again, I found myself squeezed in among hasidim anticipating the arrival of the rebbe. I could smell the pungent odor of perspiration embedded in gabardine that always filled the air when crowds like this pushed together.

There was something subtly erotic about this pressing together. It was not unusual or a breach of etiquette for hasidim to have their arms draped over one another's shoulders or to feel another's breath on your neck. Feeling the bodies of others pressed closely against you so that you lost a feeling of where you ended and they began, sharing an emotional bond with them and the longing to see or be seen by the rebbe had the makings of a deeply felt experience. In such circumstances of communion one lost a sense of discreteness. We were all one. Life in the community was a physical and a metaphysical experience all at once. One felt the community in every sense. It was metaphor mixed with reality.

The sweaty smell that so repelled me at first later called up in me all those feelings of closeness. To be sure, I did not realize all that then. I was too busy positioning myself for what would come next.

Suddenly, I felt the people around me surge forward as a door opened and the rebbe, a dark-eyed, heavy-set man (looking older than his forty years) in black-rimmed glasses walked in and sat down on the same wooden chair I had seen him enthroned in at the bar mitzvah. At that moment a young boy tried to push me aside, but he was quickly shoved away by my guardian hasid. I glanced over and saw him smile at me. Later he would tell me that the young boys didn't know how to treat guests. What he meant, of course, was that they were so intent on keeping outsiders out that they did not yet realize our value as trophies.

Obviously, I was to be given a good view; I was to report to the world out there what I had seen. My new guide signaled me with his eyes. "Look, look at this," he seemed to say, "mark it well, and don't miss a thing."

Next to the rebbe's carved chair was a large, rather ornate silver eight-branched menorah. Beside it were two tiny silver pitchers filled with pure olive oil, commemorating the miracle of the vial of oil found by the Maccabees, the religious purists, haredim of their day, who nearly two thousand years before had reclaimed the Holy Temple from the Syrian Greeks and their hellenizing compatriots, Judeans who were like Gentiles. This vial, lasting eight times as long as it was expected to, became the beacon of light that the Jews forever afterward associated with the fire of their hopes for redemption and religious return to Jerusalem. "Chanukah is a haredi holiday," one hasid explained to me on another occasion.

Kindling the Lights

The rebbe was about to light his menorah. He poured the contents of the pitchers carefully into five glasses atop five of the menorah's branches, one for each of the days of the eight-day festival. The cotton wicks, prepared in advance, quickly soaked up some of the liquid. Then he lit a candle that he would later put in a two-stalked candelabrum mounted on the wall near the door. With the candle in hand, and amid the shushing of the hasidim, he began to scream out in a high-pitched voice the words of the blessing. There was no melody, only a kind of singsong that exaggerated the enunciation of the words. After each of the two blessings the crowd in a single voice screamed back "Amen." And then silence as they watched him light the oil-saturated wicks in the lamps.

The identification with the rebbe was palpable. Next to me I could feel the hasidim near me strain to get closer, to see. There seemed three stages to the identification with the rebbe. First came the emotional bond, a feeling of being close to, even loving, him. This attachment seemed to extend also to the other hasidim. It was the affective aspect of being a Belzer. "To be a Belzer hasid," one of these hasidim explained to me, "means you are part of the family of the rebbe—all one family."

Second, there came the identification with the accomplishments of the rebbe. When the rebbe was celebrated and celebrating, so too were his hasidim. The glory of Belz, the eminence of the rebbe, was everyone's glory. This after all had been the message at the bar mitzvah. And it was true here too.

As my guardian hasid watched me watch the rebbe, he beamed with pride; it was as if he were showing off himself. "I share in the rebbe's life because the rebbe shares in mine," he told me later.

"We all share one another's lives," said another man, "the joys and the sorrows belong to everyone." That was the third element of the Belz identification: a sense of common culture, interconnectedness, empathy.[1]

At the time, of course, all I knew was that I *felt* something in that crowd, as I had felt it at the bar mitzvah and as I would feel it again in the many hasidic gatherings I would join throughout my time in the haredi world. I would feel it in Brooklyn, standing in line on the holiday of Sukkot with hundreds of Lubavitcher hasidim who wanted to greet their rebbe, Menachem Mendel Schneerson, and get his blessings and a piece of cake from his table. I would feel it at Purim in a mass of hasidim pushing to be near the Bobover rebbe's table. I would experience it in a mass of Reb Arelach hasidim who danced in a circle in front of their rebbe in his Jerusalem yeshiva. I would sense it in a crowd of hasidim gathered to pray the *Selichot* penitential hymns with the rebbe of Ger on the eve of Rosh Hashanah and Yom Kippur, the days of awe and judgment. And, I would feel it when yeshiva students and others gathered to hear a special *shiur*, or lesson, from their rosh yeshiva. I would even feel it much later when I gathered with tens of thousands at New York City's Madison Square Garden to celebrate the completion of a seven-and-a-half-year cycle of Talmud study. But all that would come later. Now I turned my attention to the rebbe's candlelighting.

When he had finished, he sat down at a small table covered in velvet and on which lay two large leather-bound books. In his hand he held a small pamphlet: the Belz service for candlelighting and some additional psalms. His son, who stood next to him the whole time, now sat down next to him at the table. The rebbe appeared to be immersed in prayer, swaying back and forth as he mumbled, in a hum that those near him could hear, the words on the page in front of him. He kept an extraordinarily serious expression on his face, alternately closing and opening his eyes. It was obviously a display of private worship for a public occasion. That was what rebbes had to do; they had to make their private feelings perceivable yet mysterious. We could not know what the rebbe thought or the nature of his devotions—but we had to see that he had them.

On the rebbe's left stood what looked like a cadre of gabbaim, hasidim appointed to assist him in any of his needs. Behind and closest to him was the chief gabbai. From among this ensemble would come those who directed the human traffic and the flow of spirit. Practically, they were the ones who gave all the signals as to when singing should begin and end, when chairs should be brought or removed, and so on. In a sense, the rebbe's will, such as it was, was often only indirectly encountered in these gatherings—except of course when he offered words of instruction and moral teaching. Rather, the gabbaim acted as go-betweens. It was almost as if the rebbe was an icon or totem whose voice could only be heard and interpreted by the hasidim through the gabbai.

This became even more vivid in the case of the Reb Arelach hasidim, about whom much more will be said later. The Reb Arelach, an offshoot from the Satmar (Hungarian) court, were in these days gathered in Jerusalem's Toldos Aharon Yeshiva around their leader, Rabbi Avraham Yitzhak Kahan, son-in-law of the sect's founder, Rabbi Aharon Roth (1894–1947). Their rebbe was now an old and sick man. His voice was faint and his body had been ravaged by stroke. Still, he commanded a following. Yet it was his gabbaim who often articulated and communicated his will to those followers.

It was they who, presumably at the whispered behest of the rebbe, selected those among his hasidim who would be called to shake the rebbe's hand or stand by his side. They determined when dancing would begin, when it would end, when it was time to sing or when the time had come to listen to what the rebbe had to say. And if indeed they were simply acting on the wishes of the rebbe, who could tell? The rebbe was, after all, barely audible and even less comprehensible. Without the gabbaim, who would know what he wanted?

Approaching the rebbe once, at the urging of the head gabbai, I waited as he introduced me. The gabbai was whispering into the elder man's ear while gesturing toward me. The rebbe's face looked expressionless, his eyes glassy. "Does he understand what is being said to him?" I asked a hasid later.

"He knows everything."

And when he had finished, the gabbai put his ear near the rebbe's lips. I could not see them move. Turning to me, he offered me the rebbe's blessing and greetings. A few moments later he again put his ear near the rebbe's mouth and then told me what he had said. Was that what he said, I thought to myself? Had the rebbe said it or had the gabbai? And did it matter? What counted was what the hasid believed. Given the predisposition to be bound to the rebbe, the question of whether the rebbe or his gabbaim actually ran the ongoing business seemed secondary. The flow of the action took on a kind of life of its own, as indeed the community did.

The Belzer rebbe's gabbaim signaled for the singing to begin. Led by a young man in thick glasses who sang a capella, the choir of young boys and men began to chant a tune. The first was "Maoz Tzur" (Rock of Ages), the special song attached to the holiday. But the tune was new. At the words "they embittered my life with hardship," the melody was especially plaintive. Over and over, the words were repeated. From one tune they moved seamlessly to another; a few in the crowd began to hum along; hasidim swayed quietly.

After about a half hour of singing, the choir stopped and a *chazzan* (cantor) moved next to the rebbe and sang several portions of Psalm 119. This psalm, the so-called Grand Alpha-Beta, used each letter of the Hebrew alphabet to sing praises of God and the Torah. The chazzan sang the verses of the letters *mem(m)*, *nun(n)*, and *samech(s)*.

> O how I love Thy law; it is my meditation all the day. Thy commandments make me wiser than mine enemies, for they are ever with me.
> I have learned wisdom from all who sought to teach me, for Thy testimonies talk to me.
> I will be made wise by my elders; Thy precepts strengthen me.
> I have restrained my feet from following every evil path that I might keep Thy word.
> I have not departed from Thy judgments for Thou hast taught me.
> How sweet are Your words to my taste, yea sweeter than honey in my mouth.
> Through Your precepts I gain understanding, therefore I hate all false ways.
> Thy word is a lamp unto my feet and a light unto my path.

These words of the psalmist might well have been the haredi credo. After each two verses the lines were sung and repeated by everyone. Ancient utterances endowed with new meanings. As we sang out the psalms, we seemed with each verse to reaffirm their truth in our lives. For the haredim this was the meaning of Chanukah, to "hate all false ways," to demonstrate that those who love the Torah, those made wise by their elders, teachers, and the past, were wiser than the "enemies." And the enemies were of course those who could not claim that the Torah was their "meditation all the day."

The chanting over, the microphone was moved by one of the gabbaim to the rebbe. From a seated position and with his body swaying back and forth as if he were still at prayer, his hand playing with his beard, he began to speak. At first, his Yiddish mumbling was difficult to make out, and I thought he might still be praying. But in time, as I got used to his diction and as he gradually raised the volume (as if dramatically building toward something), I began to comprehend the words. It was a lesson, an interpretation of an old talmudic conundrum: because Jewish law requires both the Chanukah lights and a mezuzah be put at the doorway of one's house, the rabbis had wondered what connection there was between these two ritual objects. The connection, the rebbe explained to his haredi followers, was clear.

"Oil does not mix with any other liquid. No matter how much one tries to blend the oil with these other liquids, it always remains separate." The oil, he went on to explain, represents the Jewish people who, no matter how hard some may try to mix them with others, will always remain separate, like the oil.

"The light of the chanukah candles which, as the great Hillel determined, we light in ascending number—not descending as the great Shammai suggested—is there to light the darkness for us. The most important light is the first, for it separates us from darkness. The others are the lights within lights." The darkness was all around us, the rebbe warned his listeners. We had to separate ourselves from it with our lamps. As the light symbolically separates the sacred from the profane—the Jews from the other nations—so too the mezuzah on our doors separates us and protects us. Both have stood from the beginning as signs distinguishing between Jews and others. Chanukah lights and the mezuzah both symbolize separation, and thus protect the Jewish people from corrupting foreign influences that "threaten to make us disappear." Both are, and now he spoke in his loudest tones, "a lamp unto my feet and a light unto my path!"

With a dramatic flourish, the rebbe flipped around the microphone and the choir began to sing, and quickly the crowd joined them. Faster and faster the rhythmic pulse of the song beat through the room. Their eyes on the rebbe who, with eyes closed and fist clenched, kept the time. Over and over, they sang the words of the song, louder and louder: "Rejoice in the Lord and exult righteous ones." We swayed, sang, clapped. Even the flames seemed to dance. We were the righteous ones and there was no doubt about it.

In this human drama it was hard to tell who was actor and who audience. And that seemed to me to articulate the essence of communion. Moments like this one, of singing and swaying together, of listening to the rebbe reassert the basic beliefs of the group and to reaffirm these with him, of coming close in person and spirit—even if through the mediation of the gabbaim—were the very stuff of communion.

6

At the Rebbe's Table

I was leaving the Belz yeshiva after the Chanukah celebration when my guardian hasid—a man in his twenties, born in Rumania and the first of his family to have switched his allegiance—grabbed me by the elbow and whispered in my ear: "Come Shabbes at night; you'll really see something." As it had been during the rebbe's candlelighting, his face was once again incandescent with pride. A refusal would be an affront, as if to say I had seen as much as necessary or desirable tonight. "About nine-thirty, *Shabbes* by *di nakht*," he murmured. "Come, come."

Shabbes by *di nakht* (Sabbath at night), or Friday evening, was the time that the rebbe, like most such hasidic masters, convened his followers at his *tish*. The *tish* ("tish" is the Yiddish word for "table") was any formal meal at the rebbe's table. Commonly it was the first festive meal of his Sabbath, the same meal that every traditional Jew ate in celebration of this special time of the week. But for hasidim, it was supposed to be more: both a mystical and communal experience: a communion on earth that mirrored mystical unions on high. As in their sanctuary the hasidim gathered with their master and one another, so in parallel fashion the Sabbath, the Jewish people, and God came together on another, higher level. Both were sacred unions. Not everyone fathomed the mystery, as I would discover, but many seemed able to experience the communion.

Women and very young children remained at home. Home, where the family got together around its own festive table, was the other important pole of the Sabbath. Although much was said in the literature comparing the woman to the Sabbath queen, and in many haredi quarters Friday night was a special time for unions between husbands and wives (about which more later), in most cases community gatherings—which took up much of the hasid's day—included only men. A few of the women perhaps resented this, but most took it to be an order of life, as unshakable as the laws of nature, that their role was to remain at home. As for the little children, in time the little boys would be old enough to join their fathers and little girls could look forward to the time when they could prepare a table for their own husbands and children.

Women were not actually locked at home on Sabbaths, although after preparimg the multicourse meals and caring for their many children, they might not have much sense of their own freedom. Still, they sometimes did go out for a walk with the children on long summer Sabbath afternoons, but that was a different type of community activity, something not endowed with religious or spiritual significance. And for the most part those who did get out were among the younger wives and mothers with few, and young, children. Older women either lacked the free time or the energy for such outings. If they got out, it was to go visit a mother or married daughter (or daughter-in-law) in her home.

Even on those special occasions when women did come to a rebbe's tish (as at the Belz bar mitzvah), they commonly were kept at the margins of the crowd: upstairs in a gallery or outside on the street, peeking in at a window. For them communion emanated from the home and hearth and was experienced through their husbands and children—which is why marriage and a family were an absolute prerequisite for being a haredi woman.

But the community, and the rebbe (or at times the rosh yeshiva) as its incarnation, were stiff competition for the women and home. For all the importance family gathering had for these Jews, comparatively few were the hours the men and boys might spend around the family dinner table and even fewer with their wives. Many a haredi spent more waking hours at his rebbe's tish or sitting in the yeshiva than at his own table and home with his wife.

A hasid who became disaffected with his rebbe often found that the best way for him to express this alienation was to stop coming to the rebbe's tish. For some that meant going to another rebbe's tish—although abrupt shifts of allegiance were discouraged, being too socially turbulent. It was one thing to take in an outsider like me with enthusiasm—I was being weaned from the evil outside—but it was quite another to take in a hasid from another court. That could launch —and sometimes did—destructive internecine struggles over membership and turf. So most of the time (although the number of such cases was relatively small) a hasid who became estranged from his rebbe or community (and commonly both happened simultaneously or close to it) stayed home. "I make my own tish now," as one such hasid said to me once. "My children are my hasidim, and my wife admits she is happy that I am not running off to the rebbe all the time." But while this family had one another, in time they found themselves all alone. They could not easily arrange marriages for their children or count on a community for support when the need arose. "When I am only for myself," said the great sage Hillel, "what am I?" The question still resonated with meaning in the haredi world, organized as it was around community. It discouraged disaffection and dropping out.

The Belzer rebbe did not come in to the yeshiva every Friday night to "lead" a tish. But the Sabbath of Chanukah was a special moment, and so the announcement went out through the grapevine: *"De rebbe kimt arein,"* the rebbe is coming in, *in*to the yeshiva, *in* to have a tish, and *in*to the lives of his hasidim. For many of his followers who had already moved from the old neighborhood to Kiryat Belz, this would mean a long walk—there was of course no riding on the Sabbath. But on Chanukah the nights were long. There would be time for everyone to eat at home, make the walk, and conclude his Sabbath meal at the rebbe's table. The gathering would last about two and a half hours. Then everyone would go home and complete the evening with yet another communion—this one a sexual union with the wives.

The Tish

To accommodate the proceedings, the large room of the yeshiva had been altered somewhat. That was the fluid nature of these interior spaces—they could always be rearranged to fit the needs of the moment.

Although there were some hasidim still walking around in the vestibule and outside on the street near the yeshiva, the vast majority were inside, arranged around several long tables covered in white.

Most of the hasidim sat on the bleachers that ascended like steps around the outer rim of the "main arena," wherein were the tables, around which some older men and notables sat. My host noticed me the moment I walked through the door—it was not difficult, I being one of the few who was not wearing a black coat or caftan—and with his eyes, which caught mine, motioned me to walk around the back to get close to him. As I coiled around the back of the bleachers, he sent out a signal to people near the back who located me and actually passed me from one to the other until I reached a spot next to him. What had looked to me to be just a crowd was, as I now discovered, in fact an elaborately arranged network in which people of different rank sat in set places. And because the network was so carefully arranged, it was easy to send a silent message along its lines to bring forward someone from the rear. Orders from the front had to be obeyed in the back.

I would perceive the efficiency of the process a bit later when I was called to move from one side of the crowded room to the other. Clearly, the hasidim who pushed together did not sacrifice organization for intimacy nor did they lose closeness in the need for order.

Being passed this way reinforced the growing feeling that in this place I was subjugated to the power of the community, no longer standing only on my own two legs, as it were. I was squeezed in near the man I shall call "Kirsch," who pulled me forward a bit more so that I would get a good look. In telegraphic whispers he surveyed the room for me, confirming my suspicions that this was not some random arrangement of people. He indentified the notables and told me what to look at closely and what I could scan. While he reviewed the "famous," I was once again reminded how these people inhabited another universe from mine, for while there were some here whose names and reputation I knew (a member of the Knesset, for example), most of those who were celebrities here were unknowns to me. Among them were some older men, including a wizened man who sat on a kind of throne to the rebbe's right.

"Who is that?" I asked.

"He was a hasid of the previous rebbe."

Among this new postwar generation of hasidim, this old man was a crucial living link with the past, an incarnation of continuity, an enshrined remnant of a community that was mostly memory. If one needed proof that the followers were as important as the leader for any community, here it was in flesh and blood: a follower who was now enthroned, an icon at the young rebbe's right hand. And while the hasidim might not articulate matters in quite such a sociological way, they knew that to put the oldest hasid near the rebbe was the right thing to do.

Also seated in a place of honor was a visiting Gerer hasid. With his *spodik*, the tall fur hat, he stood out from the Belzer married men, who wore the round and more common fur shtreimel, made of twelve fur tails (one of each of the ancient tribes of Israel). This man was paying respect to the Belzer rebbe by his visit. But of course his presence was also a sign of a rapprochement between Ger hasidim, so important in Agudat Israel, and Belz, who had broken away from its ranks. There might be political rivalries between the groups and even a muted competition for followers, but there were also necessary displays of respect and communion. Nothing could more obviously demonstrate that than such a visit to a tish.

Even the presence of the Member of Knesset, a representative of one of the religiously right-wing Zionist parties whose platform was associated with holding on to all the conquered territories, was a tacit show of sympathies if not alliances. While Belzer hasidim were not actively engaged in Zionist politics and formally took no stand on holding on to the territories, insiders could see by this visit that Belz had room at its table for those who saw the footsteps of the Messiah in the conquest and were not willing to give up a millimeter of the Land of Israel. The tish was a place to see what's what and who's who. It was a subtle way of sending all sorts of social and political messages to informed insiders.

Indeed, during the course of the proceedings, while pieces of the rebbe's food were distributed throughout the room, one of his gabbaim would call out the name of each and every notable and announce his presence to the rebbe (and of course to everyone else in the room as well). A few hasidim, not wanting to be overlooked or unannounced, raised their hands, as if to catch the gabbai's attention. When he saw them, he made a quick decision who would be mentioned first and who later, and then he called out the names in an order that would be meaningful to insiders.

The rebbe was standing at the head of the table, a tallis over his head. He recited (shouted, was more like it) the Eyshes Chayil, a hymn with which all observant Jews were supposed to begin the first of the Sabbath meals. The hymn extolled the glory and virtue of the Jewish woman:

"A woman of fortitude, who can find? Far greater than pearls is her value. When her husband's heart relies on her, he shall lack no fortune. . . . She arises while it is yet dark to give food to her household. . . . Strength and majesty are her raiment; joyfully she can anticipate the Day of Judgment. . . . Anticipating the ways of her household, she partakes not of the bread of laziness. . . . False is grandeur and vain is beauty; only a God-fearing woman deserves

praise. Give her the fruits of her handiwork and let her be praised
at the gates for her many deeds."

The words were striking in their Hebrew poetry, but anyone could
see there were no women here to hear this praise. They were all at
home. Of course, there was yet another level of meaning in this gloria.
In mystical tradition the Sabbath was queen and the Jewish people her
bridegroom. On each Friday night the union between the two was
consummated. The queen's glories were her mate's blessings. This too
was implicated in the hymn. Yet there was no missing the irony of the
recitation—at least to an outsider like me; in this men's club, the spirit
of women was being extolled, while women in the flesh were exhausted
and waiting home alone.

Following the hymn, this model Sabbath meal continued. Two
gabbaim stood on the rebbe's right and left. The former, the senior
(and older) gabbai, filled the rebbe's goblet with red wine from a silver
carafe. The rebbe recited Kiddush, the sanctification of the day and
the Jewish people's connection to it. "For You chose us and sanctified
us among all nations. And Your holy Sabbath, with love and favor did
You give as a heritage." Although the words were familiar to anyone
who had ever recited this prayer, somehow the sentiments seemed
more powerful here. These were indeed people who considered themselves chosen and sanctified and distinct from all others. Moderns
might be embarrassed by these chauvinistic sentiments, uncertain
about their holiness and not at all ready to stand out from the crowd.
But for these people there were none of these doubts and no discomfiture. They were ready to defend these articles of faith; their way of life
demonstrated that.

After the Kiddush, the rebbe ritually washed his hands in a bowl
brought to the table. There was constant hushing during all this,
adding to the sense of excitement and drama over what would otherwise be essentially a rather routine act. When in a stage whisper he at
last completed the blessing over his ablutions, everyone recited as one
a loud "amen" that shook the rafters.

Again, there was silence. A blue-velvet cover, embossed with gold
stitching covered two breads, one large and flat and the other large and
twisted. These challot, as they are called, were to be blessed, hand-
sliced, and distributed among all the assembled. Pulling off the cover,
the rebbe made the blessing over the bread. The twisted loaf was cut,
the remaining flat bread was rewrapped and removed almost as if it
were a swaddled baby. The rebbe ate a small piece of the loaf he had
cut and then began to pass out slices that were being cut by the

gabbaim. For the first pieces the rebbe would whisper to his gabbai to tell him who should get what. Later the gabbaim themselves would decide who received the remaining sherayim. Just as I had been passed through the crowd, so too were these pieces of bread. After the notables had gotten their bites, the process went very quickly. These last slices were cut by one gabbai, passed by a second, and then torn and passed by people in the crowd. Soon little portions were everywhere, and the miracle of these loaves was that they disappeared in a flash. After the first loaf was gone, another twist was brought out and cut. Then, when that was completely eaten, still another smaller one was brought out from the back.

When everyone had broken bread with the rebbe, word passed through the gabbai to the choir to begin the z'mirot, the Sabbath melodies. The rebbe chose the tune he wanted sung. But of course he was limited by his own traditions—traditions that made Belz what it was. Some of the tunes were sung only by the choir; others by the whole crowd. There were even a few solos that one of the hasidim sang. But they were all Belz tunes and they followed a set order.

Then after each set of songs, the rebbe would eat another course of his meal. Each week the menu remained unvaried. After the first bite of challah, he took another slice and dipped it in gravy. Then he would pass a spoon of the soupy stuff to his son, who sat at his side. Next he would distribute the remainder to his hasidim. Afterward there was both boiled and gefilte fish. This too was passed around. The rebbe broke pieces off everything so that whatever else was eaten was nominally part of his meal. There were never any leftovers to be thrown away. Even the rebbe's fish bones were sucked clean. These were usually left for the youngest boys, who did not yet merit more than a lick. After the fish the rebbe drank grape juice; custom had it that fish was not to be eaten with meat, and so the mouth was rinsed between the two courses. Later he tasted chicken soup. The soup itself was accompanied by a great many spoons; these too would be distributed. Then there came farfel—little bits of cut noodles—and honeysweetened carrots, chicken, and finally fruit compote. It was a classic east European Jewish meal. But what was once a matter of course was now a matter of high ritual, as indeed almost everything from that European world had been sanctified by time, memory, and suffering.

But there was of course something more in all of this. Nothing could so serve to cement these people together in intimacy as that sharing of food, to say nothing of having the same spoon in their mouths or licking one another's fish bones. The so-called sherayim of the rebbe were really a common meal for the multitude, a communal breaking of bread.

And what of the singing? I had been listening to it for a long time. It was there at the bar mitzvah, there at Chanukah, and now it punctuated the tish. That collective singing served to foster a feeling of closeness was obvious. Even the most distant participant could feel the way an individual was swept up by melodies, rhythms, and the words in the songs. That was of course one of the abiding reasons that hasidim had always used music. But there was something more as well.

As the musicologist Leonard Meyer once pointed out, music is freighted with emotion and meaning. It arouses certain expectations, "and provides meaningful and relevant resolutions for them." Familiar music or the melodic phrases and rhythms, songs repeated regularly, develop patterns of feeling and create emotional "norms."[1] That was happening here. The repeated singing of these familiar z'mirot gave all of those present at every tish a feeling of comfortable familiarity and reaffirmed their sense that things were as they should be, that there was continuity, that expectations could and would be fulfilled. The songs were the sounds of stability and order. They were, like the tish and the communal gathering itself, an anchor for life.

For these people in whose collective memory there had been dislocation and loss, for whom the world "out there" was always a hazard, a tide threatening to erode all that they had socially constructed, the expected order and sound of the tish was a cultural antidote. And it worked so well, they did it again and again. In the familiar atmosphere of repeated rituals and songs, there was the peace and tranquility of a Sabbath that transcended time and a Belz that seemed no less eternal.

All this, however, was not simply the result of habit and tradition.[2] In the course of the evening, hasidim might get caught up in the action, but that did not mean that there were not those who consciously and carefully manipulated the goings-on. The whispered directions of the rebbe, choices of melodies, eating sequences, decisions about who got what and whose names were called and in which order, were all part of a calculated blueprint of meaning and affect. "It's all very carefully planned," as one of the hasidim explained to me. In Yiddish the hasidim said it even more simply: "The rebbe leads a tish."

As I stood there watching and reflecting upon all the events, word was passed from the rebbe (or perhaps from one of his gabbaim) that he would like a *l'chaim* with me. Throughout the evening certain people had been singled out to toast the rebbe with "L'chaim" (To life). It was a singular honor to see and be seen with the rebbe from close up. Those summoned entered a long line of people waiting for their moment in the spotlight near the rebbe. It was a crowded line, dissolving into chaos near its end but somehow—with the help of the gabbaim—in full order as one approached the front. The crowd strained to be near the rebbe, to catch his ear, and attention was always pressing in upon it. Some wanted a blessing or had a quick and important request and looked at the tish as a propitious moment (although for serious problems one passed word through a gabbai and arranged a private meeting). People tried to squeeze their way into the line, but the gabbaim were scrupulous about who could get to the rebbe, and long before any interloper could encroach upon the rebbe's attention, he was weeded out.

There are several possible reasons why I might have been singled out for the l'chaim. First, I was the stranger, and as I have already suggested, strangers who come to admire or show deference to the world of the haredim are to be displayed to the faithful like trophies. Second, I may have been invited as an honor to my host, Kirsch. To arrange for your visitor to be close to the rebbe is a way to signal to the assembled community that you are a man of consequence. It was Kirsch who informed me, a smile of pride playing across his features, that I was called to the rebbe.

And there was a possible third reason. Throughout the evening I had been somewhat reluctant to share in the sherayim. The idea of using the same soup spoon as the others or licking someone else's fish bones had not been terribly appealing to me. But in deferring the offers of the food, I had also been simultaneously indicating my social and moral distance from the proceedings. Put simply, my admiration was not so great that I was ready to eat everything up. But this communal gathering, the tish, abhorred that kind of distance. On the contrary, it was the incarnation of communion. If the rebbe or his minions had indeed been paying attention to me, this sign of my abiding distance and lingering estrangement had to be conquered. It represented an open wound on the community's body. The person who came to observe but remained untouched, separate, or uninvolved was a voyeur. Voyeurs had to be undone. One could keep them out— that was the common way; keep the haredi world closed. But if they did come inside, they had to be consumed—even if only for the moment. That was why strangers had a much easier time gaining audiences with the rebbes. The toast that could not be refused was the way I would be absorbed.

"Here, take this," Kirsch said, handing me a cup filled with grape

juice. This would be my pass to elbow past the swarms of others and
get to the other side of the large hall and to the rebbe.

"How will I manage?" I asked, panicked that I would arrive, if at
all, with an empty glass and a purple-stained white shirt.

"Just hold up the glass," Kirsch told me, "you'll see."

"And my place here?"

"You'll have it when you get back."

The first steps were easy. All around me the hasidim had watched
the scene developing. They knew I had been summoned, had seen the
glass passed to me, and knew I was a novice at making the trip across
the room. They parted and passed me through the crowd, and in a
moment I had teetered over the bleachers and under them and found
myself at the back, beyond the rim of the gathering. Gingerly, I
walked around the outside of the circle behind the backs of everyone.
But when I reached the other side, far from my guardian hasid, where
no one knew me, I had to find a way into the circle again. I had to test
the system.

No one paid any attention to me on this side. I was beyond the
boundary of the notables. Here I would have to elbow and shoulder
my way past the young yeshiva boys who had no interest in strangers.
To them I was an interloper with no special status. My tap on their
shoulders could be ignored. I was part of the world they had learned
to turn their back on and to disregard. To get through I would have to
be aggressive. I pushed a little harder and held up the cup. It was like
a talisman, a red flag. When they noticed it, a few of the young boys
gave me room. There were a few curious whispers, but little attention.
As soon as I had crossed into the crowd, I found that each row had to
be negotiated on its own. Territory was carved out in millimeters. And
always the pushing and shoving threatened to spill the juice. What
would I do if I reached the rebbe at last with an empty glass?

At last, I found the end of the line. It stretched way back behind
the bleachers on this side. Here a number of hasidim milled about—
sheepishly, I thought—hoping to approach the rebbe. Should I wait
for them to go first? Was there an order here?

I pushed forward, my cup held high. "My cup runneth over," I
thought to myself.

"Shake hands with the right hand and wish the rebbe a l'chaim,"
someone whispered into my ear. It was one of the gabbaim who led
me out of the end of the line and toward the front.

I thought about what I might say to this man who was my contemporary. Would he ask me a question? Would he want to know what
brought me here? Would he explain why he had called me?

But in a moment it was over. I shook his hand and mumbled, "L'chaim." The rebbe barely glanced at me; the gabbaim hurried me off. My glass was empty, my role played out. Here I was not important enough for more than just a quick shake and a show. But when I got back to my perch, I was greeted with smiles and handshakes. They had seen it all. In this part of the room I was a hero.

There were some, Kirsch said to me, who called such a trip through the crowd *sakunes nefushes*, life-threatening. The phrase meant literally a "danger to one's soul." But, he concluded, the rebbe called it *takunes nefushes*, the repair of one's soul.

Now the rebbe was beginning to speak. It was more of his effort at takunes nefushes. This, the Sabbath of Chanukah, was a time to think of keeping separate from the Greeks. Jews needed to keep pure, to keep the fires of true faith burning and not to let them go out or let them burn with an adulterated oil. It was a theme of separation and isolation that still echoed from the other day and from the experience of the Maccabees.

At last as the evening drew to a close, after the grace had been said and all the z'mirot sung, the choir sang one last song. It was the "Rock of Ages," the thirteenth-century song associated with Chanukah. Five of its stanzas allude to the deliverances of the Jewish people from the exiles of Egypt, Babylonia, and Persia, and the last stanza tells of the Syrian-Greeks who with their strange ways, their hellenism, brought the exile into the Holy Land. This last stanza begins: "Greeks gathered around me . . . demolished my towers and polluted my oils." And it ends: "But from the remaining flask a miracle was wrought for the Jewish people."

Again and again, the verse was sung. The rebbe stood and linked hands with those near him and the whole table joined hands and circled. Faster and faster they went, until the whole place was hopping with it. "Greeks gathered around me . . . but a miracle was wrought." As on the day before, these haredim were recalling the siege around them, the attacks on their ways, the effort to remain pure and the ultimate triumph. The foreign ways would not penetrate their circle. They would remain a people apart.

7

This Is Who We Are

"It is from the group that individuals learn their creed," Claude Lévi-Strauss reminds us.[1] Yet, as I knew, it is from individuals that the anthropologist learns the group's creed. Until now, I had been inferring the Belz ideology, and through it a haredi view of the world, from my observations and the passing remarks people made to me. But why guess? "There can be little doubt," ethnographer Paul Radin once wrote to explain how he could draw so much tribal wisdom from his interviews of solitary Indians, "that every group, no matter how small, has, from time immemorial, contained individuals who were constrained by their individual temperaments and interests to occupy themselves with the basic problems of what we customarily term philosophy."[2] If I could find individuals such as these among the hasidim, I might by talking with them probe the haredi philosophy, creed, and ideology. One such man, I discovered, was Yisrael Eichler, editor of *Ha-Machaneh Ha-Haredi*, the weekly Belz paper.

"The distinguishing feature of the *haredi* press," journalist Amnon Levy explains, "is that in many respects its pages reflect its image of what life ought to be, not what life really is."[3] Who better then to tell me what reality was for haredim than one of the persons responsible for putting together such a paper? Like other such publications, *Ha-Machaneh Ha-Haredi* was filled with as much editorializing as news (the latter was usually just reprinted facts already available in general-circulation newspapers that many haredim refused to read because of the pictures and secular slant of the stories in them).[4] In all this Eichler interpreted for his public what Belz, and by implication, all haredi Judaism stood for, cared about, and meant. That his paper was called *The Haredi Camp* seemed to say it all. He was not simply sending a local message; his was a message for all haredim even though it was shaped by his particular experiences in Belz.

For all of his editorial hostility to the nonharedi world, Eichler, whom I had met at the rebbe's tish, was happy to talk to me. We talked for hours and met many times. And while, with his permission, I recorded each conversation, as I reflect back on them, they can be fused into one long discourse.

At the time we spoke, Eichler was thirty-two years old. Like all young haredi men of his generation, he had a yeshiva education. In journalism, however, he had received no formal training. He was an important figure in the new Belz order, encouraged in his writing by the rebbe, and carefully drafting each editorial he wrote with the sanction of the Belz leadership. When Belz entered into a coalition with the Lithuanian forces of Rabbi Schach in founding the Degel Ha-Torah party, there was talk of Eichler serving as a candidate for political office, although this never bore fruit. Still, his was a prominent voice.

We Are Not Backward

Of our many meetings perhaps the most revealing was one we held in his apartment in Kiryat Belz. Even the preliminaries to that encounter are significant. On my way there I had trouble with my car, and so I called ahead to tell him I would be late.

"What exactly is wrong with it?" he asked. He knew quite a bit about how to fix cars, he assured me. What sort of car did I have? Had I checked the battery? Was there a carburetor, or did I have a fuel-injected engine? Had I tried pulling the choke only part way out before engaging the motor? Did I know that sometimes if the accelerator was pressed all the way to the floor for several moments while I turned on the ignition this could start the car? With an eagerness in his voice that startled me, he continued to offer me all sorts of technical advice as I briefly described the symptoms.

Was there more than passing interest here? Was there a message embedded in all these questions and suggestions? Was he implying that, while he might be a traditionalist, he was certainly not an ignoramus about matters of current technology. On those matters he was up-to-date. At a later occasion he would be more explicit on the matter: "We are not backward people!" Traditionalism was not backwardism.

If I believed after the phone call that perhaps I was reading too much into his comments, what I discovered when I got to his apartment easily confirmed my original impressions. Although dressed like a man from my grandfather's generation, Eichler sat at a computer workstation in the corner of his combination study and dining room. Next to the screen was a portable radio/tape unit along with files of papers, books, and clippings. The technology was the latest. This was not my grandfather; the scene before me resembled the view from my own desk!

But Eichler's room gave off a series of alternate messages too. Holy books—*seforim*, as they were called—were one of its primary motifs. Along an entire wall of the room were shelves lined with bound seforim. A quick scan of the titles gave away Eichler's allegiances to Belz and Hasidism, but they also showed his reverence for the world of the yeshiva. While in the past large libraries of sacred texts like Eichler's might have been found only in the possession of rabbis or a yeshiva, today even the most simple Jew could own a collection of books that his forebears could hardly imagine. Having seforim spoke volumes. These were not books for reading; they were tomes to study, tools for worship, and the visible symbols of an attachment to Jewish tradition. They were the literal props of every haredi home.

Interspersed and sparkling amid the brown bindings and gold letters were the other props of a traditional Jewish home: Sabbath candlesticks, Chanukah menorahs, a Purim *megillah*, silver wine goblets, and a dish for dispensing honey on the High Holy Days. Eichler might be up-to-date with technology, but as his appearance and his other possessions showed, he was something far more traditionally Jewish as well.

Running like a bridge between today's technology and the timeless Judaica was a long table, large enough to seat the entire family at the many festive meals on Sabbath and holy days when they gathered together to eat. During the week, however, it was a repository for books, a space on which to study and work, half sacred and half profane. The table was where we met and talked.

As in all haredi neighborhoods, children were everywhere; Eichler and his young wife had eleven. Even though it was late afternoon, the older boys were still out studying in the yeshiva. Only the little ones were around now. Generally, boys and girls did not play with each other; the boys rode bikes while some of the girls played jump rope and others stood together near the steps chattering quietly. One of them was Eichler's daughter; she shyly led me up the stairs to her apartment where her older sister opened the door and brought me to the closed dining-room doors behind which their father sat at work.

Eichler slid open the doors and stood to greet me. He asked his daughter, who was almost eleven, to bring us glasses of tea. In a moment she returned with the drinks and some cookies. Then she left without a word and slid the double doors shut. As we talked throughout the afternoon, the sound of children was as ubiquitous as the chirping of birds, but except for one interruption by Eichler's three-year-old son who came to report that his *cappeleh* (skullcap) had fallen into the toilet bowl, we were undisturbed. Somewhere out of sight someone was taking care of the children.

Our conversation began exactly where we had left off on the telephone. Not that we spoke very much about the trouble with my car—that was disposed of quickly. But Eichler focused on matters not so different. He had been in the midst of preparing his newspaper column when I came in to the room. I must have had a look of surprise when I glanced at his work space. He caught it and seemed to want to drive it home. Eichler liked showing outsiders that they really did not know haredim, that their stereotyped expectations were wrong.

"You know computers? You know Wordstar?" He wanted to talk to me about the relative advantages of his word-processing program versus others. And then he showed me how he used his modem to communicate with computer networks. We talked about the details of the process. Eichler displayed a thirst for technological information; he wanted to know about faster computers, better programs, and all sorts of other electronic communication devices. As we talked, it was easy to forget that the man in whose apartment I sat and with whom I spoke was the image of another age. For a moment it seemed to me that the image was illusion.

We Are in Danger

And then—just when I was beginning to forget that I was in the precincts of the haredi world—our conversation slid into areas that reminded me that, after all, I was in another place. "You have a beautiful home," I said. We spoke in Hebrew.

"You look at the material improvements we have made in our

lives," he said, "and you think how successful we have become. But I
know that all this can be our ruin. A person who has fewer material
possessions needs far less to busy himself with the work necessary to
acquire these possessions. We would be better off just sitting and
learning Torah. To have these things—things that more and more of
our people want—not only the man but even the woman may have to
go out to work. And when the woman goes out to work, this creates a
problem of who will supervise life in the home. And the home will
require the help of the husband, which of course takes away from his
time to study. This is a great danger to us, a great danger to Judaism.
And it doesn't stop there. The young people want it too so the parents
will have to help their married children more. There will be no end
to it."

Eichler saw the threatening slippery slope; he was anxious about
falling into the abyss of modern materialism, which would be a prologue to an existence that abhorred Judaism. It was, as I would learn
again and again, one of the great fears of many haredim. They saw
their American brothers and sisters—even the ultra-Orthodox among
them—endangered by it. And now, with improving economic conditions and rising material expectations, they too were in danger of being swallowed up by materialism, a scourge that they believed they
had caught from contemporary culture. Not that Eichler thought
Jews had to suffer; he was by no means an ascetic. But he worried
nevertheless.

On the other hand, he did not believe that all was lost. There were
also important gains being made these days in the cause of haredi
Judaism.

"It's a fact that today more and more concentrations of haredim
exist; there are more and more of those who observe Torah [*shomrei
Torah*] and the shomrei Torah observe more and more, and parents
send their children to yeshivas, and even the modern Jews are influenced by this. They see what we have built—so we might say that
even with all the problems, we will triumph."

This was triumphalism haredi-style, optimism tinged with anxiety
that one was not completely safe from the corrosive effects of the
contemporary world.

We Are Not Americans

Eichler was fond of drawing distinctions between haredim in Israel,
whom he considered the genuine article, and those in America who,

although in his estimation certainly the best examples of Diaspora Jewry, were something less than truly haredi. Was this true even of those who were part of his Belz sect, I asked him? "Is there a difference between a Belzer hasid from New York and you?"

With a look of astonishment at the absurdity of my question, he shot back: "Of course, he's an American!"

And what—besides his passport—was American about a Belzer hasid from New York? I wondered whether other Americans would be as certain as Eichler was that hasidim in New York were culturally American. But Eichler was certain.

"A Belzer from New York thinks like an American. He comports himself like an American. Would he complain if a car drove through his neighborhood on the Sabbath? To whom? Would he complain about a lewd picture on a bus shelter or in the subway? Never, how could he? Would he post a sign on his business that men and women would be served at separate hours? Never. But we can and we do! We are far more demanding in what we expect of our Jewish lives.

"If an American wants to be a haredi, he has to come here. Here is where he can be true to his principles."

He was right. The American ultra-Orthodox Jews who would do battle against those who did not observe Sabbath, who wanted to throw a stone against its desecrators, got on a plane and threw their stone here in Jerusalem. In America, haredim—such as they were— limited their struggles with modernity to intramural jousting with other Jews. They railed against the Conservative and Reform Jews— although only within their own precincts; they almost never went out on the attack—but they essentially left general American society alone. Although they claimed not to approve of it, they were affected by it. Except for Lubavitcher hasidim with their so-called Mitzvah Tanks and outreach programs to other Jews, most ultra-Orthodox Jews in America kept to themselves. And even the Lubavitchers targeted only other Jews (although their messianic fervor was lately moving them close to the edge of the Jewish world). Haredim, for the most part, were not out to change America; it was beyond them. They were after all still in a stance of powerlessness in exile, waiting fror a Messiah who would bring them back to the glories of another age.

But haredim in Israel—for all their talk about their still being in exile and awaiting the Messiah—had taken an activist, assertive stance. They were ready to be masters of their own fate. They were ready to insist on their own view of what it meant to be a Jew and assert it as the dominant view.

Did this not make them like other Israelis? I wondered aloud. Was not a key element of Israeli existence and Zionist doctrine the notion that Jews could decide about themselves for themselves? Did not having this power epitomize the end of exile?

Eichler smiled. Perhaps there was something to this argument. Yes, he supposed to some extent they had become like Israelis. But they added one more element to this, and a crucial one: the ways they fought for were the right ones, mandated by God and Jewish tradition. They were not simply pushing some corrupted Zionist secularity. They were asserting the ways of yisrael sabbah.

"It is a loss of orientation," Clifford Geertz argues, "that most directly gives rise to ideological activity."[5] To the haredim much of contemporary life—and particularly the last half century—have been times of profound loss of orientation. These rapid and far-reaching changes made tradition more important, a matter of ideological concern.

We Are Vulnerable Too

The idea that there was something that made even haredim part of Israel displayed itself in another part of our conversation. Eichler talked about power and vulnerability. Like many of the other haredim with whom I spoke in Jerusalem, he reminded me of how exposed they all were to attack. But the attack on which he chose to focus first was not the ideological one from the nonharedi world. Instead of stressing those sorts of battles that filled the columns of his newspaper, he talked about the dangers that came from the Arabs.

Mea Shearim, Geula, and many of the haredi neighborhoods were, after all, situated along what had from 1948 until 1967 been the cease-fire lines. For twenty years houses, streets, and the people who lived here were shelled by Jordanian forces. For those of Eichler's generation that constant bombardment was an unforgettable memory. And the continuing hostility of the Palestinian uprising and surrounding Arab countries echoed that memory. Both confirmed a message that many of their fathers and mothers—refugees from and survivors of the Holocaust—had impressed upon many haredim throughout their early years: the life of a Jew was a precarious one.

To talk about the threat from the Arabs was to focus on something that united all Jews. Eichler was subtly, perhaps unconsciously, affirming that he was an Israeli, and that this physical vulnerability was what had created the common culture if it existed at all. All Jews in that sense were in the same boat.

This was a version of an argument heard many times in the haredi community. That argument recalled that Hitler and the Nazis had not distinguished between the assimilated and secular Jews on the one hand and the segregated, observant on the other. There was no escaping Jewish vulnerability for any of us. In an existential sense, we were indeed all in the same boat.

But surely the situation was different now, I suggested. Now Israel was protected by a strong army, Jews were no longer helpless victims. This was one of the great triumphs of Zionism; it had prevented Jews from standing helpless in the face of threats from others. At least now and here, in the Jewish homeland, Jews were safe.

"Ah," said Eichler, that was my basic mistake. "Perhaps they will protect me the way they will protect the Arabs of Abu Ghosh," he said, referring to those Arabs who were nominally Israeli citizens but whose loyalties many Jews doubted. To Eichler, Israelis likewise looked upon haredim as less than full-fledged citizens.

"They will protect us but with less than full enthusiasm. I do not count on their protection."

To Eichler haredim were of course doubly vulnerable: first, they were likely to suffer as Jews—a threat that came from the outside world—and then they were subject to attacks from their own secular Jewish counterparts, the Zionists and the state that many believed hated them for their particular way of being Jews.

"Maybe that's because you and others like you refuse to serve in that army," I suggested. In Israeli society the army had become the great integrative institution. As the young graduated from high school and confronted the universal draft, they became caught up in the quest to join the best units. As all young people went through this military institution, they were forged into Israeli civilians. Each would come out of the army with a sense of his or her place in Israeli society. Haredim, who like Arabs did not go through the process, remained unintegrated into the society—or so it seemed. They remained outsiders who held on to their deferments from military service by staying within the protective walls of the yeshiva.

"My father won his stripes fighting in the armed forces," he shot back. "He helped force the British out of Palestine and participated in many battles. Even after the state came to be, he fought in the Yom Kippur War." There were many like Eichler whose fathers had served in war.

"And what about you?"

"I could never join. My father thought he was fighting for Am Yisrael [the nation of Israel] not for the state. But I would be drafted into the state army. What was possible for my father is no longer possible for me.

"The army is now a force that pulls people away from being Jews; it no longer protects their being Jewish." He knew, as did other haredim, that the army and Israeli society had made this place safe for Jewish bodies but "dangerous for Jewish souls."

These soldiers were not the Maccabees preserving what was pure against the hellenizers; they were the hellenizers. Haredim were the true Maccabees, as the rebbe had pointed out.

And yet people glorified the army. Even the haredi world, who thought themselves insulated from the attractions of a secular Israel, were inevitably tempted by the army sometimes. There was no denying it.

"A student in the Belz yeshiva recently expressed an interest in going into the army." Lately, as haredi political parties jockeyed for position in the inevitable coalition talks to form a new Israeli government, there had been talk in the press and the public demanding that haredim who wanted a greater voice in defining the nature of the Jewish society serve in the army in greater numbers. Some well-meaning young men were coming to feel that they would make their moral demands more forcefully if they voided this criticism so often lodged against them. They would show the world that they were no less willing to risk their lives and therefore could be no less listened to when they made their demands.

There were all sorts of excuses that the yeshiva people and other haredim who avoided the army had made: excuses that said the Jews were defended by the study of Torah and observance of God's commandments no less than by carrying arms. But that argument often fell flat when the risks of the two battlefronts were compared. The young boy from Belz who thought about serving in the army was wavering in his resolve. He needed to be propped up.

Eichler continued: "But just then I read an article by Amnon Dankner."

Amnon Dankner is a journalist for the labor-socialist newspaper *Davar*. Although born into a religious family, he had abandoned those ways. And now like many an "apostate," his enmity toward haredim was well-known, perhaps most vividly captured in an open letter to them that he once published and in which he said, among other things:

> I want no dialogue with you for I have nothing to say to you. I want no part of you. For me, you are banished and outcasts. . . . I will protect my soul and the souls of my children from you, from your evil, primitive, mindlessly brainwashed spirit. I will speak and write

against you in every place, because you are the greatest danger to my existence here.[6]

"I showed it to this Belz boy. Do you know what Dankner wrote?" Eichler said. "He wrote that he smoked his first cigarette on Sabbath while in the army." The army had led to the creation of this enemy of the Yidn, to his breaking the laws of Sabbath.

" 'And this is what you want to be part of?' I said to him. 'This is how you will protect Yidn?' and that ended the problem of his going to the army."

We Are Becoming More Haredi

"We have become far more haredi since I was a child," Eichler admitted. "We had to. I will tell you the truth—I see the haredization of this generation as greater than that of mine, and this is a very interesting thing. In my mind the alienation between the religious and the secular is what strengthens us. Every Dankner whom we have to confront forces us to be stronger."

It was not always that way. "Once we were part of the same family. Once the Dankners lived with us. Once there was no religious family or home in Israel that did not have a secular Jew in it. They lived together with us." Sometimes this encouraged extremism, as the newly secular people tried hard to show they were abandoning the old ways. Inside Mea Shearim one could see the desecration of the Sabbath. "This was *not* some secularist from outside who invaded Mea Shearim," Eichler explained. "The sons of Mrs. Shosha came on Shabbat morning with big cigarettes to the alleys of the synagogues and stood tall and the boys who carried seforim cowered off on the side against the wall."

Worse still, these boys with their forbidden cigarettes on Sabbath were already members of the Haganah or Etzel; they were heroes, regular guys. They seemed to hold the keys to the future. And they made it clear that the 'smart' guys left the yeshiva.

"There was a great crisis. Out of full classes in Yeshivas Etz Chaim there remained only a smattering of students. . . .

"So at first we were all weak, afraid that we would be overpowered by the secular boys and their ways. But now over the years we and the secularists have separated physically—we have our own neighborhoods and communities—and we have separated culturally. Dankner has gone to *Davar* and I remained at *Ha-Machaneh Ha-Haredi*. And that is what has fortified our population. There have been fewer and fewer dropouts from our world. And now *they* are often the ones who have the dropouts. They are the ones whose sons have lost faith in the ways of their fathers. What is there left of that secular Zionism? They leave Israel by the thousands. They feel nothing that holds them here and nothing that keeps them Jews.

"But we fought back by not disappearing, by not giving up our ways. We did not all cower. So today we do not have to let a car drive through our neighborhood and desecrate the Sabbath. And we do not have to bend to each one of their Zionist rules."

We Choose Our Way of Life

"But make no mistake. Even according to them, I have a right to live my life my way. Just as one man can complain when another makes noise on his street at night, so I can complain when he disrupts the life on my streets. 'The Majority rules,' they say. Well, on these streets we are the majority and we have a right to rule."

There was something exquisitely modern about this argument that within their own domains persons and communities have rights to live life as they see fit. Haredi ways were an optional lifestyle. Eichler defended his right to live his way of life with the principles of tolerance and pluralism; values that the modern secular world itself championed. "Modernity pluralizes," as sociologist Peter Berger contends.[7] Eichler would make an argument for pluralism many times. In the pages of his newspaper, celebrating the tenth anniversary of the Machzikey Ha-Dat organizations (through which Belz institutionalized its own, competitive, supervision of haredi standards of practice) he would argue:

> Just as no one would question or challenge the right of every hasidic group or congregation affiliated with a particular yeshiva, city, community, land, etc., to establish its own bes medrash, school, or neighborhoods, so no one can deny their right to establish their own courts, judges, systems of kosher certification and ritual slaughter so long as there are sufficient worshipers in the bes medrash, enough students to keep up the study in the schools and ample customers for their products. . . .[8]

Eichler used pluralism as the basis for legitimating his "marches on the path of Torah."

"In the past maybe there was only one small community, one little village of a hundred families with one school, one burial society, rabbis, synagogue, religious court, ritual slaughterer, a community leader —so we all came into this one unit. But today we are many.

"Of course, if you think all haredim are one, you are making a mistake," he added. "Today we all recognize that the large and holy population, with its tens of thousands of souls, may Heaven protect them, which we generally designate 'the haredim,' does not constitute a single community."

I heard similar arguments from other haredim. As one hasid put it, distinguishing between his kind of Judaism and that of the world of the Lithuanian yeshiva: "We negate their approach in principle; the goal may be the same but the approach is not and it's time the secular community recognized that we are not all alike."

We Are the True Jews

The more we talked, the clearer it became that for Eichler and people like him the world was divided. There were various kinds of insiders and outsiders. But the lines were not always clearly drawn.

On the one hand, secular Jews were just like goyim. "I have to teach my children that the secular world is filled with goyim. When my children see someone driving on the Sabbath, how can I tell them this person is a Jew? I have to tell them he is a goy because otherwise they will begin to think it is possible for a Jew to drive on the Sabbath."

"And what should be the essential characteristics of the people in your community?"

"We want to produce talmidey chachamim [scholars], great believers, anshei chesed [people of kindness], erlicher Yidn, Jews who will find it possible to live with the Holy One, Blessed be He, from the time of their birth. That is the utopia for which we yearn. The minimum is to observe all God's commandments with devotion and intention."

"But there are Jews who manage to go into the secular world without ending up desecrating the Sabbath, who can be erlicher Yidn and anshei chesed," I protested.

"Look at the streets around you; look in the university where you work," he said. "The last two hundred years of Jewish history prove you are wrong. The encounter with the outside world is dangerous."

"And haredim cannot pass the test?"

Eichler held up one of the diskettes from his computer. "Look at

this. It has seven hundred thousand spaces for memory. Very powerful. But if I know nothing about it, I see nothing. How can I test its
power? Suppose I throw it out the window to see how it survives the
fall—I will not really learn anything at all about its power or capacity.
That is the wrong test! As the diskette cannot be tested by being
thrown out the window, so the haredi Jew cannot be tested by his
encounter with the modern world. To tell me about haredim who are
broken by a situation for which they are not built is to tell me nothing.
Because I am a talmid chacham or erlicher Yid, does that mean I can
eat glass without slicing my belly? No—glass is a dangerous thing; it
has been proven that many people who eat it have been injured. I
therefore am not about to go and eat glass."

He looked into my eyes with what seemed a melancholy expression:
"Life in the world you come from is like eating glass. We have to keep
our distance from it."

We Keep Our Deviations Out of Sight and We Know Our Limits

What about him? Eichler claimed he was one of those people who
managed to absorb much from the outside world without being
harmed. "I read all sorts of materials that I would not allow my son to
read," he admitted. "I don't show anyone else when I read these sorts
of materials."

It was known that many haredim would sneak off to the National
Library or other places where they could get their hands on all sorts of
things that they could or would not read within the boundaries of their
world.

There were even people among the haredim whose deviations were
far more ominous. These included haredim who visited prostitutes but
who always did it under the cover of darkness. Someone once noted
that at 2 A.M. among the few people out on the streets of Jerusalem
were haredim going places they would never dare go to in the daylight.
Indeed, there were even advertisements for call girls in the Israeli
papers (not the haredi ones) that announced that the girls were ready
to service the "religious."

Yet the embarrassment and the shame that kept the deviations out
of view were, Eichler claimed, also the sign of the community's
strength. In keeping the activities secret the deviants were also protecting the community by not publicly flaunting their breach of norm.
As long as people felt constrained in their behavior, even if that con-
straint was for a few only a matter of managing the impression they

made upon others who counted, these were nevertheless limits that the other Israelis did not feel.

"That's why we dress and look the way we do. How far can we move from our world looking like this?"

Community, norms, and tradition were a protective apparatus, even when there was intellectual wandering. "I'm not worried about my reading leading to heresy because I already have immunity. My way of life, where I live, my community gives me that immunity."

"But I feel the same thing," I countered.

"Ah," he smiled, "but there are some things I will not read, places I will not go. I can't cut my beard or earlocks and disappear into the crowd. You can take off your skullcap and do anything you want to do. I don't tell myself, 'You're strong enough to read anything. Go anywhere.' And what about you?"

In everything he claimed to be and said to me, it seemed to me that Eichler was a combination of opposites, a synthesis of what Oswald Spengler in his *Decline of the West* defined as Apollonian and Faustian man.[9] As an Apollonian, he conceived of "life as under the shadow of catastrophe always brutally threatening from the outside," while as a Faustian he had a picture of himself and people like him "as a force endlessly combating obstacles."[10]

"And you?" he asked again. "Are you strong enough to read any-thing?"

He paused. I said nothing.

"To this you have no answer. But we know, we know the limits."

8

Purim: This Is Who We Are Not

In their discussion of the way in which a society's views of the world, *Weltanschauungen*, are forged, Peter Berger and Thomas Luckmann point out that "only a very limited group of people in any society engages in theorizing, in the business of 'ideas,' and the construction of *Weltanschauungen*."[1] But, they add, in one way or another, everybody in that society participates in actions that reveal what those ideas or philosophic views are. To get at these worldviews in haredi society, conversations with people like Yisrael Eichler were useful, but nothing could take the place of watching people in action.

While not everything that insiders do reveals the governing ideas of their society in the same way, some moments and activities seemed undeniably to reflect outlook. Like the Belz bar mitzvah and rebbe's tish, holidays were particularly notable in that they were times of social effervescence, when collective life became "more frequent and active" and what people believed became "especially apparent."[2] While haredim of course celebrated all Jewish holidays, some of these, especially the ones that hovered somewhere between being mundane weekdays and full-fledged religious holy days, were occasions when the haredi version of the holiday seemed significantly different from the way the rest of the Jews celebrated the day. Besides Chanukah, there were also Purim and Lag b'Omer. Both raucously turned life inside out, which is perhaps the reason they offered a glimpse of interiors otherwise hidden away.

Partly sacred and partly profane, Purim [3] in Israel comes at the end of winter and commemorates the deliverance of the Jews of ancient Persia from the genocidal decree of the Vizier Haman. According to the megillah (*the Scroll of Esther*), the traditional account of these events, Haman's plans were undone by Mordecai the Jew and his cousin Esther who, as queen to the Persian King Ahasueras, was able to intervene on behalf of her people.

While this is the traditional Jewish explanation for the origins of the holiday, there are some scholars who argue that in fact the holiday precedes the scroll and simply enshrines the principle of Jewish salvation from all those who have tried to destroy the nation. And indeed, Jewish tradition is filled with many local "Purims," each with its own "megillah" commemorating the deliverance of the Jews in question from disaster [4]. Some of those scholars who see Purim in such relative terms argue that it arose in Persia as a Jewish counterholiday to many of the pagan winter festivals. Others cite the absence of any evidence of a king named Ahasueras in Persian records as well as the similarity of the names Esther and Mordecai to the ancient Babylonian gods Ishtar and Marduk as evidence of a linkage with precursor non-Jewish traditions. They note the Talmud's admission that the celebration of Purim was not immediately accepted throughout the Jewish community [5] as additional proof of resistance to the integration of these pagan rites.

Still other scholars, noting that Purim was once called Mordecai's Day, argue that it may have merged with another holiday, Nicanor's Day. Nicanor's Day, which in the ancient Jewish calendar precedes Purim by one day, celebrated the Hasmonean victory over an invader who sought to desecrate the Jerusalem Temple and the Jewish way of life. That event today is associated with Chanukah. Chanukah and Purim are thus linked together as holidays that celebrate respectively the spiritual and physical survival of the Jews. Indeed, just this connection, some scholars argue, is what has kept Purim in the sacred calendar. Were Jews not being attacked repeatedly and their survival not continually in question, Purim might have receded as a holiday. But the course of Jewish history has made Purim a living symbol of Jewish survival against all odds.

Whatever the historic facts, to celebrate the occasion of this miraculous deliverance annually, Jews ritualistically reread the story of the events that have become enshrined in the Scroll of Esther. Once in the evening and another time the following morning, they gather in the synagogue or another public place and listen to every word in the scroll. In addition to this central ritual requirement, the celebration of Purim obliges Jews to mark the occasion by giving charity to the poor, exchanging gifts of food with one another, and eating a festive meal. Jewish law as well as rabbinic interpreters have elaborated on all these obligations by indicating how and precisely when the megillah must be chanted, the minimum of charity that must be given, the nature of the sorts of foods that should be exchanged, and the timing and substance of the festive meal.

Beyond these religious obligations, a variety of customs have become attached to Purim over the ages. Most of these focus on joyous celebration. These include responding with raucous jeering (commonly with noisemakers) to blot out the recitation of Haman's name during the reading of the megillah and getting drunk at the meal until "one cannot distinguish between blessing Mordecai and cursing Haman."

Indeed, in many ways the revelry has marked Purim as a holiday of inversion—a time when what is commonly prohibited becomes permissible. Thus, for example, those who are normally engaged in serious study are encouraged to engage in merrymaking. The sober discussion of Torah is replaced by a satirical discourse, "Purim Toyreh," often offered by a jester, a "Purim rabbi," who takes the place of the true rabbi.[6] In some quarters among Ashkenazic Jews a "Purimshpiel," Purim farce—frequently a satire on some biblical or Jewish theme—became a part of the community celebrations.[7] Often the play is also a form of inversion, when themes normally treated with the utmost gravity are presented in antithesis. These include relations with outsiders (goyim), sectarian internal conflicts, and even the difficult demands of ritual and religion. Some dramas even lampoon difficult theological issues such as the triumph of evil over good or the rule of the righteous by the wicked. On Purim what would otherwise be unspeakable heresies or at the very least iconoclasm becomes the stimulus for uproarious laughter.[8] For example, one striking play put on by the Bobover hasidim a number of years ago mocked the apparently arcane rules of Jewish dietary laws and used the story of Daniel in the lions' den as a kind of funny story of Jews outsmarting their Gentile oppressors.

But of course one need not be a psychoanalyst to realize that behind the laughter is a world that the people must find enormously difficult to maintain under normal circumstances.[9] The repeated themes that focus on the precariousness of Jewish survival and the difficult demands made by God and man upon the Jew are impossible to miss;

the people laugh about what would otherwise make them cry. What haredim tremble about all year, they joke about on Purim.

Masquerade

One of the most prominent Purim customs—particularly among the children who are the central beneficiaries of this celebration of Jewish survival—is the masquerade. The precise origins of this practice are cloudy, a matter of some scholarly and rabbinic debate, but its significance seems clear. Like all else about the holiday, the masquerade is an opportunity to display an inverted reality, to exhibit what one is normally *not*. One masquerades in what assuredly is the opposite of one's true identity.

For someone trying to find out who the haredim were, Purim might therefore be a perfect time. To find out who the haredim were, all one had to do was to reverse the masquerade. Moreover, by seeing how the haredim displayed what they were not, I could also discover how much they knew about, and how they perceived, alternative worlds. Finally, because so much of the masquerade involves being seen, much of the action takes place out on the streets, in full view of the public. I would only have to join that public, wander along the streets of the haredi neighborhoods, in order to see what there was to be seen.

As I made my way to Mea Shearim and the streets that were the heartland of haredi life in Jerusalem, I passed through the downtown area where many altogether secular Israelis were also in costume to celebrate what had become a kind of national day of merriment, something of a Jewish analogue to Halloween. The downtown was a tableau filled with people dressed as punk rockers, astronauts, and freaks of all sorts. Looking at them, I thought of the way my friends and I used to dress up on Purim. We became what we could never be in real life. So my friends and I dressed up as cowboys—I was Hopalong Cassidy —or Batman, Superman, or Captain Midnight, characters far away from our everyday reality. The freaks and astronauts and punk rockers were, I supposed, the contemporary versions of the same thing.

But in my modern Orthodox Jewish community there was another, quite popular Purim costume: we dressed up as hasidim. People would put on false beards and earlocks, mock caftans and something like a fur shtreimel, looking for all the world like the Jews we would never be willing to look like in real life. Would the alternative worlds depicted in the haredi neighborhoods have them dressing up as us?

The streets of Mea Shearim were filled with children and parents.

Many carried packages—*mishloach manot*—of foods to be ritually exchanged with their neighbors. The parenting role of haredi fathers stood out. While mothers were presumably at home preparing the festive meal or filling the baskets in which the *mishloach manot* were carried, fathers walked the neighborhood with their costumed youngsters in hand, making deliveries.

Because concern with and control over children is crucial to the haredi community and because they were with their fathers, I assumed that whatever costumes the youngsters had on were worn with at the very least the tacit approval of their parents.

From the desk of the exalted scholar and head of the court, may he live long and well, the master and zaddik of the court of justice, may he live long and well.

TO WARN AND TO BE WARNED

It has come to our knowledge that in the last number of years there have come on Purim to the environs of Kikar Shabbes invaders dangerous to [the standards of] modesty. They walk about in covers that cover nothing.

Hence comes our warning to warn the elders to warn their children and others: **TO DESIST AND PREVENT** loitering in the above-mentioned area by those who would gaze upon them and observe their actions which are so dangerous to modesty and the purity of Israel.

He who protects his soul will distance himself from them and make them distant from him.

AND IT IS GENERALLY APPROPRIATE THAT ON PURIM PARENTS KEEP A WATCHFUL EYE ON THEIR BOYS AND GIRLS, AND PREVENT THEIR BEING FOUND ON STREETS AND IN PLACES WHERE MANY ASSEMBLE AND WHERE IMPEDIMENTS TO PURITY MAY BE FOUND, HEAVEN FORBID.

and those who listen to our words will be blessed with an everlasting joy upon their heads.

The adult's concern with costumes was prominently displayed on a broadside posted on a wall near Kikar Shabbes, the main square in the neighborhood.[10] Like many of the locals, I read the bottom first, to look at the endorsements and find out who had published it. The poster was signed by a number of well-known haredi rabbis, including Yisrael Moshe Dushinsky, Yisrael Yaakov Fisher, Binyamin Rabinovitz, Avraham David Horowitz, and foremostly, Yitzhak Yaakov Weiss, chief judge of the religious court of the Eda Haredis. This was an august and influential group. Even though this was a day of revelry and joy, the warnings of men such as these rabbis had to be regarded seriously. Yet the fact that the poster had been printed ahead of time also indicated that what it railed against was regular and predictable. The rabbis put their message on a poster.

Obviously, the masquerades and merrymaking were threatening, impediments to the insulation of the haredi culture. Parents had to watch their children and prevent the invasions that were endemic to Purim celebrations.

Kikar Shabbes, at the entrance to Mea Shearim, was filled with people, but many had taken the rabbis' warning and remained deeper inside the alleys of the neighborhood. To get to their masquerade, I would have to go farther into the heart of the neighborhood. Walking into the courtyards of the Hungarian Houses, inside the market of Mea Shearim near the main synagogue, in the open places in front of the many yeshivas, I found the masquerade parade. Standing unobtrusively against one of the walls, I took out a small pad and registered all the costumes I came across.

And what is the picture of the haredi community that emerges out of this tableau? What all the costumes share in common is that they represent expressions of an alter-ego identity, a chance to be something altogether different. Purim being what it is, on this day, at least in masquerade, even the impossible becomes possible.

So children can become an animal—and not just any animal but one that is dangerous, frightening, and altogether foreign or exotic in these parts. I saw gorillas and wolves. And they can become clowns, witches, trolls, and other monstrous-looking creatures that in masquerade are no longer dangerous and terrifying. The dressing up (and playfully scaring one another) offers them an opportunity to enter into their fears and diffuse them in play.[11] In this haredi children were not especially different from other youngsters who wear similar costumes. Indeed, the fact that for all of their haredi experience these children remain children—not so different from their peers, sharing some of the same fantasies and fears and finding play as a way to handle them

—is of course revealing, for it implies that for all the effort that haredim make to insulate their offspring from what goes on outside their domains, the haredi world is not in every aspect set apart. But there are other costumes that do display the special character of haredi life.

If the masquerade is an opportunity to be what one normally cannot be, what do we discover the haredim cannot be? Besides being animals and monsters, they cannot be adults. In traditional Judaism and especially in its traditionalist haredi incarnation, adult status is strictly separated from childhood. The adult has different religious obligations and prerogatives. He even wears different clothes. The men wear the long black (or sometimes gold-striped) caftans and black broad-brimmed hats, and the hasidim among them wear fur shtreimels or the taller fur spodiks. The women, commonly married, cover their hair with a variety of kerchiefs or wigs. None of this is common among those below thirteen. But on Purim even the very young can dress up in their parents' clothes and become them in masquerade.

It is no surprise to find these sorts of costumes among the most ubiquitous, for while they allow for a break in the normal, they nevertheless eliminate the more dangerous radicalism of Purim; they subtly turn this day of inversion—always a threat to a highly controlled environment like the haredi one—into an opportunity to reaffirm a pattern of life lived the whole year through. Wearing what will be the everyday garb of their future, the children (and the parents who helped dress them up) say, "We cannot yet be adults, but today we shall try on what we one day shall truly become." Purim in its now controlled playfulness allows children to use the occasion to play at a role and try out behavior they may some day permanently take on, "to practice it in an intermediate reality between fantasy and actuality." [12]

Normally, they cannot be Queen Esther or Mordecai or any of the Bible characters or High Priests in the Holy Temple, but on Purim they can become them. Today they can step back *into* and dress themselves in Jewish history, or at least the idealized traditional image of it. This too is a favorite sort of costume, bought or made up by the parents for their children. But like the masquerade as an adult haredi, it is tame, limiting the inversion, and turning the wild day into an endorsement of Jewish ways and an idealized Jewish past. To want to look like Queen Esther or Mordecai or King David or Aaron the High Priest is to remind us that these Jewish characters are heroes larger than life. Compared to the punk rockers and Ninja Turtles I found in the downtown streets, these costumes unmistakably celebrated a far more obviously Jewish heritage.

But the children are not only dressed up like little haredi adults or characters from Jewish tradition and the megillah. They wear many other masquerades as well, and these reveal the inverse in a far more dramatic way. These other costumes are the images that come from other domains. These are the alternative identities that on all other occasions would be unacceptable and impossible.

On days other than Purim haredim cannot be university graduates, for this would take them into the intellectual and social domains of the prohibited. The university is the antipode to the ghetto. But today I see a boy in mortarboard cap and black academic gown. On all other days girls cannot be coquettes or alluring females, painted in makeup, for this would be immodest and licentious. But today I see a French mademoiselle and a girl ostentatiously festooned in jewelry and covered in cosmetics. Throughout the year they cannot be Arabs, for this would mean to be a Gentile, freed of all the rules and regulations that come with being a Jew. But today I see a Jewish boy in kaffiyeh and flowing robes. They can never be movie stars or comedic entertainers whose entertainment and humor come from another universe, from among the goyim. But today I come across Harpo Marx in Mea Shearim. They will never become a Magen-David Adom (Israeli Red Cross) nurse, a role inconceivable to haredi girls who cannot engage in the immodest and therefore prohibited physical contact with unrelated males this would entail, nor will they be doctors, whose training process and initiation would take them too far out of their protective environment. But today I find earlocked boys in white coats and little girls carrying stethoscopes and wearing white nurses' caps.

Living in their exilelike pose of dependency, haredim cannot be in charge of the government—and certainly not of a non-Jewish one concerned with the welfare of all people and not just those who live in their enclosed minority community. Yet today I see them dressed as commissars and kings. They will never be in the army in general and particularly not the Israeli army, but today I see them as GI Joes or boys dressed as IDF soldiers. Although these people who value the scholar over the soldier will not be warriors of any sort—be they freewheeling gunslingers who follow where the buffalo roam, paladins of ancient days, or any other toughs—today I see cowboys, knights in plastic armor, and cossacks. Only on Purim is all this possible. On the day when opposites are the rule, when the village fool can play the part of Purim rabbi, the unthinkable is visible. And these youngsters who as adults will never agree to join the army or use a gun are today shooting up the place with enthusiasm.

Of course, the outside world represented in these costumes is a caricature, made up of cowboys and cossacks. To make it too real is to make it too attractive. Indeed, that is what the posters from the self-appointed community censors that warn parents against allowing their children to wear certain costumes, particularly those viewed as sexually immodest or sacrilegious, are meant to ensure. But what the broadsides forbid is what nature wishes to do. And that is why the same posters appear each year, their message always relevant and never completely observed.

And what is there to be said about the children (some as young as nine or ten) openly smoking cigarettes, something I found in lots of places? There seemed to be no effort to stop them. Huddled together, they handed around smokes, looking like conspirators in crime. This might be seen as the children's expression of doing the absolutely forbidden, the child's equivalent of getting drunk. Now this is not to say that the adults do not smoke in these communities. They do. In a way, the smoking represents the vice of adulthood, and on this day the children are allowed to emulate even the vices of their elders. The smoking is thus at once an inversion and paradoxically also an expression of continuity.

Both inversion and role playing make the day a chance for affirming the haredi way of life, the former by reminding people what they are normally not and the latter by showing them that the next generation will follow in their footsteps.

9

Mass Pilgrimage

Lag b'Omer, a minor Jewish holy day in the spring, is the thirty-third in the forty-nine ritually counted days—called the "Omer"—that come between Passover, the commemoration of the Exodus from Egypt, and Shavuot, the traditional anniversary of the Jews' receiving the Torah at Sinai. According to tradition, during the first thirty-three of these days, many of the greatest Jewish sages died, twelve thousand of them students of the great Rabbi Akiva. The story is recounted in the Babylonian Talmud (Yebamot 62). To this day their deaths continue to be mourned during the Omer. That mourning is marked by the observant in a variety of ways, the most prominent being that no weddings or other celebrations are held during these days, and—in the customary Jewish sign of bereavement—no hair is cut. The thirty-third day, Lag b'Omer, is different. According to accepted lore, on this day the rabbis stopped dying. Others note that on Lag b'Omer in the second century and during the Bar Kochba revolt against the Romans (132–135 C.E.), a dramatic turn of events occurred, leading to the victory of the Jewish zealots over the Roman occupiers of Jerusalem and Judea.[1] And thus Lag b'Omer became associated with joy, or more precisely, an end to mourning.

There are mystical associations with the day as well. This day is filled with the promise of redemption and an end to suffering. It is a day echoing with messianic hopes, not unlike those that accompanied the victories of Bar Kochba (whom the sage Rabbi Akiva thought was the Messiah himself). And on this day, Rabbi Shimon bar Yochai, the last and perhaps most famous of Akiva's students, champion of the revolt, twelve-year fugitive from a Roman death decree, and according to traditional belief the author of the Zohar, the prime text of Jewish mysticism, died.² But—so the story goes—just before his death in the Galilee, he revealed to his students some of the greatest secrets of the kaballah. And when he died on Lag b'Omer and was buried in the mountains, a voice from heaven called out, "Arise, come, and gather to commemorate Rabbi Shimon Bar Yochai."³

For a time, Jews made pilgrimages to his burial place, a cave on Mount Meron, just outside of Safed, city of the mystics. In time, the practice fell into neglect until Rabbi Isaac Luria, the famed "Ari," a mystic who settled in Safed two years before his death in 1572, reinstituted the Lag b'Omer pilgrimage to Meron. (The Ari was not alone in this; many of the sixteenth-century kabbalists of Safed are known to have observed annual memorial pilgrimages—called *yoma d'hilula*, Aramaic for "day of celebration"—to the graves of revered rabbis, many of whom were buried in Safed.) Coming to the tomb, he would, among other things, ask the deceased to act as a *mailitz yosher*, righteous intermediary in the heavenly court. "The grave of the *zaddik* was considered an especially efficacious place to pray, and where prayers are more likely to be heard."⁴

The Ari, whose mystical readings of Judaism form an important basis for much of hasidic practice and many of the founding beliefs, still carries enormous weight in haredi circles in general and among hasidim in particular. Among them, the idea of a pilgrimage to Meron is still among the most sacred of journeys.

Another one of the Ari's well-known mystical dicta was that "children are like trees in the field." As fruits of new trees, according to sacred law, may not be harvested for the first three years of blooming, so the hair of young children, in particular the boys, may not be cut for the first three years of their lives. In a practice that mixes together many of these Lurianic traditions, many hasidim have taken to bringing their three-year-old sons to Meron on Lag b'Omer for their first haircuts. There, outside the tomb of Rabbi Shimon bar Yochai, the locks are clipped and blessings recited. The occasion has become a pilgrimage of enormous importance, and the first haircut—the *chalaka*, as it is called—has become a community celebration and an important rite of passage.

Not only hasidim consider a trip to Meron and the tomb of Shimon bar Yochai on Lag b'Omer an important act of piety. The tale is told that Rabbi Hayim ben Attar (d. 1743), Moroccan-born holy man and scholar to whom many Jews of Middle Eastern and North African origins attribute miracles, also visited Meron on Lag b'Omer.

"When he reached the foot of the mountain from which one ascends to the tomb of Shimon bar Yochai, he got down from his donkey and crawled on hands and knees, crying: 'Who am I, the lowly, that I dare come to the place of the torch's flame, the place where the Holy One Blessed be He and His host are present!' "[5] Still today Sephardic Jews, and especially those from North Africa and the Middle East, follow in his footsteps and come to Meron, also expecting miracles.

And indeed Jewish folklore is filled with tales of being healed, the birth of children to the barren, changing fortunes, and like miracles by those who have made the Lag b'Omer pilgrimage to the tomb in Meron in order to celebrate the anniversary of Rabbi Shimon bar Yochai's revelation and death. Thus, not only those who have children who are to get their first haircut, but all sorts of Jews in search of miracles—many of them Moroccan—come to Meron on Lag b'Omer.

Getting There

For weeks posters were plastered all over haredi neighborhoods about bus service to Meron on Lag b'Omer. As in years past, thousands would be making the trip. In Jerusalem two bus companies set up a special express shuttle service to the tomb and back. The larger of two—Hoffman's Buses, with offices in Jerusalem's Geula quarter and B'nai B'rak—was leasing vehicles and drivers from Egged, the national Israeli bus cooperative. While most travelers used this service, another company—Mahir Yerushalayim, with offices in Mea Shearim —was offering a competing service with its own buses and drivers. Both companies essentially offered the same ride to and from Meron, with separate seating for men and women and a charge of thirty-five shekels for the round trip. Buses ran every twenty minutes from one in the afternoon of the day before until nine-thirty Lag b'Omer night.

But what made Mahir's buses more attractive to some haredim was that, as advertised, it did not use Egged buses and drivers who were known to sometimes work on and thereby desecrate the Sabbath. Mahir's buses—shiny new Silver Tiger Volvos—and drivers never made such transgressions, and the presumption therefore was that those who chose to travel with them would by this—if only in a small way—be striking another blow against the religious compromisers and Sabbath desecrators. Accompanied by a Lubavitcher hasid from Jerusalem who acted as my guide, I took the Mahir bus.

Who Sits Where?

Purchasing the tickets, we found seats on a nearly full bus parked on Mea Shearim Street. Already inside were hasidim from various groups and even a few Lithuanian yeshiva types. I was the only non-haredi aboard. Nearly all the men and boys sat in the front; women and girls were in the back. While in most cases husbands and wives who entered the bus together sat separately (though, according to Jewish law, they need not have), the norm of the community was separation of the sexes in public. In spite of the fact that the women sat in the back, when the ticket agent walked through the bus collecting fees, it was more often the women who paid for their men. They might be sitting in the back, but they held the purse.

There were three elderly couples who sat together. No one voiced any objections to this situation. People knew, as my guide put it, "the old folks abided by different standards of behavior sometimes."

Just as we were about to set off on the trip, eight women tried to get aboard to fill the remaining seats. But most of the empty spaces were in the front where the men sat. An argument erupted about who would fill those places. Because they would not sit next to any man who was not their husband (and some would not have done even that), the women wanted some of the single men to move off the bus or at least shift seats so they could find room. A few adjustments were made, but only a couple of women got on our bus. The rest had to turn around and wait for the next bus. Haredi women had a hard time traveling about; they always seemed to encounter problems like this one. The matter of mixing the sexes was not to be compromised, and most of the men would not be moved. The implication was that if women wanted to leave home alone, the men were not going to make it easy for them. We waited for a few more minutes until the people who could match the seats available came. At last, everyone in place, the bus pulled out with its full load of forty-two.

Hair

On the bus were some little pony-tailed boys who looked as if they were on their way to Meron for their first haircut. Anticipation, anxiety, bewilderment, and excitement animated their faces. For some this was simply a long outing, one of those rare occasions when the family left the environs of the few streets that constituted their entire world. For others it was a day filled with changes that they still did not quite comprehend.

As for the women on board, all of the married ones complied with the haredi standards of modesty, which asserted that *"sa'ar b'isha erva"* the sight of a (married) woman's hair is an impropriety, tantamount to seeing her naked.[6]

The matter of a married woman having to cover her hair is by no means a simple one, although haredim distinguish themselves from other Jews by their scrupulousness on this point. A key source for this practice comes from the Jewish Code, which warns that one may not recite the Shema prayer in front of a married woman whose hair is uncovered because her locks are an element of her nakedness and as such sexually arousing. The modest woman hides them away.

Although married haredi women were scrupulous about covering their hair, "the customs of a community always have a particular style"; different women went about this in varying ways.[7] The style of covering her hair was not an arbitrary choice; each one signified a level of stringency and an attachment to a particular community's norms. And there was in all this a kind of symbolic hierarchy that haredim had developed.

The more a woman looked vaguely like her contemporaries in the outside world, the less haredi she was assumed to be. At one extreme were women with black kerchiefs covering their shaved heads. These were predominantly the wives of Satmar or Reb Arelach hasidim and the women of the Eda Haredis or Neturei Karta, known to be strictest in their haredi ways. Next, a bit less austere-looking, came women who wore colored or patterned kerchiefs atop shaved heads. Then came women who wore colored kerchiefs over their own, trimmed hair. At the next step were women who wore kerchiefs or crocheted caps over their clipped hair but who allowed a bit of that hair to show in front over their foreheads. Finally came the women who wore wigs. Some wore hats atop the wigs and others not. And even among the wig wearers there were those who wore locks that were made of human hair and made to look like their own (which was why they often wore hats on top of them), and there were others who wore synthetic perukes designed to look obviously fake. While both wigs were meant to display religious observance, those made of human hair could also camouflage it, which was why some rabbis railed against them. The bus contained women from almost every group.

Although all the women had their heads covered, and each wore a high-necked, long-sleeved dress, even on the warm spring day, to cover all hint of nakedness, they did manage to find ways of displaying their femininity and attracting attention. It was in the way they wiggled when they moved or even more in the way they decorated themselves. Dressed in their finest, many of the wigged ladies sported large brooches, sparkling necklaces, diamond rings, and jeweled bracelets. Even those in austere black kerchiefs had pierced their ears, in which they wore small but glimmering earrings.

Although seated in back, the ladies would occasionally come forward in the bus to give their husbands the child or bring a bottle or ask a question. But this did not happen very often.

Passing the Time

As we began what would be a long journey, a number of the men and boys took out material to read. In haredi thinking, it was wrong to be idle, especially when one was on a pilgrimage. A number of the men began reading *Mesilat Yesharim* (Paths of the Righteous), an early-eighteenth-century volume by Moses Hayim Luzzatto. The book was filled with ethical teachings meant to pave the way for spiritual repair and mystical communion with God. For the four hours it would take us to get to Meron, a man could repair a great deal of spirit. A few others pulled out copies of a text on Jewish law, reviewing the ordinances of Lag b'Omer. Pointing to one of them, my guide whispered: "At home he sometimes reads Sherlock Holmes." But such interest in the prohibited literature from the secular world was not to be displayed in public. In the seat in front of me a slim young man in his twenties slipped out of his pocket a pamphlet filled with stories of hasidic masters. Behind me I could see several of the older women, and a couple of the younger ones with shaved heads, open pocket editions of Psalms, which they now whispered.

Just outside Jerusalem, as the bus began its descent toward the coastal plain from where we would turn north toward the mountains of the Galilee, a man sitting behind the driver announced that it was time for the recitation of the Prayer for Travelers. On cue, everybody recited the prayer, which one was supposed to say whenever leaving the city limits.

This concern about the ritual and religious practices of fellow travelers was expressed again on the ride home when one man took the microphone just as we neared Jerusalem to announce, "Dear congregation, you are all reminded to still recite Ma'ariv and to count the Omer." These sorts of communiqués would never take place on a standard bus ride; and they reminded me that I was inside a community where another set of routines and interpersonal obligations were in effect.

My hasidic guide turned to me. We were leaving Jerusalem very late; his wife had gone up earlier with a group of women who were preparing refreshments for the thousands of pilgrims. She was trying to transform herself into a *zaddekes,* a pious and righteous woman. Preparing the food was only one part of this. She had also taken on a regimen of study that she pursued regularly with other women from the neighborhood. And she now also periodically observed a *taanis dibur,* days during which, to enhance her soul, she desisted from speaking. Sometimes, she altogether stopped talking on Sabbaths; that way no word of gossip or evil could pass her lips on this holy day. Her husband suspected that she might also be regularly fasting twice a week—on Mondays and Thursdays, but he was not certain, as she was asleep when he left the house early in the morning and out studying or asleep when he returned at night. She wanted him to become more of a zaddik, which would mean he would spend his entire life learning Torah, but he had a job as an administrator at one of the local yeshivas and that helped pay their many bills. Besides, he admitted, "I really don't have what it takes to be a scholar, to sit and learn all day."

"You know it's odd," he admitted, "normally, with us, it's the man who's learning and pushing himself to take care of his spiritual growth, and the woman who cares about the more down-to-earth matters. But with us things have become reversed. I am more and more concerned with *gashmius* [material matters] and my wife is becoming absorbed totally in *ruchnius* [spirituality]." This was a change in the order of life in the haredi world.

"Of course, she cooks and sews—just like all her women neighbors." But her greatest concern was to enhance the spiritual life of the family.

I had heard a similar story from another haredi, who also had begun by saying: "I'll tell you, life here has become changed." He told of a haredi couple who had recently divorced, once a rare event but of late far more common. "She was upset at her husband. All day he was supposed to be learning in a yeshiva, but each night when he came home, he read the paper. He didn't give her any attention, didn't tell her how good her meals were and how they helped him study better. After all, she was working very hard to allow him to grow spiritually.

"Eventually, she began to doubt that he was really studying in the yeshiva. How could he want to read the paper if he was so immersed in Torah learning? She had very great spiritual expectations of him."

"Too great expectations perhaps?" I wondered aloud.

"Could be. Anyway, she thought, maybe he was not really learning at all, and if so for what was she working? This doubt undermined the entire marriage."

Once again, I sensed that I was getting a glimpse of another order of reality as I listened to these stories. To be sure, tensions between husbands and wives could express themselves in many ways. In the world I came from, if my wife ever stopped speaking to me, it would not likely be because she was practicing a taanis dibur; or if I was reading the paper instead of paying attention to her, this would not be framed as a diminished religious spirituality. Rather, the problems would have been articulated as a breakdown of communication between wife and husband, an underlying sense of unfulfilled expectations. But here the problem was seen in haredi religious terms in the context of a concern over spirituality. Haredi life framed reality differently.

Arduous Journey

We were in Afula, ready to turn toward the Galilee. The bus driver made a fifteen-minute rest stop at a gas station. Most people left the bus, some to go to the bathrooms. Those who stood outside the bus gathered in little groups. People chatted comfortably with me. After all, I was joining them on a pilgrimage, and I was accompanied by a hasid. Perhaps I was a penitent, on my own road to spiritual repair. Obviously, I was not a hostile. With only haredim around me for hours, I had almost forgotten that I was not one of them.

The trip took much longer going this way, everyone around me admitted. "To bad we couldn't go via Jericho," said one man. We talked about the relative risks and advantages of taking our roundabout route versus the more direct road through Jericho and the Jordan Valley. Buses were taking the long route that avoided entering the occupied territories.

"Yes, but remember Rachel Weiss," responded another. Several months earlier an interurban bus passing through Jericho on its way to Jerusalem had been attacked by Arabs hurling a petrol bomb and Rachel Weiss, a haredi passenger, and all her children had been burned to death. Many haredim considered these deaths in the valley, which occurred in the midst of a bitter political campaign that pitted hasidim against misnagdim, as divine retribution for the intracommunal discord—the "baseless hatred"—among them. For haredim, nothing "just happens"; everything was a sign of divine concern for them. Haredim were, after all, the ones to whom God paid special attention. In this world where the supernatural interferes with the rational, the fact that a haredi woman was killed taking that route was enough for many to stay away from it.

"Besides, the more arduous the pilgrimage, the greater the reward," someone else added. This was the haredi version of "No pain, no gain."

We got on the bus again to turn northward. The ride was tortuous, almost two hours longer this way. At last, the bus began its slow circular climb through the mountains. Cars and buses were everywhere along the narrow mountain road. Among some Moroccan Jews there was a custom of sleeping in the woods near the tomb. We could see some of their campsites from the road. The closer we got to Meron, the more such campsites we saw. Suddenly, we stopped.

A few of the younger haredim—*avrechim,* they were called—got off the bus. "Are we there?" I asked.

"No, this is where the avrechim get off. They don't want to walk through the main entrance," my guide told me. "There's a lot going on there that is not exactly spiritual, as you will soon see."

There was a path through the woods that allowed one to climb up the steeper back side of the mountain and get to the tomb without passing the thousands who came through the main entrance. Most people did not go this harder way. Women certainly did not. The symbolism was unmistakable. The hard road was for those who avoided contact with the immodest, the impious, the women. To make the journey this more demanding way was good; it was a sign of their religious toughness. Avrechim who wanted to demonstrate how haredi they were took this harder path.

But of course taking the hard road was also a way that these young men, barely past puberty, could demonstrate that they were heroes. And wasn't that something that adolescents liked to do in all cultures? Here once again I could see these universal human characteristics framed in religious terms.

To be sure, the matter of mixing with the others—particularly the nonharedim—who celebrate this occasion and venerate Rabbi Shimon bar Yochai was of special concern to the haredim. Many of them had a low estimation of these Sephardic Jews whom they called a variety of not always complimentary names. Their approach to the rabbi and to the occasion struck quite a number of haredim as primitive and crude, superstitious and sacrilegious.

The bus moved on. People began to prepare to disembark. Some men turned around to signal their wives with a few quick gestures. People stood to gather up their belongings and children. A few more turns and we would be in Meron, during the rest of the year little more than a few houses on the side of the hill, but for today, capital of the Galilee. Behind us there was a caravan of buses and cars as far as the eye could see.

At the Foot of the Mountain

At last, we arrived at the parking lot at the foot of the mountain. Even though it was already late afternoon, the place was still filled with buses, cars, tents, and people milling about. Some joined an interminable column of people on their way to the grave site, while others came from another line of people returning, trying to find a bus or car that would take them home. Quite a few were looking for their family members who had somehow become separated from them in the crowd.

At the edge of the lot, just beyond the police headquarters, there was a variety of snack bars selling everything from shish kebab to pita and falafel. There was also a booth with lottery tickets (presumably, a ticket brought to the holy rabbi's tomb for a blessing could be a big winner). Along the promenade were a seemingly endless array of booths and stands offering everything from free juice drinks and cassettes of inspirational songs or talks to blessings and amulets. It was a kind of spiritual flea market. Bearded men behind microphones proffered blessings, a prayer for the sick, or a supplication for the souls of the departed in return for charity. Next to them entrepreneurs were selling complete sets of the Zohar (in "three easy payments"). And on the other side were stands that sold earrings, T-shirts, and hand-dipped candles. The sacred and the profane mingled here in ways that many of the haredim found disturbing.

"You see; this is what the Sephardim do," my guide said to me. And indeed the scene was a kind of paradigm of the uncomplicated piety of these people for whom sacred and profane seemed to mix easily in a kind of ethnic and folk religion. But these sorts of appreciations of the Sephardic folk religion were beyond the haredim; they were scornful of what they perceived to be a corruption of Yiddishkeit. They had tried to remake some of their rabbis in their own image in the yeshivas, but the simple people still remained am ha'aretz (ignorant).

In the Footsteps of the Haredim

As I began to walk the promenade and in the direction of the tomb, I saw different groups, each looking for their own way to navigate the pandemonium. Most of the haredim on my bus turned away from the promenade. They took other paths. But these were not just other walkways; they were alternative approaches to the very act of pilgrimage. The avrechim had completely bypassed the entire area. Those not quite as hardy had their own ways of getting around the scene. As soon as they got off the bus, they were quickly herded aboard a waiting minivan that for a fee would transport them past the promenade and drop them off right next to the grave. A less expensive option required one to start up the promenade but after a few steps take a side path that weaved through some of the cottages of the town and avoided the most honky-tonk sections of the promenade. This required only a brief encounter with the sideshow, a chance perhaps to buy something or get a drink, a brush with the excesses of another world. There were those who did not turn aside and took the opportunity to pass through the gauntlet of hawkers and religious barkers, who had come here not just on pilgrimage but for a holiday in the country, who under the cover of this "religious occasion" could step over the boundary of their own narrow four cubits of life. After all, Lag b'Omer was a day when Jews celebrated by going on hikes and outings in the country.

To be sure, people were prepared for this scene, warned about what awaited them by flyers that fairly littered the streets of Mea Shearim. One, distributed by a van company that offered rides from the lot to the tomb, prominently mentioned the fact that the path that allowed one to avoid the promenade and the parking area reserved for their bus were coterminous; this of course served to endorse the bus company's services. The text of the flyer began:

With the help of Heaven

AN IMPORTANT ANNOUNCEMENT

FOR THOSE GOING UP TO MERON ON LAG B'OMER

For those going via *Megiddo*. That they may be prevented from mixing

We are announcing the following details:
★ It is necessary to park in the lot next to the grave of Rav Hamamnuna Sabah, on the side of the road. . . .

The rest of the flyer gave details of how to ascend the mountain via the various bypass paths, noting which were possible for the young and which for the aged and how long each path would take to climb. On the rear was a scrawled map. By demonstrating such sensitivity to matters of concern to the haredi population, the company signaled its affiliation with that community. And among haredim, the notion that "we support our own," financially and morally, was a deeply held principle.[8]

Most of those on my bus, and other black-frocked haredim, took the modified bypass; but in deference to my interests my guide, his son who also accompanied us, and I took the main path. The twelve-year-old boy gaped at the sight. The barkers, the music, the sideshow mystics, the strange parade of pilgrims all made this an outing he would not soon forget.

At a few of the booths people had set up cots. For them this was not just a chance to do some business; it was all part of the holiday excursion. Political parties, hoping to attract supporters from among the pilgrims, had also set up boxes. But these were mostly directed at Sephardic voters who the organizers knew would make up the bulk of the constituency on the walk. In one particularly elaborate stall erected by the Likud candidate for the upcoming national labor-union elections (broadsides for which were on every tree or post available), a small color video monitor on which an election ad was running had been set up. The curious gathered around to watch. Heavenly matters could wait.

But not only the politicians had this sort of elaborate recruitment setup. Nearby, under a clump of trees, next to some picnickers who

were beating drums and singing songs from Morocco, Chabad hasidim
had set up a trailer—they called it a "Mitzvah Tank." Inside, visitors
were being introduced to some basic tenets of Jewish observance,
given leaflets about Chabad Hasidism, and, if they were adult males,
offered an opportunity to don tefillin, the black-leather scripture-filled
boxes worn by males at morning prayers. This was a ritual whose daily
practice, the rebbe asserted, it was his hasidim's mission to encourage.
A line of people had formed outside. Just as the curious were ready to
watch a video of a Likud political candidate, try a new kind of snack
on a sesame-seed bun, have their loved ones blessed by an itinerant
preacher with a microphone, or consider buying a set of the Zohar, so
too they were ready to step into a Mitzvah Tank and try a taste of
hasidic Judaism.

Peter Berger once argued that in the modern world religion, originally considered a matter of fate, had become a matter of choice, where
it had to compete for attention in the marketplace of other life choices.
"In other words, there comes to be a smooth continuity between con-
sumer choices in different areas of life—a preference for this brand of
automobile as against another, for this sexual life-style as against another, and finally a decision to settle for a particular 'religious preference.' "[9] Here before me, on this mountain in Meron, was the
marketplace Berger described.

Leaving the Chabad outpost, my guide at last felt compelled to take
the side spur. "I think we've seen more than enough," he said and
grasped his son's hand.

Before I turned away with him, I jotted down some notes about
who I could see. As I looked out on the vista before me, I discerned at
least four categories of people: haredim, of all types; elderly pious
Sephardic Jews, who were repeating the pilgrimage patterns they had
established in Morocco, Tunisia, or other countries of origin; younger
and more this-worldly Sephardic Jews, the second generation who still
came out for such once-a-year carnivals; and gawking tourists and
observers like myself. Clearly, these different people all saw the occasion in their own ways. This was by no means a single event, as the
variety of characters who participated in it dramatically revealed. But
it was the haredi version that interested me. I followed my hasid.

At the Tomb

After many turns we reached the outer courtyard of the array of
buildings in which the grave of the holy man was to be found. Not

only was Rabbi Shimon bar Yochai buried here but so too were a variety of his rabbinic contemporaries. And even the great sages Hillel and Shammai of mishnaic fame were said to be buried nearby, on the other side of a deep ravine. There was a holy man for every season here.

Just before the entrance to the main set of buildings built over the tombs—what Jews called the *ohel*—the line of pilgrims slowed and the crowd became even thicker than down below. Taking advantage of the situation, a kind of queue of beggars had arranged themselves. "*Zedaka tatzil mi movis*" (Charity saves one from death), one was announcing, his hand jingling coins. Others whispered the more common phrase of Jewish mendicants: "*Tizkeh l'mitzvahs*" (May you merit the performance of other good deeds). The poor knew that wherever the community gathers, there they could find handouts. Indeed, there was nearly no gathering—except on Sabbaths and major holy days, when the handling of money was prohibited—where one did not find the poor in attendance.[10] Many collectors had hands bulging with bills of all colors, denominations, and nationalities.

Just beyond the poor people, the crowd began again to divide itself. The Sephardic Jews, many of them dressed in white, moved to the right and the haredim, most of whom were Ashkenazic Jews dressed in black, turned to the left. I was swept along with the black coats. Once inside the courtyard outside the tomb, our crowd once again split asunder, women going to the right, on the other side of a divider that had been set up to separate the sexes, and men to the left. Yet while the haredi men and women remained separated, the crush of people and the carnivallike atmosphere made contact between the two sides easy. Besides, at the rear of the women, there were the mixed crowds of the Sephardim.

On the haredi men's side were lines of people waiting to ritually

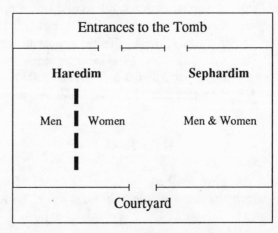

lave their hands. There is no place that a haredi comes to that he considers to have some ritual importance that he does not pour water over his hands, a kind of shortened form of dipping in the mikveh. While these ablutions are clearly an effort to recall the ancient practice of ritual purifications and bodily immersions that were once a part of the religious way of life in the holy land, a way of marking the transition from profane to sacred activity, they also served as activity markers. As people rubbed their palms together to dry them, I could feel their anticipation and almost imagine them saying, "I'm washed and ready for what's next."

Several entrances opened into the actual ohel. There, under a domed roof, was a catafalque surrounded by a fence. As was the case outside, the two groups had each staked out their own sides.

Along the outer rim of the ohel there were rooms reached by several staircases. Normally places for storing everything from prayer books to velvet coverlets for the tomb and chairs for worshipers, many of these rooms today were being used by pilgrims for rest, private prayer services, and haircuts.

Their hands washed, the haredim now turned to one of two activities. Some tried to push their way through as close to the tomb as possible. There they would pray, recite psalms, and worship. Many of them tried to lay a hand on the catafalque while they whispered the words of their litany. Others, however, were caught up with the special activity of the day: shearing the hair of their young ones. It was around this ritual that little family bands gathered and on which most of the attention seemed to be concentrated.

Haircut, or Chalaka

Although the bedlam here at first seemed even greater than down below, even amid the pushing and crowding, I could see there was an order to the proceedings. After washing their hands, many of the fathers gathered up their young sons, all dressed in their best, and moved toward a perpetual circle of dancers. In celebration of this milestone in their lives, all the families were reveling in the occasion. Holding their long-haired moppets aloft, fathers might bring the boy to the gate separating the men from the women. Here they might give a variety of friends and honored guests the privilege of taking a snip from the bewildered young boy's hair while his mother and sisters and even a grandmother or two watched. Following the snip, they would drink a l'chaim toast, which would be offered all around. The women held the provisions. Anyone nearby might be offered a chance to sip the brandy or other liquor. On this side of the divide, everyone was family for now. The women nearest the fence (and there was as much pushing on their side as on the men's) often pulled out plates filled with sweets and cakes, which they handed over the divider to those in their party.

Then the father, holding a hank of hair in one hand, would lift up the child—sometimes placing the father's or grandfather's shtreimel upon his head (a number of the three-year-olds were attired in tiny caftans too)—and enter the circle of dancers who whirled and whirled to a tune whose refrain celebrated "Bar Yochai."

Seeing me with camera in hand, a number of haredi men, often at the prompting of the women, asked if I was a "photographer," and then requested me to take a picture of the shearing. These same people whom, had I wanted to photograph them on the street might have objected, were now clamoring for me to take all the pictures I could. Those who thought that haredim objected to being photographed because they ascribed to the belief that one must not make "a graven image" were clearly mistaken. At their weddings, there were often no fewer video and still cameras than at such affairs in other communities. Shops throughout their neighborhood sold film and advertised their portraiture with photos of haredi families. The objection to being captured in a picture on the street was simply another part of the cultural battle with the secular world. "You cannot come into our places and capture us on your film as some sort of curiosity," they seemed to be saying. "We are not here for you. We will not be your ornaments."

But when they wanted the pictures, when they were calling the shots, you could shoot all the pictures in the world. "Don't forget to take off the lens cap," one man warned me. I took a number of photos and was given a number of addresses and phone numbers for providing the photos when developed.

While the men and boys danced in the circle, the haredi women who stood nearby gazed unblinkingly at them as if to conspicuously reflect the joy that their menfolk and children exuded in their dancing. If the men's goal was to get into the circle, the women's was to see their husbands and sons as clearly as possible. Occasionally, a woman would call something over to one of her men.

I pushed up the stairs with a slowly oozing crowd of fathers and sons who moved away from the plaza and circle of dancers and went to the roof for the chalaka. For a while I balanced on the steps to get a better perspective on the proceedings below, but I was pushed onward by the crowd and the ushers who had been sent by the Ministry of Religion to keep order here.

Along the roof surrounding the courtyard there were lines of people standing on two sides of a huge torch of burning coals in a barrel, meant to look like a giant memorial flame. As was the case below, the sexes were separated. But here the females were all young girls; women did not climb up on roofs. My guide told me that his sixteen-year-old daughter had come up ahead with her girlfriends to recite psalms at the tomb and then talk and watch. She might have been one of these girls. For them this was one of those rare occasions in the year when they had a chance to get out of their neighborhoods and see some excitement. While they might only be watching, at least they could climb up dangerously high. Jammed against the fence that encircled the roof, they gazed down for hours. At a rebbe's tish or other synagogue affair, the view was never as good; at those events they were usually squeezed into partitioned, upstairs galleries or forced to peek in through windows. Only weddings, when they got to dance (of course, only with other girls), were as exciting.

In a little arched chamber along the roof, a minyan for the afternoon prayers was forming. Someone grabbed my elbow and drew me inside. It was my guide. There was barely space to move in what seemed more storeroom than a place to pray. Against the wall and squeezed under an arch was an old man half asleep on a cot. Inside the room haredim of all stripes mixed easily. We managed a fairly quick and cursory prayer. For all of the religious fervor one might have imagined associated with pilgrimage, these prayers were rather perfunctory. Clearly, pilgrimage and piety, even among these men who sought to distinguish themselves from the less "religious" on the other side of the divide, were not the same. Ritual was at once routine and supercharged here. The everyday ritual, like the recitation of the afternoon Mincha prayers, was routine; while the singular events like celebrating the chalaka were supercharged.

The prayers over, everyone except the man on the cot slipped out of the room. Just beyond the door three hasidim, their hands on electric clippers, razed the heads of the little boys. It all went very quickly. Some of the boys, a shocked expression on their faces, stood silently as their long locks were shorn. Others screamed in fear and cried bitter tears. As the locks tumbled from their heads, their fathers gathered them up and stuffed them into little sacks. At first, I was told the bags were taken home, weighed, and an equivalent amount given by the parents to charity. This was a nice idea, another hasid told me, but he thought that in most cases the locks were saved for sentimental purposes.

There was nothing especially elaborate about the shearing. The barber simply zipped across the entire head, leaving only the locks around the ears untouched. But if I thought I was seeing boys getting a haircut (and the image of the Jews having their hair razed in the concentration camps kept bursting into my thoughts), the fathers and other participating adults saw matters differently. They were not focusing on the locks that were disappearing; their thoughts were rather on what was emerging. As one father said to his little boy, "In a few minutes you'll be a nice little Jew; you'll have new *peyos*," referring to the earlocks that would soon stand out vividly against the child's razed head. What I saw as the losing of locks, a razing that reminded me of the Nazi degradation of Jewish identity, these people perceived in an altogether different way. For them the whole event meant the *gaining* of earlocks, the enhancement of their image as Jews. As a hasid said to me on the bus later, until now the peyos they had were not visible; now at least they could be seen, visible markers of their haredi Judaism.

When the cutting was all over, congratulations were exchanged, and some fathers took out a bottle of liquor, cake, and glasses, and offered drinks all around. "Make a blessing," they would say. As for the boys, most of those who were not crying rubbed their hands back and forth along the fuzz atop their heads, trying to take in this new image of themselves. Only when they got home would they have a chance to really see what they looked like. And when they did, they would discern that they would never again be looked upon in quite the same way as they had once been. It was the end of that period of childhood in which they ran wild—as wild as their hair had grown. Now they would begin to be haredim, restrained by their appearance and soon by their education as well.

Among the Sephardim

I elbowed my way back down from the roof to get into the room where the catafalque was. At first, I tried to push my way in on the haredi side, but the crowd was simply too thick. Once at the grave, the haredim did not want to move away, at least not for someone who looked like me. I decided, therefore, to go outside the courtyard and reenter through the Sephardic side. This brought me behind the haredi women. Here I could see how they separated themselves from the Sephardim. They did it by creating an invisible but undeniable line of inattention, never looking at what went on behind them but facing only toward the haredi men.

Against walls and under the cupola over the grave on the Sephardic side, I found aged men and women collapsed on thin mattresses spread

along the floor. Most of these people looked tired, even afflicted. Many
had been there for days. Looking at them, I got the feeling of being at
Lourdes or some other such holy place where people went for miracle
cures. The notion that many of these people viewed this visit as a
remedy for their afflictions was reinforced by the ubiquitousness of
amulets, holy candles, and other such talismans placed around the
grave near each worshiper (and for sale at a stand near the tomb in
case anyone came unprepared).

Even the usual prayers, which were whispered or sung on the haredi side, sounded more like recited incantations here. It was not that
the words were different but only that in this context they took on a
different character. Among the Sephardim, the religious and the popular, ethnic and spiritual seemed laminated onto one another. Only a
few meters away from the haredim, I had entered an altogether different kind of place. If I needed evidence that people and their activities
define and determine the character of a place, this was it.

Community Tensions

While the scene seemed to reflect a kind of tacit pluralism, a willingness of each group to allow the other to revere the rabbi and celebrate the occasion in its own way, there were hints of tensions between
the two. Pluralism did not mean tolerance. The haredim, after all,
made it abundantly clear that they wanted as much as possible to avoid
contact with the Sephardim, whose expressions of piety they considered unseemly at best if not altogether idolatrous and licentious.

Not only were there comments about the *frankim,* as they were
called, a reference to the Sephardic followers of the false Messiah Jacob
Frank; there were also posters and leaflets that articulated the issues
and tensions. One issue over which tension was evident resulted from
the different conceptions that each community had about how one
properly demonstrated piety. There was haredi discomfiture about the
mixing of the sexes and "superstition" on the other side of the divide
at the tomb. There was also concern that piety was unrestrained and
running amok. Nearby in Safed some women were disrobing and immersing themselves in the mikveh of the Ari, where men might happen
along as well—an unacceptable situation. Distributed everywhere was
a flyer that warned them to desist. On it was a picture of Yitzhak
Kadourie, the revered Kabbalist, and Rabbi Abraham Leifer of Pittsburgh and Ashdod, along with letters from them and signatures of at
least twenty-one other prominent holy men. "Said the sages," Rabbi

Leifer's reprinted letter began, "wherever there is a barrier around licentiousness, there will you find holiness. Therefore I turn to the holy nation to defend holiness and purity which is the essence of our heritage. . . ." But in bold letters and at the top of the page beneath a picture of the venerable sage and mystic was the heart of the message:

A SERIOUS WARNING

To women who believe that immersion in the mikveh of the Ari, may his memory be a blessing, will cure them of ills, and provide other remedies: THIS IS FALSE. On the contrary, there is a serious prohibition to immerse there; it is an act of great licentiousness. In particular the mikveh of the great and holy Ari must not be defiled by women.

And those women who hearken unto us will truly be blessed from heaven and healed and saved.

Amen, and so may it be G-d's will.

Excerpts from the letters of other rabbis endorsing the call were reprinted on the back. "We have in our hands, many more letters from rabbis which prohibit this practice," the authors of the flyer added and concluded with an expression that has become a motto of the Sephardic Shas Torah Guardians political party: "And with the Help of Heaven we shall see the return of the crown to its former glory."

There was no mistaking the targets of this letter, who the women were. This was a warning from the haredim to their misguided (at best) and sacrilegious (at worst) Sephardic compatriots. And if they had found holy men who approved this practice, then they should know—and these words on the flyer were underscored: THERE IS NO "RABBI" IN THE WORLD WHO HAS THE POWER TO INSTRUCT A WOMAN TO TRANSGRESS THAT WHICH OUR SAGES IN THE CODES HAVE INSTRUCTED US.

Going Home

A little after 7 P.M. we started back toward the buses. Being hungry, I stopped for a snack at a stand. It was a place for fast food—not unlike dozens I had been to before in my life. But when the girl behind the counter handed me my sandwich, she also and automatically brought me a cup of water for me to ritually lave my hands in accordance with the strict dictates of Jewish codes that say bread may not be eaten without preliminary washing. This was not a service I had ever received at a roadside kiosk. Here, in this setting, even the outdoor stands were, however, ruled by a different taken-for-granted order. The haredim had succeeded in recreating the world in their own image.

It was time to catch the bus. Heading for the Silver Tiger, my guide and I sat down in two of the only seats left. Behind us was a man with whom I began to talk. He was dressed in the same black frock coat as most of the others. After we had chatted for a while, I asked him what sort of hasid he was. He said he was not actually a hasid.

"Are you a misnagid?" I asked. No, he said, he was a Jerusalemite, someone who found a way to hover between the two. And then with a smile he added: "You know the difference between a hasid and a misnagid?" It was one of those riddles to which there are as many answers as imagination allows.

"What?"

"The difference is only one rebbe." He laughed. "You see," he said, "to a hasid all the other rebbes are worthless except his own. And to the misnagid all the other rebbes are also worthless, but so too is that one rebbe that the hasid reveres."

As we pulled out of the parking lot and began our descent toward the valley, the sun dropped quickly and soon we were all sitting quietly in the darkened bus. Then, softly at first but with gradually increasing volume, the first three rows of passengers, a group of Klausenburger hasidim, began to sing. In time, they began to clap, and soon many of us on the bus joined either in the singing or the clapping or both. For more than nine hours I had been among these people. Now in the dark, where the difference of my appearance no longer stood out, and amid the singing and clapping, I felt the barriers that always separated me from them somehow melt away—at least for the moment. There was something about the day and the time and the place that enclosed me in their circle. There were still another two and a half hours or more to go before we would be back in Jerusalem.

The Movable Community

As I sat in the bus surrounded by these people, I reflected on the events and meaning of the day. For the haredim with whom I shared the time, this day "away" from their homes, out of the geographic limitations of their ghetto, was not really an escape at all. In a sense, the "religious" and "cultural" festival in Meron only *seemed* to provide an opportunity to leave the boundaries of their world. In fact, they had not left it all; it was there with them in the bus. It surrounded them at the tomb (and what was not theirs they found ways to avoid or keep at a distance). They had transformed Meron by their coming. They had even redefined what a fast-food stand was like. Precisely by moving *en masse* to these places, they had still been able to remain within the protective framework of haredi society. They had made their world portable by embedding it in community and practice and not in place. This was what made the mass pilgrimage such an ideal outing for the insular haredim.

Such movements of the community were not limited to pilgrimages. Haredi vacations, such as they were, were often quite similar. A haredi left B'nai B'rak for Jerusalem or vice versa; or both went to Safed to sit among other haredim and continue the same activities they normally did at home. Or entire groups went to the Dead Sea, to their own separate beaches (where men and women remained segregated), took the cure, and returned home. And even those who went abroad commonly went only to places where there were large concentrations of other haredim. Thus, when I traveled to Arosa, a village in the Swiss Alps, to see the hasidim on vacation with their rebbe, I found a part of the town black with them: they had their own hotel where they sat and studied texts in between the meals and the thrice-daily prayer services. The hotel inside looked no different than their places back home. The setting might be Swiss, but the content was all haredi and Jewish. Even in the United States there are whole villages in the Catskill Mountains of upstate New York or the White Mountains of New Hampshire that are little more than transient twins of ultra-Orthodox communities in Brooklyn. Place may shift, but community's framework remains intact.

Extremes Meet

In his introduction to a volume of essays that articulate various elements of the ethnographer's craft, James Clifford reminds his readers that "the ethnographer's personal experiences, especially those of participation and empathy, are recognized as central to the research process." [11] As we bumped along in the bus and people began to sing religious songs and clap, I listened to them distractedly, measuring the dimensions of the day in terms of my experience. For the ethnographer dimensions of the day in terms of my experience. For the ethnographer personal experience and empathy are in themselves insufficient if they do not lead to insight. Or in any case, if they do not, they are not relevant to his account.

About halfway into our return trip, near Hadera, our bus made a stop. Again people needed a toilet, a stretch, a drink. The driver pulled into one of the large gas stations along the road. At its side was a small kiosk with a few dirty tables. It was the sort of place that served the lowest common denominator, a place no one—certainly not the people on my bus—would choose to go to but which, caught on the road at night and needing a stop, they could not afford to pass by. Descending from the bus, I realized that for me this stop was my first encounter with the "outside world" during the last ten hours.

We all got off: the men in black hats, coats, and beards, the little boys with their new earlocks, the women in kerchiefs and long dresses. And then, seeing us from a distance, the kiosk attendant started to call out, half laughing and half trying to draw us to his stand, "Hey, hey, Agudat Israel, kosher, Badatz [the name of the haredi organization that certifies food as kosher]." The others around him echoed his call, clapping and laughing. It was as if we were creatures from another planet who could only be enticed by hearing these "magic" words that would attract us. How different this reaction was from the one at the last kiosk where water had been brought to lave our hands.

Getting off that bus in the dark, surrounded by the haredim, I still felt as if I was one of them. In the darkness, my difference did not stand out. The songs, the sense of intimacy and closeness that came from the long trip and common experiences, still reverberated in my consciousness. And suddenly from out of that sensibility I perceived how far away from this world I was in now that kiosk with its mocking salesman stood. The snack I might have grabbed at any other time now suddenly seemed a betrayal. Like the others on the bus, I stayed far away. For that one moment, there in a gas station in Hadera, perhaps more than I had all day, I could feel what it must be like to be a haredi, passing through or even alongside the outside world. I felt the malice, the experience of being an object of derision, as if I were on the haredi side in the culture war. The kiosk man was the goy, and I saw him that way. That he was legally a Jew did not matter. "Goy" was an ontological reality, not a legal category now. He was inhuman, mocking, and far away from the community of erlicher Yidn among whom I found myself. Indeed, that he was a Jew made the anger and pain even worse: how could he treat us with such contempt? I had, at last, if only in my mind, gotten inside the haredi community.

Third Meal

If any group could withstand the cultural siege around them, keep the outside world at bay, and remain pure in the zeal of its haredi ways, it would have to be the Reb Arelach hasidim. These Jerusalemites whose yeshiva was at the far end of Mea Shearim Street were reputed to be the most extreme in their opposition to Zionism and their contempt for contemporary Israel. An offshoot of Hungarian Hasidism, the Reb Arelach were a group who helped fill the ranks of the Eda Haredis and Neturei Karta. They were always finding fault with Agudat Israel and what they viewed as its half-hearted and therefore impotent antagonism to the world outside. They never voted in Israeli elections and remained unwilling to make even the most minor compromises with secular culture. Their women, with their severe-looking black kerchiefs tightly bound over shaven heads and black stockings covering their legs, and their bearded men, with black-and-gold-striped caftans and long, wild earlocks, were the face of zealotry. I might visit Belz hasidim or talk to Lithuanian heads of yeshivas, but until I had penetrated Reb Arelach society, I supposed, I would never get to the extremes of the haredi world. The sense of belonging that my Lag b'Omer trip engendered within me nurtured the belief that I might gain entrance to their world.

Having discovered that getting inside Belz was easier than I might have anticipated, I used much the same approach with the Reb Arelach. Like many haredim, Reb Arelach choose to look upon individual Jews who come to them as seekers who can be brought closer to what they believe to be the authentic Jewish way. As always, the seeker has to be willing to present himself as nonjudgmental, curious, and willing to learn if he is to be allowed entry. I began visiting on Friday nights, observing the rebbe's tish, and then I came to other synagogue services, spent time in the neighborhood, and talked to whoever would approach me. In time, I established relations with a number of these hasidim. They would take me into their cultural domains and show me their ways of life. It would take a long time before I could put my observations of who and what they were into a meaningful context. That happened, perhaps for the first time, on a Sabbath afternoon at twilight. It was then I encountered something of the meaning and essence of Reb Arelach community life. The occasion was *shalosh seudos*.

Shalosh seudos is the third of the ritual meals that help organize the twenty-five hours of the traditional Sabbath from Friday sunset to Saturday nightfall. More than that, it turned out to be one of those special moments in a group's life that provide a window of cultural understanding and the opportunity to interpret some of its essential qualities. Put simply, it is an exquisite example of what has been called the process of cultural performance, an opportunity for a group to exhibit—to itself and others—what and who they are.[1]

How can I claim to find so much in a single event? Should I not rather present a multiplicity of images or a variety of encounters and practices that by their sheer numbers reveal the Reb Arelach? In a sense, I do, for the shalosh seudos is not just a one-time happening, but a repeated and regular ritual during which these people, each week and almost always in precisely the same way, express who and what they are. In some ways it seemed to be "the concentrated expression of the whole collective life."[2]

At the start, I did not pay special attention to the shalosh seudos because I realized how important and revealing it was. That came from later reflections. At first, I was simply struck by the inherent drama of the occasion and sensed that something significant was happening here. Culture sometimes emerges most vividly in small details and single instants. "Exploration," as Lévi-Strauss once put it, "is not so much a covering of surface distance as a study in depth: a fleeting episode, a fragment of landscape or a remark overheard may provide the only means of understanding and interpreting areas which would otherwise remain barren of meaning."[3] The trick, of course, is to be ready at the right place and time and properly tuned in to what is happening.

Sabbath and Shalosh Seudos

To begin to make sense of the Reb Arelach version of shalosh seudos, it is necessary to understand something about the nature and meaning of Sabbath in general and the ritual of shalosh seudos in particular. For Jews, especially the traditionally observant among them, the Sabbath is not simply the day of rest. The midrash calls it an opportunity to have a taste of the world to come, a chance to enter another time realm, to transcend the regular linear scheme of existence, where days pass one by one into the past, never to be retrieved. While without the existence of a Sabbath, days would move inexorably into the eternal yesterday, Sabbath turns all the other days into units of a seven-day week that cyclically repeats itself.

Second, unlike the weekday, which is dominated by the profane—although it is enhanced by the observant Jew with events of a sacred character—the Sabbath is a time in which the sacred is the dominant element, even though there are elements of profane existence that take place within it. The significance of the difference is that on the Sabbath, expressions of the profane—such as they are—seem intrusive and are accordingly stripped, sometimes tacitly and sometimes explicitly, of legitimacy. What might be appropriate conduct during the week, indeed harmlessly profane, becomes a Sabbath at best tolerated and at worst a transgression.

Third, this day that stops and transforms time and redefines behavior has its own temporal rhythm: there is its dramatic moment of onset, Kaboles Shabbos, linked with the setting of the sun; its development, filled with the Sabbath's many ritual and social activities; its denouement in the late afternoon at shalosh seudos; and its coda at nightfall around Havdalah, the ceremony of separation, after which comes the M'laveh d'Malka, the celebration when the Sabbath "Queen," the spirit of the day, is bid adieu. While various groups of Jews fill the Sabbath in different ways, the basic pattern of the day remains the same, and its stages are easily recognized among those who maintain its ritual elements.

For the Reb Arelach, Sabbath preparations are completed in the waning moments of the week; and then, as the sun sets, candles are kindled and the sanctity of Sabbath descends. For the men this commonly means a dip in the mikveh, an act which marks the beginning of their final preparations for the holy day. When the hasid emerges from the waters just before sunset as if born anew, cleansed of his profane being, he transforms his external appearance. Donning his special golden coat, wrapping himself in the white and blue waistband reserved for the sacred days and, if over thirteen, putting his fur and velvet shtreimel on his head, he makes his way to the synagogue for Kaboles Shabbos in the Toldos Aharon Yeshiva.* Following the prayers he goes home for the first of the three ritual feasts. The faithful recite prayers that are acts of sanctification by which the profane is marked off both in space and time. As with the Belzer hasidim, the meal commences at home and ends in the yeshiva around the rebbe's table.

For many of the hasidim, the Friday night tish is the highest of the Sabbath's several dramatic peaks. That such a climax should come so early can be explained perhaps by the fact that Friday evening is the time when the charm of the new Sabbath must be most compelling if it is to be potent enough to make one forget the weekday and undo the effect of the profane world that for six days dominated consciousness. Friday can turn into Sabbath only with the greatest and most sensational efforts. Indeed, in almost every incarnation of Judaism, although perhaps none more so than the haredim, the onset of a holy day is a time of deep contrasts and active and dramatic sanctifications.

Saturday morning and early afternoon, when Sabbath is in its full flow, is for Reb Arelach hasidim—as indeed for many other traditionally observant Jews, those who in the common parlance are called *shomer Shabbos*, Sabbath observant—a time filled with the routines of sacred time. These include the review of sacred texts (particularly the biblical portions allotted by tradition to the Sabbath in question), extended and additional prayers, and a second ritual meal accompanied by much liturgical singing. The Sabbath day is also a time of coming back to spiritual sources—cultural, religious, and familial. This is a time to sit with the family around the Sabbath table, a time for some parents to teach Jewish texts, songs, values, and other essentials to their children. The afternoon is when the community comes together, a time to visit with friends. And it is also a chance for still others to fall into deep rest or at least to catnap. The rhythm of life is slowed perceptibly, or at the very least, time seems to move at a different pace from the rest of the week. Although nominally a day of

---

* The Reb Arelach hasidim allow unmarried males over the age of majority, thirteen, to wear a shtreimel; other hasidim limit this to the married males among them.

rest, it is more precisely a break from the labors of the temporal and ephemeral and an opportunity to be caught up in the service of the spiritual and eternal. Of course, if this goes on too long—as for example when holy days run consecutively with Sabbath and contrasts between the days disappear, or on the very long days of summer, when the Sabbath seems to be unending—the different pace threatens to become tiresome and Sabbath rhythms can become rather tedious.

Finally, in the twilight of the day, after the recitation of the afternoon prayers—in the midst of which a reading of the next week's portion of the Torah hints that while this day is ebbing there is yet another Sabbath to come, a promise of eternal return—comes the last meal. Although commonly short on food but rich in symbolism, shalosh seudos marks the beginning of the end. As Friday night activities explicitly mark the transition from the fast and profane week to the slower and sacred Sabbath, so late-afternoon activities on Saturday retard the onset of that profane week and draw out the Sabbath.

In the Kabbalah, the mystical tradition that informs much of hasidic life, Sabbath is not only a taste of the world to come; it is in fact a time of coupling: for earth and heaven, the human and the divine, and for husband and wife. It is a time of *devekut*, the cleaving of the human with the divine. And as such, it is—as one hasid explained to me—"a time of *ravin*," a time of divine favor auspicious for communion. But if the Sabbath is a time of increasing attachment to God, its conclusion, the moments of the shalosh seudos, is *rava d'ravin*, the most favorable hour for this communion. When the power of the holy day would seem to be waning, the mystics say that, on the contrary, it is most intense. Just when one might be tempted to move back into the profane atmosphere of the weekday, then according to the mystical tradition does Sabbath become most appealing, for it staves off this inevitable deterioration and spiritual decline. For those who manage to stay within the eternal holiness of the Sabbath, the haredim who hold off the week from coming too soon, there is the greatest reward. According to the Kabbalah, there is at least one more reason to delay the end of Sabbath. As long as their descendants remain within the Sabbath and its observances, the souls of the departed, whatever their sins in life and their consequent divine punishments, are given respite from the fires of hell. Or, put differently, the observance of the Sabbath is the way humans conquer the ultimate horrors of death, for through it they can provide the departed (and themselves) with a sort of eternal life, a taste of Eden.

Thus, the beginning and end of Sabbath are occasions when the temporal and eternal are engaged in a struggle for control. And at both these times the hasidim get together with their community and their rebbe. The gathering is meant to help the individual rise above himself.

As a young boy sitting in the gathering darkness of my parents' living room, listening to my mother repeat melodies that her father, an Ostroviecer hasid, had sung around his Sabbath table in Poland, I had been first exposed to this. And yet, in a constant counterpoint to this relaxed Sabbath atmosphere, even when its charms were most vivid, there was for me the electric lure of the profane week. Even though I knew that the close of the Sabbath constituted moments of special importance and sanctity, a time during which the grandparents I never met were "getting their heavenly rest," by the last moments of later afternoon I could not help but start thinking about Saturday night and all its promise of profane pleasures. In my world the erosions of the weekday almost always conquered the enhancements of the Sabbath during its waning moments. Were the Reb Arelach immune to these feelings? Could they hold on to Sabbath longer and more easily? I knew they were famous for ending their Sabbath long after most of the other haredim ended theirs. And that too was a reason I went to shalosh seudos.

The Reb Arelach

The Toldos Aharon Yeshiva, where the shalosh seudos takes place, is both the spiritual and the communal center for the community. It is a stronghold of tradition. While Reb Arelach hasidim, like other Orthodox Jews, believe formally that the *axis mundi*, the center of the world, is on the Temple Mount, just beyond the Western Wall, where the Beis Ha-Mikdash, the Holy Temple, once stood, their own building in the western part of the city is their Mikdash Me'at, Little Temple. They have emblazoned on the stitching of the ark cover that hangs on the all-important eastern wall of their sanctuary representations of the holy vessels that were contained in the Temple. Above them in large Hebrew letters are the words with which God was to have commanded the building of the Tabernacle: "And you shall make Me a holy place and I will dwell in it." As the Belzers see their yeshiva as a kind of incarnation of the Temple, so too do the Reb Arelach see in their center such a holy place. Of course, like all defenders of the faith, they await the miraculous rebuilding of God's Holy House. In the meantime, however, it is through here that their devotions pass— of course, as for all hasidim, via the person of the rebbe—and ascend to God as they once did from the Holy Temple. Indeed, formally, the Reb Arelach have stopped going to the Western Wall and site of the Holy Temple. The rebbe said they should wait here, in their yeshiva, for the Messiah to bring them to the site of the Temple.

The Reb Arelach take their name from Rabbi Aharon (Reb Arele) Roth, a man who in the years before the Second World War began to gather disciples around him in Satu Mare,* a city in Hungary and led them to a particular blend of Hasidism that he had developed out of his exposure to a variety of hasidic masters. Each year in early winter the members of the group reaffirm their willingness to remain as a *chevraya*, or sect, committed to their own doctrines and practices, and to the leadership of their *admor*, the Hebrew acronym used to denote "master, teacher, and rabbi." Roth, the first admor of this group, which was relatively late in developing within Hasidism, stressed the importance of piety and prayer, emphasizing feeling even more than scholarship, and the need to separate from the surrounding and threatening world of temptations and impurities. This motif became even more pronounced after the Reb Arelach established themselves in Jerusalem under the leadership of Avraham Yitzhak Kahan, Reb Arele's son-in-law, the current rebbe and today a man in his eighties.

One of the Reb Arelach, whom I will call Shalom Nisan, explained to me: "Reb Arelach don't need to think; they just need to experience, and they experience very deeply, very organically. Things are and that's it. Don't ask why and how or how would it be if it were different. There's a basic lack of a need to think things over." For the Reb Arelach, Shalom Nisan explained, doubt is anathema and that is what thinking may bring. "*Safek* is 'Amalek' in gematria," he explained, noting that the letters that spell out the word "doubt" [safek] are kabbalistically equal to the name Amalek, the Jewish incarnation of evil, the nation's greatest enemy. Reb Arelach are supposed to live without doubts, taking for granted the established truths in their world; they are expected to have no interest in reexamining these.

To ask a question about the established is to ask a *maskilisheh kasheh*, a question that comes from another universe of discourse. Those who ask such questions are maskilim. While in modern Hebrew "maskilim" is commonly interpreted as "the enlightened," in Reb

---

* This village, sometimes called Satmar by Jews, was also a center of Satmar Hasidism, from among whom the Reb Arelach emerged. That "Satu Mare,"—a place associated with intense expressions of hasidic Judaism—is Hungarian for "Saint Mary," is of course one of the smaller ironies of contemporary Jewish history.

Arelach terms the meaning of the word is inverted. The maskil is not enlightened but rather confused, beyond the meaningful universe of discourse; he is the menacing and uncomprehending outsider. Maskilim ask superfluous questions at best and ones that undermine faith at worst. Those who know the truth need not ask; they simply need to declare the already known. As a result, for the Reb Arelach, Jewish erudition, which for much of the traditionally Orthodox world is paramount, is relatively downplayed. It is enough to repeat the words of the Torah.

Indeed, Reb Arelach spend much of their time not in intellectually plumbing the depths of talmudic texts—as many of their haredi counterparts do—but in exercises of piety such as prolonged prayer or spiritual meditations. They absorb themselves in extensive displays of devotion, such as inspired singing or bodily expressions of spiritual arousal. Even when engaged in such corporeal matters as eating, they recite special prayers (in addition to the standard benedictions before and after meals) to affirm that they are not consuming the food for bodily pleasure but as part of their service of God. There are also exercises for eating such as taking the food slowly to the mouth, putting it back when you feel that you want it too much, and so on. And even their daily study of talmudic texts—in which the teachers are often not themselves Reb Arelach—becomes more a form of worship than of scholarship.[4]

In addition to their emphasis on the spiritual and mystical is an ideology that comprehends the world beyond their own as at best irrelevant and at worst threatening and evil. Reb Arelach realize, of course, that this outside world forces itself upon them, at times even tempts them mightily. But as Shalom Nisan explained: "We know what that world is; it's goyim and *pritzos* [whores]. The people who come from that world are *fremde* [foreigners]. The world is black and white. We are white." And so all kinds of efforts are made not to engage themselves with the outside world, to prevent its corrupting them. Reb Arelach do not like to move very far beyond the borders of their neighborhood.

The contaminations of the outside are located not only in space but also in time. "Today is the worst period of history," as one Reb Arelach hasid explained. "The world has reached fifty levels of impurity, while in Egypt [once the lowest plane of our Jewish existence, the period of bondage] we reached only forty-nine measures of impurity." To the Reb Arelach these kabbalistic concepts are more than mere metaphor; they are recipe knowledge, guides for life, defenses against deterioration. Taken seriously, they lead to action. Not only do they foster insulation and isolation from the outside, but consequentially they lead also to a vigorous battle against those who would impose that outside world and its values in a missionizing way. And the missionizing of contemporary culture is cunning. Its very existence declaims its claims of superiority. Only a constant attack against this ostensible superiority can successfully unmask it for what it truly is. The attitude toward this outside world is not so much anger as contempt. In effect, to the Reb Arelach—as one hasid put it—the outside world is precisely the opposite of what it imagines itself to be. What it thinks is good is really bad, and what it values is worthless. Where the outsiders see light, the Reb Arelach see darkness; and what outsiders might perceive as the darkness within the world of the Reb Arelach is, as they see it, true light. Or at least, so they say.

All this and more is embedded in shalosh seudos, for it is meant to serve as a ritual and social barrier that staves off spiritual erosion and the outside world. As such, it could be for the Reb Arelach a moment that perfectly articulates much of what consumes them: the need to hold out against a mundane reality that threatens to end the world they inhabit. In a sense, the Reb Arelach—were they to reflect on the metaphor of their situation—could view themselves as Sabbath in the hour of shalosh seudos while the world that surrounds them is the profane, Saturday night. And the longer they hold on to that Sabbath, keeping it from turning into the profane Saturday night, the more successful they are at staving off the erosion of their way of life.

Shalosh Seudos at the Reb Arelach

According to Jewish law, the recitation of the afternoon prayers, Mincha, must occur sometime during the last third of the daylight hours. Precisely *when* during that interval it is to be said, however, has become a matter of some debate. For some the ideal time is the earliest possible moment; others argue that it should be said just as the sun is beginning to set, while still others contend that it should come at the latest possible moment. These determinations are based not only on interpretations of the law but also in many instances—especially among the hasidim—upon kabbalistic principles or esoteric traditions. Within this world, distinctions such as these—which to outsiders might seem like trifles—are often ways that groups have of marking themselves off from one another, and as such they are crucial details. With geographic distinctions no longer as clear as they were in eastern Europe, group customs become more important: the time a group decides is the correct or most auspicious for Mincha (or any other) prayers—and the actual distinctions may be matters of minutes—has these days become one important way it distinctively defines itself.

To know when it is time to pray is critical for the believer. If one is in quest of the most felicitous hour to find favor in God's eyes, to be wrong even by a moment may make all the difference in the world. Prominently displayed on the wall in the Toldos Aharon Yeshiva (as in most such places) is a framed listing of the precise times of prayer, along with a legend that explains the religious sources for these times. Thus, time is reshaped in the group's image.

The Reb Arelach recite Mincha relatively late in the day. Yet, while this is supposed to be a special moment of the spirit, it begins in a way that might be considered indecorous by the uninitiated. The prayers are at first barely audible, recited amid a hubbub during which dozens of small children, loudly at play, are running about the room, while their elders are walking in and out of the sanctuary, carrying on conversations, or beginning preparations for the shalosh seudos that is to follow. Even the chanted reading of the Torah goes on amid apparent pandemonium.

But for the Reb Arelach what appears as pandemonium from the perspective of an outsider who assumes that only one focus of activity should be maintained at a time—particularly if that focus is sacred activity—is simply the way things are supposed to be. As an event, Mincha is a series of subtly shifting and simultaneous involvements all of which may go on at the same time but not all of which are endowed with the same level of significance. Such capacity for simultaneous involvement or polychronicity is an element deeply embedded in Judaism, which mixes community with worship and envelops ritual with communal bonding and expression. The synagogue is after all a house of assembly at the same time it is a house of prayer.[5]

People arrive at Mincha somewhat spent from the activities of the last twenty-three or so hours. This is because for Reb Arelach hasidim the Sabbath is packed with things to do. Beginning with the dash to conclude preparations before sundown, the extensive and intensive Friday prayers, the rather rushed meal at home from which the hasidim hasten to the rebbe's tish, the men and most of the older boys have hardly a moment's respite. Following the tish, known to be one of the longest in Jerusalem and which can often end close to midnight, and during which a number of the older men begin to nod off, the younger married men come home and "perform the mitzvah." In an echo of the mystical union that Sabbath symbolizes, the hasid and his wife engage in a conjugal union whose origins are steeped in kabbalistic ideals but whose practice becomes simply one more of the services that must be performed on Sabbath. At last, exhausted, they fall asleep.

Rising only four or five hours later, the Reb Arelach hasid spends a relatively long morning engaged in prayers, *davenen*.[6] Prolonged beyond the time it would take to simply recite the words, davenen is carried out with displays of devotion and intensity, a large part of which consists of exaggerated swaying and screaming meant at least in part to exhibit the fact that the worshipers are swept up by the litany of supplications and devotions. While Reb Arelach are renowned for their long davenen, their prayers are particularly extended on Sabbaths. This also takes its toll, being both spiritually (for those who are so moved) and socially (for those engaged in active impression management) draining. Following these morning prayers and the long and heavy Sabbath meal, some visit relatives and friends while others collapse into *menuchas Shabbos,* Sabbath rest. Because of all this, one should not be surprised that at shalosh seudos, yawns pass like a wave through the crowd, and throughout the proceedings hasidim can be seen crumpling against one another or dropping their heads on the table around which they sit.

The meal does indeed have a formal beginning. This comes when the rebbe, dressed in a white caftan and standing at his place near the head table, turns away from the hasidim, washes his hands, and then flamboyantly raises and slowly dries them while reciting a blessing. Turning back toward his hasidim, he sits down and cuts the challah slowly, after which he slowly chews a small bite on which he shakes some salt. One of the gabbaim cuts the rest of the loaves and then the rebbe himself distributes the remaining slices. But unlike the case on Friday night where everyone has already broken bread at home and now shares with the rebbe, at shalosh seudos in addition to the rebbe's bread, many of the adults also have their own set of rolls, or *matzah,* over which their private benedictions are made.

And while this act by the rebbe is the formal beginning, in fact, even before Mincha has been formally concluded quite a few of the hasidim have already washed their hands and broken bread. The fact that quite a few hasidim do not wait for the rebbe's blessing and his first bites of bread before beginning their shalosh seudos or that they continue to carry on conversations or engage in private byplays among themselves (and quite a few will continue these other involvements throughout the proceedings) may be logistical—if they waited till later, this part of the proceedings would take much more time as everyone lined up to wash hands. Or it may indicate a waning of an aging rebbe's authority.

During the meal come songs, a few words from the rebbe—commonly on the subject of that week's Torah reading—more songs and finally another laving of hands and grace after the meal, followed by the Ma'ariv prayers that inaugurate the new week. But it is not simply this basic structure that is important here. Rather, what is culturally and socially significant is the way the Reb Arelach hasidim act out and embellish this ritual, how they stamp it with their own concerns and character, how they make it their own.

This they do in a number of ways. The first, perhaps, is the way in which they fix the ritual inside their space, how they use it to transform their place.

Fixing the Space

Within the Toldos Aharon Yeshiva—as in so many other places like it—a large central room commonly serves a multiplicity of purposes. During prayer it becomes a sanctuary. When it is a yeshiva (literally, a place where one sits), the room becomes the *bes medrash*, the study hall where males sit together around tables and over open books. And at other times—usually before or after it serves as study hall and place of prayer—the chamber becomes a place for communal assembly. As the activities in the room change, so too does its appearance. And the Reb Arelach themselves see to it that a match between action and space is accomplished. It is as if the building were really a stage in which the players are responsible for not only the action but also the setting.

In the interval between Mincha prayers and the shalosh seudos, a number of hasidim begin to turn the tables (literally as well as figuratively) on what they were doing. What was a prayer stand laid east to west, a place to lay one's holy book, becomes a shalosh seudos table running north to south. Not all the tables are thus turned; the rebbe's table remains constant, laid east to west, thereby forming a T-shape with all the other nearby tables. Simultaneously, the *bimah*, or podium, at which the Torah was just read and which was then at the heart of the sanctuary, is rolled toward the back corner of the large room. Here what was once the center of attention—at least in principle—becomes a kind of alcove for conversation and an obstacle to be worked around.

Concurrently, breads, slices of orange, plates of herring, and hot tea are brought out and placed on the tables. Bringing the tea becomes an especially elaborate affair. Each hasid appears to have his own glass for tea. The trick seems to be to bring the steaming tea in a glass filled to the brim from somewhere in the back of the room to one's table without spilling it, even as one is jostled as he moves through the milling crowd. Often the task becomes even more challenging, as in the frequent cases where one young man (it is usually young men with steady hands who do this) brings several glasses for himself and others. Even some of the little boys, those older than about ten, whose peers in the contemporary world outside these precincts would be unlikely to be drinkers of hot tea in a glass, can be seen emulating their elders and carefully walking their steaming drink to the table.

In an unspoken but unmistakable way all these moves—from facing one direction (toward the holy ark) to facing another (toward the rebbe's table and one another), from holding prayer books to holding glasses of tea, oranges, or bread—demonstrate physically and symbolically the change away from prayer to assembly. And indeed the preceding hubbub during and around the prayer indicates no less that shalosh seudos is really the major activity of the afternoon. Prayer was only the prologue.

To confirm the observation that these moves are more than functional, one needs only to watch the children. To the young, not yet jaded by years of ritual repetition, the drama of the occasion and transition still retains some of its freshness. Hence, the excitement in their faces and movements is more obvious; it serves to underscore that "something new is happening." With obvious gusto the children rush to push the bimah toward the back or help to revolve the tables. Similarly, they race to grab the sliced oranges or pieces of bread. "Shalosh seudos, shalosh seudos!" some of them call as they get things ready.

The Tish versus Shalosh Seudos

Shalosh seudos is of course not the only Sabbath meal with the rebbe and the others in the community. But it is very different from the Friday night tish. For example, as in Belz, Friday night's entire proceedings radiate from the rebbe's table: from the opening words of his Kiddush, through the distribution of food, to the last echoes of the final prayers and songs. But at shalosh seudos the rebbe is a distant presence. Even the seating is different: on Friday night all the tables are like branches that lead from him, while on Sabbath afternoon the hasidim create their own separate centers of activity, seated around long tables, cafeteria-style. If Friday night the group experiences itself almost exclusively through the medium of the rebbe, on Saturday afternoon the contact is far more diffuse and relaxed. The physical situation on Friday night forces the hasidim to look constantly at the rebbe and at one another, holding them tightly at attention with their fronts very much on display. The situation allows very little in the way of other involvements.[7]

One hasid described the Friday night tish this way: "Everyone is very much aware of what is going on because you are in this circle." Everyone is on stage, forced to perform their devotions and reflect their engagement in the most public way imaginable.

Shalosh seudos lacks this single focused circle where everyone is on display before the entire group. Hasidim who opened books (the codes of Jewish law, hasidic texts, or the Bible) during Mincha—sometimes looking at them, other times gazing over them into space, sometimes carrying on conversations above the page—continue to do so now, while still others cluster around the rebbe. Moreover, because everything takes place around smaller tables, and for a time in very dim light, shalosh seudos allows a lower level of exhibition, restricting the display to those who share the same table.

Something less than prayer and more than simply a meal, squeezed in at the twilight of the day between the sacred and the profane, shalosh seudos is, like the twilight itself, betwixt and between, liminal, a time of transition. In a sense, the shalosh seudos stands somewhere between the family gathering with its intimacy in the home and community assembly around the rebbe's tish. It provides intimacy with one's peers in the presence of the rebbe and all the other hasidim. But the rebbe and the others remain only a part of the resonating background of the aural landscape and only peripherally part of the visual one. As anthropologist Victor Turner has argued—and no better case could be found to support his contention—"in liminality extreme authority of elders over juniors often coexists with scenes indicative of the utmost behavioral freedom."[8] Simply said, whereas the tish is characterized by restraint and fixed displays, shalosh seudos is distinguished by freedom and repose.

Walking About, Shtippen Zoch

At the start of the shalosh seudos there continues to be—as there was during Mincha—a great deal of movement. Many people are still pacing about the room. At first glance, the purpose of the walking about may be hard to decipher. But what *is* clear is the *way* the walking is done. The proper walk always gives the impression that one is purposeful, on his way to get somewhere or something and not just ambling about (strangers amble aimlessly). During Mincha the evident purpose of the walk is to get to one's seat to pray or to the shelf to get a prayer book or tome to study. After the conclusion of the service, the movement is apparently accounted for by the ritual need of the hasidim to lave their hands before taking bread. Later still, it is stimulated by the fact that many go toward the rebbe's table to get his gleanings or to share in his presence and better hear what he has to say. Then it is prompted by the need to get tea and by the desire to change seats or to talk with friends and share news—also an important feature of the proceedings. Indeed, the walking is purposeful—though the purposes are not always what they seem at first.

But it is not enough to look purposeful. One has to touch and push too. The hasidim call it *shtippen zoch*. Unlike, for example, Americans who have been taught to pass through a crowd with a minimum of physical contact—for to an American, body contact is to improperly invade the personal space of another (when it happens, Americans are expected to beg the pardon of the one they have jostled)—a hasid walks through his crowd by touching or even jostling many of those he passes near; and he never acknowledges the contact with a request to be pardoned.[9] Ostensibly, he does this shtippen zoch to make his way past the others, but in effect the laying of hands upon another constitutes a subliminal expression of intimacy. It is almost as if everyone had to rub shoulders with and touch everyone else, *feel* them, as part of the joining in this communal meal and experience.

Looked upon from a distance, the walking about appears to be not only a weaving *through* the crowd but also a weaving *of* it. It is a way the people tie themselves together during the gathering. When one can lay hands upon and lean against others—even strangers (for I was touched no less than others)—without comment and negative reaction (in marked contrast to what is absolutely prohibited between men and women, including one's own wife at times), the significance of this contact cannot be overlooked. It seems to say that here in the group more than anywhere else perhaps we are a single body. This was what I had already experienced at Belz and felt at Meron. But here, perhaps because it was less frenzied, the sight of one man's hand draped over another's back, or one's shoulder propped up against another's, of people collapsing against one another was striking.

To be sure, the Reb Arelach would certainly not explain their walking about and leaning against one another in this way. Their touching had to remain automatic and unconscious lest it become something sensuous and pleasurable and therefore prohibited. Indeed, the community has a very aggressive mechanism for handling those who purposefully seek physical (homosexual) contact with their fellows—Reb Arelach are among the most prominent of the ruffians of the Modesty Patrol who beat and intimidate perceived deviants. A man once caught rubbing himself improperly against young boys was severely beaten up by the powers that be, while another pedophiliac had the windows of his shop broken and found himself publicly shamed. Nevertheless, though the meaning of shtippen zoch may remain subliminal, a means to an end, it is not without meaning.

Eating, Singing, Tradition, Zeal, and Youth

As the walking about begins to wane, the eating ensues. But this is not an eating that grips the attention of the hasidim. In a mirror image of their rebbe, who appears to nibble indifferently on pieces of challah and herring or diffidently takes a small sip of tea, the hasidim eat their few morsels in a distracted fashion. This is for many precisely the right expression to show that for them the actual eating of the food is not the essence of the meal.

The way they eat contrasts sharply a short time later with the attention they give to the singing with which they fill the major part of the proceedings. As the movement of furniture shaped the space and the walking about reshapes the crowd, so the singing fashions the atmosphere and forms the mood. But like everything else about this occasion, the singing does not begin all at once. Rather, a few of the hasidim sitting near the rebbe—the inner circle—start languidly to sing. In fact, those who sit closest to the rebbe are those most caught up with formal proceedings. At first, the songs are soft, rather slow, lachrymose, and not sung in as organized a style or as unified a manner as on Friday night. What is a single large chorale at the tish begins here almost like a rising buzz of conversations. Only gradually does the singing begin to absorb more and more people. As before, the children in their enthusiasm stimulate the transition. When *they* start to sing, their voices fill the room and act like a magnet for the others to raise their voices as well.

Those between the ages of seven and twelve sit on the southern side of the room, the younger children sit in the western wing, and the rest of the hasidim are arrayed between them. On the extreme margins, beyond the buffer of young children, sit those who are most marginal.

The songs are set by Jewish liturgy; the melodies come from the Reb Arelach. Both have been collected and inscribed in the tradition over generations. Change is abhorred. To Jews like the Reb Arelach, just such repetition week after week and generation after generation is the quintessence of what they are all about. In a world where change is endemic, the capacity to remain constant represents the mark of distinction and indeed the superiority of this people. The steadfast refusal to change—in songs, appearance, ritual—is the symbolic response to the strain that contemporary life puts on the tradition. And that response must be repeated at every occasion possible—and certainly at such meaningful events as the Sabbath gatherings in the yeshiva.

Yet for the tradition to live—to act not only as a model *of* a way Jews have defined themselves for generations but also as a model *for* the maintenance of continuity—the songs must not simply be repeated; they must be recited with the enthusiasm of a first-time experience. That of course is the paradox that everyone who strives actively to maintain traditions encounters. What is repeated becomes routine and sometimes even banal. And that precisely is the dilemma of haredim like the Reb Arelach: how can they sing these same songs exactly the same way each week, yet always with feeling? From whence comes fervor—*hislahavus,* the hasidim call it—when they are tired and drained? Can the zeal of a beginning come in the twilight of the day?

As one hasid explained: "If you're looking at it from the outside, maybe you don't grasp it. But basically, for someone who is inside, the feeling that he gets is very much of boredom and of a kind of emptiness. Yes, shalosh seudos is supposed to be rava d'ravin, but that does not mean that every time you get it. And even if you are touched, that might be once in a very long while and then it might not last more than two minutes. And even then it doesn't mean that you're not also bored some of the time."

The expectation outsiders may have that hasidim, who by doctrine insert spirituality into their existence, are always turned on by their spirit loses sight of the limited capacity that human beings have for sustaining spirituality.

To be sure, this problem of making a tradition live for those who are too practiced in it does not only come up in the case of shalosh seudos; it comes up repeatedly and is one of the essential predicaments of Orthodoxy. It is one of the elements of the religious angst that is part of haredi existence.

And how do the Reb Arelach deal with the problem? Here is precisely where the *children* play a crucial role. For them the tradition is new; in them the fires of enthusiasm burn more powerfully. They know (because they have been taught) that the repetition is crucial.

For them the ability to repeat is evidence of their initiation and belonging. It is the stuff of familiarity but not yet of routine. Their singing is filled with fervor—even if it is an immature fervor, unenhanced by a deep understanding of the poetry or the mystical and religious themes embedded in it. And that ardor, enthusiasm, and youthful zeal that emanates from the heart of the room where the youngsters sit seems to be what moves the hearts of the others in song. As the children sing louder, so do their elders. And slowly but surely the room becomes filled with the voices of both as each feeds on the other's feelings. "And a little child shall lead them." (Isaiah 11:6.)

Here in microcosm then is the role that the young play in the world of the Reb Arelach and others like them. They are at one and the same time the recipients of the tradition and its carriers. As long as there are lots of children, then, the future of the tradition is assured. Yet while it is these young whom the elders must surround and protect from the contaminations and corrosion of the outside, it is really the young who maintain the zeal of the tribe for the elders. Their purity and zeal must be preserved. For if the young cannot sing the songs with the pure zeal of the initiate, then the old too will have difficulties sustaining the tradition. So the children go to extremes: they sing louder than the adults, run where the adults walk about, and more dramatically mark the transitions that their elders experience in a more faded fashion. And they are rewarded for all this by becoming the center of concern.

Says the midrash, which the Reb Arelach cite in their guidebook to educating the young: "Sons save their fathers from disgrace, shame, and the mortification of hell." And adds the Great Rabbi Eliezer, whose dictum they repeat in their guide to education: "Take care to have children and raise them in the ways of Torah for on their account will you merit the world to come.[10]

In the larger sense, the education (socialization) of the young has become the raison d'être and central preoccupation of many of the haredim. It is not insignificant, for example, that a number of fathers sit with their sons before and even during shalosh seudos and "farher them," listen as they review their understanding of the week's Bible reading. Education is at the heart of the relationship between generations here. All youngsters are by definition tinokos shel bais rabban, the children of the rabbis' school (just as all their elders are attached to the yeshiva). For the student and the child are both persons who remain unsullied by the real world and insulated from its destructive influences. Only they can be counted on to remain zealots in every sense of the term.

But why do the youngsters lead at shalosh seudos and not at the tish? Because it is precisely now, when the elders have difficulty getting into the swing of things, that they are needed. And only now in the liminal interval of twilight, can the children feel so free and the order be reversed.

The King Forever

As they sang the songs, these people like those at Belz fused themselves into a single voice. At last, they reached the first of several crescendos, when everyone stood to recite the words "God is the King forever and ever." Now the rebbe, who had been sitting quietly on his wooden armchair at the head of the table, spoke. It was a brief *d'var Torah*, a word of instruction.

When the rebbe speaks, his hasidim must be attentive. Reacting to a signal from the gabbaim, many people began to cluster around the rebbe's table. Some climbed onto benches to see him and take in what he said. A few of the younger boys near the back even stood on the tables, at times nearly trampling upon the holy books that remained side by side with the dishes and crumbs.

And what did the rebbe have to say? If my ears were any guide, few of those who stood near me at the back could possibly hear the five minutes of the rebbe's discourse, although they knew from experience what it would be about and what its purpose was. In his dotage, the rebbe has a weakened voice, making his speech indistinct. And what of those who did hear him? I asked one what the rebbe said. "The talks that the rebbe gives at shalosh seudos are very hard to follow; what he says does not always hang together that well." If that is so, what were these elaborate displays of attention?

As rebbe, no matter what he says, he remains the crowning glory of the group. Nothing so much expresses that greatness as his words, be they blessings, guidance, or teaching. If they are incomprehensible, so what? This was a symbolic taking in of what he said. In this context, and indeed in many collective encounters with the rebbe, attentiveness does not always equal comprehension. It connotes instead veneration.

There is perhaps another way of understanding this attentiveness to words not always comprehended. Bronislaw Malinowski once defined a kind of "speech in which ties of union are created by mere exchange of words." In this sort of talking, which he called "phatic communion," Malinowski explains, "the meaning of its words is almost completely irrelevant." [11] What does count is that the very act of this sort of speaking binds people together. Now while Malinowski was describing communications that include "inquiries about health, comments on weather," and any other similar cordial exchange, this definition of phatic communion also provides a way of understanding these sorts of talks by the rebbe. It is not so much what he says but the occasion of his saying it that serves to bind speaker and listeners together. It is a communion without explicit content, but a communion nevertheless. To pay attention, even if one does not quite know what the rebbe is saying, is to show everyone concerned that a bond exists here. And the greater the attention, the stronger the bond. Once, perhaps, the talks aroused deeper emotions—when they were understood and inspiring. Yet still today they can retain the resonances of communion, even if only a phatic communion. The rebbe is, after all, their king forever.

When he finished speaking, those closest to him shouted "Amen," an affirmation that everyone else repeated. And why "Amen"? Because for the hasid the rebbe's words are the medium of holiness, his pronouncements are tantamount to pure religious expression; they are sancta. And blessings are always answered with "Amen."

Lights Out

The shouted amen launched more singing. Then as the last beams of sunset dropped below the horizon, the lights in the large room were extinguished. Suddenly, there was only darkness. For a brief moment the only light in the room radiated from the memorial oil lamps and the eternal flame (symbols of the past and the promise of the future), which twinkled like stars where they hung down from a corner of the ceiling near the front. In the momentary blackout children screamed —perhaps in fear of the darkness, or in glee. And then to remove the darkness, a single, rather weak, fluorescent light went on, casting a white, moonlike pall over everything. In the half-light, gone were the childrens' screams; instead, a stillness spread like the shadows throughout the room. Once again, a transformation had occurred and once again the children were the ones who underscored the metamorphosis—this time by their screamed outburst and ensuing silence.

This was supposed to be the twilight of the Sabbath. But what had once been a natural event—the dying day flickering its diminishing light through the windows or doorways and gradually giving way to the darkness and profanity of the week—was now staged, orchestrated by a preset timing device that switched off and on the lights in a crude imitation of nature. The thick stone walls with tiny windows in them that enclosed these people in the building let in very little light from outside. In their protected environment, the Reb Arelach were responsible for their own light. They manipulated nature.

But if this meant that they were cut off from the natural light, it also meant that the Reb Arelach could "stop" the setting sun, for they could extend their fluorescent twilight as long as they needed it and prolong their Sabbath day into the night—which they did for an hour and twelve minutes longer. This was modern technology in the service of tradition.

The dim light, even if artificial and staged, managed to evoke an atmosphere of intensified intimacy. In the shadows the men and boys, seated again, unselfconsciously leaned on one another, lowered their voices, and sung the slow, soft songs of the hour.

As one hasid explained: "You get to relax in the darkness, and you're not being judged for how hard you sing. You can just let be, *holoch yelech* [what goes keeps on going]."

"It's just natural, very organic," another added.

The Ideological Element: Us versus Them

But was that all there was? Was this simply a collective celebration of the mystical and social bond between man and man, man and God, man and the occasion? Or was there something else being performed in this cultural event? And how would one discover this something more?

One place to look was beyond the frame of the Reb Arelach, to step outside the boundaries of the yeshiva. To put it differently: to understand some of the significance of what was going on inside, it would help to know what was happening outside during all this time, where another reality was the order of the day. This is because, like so many haredim, the Reb Arelach cannot help but define themselves in contrast to their surroundings.

On one level the question of what goes on outside during the shalosh seudos is of course not one with which the Reb Arelach need concern themselves, for they have created their own domain, captured their Sabbath within the four walls of their yeshiva and fashioned it in their image; that is all they know or need to know. Yet on another level they know that something else is going on *out there*. And they need to know and show that they are definitely *not* part of it.

"Out there" of course has many meanings. It is most immediately the neighborhoods that make up Mea Shearim, the streets, alleyways, and courtyards where traditionalism is king. But beyond Mea Shearim it is the world of contemporary Israel where Saturday night and not Sabbath is sovereign, where now overwhelms them. In those further reaches of the outside world, where the immediate conquers the transcendental—especially on Saturday night—the Sabbath, fragile to begin with, was already beginning to give way to the week. In the distance one could hear the sound of buses and feel the rumble of a city rising from the slumber (for its secular citizens, a somewhat enforced slumber) of Sabbath rest and bestirring itself into its Saturday night incarnation.

Closer to home, in Mea Shearim, the Sabbath was much slower in its departure, in part because here there was nothing especially appealing about Saturday night. Yet even here the barriers that haredim set up on Friday afternoons to keep out unwanted cars and warn strangers that this was a domain of tradition were already being removed. One after another, synagogues emptied out and the streets filled as men and boys went home to their wives and mothers and to recite Havdalah. The now dark and empty synagogues were silent, almost melancholy reminders that all that was Sabbath was over. One sensed that soon many of the city buses that for the last twenty-five hours had remained parked by state law would soon be back on the road here, sweeping away the last vestiges of Sabbath stillness.

To keep the Sabbath going—as the Reb Arelach did—when all around Saturday night was trying to get in was thus an ideological and symbolic statement. It was a way of suggesting to the secular city that "we here have a different clock and can determine the domains of the sacred and profane independently of all the rest of you."

And it also sent a message to other haredim. As the hasid who extends his prayer longest demonstrates to the worshipers around him that he has been most caught up in its ecstasies and agonies, that he is most pious, so by stretching out their shalosh seudos and putting off the weekday the Reb Arelach showed their nearby neighbors in Mea Shearim that they were more haredi. "You all may be finished with the Sabbath and delivered into profanity," the Reb Arelach seemed to be saying, "but we, and we above all others—even those who are our neighbors—are still surrounded by the holiness of the Sabbath. And we alone will determine when that is over." So after all the other groups had gone home from their yeshivas and synagogues, the Reb Arelach were still sitting and singing at shalosh seudos, flaunting their distinctiveness. This is ideology as a form of culture.

Why do they need to do this? When a group experiences cultural strain, when it feels that its way of life is threatened, its performance

of that way of life becomes an act endowed with ideological significance.[12] Since the demise of the traditional world, as described earlier,
haredim like the Reb Arelach have felt threatened in this way. That,
after all, is an essential element of being haredi and traditionalist.

But this shalosh seudos is not purely a reenactment of the traditional third meal of the Sabbath. To sit in the still darkness of Sabbath
in a Mea Shearim just a few minutes away from downtown modern
Jerusalem is not the same as doing so in some isolated Jewish hamlet
in Europe. Rather, it is the present made to look like the past. Today's
long shalosh seudos is a stylized reaction to the intrusions of the modern world, an ideological stand against Saturday night. By the time
shalosh seudos and (for those with enough energy to come back for it)
the M'laveh d'Malka are over there is no Saturday night left. It has
been wiped out.

Rebels Among the Reb Arelach

If shalosh seudos implied an ideological stand—like so much else
about the traditionalist, haredi community—what about those who
were *not* caught up in it? Were there such people? Were they rebels? I
came in assuming that among the Reb Arelach everyone felt committed and attached to the same sectarian way of life, to the rebbe and the
community. I imagined everyone was supported "by an actual experience of common feeling." [13] But I was wrong.

At the Reb Arelach, as I discovered, there are some fellows whom
some insiders call "Shababnikes." Although the name probably comes
from the Arabic *shabab* for "troublemaker"—many Arabic terms have
entered contemporary Israeli usage—the haredim, not surprisingly,
assert a Jewish origin for it. They say it comes from an acronym
[s-b-b] for the biblical phrase (Ecclesiastes 11:9) *"Samach bachur
b'yaldutecha,"* meaning "Rejoice, young man, in thy youth." The Shababnikes are the "good-time boys," who, rather than embracing tradition with youthful enthusiasm, exploit their youth for its freedom.
In the haredi context they are rebels.

Among the Reb Arelach, rebellion could take a number of forms.
In some cases it was intellectual: thinking unthinkable thoughts, looking at the world like a maskil, or reading forbidden things. This included those who read and thought about popular novels and the
secular press (a mild kind of deviance) as well as those who looked at
pornography or spent their time reading the books found in universities (these two were much the same kind of sin). In other cases it was

behavioral: trifling with the tradition, abrogating norms, and expressing an explicit or implicit disdain for the ways that the Reb Arelach
have accepted as imperatives. This could, for example, mean being
careless about dressing in the right caftan, not coming to the tish on
time, or even eating with gusto. And then there was perhaps the most
serious rebellion of all: the ideological breach.

And what was the greatest ideological breach? It was very simply
to allow another world to penetrate one's spirit and consciousness. It
was to become one of *them,* the outsiders. Outsiders include being a
different kind of hasid, or worse still, a member of an antihasidic
group, or worst of all—Heaven protect us—part of the world of contemporary Israeli life. Ideological breaches often went with intellectual
and behavioral rebellion. They might take the form of going to and
enjoying another rebbe's tish or, as in one well-known case, of a Reb
Arelach Shababnik going mountain climbing while he should have
been in the yeshiva. In the worst-case scenario, it meant leaving the
Reb Arelach altogether. A few young men did that too.

To be a Shababnik was to be no longer within the magic circle
around the rebbe. But Shababnikes do not always go to the ideological
extreme of alienation. They do not all drop out. Many stay, living on
the margins of the community, flirting with their estrangement. And
where are these people to be found at the shalosh seudos?

In sharp contrast to the young zealots in the center of the room who
are their polar opposites, or the *shayne yunger leit,* nice young people,
who huddle near the rebbe, these boys gather near the door at the far
end of the room, at the greatest distance from the rebbe. There, at the
edge of the circle, while everyone else seems caught up in the proceedings, they sit—heads together—almost oblivious to, or at best margin-
ally involved with, all that passes around them. They chat, joke, or
gaze off into space. A number of them even remain seated and huddled
together while the rebbe speaks, not even making a pretense of turning
their attention toward the front. And as if that disregard were not
enough, they are absorbed in eating nuts, sunflower seeds, or pista-
chios, scattering and piling their shells all about the table in a tangible
expression of their alienation.

And why nuts, of all things? Why not eat the herring, the bread,
the fruit? What is the significance of these nuts that no one else in the
room is eating?

For that one needs to know Israel, the world outside. Eating nuts
and scattering their shells about is the quintessential expression of
contemporary Israeli youth. What gum chewing and snapping is, or at
least was, in certain quarters of American street life, munching and

shucking nuts is for Israel. To sit at the rebbe's shalosh seudos—behind the walls of the Toldos Aharon Yeshiva, where one is presumably isolated from the Israeli street—shelling and munching nuts, is to associate oneself (even if only subtly and tacitly) with that modern Israeli street. It is to share a different consciousness, to turn away—if ever so slightly—from the community.

Now eating nuts like this might be a relatively minor infraction of the norm during the week. There is after all nothing wrong with it except for the fact that the Reb Arelach's shalosh seudos menu does not include it. And in the privacy of one's home, having nuts this way might not even be an offense at all. But doing it here and now and while everyone else is otherwise engaged becomes almost transgressive.

Efforts have been made to rein in the Shababnikes, to get them to turn their attention to the rebbe, but with no success so far. They still sit in the back—golden-coated rebels perched on the edge—an all-too-dangerous model for the younger children.

Lights On

Are the Shababnikes the only ones in touch with the outside? Are the rest of the Reb Arelach really successful in keeping Saturday night at bay? Is the Israeli street so far away? When the lights came back on, I would see.

Now these lights could only come back on when the Sabbath was over. To turn them on any earlier would be to desecrate the holy day and rush it out. The Reb Arelach took a long time before turning them on. But when at last they did come on, what happened?

Anyone expecting a palpable melancholy sigh bemoaning the fact that Sabbath was at last over would have been disappointed. Instead, with the sudden flash of light came a shout of glee from the children and a perceptible lightening of the atmosphere among the adults. I recognized the emotion; it was the one I had when in my parents' house the lights went on for Saturday night. Perhaps I was reading into their behavior my own feelings at Sabbath's end, my readiness for Saturday night and all its promise. Yet there were undeniable nuances in the smiles, in the rush of many to get out, in the sight of a number of the men drawing deeply on cigarettes that they could not smoke during Sabbath and which they now lit up, in the sitting up and signs of awakening in the room that all made me feel that this was another transition and one that not everyone was sad about. So maybe all that extension of the Sabbath was something of a pose. They might be proud to have a longer Sabbath, but they were also glad when it was over.

To be sure, the finale of Sabbath *is* supposed to be a happy time—even in traditional circles. When the prayer of Havdalah is recited, everyone shouts "For the Jews there was light, happiness, and joy"; with this the week formally begins. But in the liturgy and Kabbalah, it is also a time of anxiety over what happens when the Sabbath sanctity dissipates. "Fear not, my servant Jacob [i.e., Israel]," is the verse repeated in the most famous hymn of the M'laveh d'Malka that concludes the day. But where was the anxiety and where the melancholy?

Even before the Havdalah had been recited or the Ma'ariv prayers completed and the Sabbath formally ended, the vestibule outside the sanctuary was filled with dozens of hasidim leaning against the walls and pillars in a gesture of ease, a pose not altogether different from one I would see only a few minutes later downtown among the scores of Israelis who stood on street corners looking for Saturday night action. Cigarette smoke billowed through the room. Were they ready too for Saturday night action?

As Shalom Nisan explained, the Reb Arelach are aware that "the outside world is nice, perhaps even nicer than they give it credit for—though very far from an ideal world." It beckons them, even from the interior of Toldos Aharon. Yet it remains off-limits and to a great extent without content. Even if the Reb Arelach were to embrace Saturday night, where would they go and what would they do with it?

That is the irony. Reb Arelach hasidim look forward to the week, are happy when it comes, but they are not sure why. Sabbath, after all, is their fullest day. "In here," one of them said to me, "when the lights come on, you're happy for the change right now, not for what is going to happen, because you know nothing unexpected is going to happen. But of course you don't think too much about it because if you did you would be in despair over the routine."

A Less than Perfect Isolation

As I walked home from Toldos Aharon and thought about what I had seen, I realized that I had discerned these cultural interferences from Israeli society not only at night but even during the afternoon. Although Hebrew is the national language of Israel, Reb Arelach, like many other haredi Jews in Israel, commonly speak Yiddish among themselves. There are at least two reasons for this. The first, and most often given, is a theological one: Hebrew is considered by the haredim to be a "holy tongue," the language of prayer and study, the idiom in which God addressed His people, and therefore not to be used for *d'varim b'tailim*, temporal and mundane words. The second reason for the Yiddish is more social and political. If Hebrew is the language of the contemporary Israeli street, then Yiddish is distinctively the language of the traditionalist Jewish street. To speak Yiddish, an alternative Jewish language and one tied to the Diaspora, the cultural crucible in which the consciousness of the haredim was formed, is to remain bonded to the society that refuses to be part of the contemporary scene and which maintains that though it is *in* Israel it is not part *of* the place and is still in a state of Diaspora.

That Reb Arelach speak Hebrew when they encounter outsiders is no surprise. They must, after all, live in contemporary Israel where bus drivers, postmen, and officials speak Hebrew. But that they should speak Hebrew among themselves—as I heard them do during the shalosh seudos—suggests that at least in the domain of language the Israeli street has made its way into their consciousness. Yiddish remains the predominant language, the official lingua franca, but Hebrew interferences exist.[14]

The food too reflects cultural interplay. The menu of the meal that remains essentially unchanged from week to week was established by traditions that are themselves the result of the interweaving of various cultural influences. The challah traces its origins to the shewbread fixed by law to be part of the Temple rites, a ritual itself echoing the manna that the Israelites ate in the desert, while the twisted shape of the challah is undoubtedly a variation of breads that were part of European culture. The herring and the glass of tea are clearly of European origin. They are to eating what Yiddish is to speech: they are gustatory reminders of another world. It is as if the Reb Arelach say, "We still eat the herring of the Old World and drink our tea the way they did back then." These foods have for so long been part of the hasidic table (whose origins after all were in eastern Europe) that they are taken by the Reb Arelach as being indigenous.

But there was one more item on the menu, and it was very different. Near the end of the evening, when the children had sung their hearts out, a few of the older hasidim walked around distributing *waffelim*, sugar-coated wafers, to each of them. It was a treat that all of them scrambled to get. But these were the very same wafers that every contemporary Israeli child craved. The carriers of Reb Arelach traditions were being given the Israel prize.

How did those in charge of these matters know what treat would appeal to the children? Surely they knew by knowing what Israeli children like. And they knew that *their children were no different.*

To be sure, were the Reb Arelach to reflect on all this as I have and perceive the symbolic meaning of these foods, they would probably abandon them and choose instead to give their children something far more particular to their own domain. There is no guarantee that at some time in the future they will not discover that these sugar-coated wafers are "not kosher," and forbidden. But maybe they will not need to; after all, little boys who have sugar-coated wafers still become *shayne yunger leit* who eat herring and drink tea in a glass.

Education

Avid carriers of the tradition, children were part of everything I encountered in the haredi world—guarding the entrance to the mikveh; laughing, running, dipping into, and animating the atmosphere inside it; the occasion for celebration at the Belz bar mitzvah; squeezed along the rafters and packing the benches at every rebbe's tish; the voices that sang on Chanukah and the faces that masqueraded on Purim; essential to the Lag b'Omer pilgrimage; the voices and enthusiasm sustaining the Reb Arelach at shalosh seudos. Among the most ubiquitous of local stores were those selling children's supplies: everything from diapers to toys. The myriad bookstores in the haredi neighborhoods carried a liberal supply of children's picture books. Strollers or prams pushed along by women of childbearing age were among the most common of sights; a woman without one looked incomplete, a mere girl. Adults or older brothers and sisters were often trailed by or holding the hands of two or more children, and laundry lines crisscrossing the courtyards were regularly festooned with children's clothes. In the early mornings and afternoons loaded yellow school buses swarmed through the streets, bringing youngsters to and from the schools, while those who came on foot streamed hand-in-hand over the crosswalks where adults guided them through the heavy traffic. During breaks from learning, little boys, their faces framed in earlocks, their heads closely shaved and crowned by large velvet skull-caps poured into attached yards or large perimeter alleys, chasing each other, playing and yelling at the top of their lungs. At separate school-yards, little girls, often with long braids and long-sleeved, high-necked dresses, perched on stoops or played around doorways. And when all the children were in class—which was most of the time—the sound of their voices repeating lessons, praying, singing songs, or reviewing some other sacred text came floating out the windows, permeating the air in and around the places where haredim lived. These voices and the children from whom they came were the humming engine of the haredi world. Although I had been looking at them only obliquely, as a secondary aspect of haredi life, children were clearly at its center.

The haredim, of course, understood this unequivocally. Everywhere there were signs of the importance of children to them. It was not just in the large families of seven, ten, or more—few if any haredim openly practiced any sort of birth control, a reflection of their scrupulousness about fulfilling the religious obligation to "be fruitful and multiply." Nor was it only at the many benchmarks of haredi life that revolved around them. It was literally in the signs written on the walls, in the posters and graffiti that covered the haredi city, the streets in and around Mea Shearim and Geula, the center of B'nai B'rak, and wherever concentrations of these Jews could be found. One phrase painted on almost every block seemed to say it all. Some said the Neturei Karta scribbled it as a rebuttal to the efforts of the Ministry of Education to dictate what must be done in their schools. Others claimed it was posted by zealots among the Reb Arelach who were alarmed about the menacing influences of outsiders upon their children. And still others explained that it was simply a general expression and a necessary reminder of what mattered most to haredim, a cry from the heart, so it did not really matter who actually wrote it because everyone here believed it.

The scrawl on the wall was chilling in its simplicity: DO NOT TOUCH MY MESSIAHS. More than simply a line from Scripture (I Chronicles 17:22) or a citation from the liturgy, this line that haredim howled whenever they perceived their young—their anointed princes—under attack from the world outside was a slogan that summed up all they were about. Sometimes the sentiment could be even more explicit, as a large poster I noticed once, plastered all over the walls of Mea Shearim's Hungarian Houses, a few meters away from the Toldos Aharon Yeshiva, graphically illustrated.

TONIGHT! The 20th of Tammuz at 8:45 there will be a meeting, *with G-d's help*, of parents and educators.

ANYONE WHO CARES ABOUT HIS SOUL
AND THE SOUL OF HIS HOUSE
WILL NOT IGNORE THIS MEETING!

The Committee for the Purity of Our Camp

Now there probably was no such formal organization of parents and educators as that which with great hubris signed itself "The Committee for the Purity of Our Camp." This was simply a provisional name for one of the countless ad hoc haredi groups that continually sought to keep pernicious influences of the outside world away from their children.

They wanted to keep to themselves morally, physically, and socially. For them purity required separation. *Hisbadlus,* they called it. But this was by no means a new haredi aim. As Alexander Friedman, secretary of the Polish branch of Agudat Israel put it already in 1935, "spiritual isolation will protect our sons and daughters from the sickness of heresy, license, and secularity."[1] Why the need for such segregation?

"It is known to all," wrote the Hafetz Hayim, one of the founding fathers of the haredi point of view, "that this generation is continuing to collapse [morally] each day."[2] "We live in a terrible and awful time," as Rabbi Eliezer Schach, head of the Ponovezh Yeshiva in B'nai B'rak and contemporary voice of a large segment of the haredi world, put it more recently; "there is no day whose curse is not greater than the one before it."[3] From the days of the Hafetz Hayim to the days of Rabbi Schach, haredim have perceived the world to be in a process of moral decay. Worse still, this corrupted world seeks to invade the protected environment haredim have constructed for themselves. And it endangers the weakest most. These are the young and the impressionable.

That was why the Committee for the Purity of Our Camp was addressing its concern about safeguarding "souls" primarily to parents and educators. Parenting and education were at the front lines of the struggle against moral decay. The Bible in Deuteronomy (6:7) made that clear when it invoked a fundamental obligation to "teach it diligently unto your children." Scripture explained it further: "Train the young man in the way he should go, and when he is old he will not depart from it" (Proverbs 22:6). The codes were most specific: "Every father must educate his young children in all the obligations, whether they be commandments from the Bible or those of the rabbis, each and every obligation according to the understanding of the young boy or girl. [And thus] one protects and separates them from all that is prohibited."[4] And more recently, in the words of the Hafetz Hayim in his commentary on those codes: "He who does not root in the heart of his children after him the faith in God and His Torah and commandments and does not care whether or not his children go in the ways of God, does not at all fulfill his obligation as a Jew."[5]

Among haredim, education was everything: the purpose of Jewish existence and at the same time a barrier against its decay. It was the essence of what they believed was demanded of them as Jews. To this end, they created a network of schools that embraced life from youth to age and that, whenever possible, evaded the harmful influence of secular education—what was called by insiders "alien wisdom" (*chochmos chitzonios*). In their schools the young were turned into haredim. They were taught to speak and write in a separate haredi version of a Jewish language that kept outsiders at bay—Yiddish, encrusted with acronyms and insider expressions, even more than modern Hebrew. They were confirmed in their distinctive appearance and dress that made assimilation in the outside world impossible. They were introduced to their own customs, folkways, values, and versions of the life that made them conscious of their own traditions, which were also presented as the true Judaism. Anything short of that was "putting darkness into light."

In an open, modern, urban, and pluralist society—such as the one surrounding today's haredim—where all sorts of influences threaten to besiege and bombard unprotected individuals, the school is a sanctuary, a cultural stronghold, a sheltered environment where external influences are institutionally controlled. Of course, even before the start of school, these children unconsciously have absorbed a great deal of what it means to be haredim. The way they dress or groom themselves, for example, the demands they have already accepted as natural—including having to recite blessings before eating or after defecating (that is, bracketing their newly gained autonomy over their bodies with a series of ritual and religious practices)—are all reflections of their culture and society. But it is in the school that they first directly encounter the formalized world of Jewish learning and join their peers in a framework that harnesses and tames their exuberant childhood imagination and predispositions, replacing them with haredi morals and válues.

However, while the underlying impact of schooling may be socialization to haredi ways, haredim conceive of what they do very simply as *lernen Toyreh* (studying Torah). "Torah" denotes Scriptures, Talmud, midrash, codes, commentaries, and in some cases even parable and folktales. Immersing oneself in it is tantamount to being a better Jew, coming closer to God's will, and protecting oneself from corruption. "There are many ways to bring oneself close to the Holy One, may He be blessed, but all the ways are risky and only the path taken by way of the [study of] Torah is the secure way."[6]

As Eliezer Schach rhetorically asked: "What is the secret of our existence?" Generations of persecution and pogrom had not succeeded in wiping out Jews and Judaism. "They can kill us, but our sons will continue to cleave to the Torah." Through this, "the Jew lives forever."[7] The school, more than any other place, was where this process was set into motion. Here first steps in the fashioning of the consciousness are taken. Here children begin in earnest to transform themselves into the anxious haredi Jews that their parents and teachers expect them to become.[8] Here, as one haredi educator put it, they enter "the road that our fathers and our teachers have trodden upon forever."[9]

For all these reasons schools are everywhere in the haredi world. Kindergartens, primary and advanced yeshivas, or kollels, as well as synagogues that between their morning and evening services have been converted into study halls, are omnipresent. And nearly every one of them appears to be bursting at the seams. While many schools are being enlarged, and often the newest building on a block is a yeshiva, most commonly the physical plant of the school is hardly more than a few rooms.

Although Jewish tradition suggests that a child need not begin learning Torah until the age of five years, the trend among haredim increasingly has been to advance the time their young go to school. From the time they are barely out of diapers until well after marriage, at least for males, life means going to school every day, except on Sabbath and holy days (and even on these days the obligation to study Torah is not rescinded).[10] While there is a summer vacation, called *bayn ha-z'manim* (between terms), it is relatively brief, lasting normally from the Ninth of Av until the first day of the next month, Elul (roughly equivalent to the month of August).

In part, this expansion of schooling is explained by the instrumental need to share the task of caring for the many children in the average haredi family. With a high birth rate haredi parents simply cannot cope without the support and assistance of schools that help them raise their children. And it is also one reason that schools for girls—an institution that in the last forty years has grown in popularity but was unthinkable a little over a hundred years ago when females were still considered to be exempt from the need to concentrate on Torah learning—are now an accepted feature of even the most Orthodox communities.[11] Moreover, the idea that the responsibility for education is to be shared with a teacher outside the family is deeply rooted in Jewish tradition.

Learning Torah is not a part-time occupation but rather a full-time preoccupation, contiguous with life itself. Jewish learning, especially for males, is considered to be an endless religious obligation superseding all others. This notion is based on at least two well-known proof texts, one scriptural and the other talmudic. In Joshua (1:8) the message is simple: "This Torah shall not depart out of thy mouth; but thou shalt meditate upon it day and night." In a contemporary gloss on this imperative, Rabbi Schach explained that in order to "be strengthened," every Jew "is obligated to set a time to study each day, so that these days are not lost forever."[12] Whether or not the school is really the impenetrable fortress and protective shell that many, like Rabbi Schach, have claimed it is, to haredim it has become the ideal Jewish environment, and the scholar, the talmid chacham (literally, "the wise student") has become the ideal Jew. Here the chain of being and continuity with the past is most vividly experienced. "Always, when the Jew is not cut off from the heritage of his fathers, then he is linked with the rabbis of the Mishnah and all the zaddikim, with Abraham, Isaac and Jacob—they live."[13]

Tinokos Shel Bais Rabban

In the parlance of the haredi community, "tinokos shel bais rabban" is a talmudic phrase that means "the littlest children." Also called the anointed ones or "messiahs," they are, according to traditional doctrine, the most precious of all children, still pure and free of all transgression. For Jews there is no such thing as original sin; children begin as a tabula rasa on which the tradition can and must be inscribed. And yet, while they are free of sin, they are not free of the tendency to sin. On the contrary, they are at risk both from internal and external sources. On the one hand, children are susceptible to domination by their inner tendencies of base instinct. On the other, they are most easily attracted by the corrosive influences of the outside world.

"What is the way of youth? Not to study and not to pray but rather to sit in idleness and chase after lustful passions." [14] To avoid this fall, the child must be molded and fashioned from the outset in order to root out the evil in him and to create a fence around him so that he is not damaged. That fence is fashioned from religion and custom. Why is this important? After all, why not allow the youth his period of license and liberty and then, when he matures, transform him into a haredi? Because, as one haredi educational guide puts it, "All that is implanted in the little heart will remain there until one has aged." [15] Being haredi requires habituation; it is a pattern of existence that begins even before consciousness and lifestyles are formed. "The acts of the fathers are a sign to their sons." [16] One generation serves as the template for the other. And that means paying special attention to children, even the youngest of them.

As haredim demonstrate again and again, their young are their most precious treasure. Said the Talmud, "One does not neglect the tinokos shel bais rabban even for the purpose of rebuilding the Holy Temple." Commenting on this in the sixteenth century, the Maharal of Prague, Rabbi Judah Loew, concluded, "From this we learn that the sanctity of the children is greater even than the Temple." [17]

Not only are they uncorrupted by life and its compromises, they are also the incarnation of continuity: the human sanctuary, recipients of tradition and its carriers. Whatever patterns of life the haredim may have managed to develop, these endure only as long as they are passed on to children who continue to maintain them. "The world only exists for the sake of the tinokos shel bais rabban." [18] The adapted haredi gloss on this talmudic dictum might be: "Our world only exists for the sake of the tinokos shel bais rabban. The elders exist by virtue of the merits they gain from teaching the young, protecting them, and raising them for Torah." [19]

What Is to Be Taught?

What makes up the curriculum of the haredi schools, especially in the primary years? A universally agreed upon and formal haredi curriculum is probably an impossibility—at least in part because, as already noted, haredim are not monolithic. Not only are there distinctions between Lithuanians (misnagdim) and hasidim, but even among hasidim there are a variety of approaches, many of which are reflected in education. Nevertheless, when considered in its broad outlines, the education that haredim receive, especially when contrasted with what others are exposed to, does have some basic common elements. First are the texts: The "plain bread" of Talmud is a staple in the higher grades—usually sometime after eleven years old. Before that comes Scripture. And perhaps earliest of all come stories drawn from the tradition. By the later years of yeshiva, the Talmud is the framework for all sorts of other discussions, including matters of ethics and esoterica that may even include some mysticism (although this is limited to a select few) and specialized rabbinic literature.

But there is another side to the haredi curriculum, such as it is. First here comes the matter of faith. "A father must implant the faith in the heart of his child." [20] That faith need not be based on reason. Indeed, "one should accustom the child [to believing] without reason and explanation, and then even when he ages and his rationality is strengthened and he can think about matters sensibly and get to the truth of matters, he will not depart from the true path and observance [even when it does not make sense to him]; or when he cannot understand the sense or reach the depths of truth, if he has been trained in such faith from his youth, he will not depart from the faith, and will not depend [only] on his understanding." [21]

Second is the matter of fearing God. "It is a commandment of the Torah to implant the fear of Heaven in the heart of children from the time they are small so that they might be God-fearing all the days of their lives." [22] As the Psalmist put it, "The beginning of wisdom is the fear of God." [23]

Then there is the element of holiness. For the haredim this means practically separating the student from all that is prohibited, "especially from the sins of youth, which needs extra watchfulness, care and energy." [24] Making the child holy—a moral creature—is no easy task: "There are children who in their nature are base and wanton, who cannot be affected by words, and even when they are instructed with words meant to strengthen either their resolution against their base passions or their fear of Heaven it is like talking to stones, for they have no feelings." [25]

While there are many concrete examples of this base character, primary among them being lust and licentiousness—in the very young this takes its expression in their touching themselves in prohibited places. "Warn your little boys of five or six (or even younger) that they should not touch their holy *bris* [penis (literally, "covenant of circumcision")] even at the time that they make water, nor should they touch that of their fellows, nor even look there." [26] With age, this taboo includes feeling lustful passions or looking at sights likely to arouse them, something demanding constant vigilance.

To help them maintain their holiness, the young must be taught a protocol of life. This agenda is called *Seder Ha-Yom*. This means knowing about the holy days, rituals, customs, where one may go and what one may eat, how to act in various contexts and in general what are the proper human qualities, the importance of Torah, attendance in the synagogue, and self control. The mandate to keep themselves under control is often articulated in terms of the commandment to honor their parents, for "it is the parent's obligation to guard his children to see to it that there not be within them an evil nature and wickedness." [27]

Yet while many of these obligations of education are incumbent on the parents (indeed it is primarily as a teacher that a parent earns the respect due him or her), it is the teacher whose role is paramount, as even the youngest children quickly discover.

The Teacher, or Rebbe

In Orthodox Jewish life, teachers or rebbes, as they are called, have always been endowed with an often larger-than-life authority. They must be treated with reverence and respect, sometimes even in precedence over one's parents. Says the Talmud, "Anyone who teaches his fellow's child Torah, it is as if he gave birth to him." [28] But teachers do more than act *in loco parentis* or embody the community's norms and mores; they are at times stand-ins for God. Said Rabbi Eleazar ben Shammua: "May the fear of your teacher be like the fear of Heaven," for "anyone who teaches his fellow's child Torah is privileged to sit in the council of Heaven." [29] And while there are some who have reinterpreted these dicta in other ways, the fact remains that for many haredim the teacher or rebbe is a sublime figure.

And who makes the best teacher? As one haredi parent explained, while training in a teachers' seminary was useful and she certainly wanted people who knew what the job entailed, the best teachers, she thought, were the ones who came from families who had a tradition of teaching passed down through the generations. Of course, after a while, everyone got better with experience.

Although most scholars aspire to be a rosh yeshiva, the head of an academy, even the primary-school teacher, the melamed, is esteemed —although often more in principle than in practice, which is probably why the Lubliner Rebbe, a hasidic master of the nineteenth century, once pointed out: "If people knew the status that the melamed has in heaven, everyone would rush to teach the little children." [30]

If adults do not necessarily view the melamed as the incarnation of the ideal, the tinokos shel bais rabban do. In kindergarten, at a time when they begin to move from helpless childhood into the relatively greater autonomy of the juvenile era even as their capacity to make the correct intellectual connections remains often incomplete, the teacher seems the incarnation of complete and unfathomable wisdom.[31] As the child is told again and again by everyone, "The rebbe knows." And he knows about everything. Unlike them, he seems to see how things are all connected.

Often the most common question a child is asked either at home or by members of the community is: *"Vus hot der rebbe gesugt?"* (What did the rabbi say?) In a sense, the reiteration of lessons learned from one's teachers is one of the enduring patterns of haredi Jewish intellectual life. Life often becomes a series of citations and quotations, each of which is appropriate to the needs of the moment.

Teachers, and in particular primary ones, are thus key figures. And when schools need them, haredim announce in their press and broadsides throughout their neighborhoods: "Help! The children of Israel need you! Come, while there is still time, and save the children of Israel from spiritual destruction."[32] This is no idle or exaggerated call. For haredim the teachers are the first line in the offensive to save those who are the "true Children of Israel" from spiritual destruction. After all, in the haredi world—as indeed in all culture, "predecessors and successors are as much made as born."[33] And it is the teachers who make them, acting as the bridge between past and future.

12

A School for
Little Haredim

For a long time I searched for a way to enter one of the many classrooms I passed in my wanderings about haredi neighborhoods. Since I would be neither rebbe nor pupil and since my appearance was manifestly nonharedi, I would have to find a place that would not only let me in but would also allow me to come so often that I would become part of the woodwork, looking but not really seen. As an anthropologist, I had long ago discovered the amazing capacity people seem to have to ignore observers if they become fixtures of a setting.

My opening came through a man whom I knew and who worked in the business office of a haredi yeshiva complex.[1] This yeshiva, Lithuanian in its origins and its formal affiliation, had a relatively small yet comprehensive network of schools that provided everything from gan (kindergarten) to kollel. Its elementary school was particularly popular for a variety of reasons, not the least of which was the reputed warmth of the teachers and their success in training their very young charges in the "Torah way." They took what seemed barely more than toddlers and turned them into "little Yidn." The gan was also favored by many because it accepted even those under three years old, a service in great demand by many of the parents with large families.

The gan served a predominantly nonhasidic but haredi clientele. Many of the children's fathers studied or taught in kollels that were not affiliated with one or another hasidic grouping. And yet, perhaps to illustrate how contemporary life and the minority status of haredim has thrust them together in many ways, all of the teachers and staff in the gan were themselves hasidim, as were many in the elementary school, including my friend who managed to get me an appointment to talk with the rosh yeshiva. After a long conversation, he gave me permission to sit in at the gan and some of the lower grades of the elementary school for as long as I needed in order to see how the haredi perspectives, which in our conversation the rosh yeshiva claimed for his school, were acquired by youngsters in it.

A message was swiftly passed down the chain of command, and in a few days I was escorted to the yeshiva, where I met with the principal. A bearded man in his fifties, dressed all in black but with the relatively shorter sidelocks of the Lithuanian school, he seemed less than enthusiastic about my presence. I was neither a parent looking for a place for his children nor a teacher looking for a job, and I was obviously an outsider who did not share in the worldview of most of those with whom he came in contact. Although he never said so, I suspect the principal believed I was sent to spy on him and his methods. But if the rosh yeshiva wanted me to be allowed in, he of course muted his objections. In the world of the haredi school, authority in general and the authority of a rosh yeshiva in particular, meant much. There were few real independents, deciding things for themselves; everyone was part of a chain of being. And that structure held. The principal asked for a few days to prepare his teachers for my arrival. Just what that preparation was, I never learned. Nor do I know how he could prepare them for a visit whose purpose he claimed not to understand. Still, in the end, all permissions in hand, I went to kindergarten.

As for the principal and me, each of us maintained a kind of studied distance from the other. Because the school was divided into three locations which, although within walking distance of one another, were on different streets in the neighborhood, and because the principal's office was in only one of them, I would be able to spend time in places where we would seldom come into direct contact. As a result, his suspicions became irrelevant—at least until, finally, when the teachers were threatening a strike over wages, he asked me to leave. Saying nothing about the labor dispute (which perhaps he did not want me to witness or maybe even thought I instigated), he claimed that some of the teachers found my presence a disturbance in the classroom. Although this might have been true, none of them confirmed this fact. Still, by the time I was asked to leave, I had already spent several months in the gan and elementary school and had seen all I could see.

At the start, I was an exotic outsider. Often, when the teacher was out of the room or in the courtyard, the children would come close to and touch me to see if I was made of the same stuff as they. One boy grabbed hold of the satchel I carried, inside of which were my note pad and tape recorder: "Why do you carry a case?"

Notebooks and tape recorders were common enough, but in the world they inhabited, grown men did not carry such bags; pouches were only for little boys.

"Are you a mother that you wear a ring?" a boy asked, touching my finger. In their universe only mothers wore wedding rings; there was no tradition for the males to wear one.

"Do I look like a mother?"

They laughed.

Two boys pulled at my knit skullcap; theirs were velvet. They stared at my sandals and toes; adult haredi men never wore sandals—the footwear of the chiloinim. As exotic as they seemed to me, so I seemed to them.

"Where is your camera?" a boy asked. Only tourists or photographers came from the outside into their world. I must be one of those. "I don't want to be photographed," he added. These little boys had already learned they were "picturesque."

"But I have no camera," I replied to an obviously disappointed little boy who was gearing up for a conflict, a kind of small-scale imitation of his elders, who also warned tourists not to shoot their cameras at them. He wanted to set the boundaries of our relationship.

Of course, as I had seen again and again, haredim do get photographed—collecting pictures and photos of great rabbis was one of the recent fads in this world, where baseball cards had been transmogrified into so-called rebbe cards. But haredim did not allow outsiders to capture their likeness. Although inchoate and not fully articulated in his consciousness, this attitude was part of what this youngster had learned: outsiders do not get to take pictures unless asked to by insiders.

As the days passed in the gan, I became, in the words of the teachers, *ha-dod*, the uncle, a familiar stranger. I was "near and far *at the same time*," not quite "the wanderer who comes today and goes tomorrow," but rather "the person who comes today and stays tomorrow."[2] Although never ceasing to be foreign, there was enough about me that became a familiar figure of the setting so that soon the children —no less than their teachers—seemed to take me for granted.

I was the uncle, and each day I became him more and more. I would overcome any unease I at first felt. After all, I discovered that for all of their exotic appearance, these little boys were not all that different from the ones I had at home: exuberant, mischievous, and curious. What differentiated them from my sons besides the externals of appearance, however, were the things they knew about, took for granted, and those that seemed foreign. And for them my differences seemed rather quickly to melt away until I was nothing to look at. And then, having disappeared, I was able to see beyond the exotic into the quotidian. I needed no camera for I became the camera.

Inside Kindergarten

Located in two small buildings connected by a courtyard, the three classrooms of the gan were peopled completely by males. Even at the earliest ages, education among haredim is strictly segregated by sex. More than that, males will have only male teachers—even in nursery or kindergarten—and of course females will in most cases be taught by other women. (Because women in the haredi world did not work outside the home, there had once been a dearth of female teachers. Indeed, when increasing numbers of women began to get formal Jewish educations about a hundred years ago, they were frequently taught by male teachers. However, the explosion in the number of schools for women in the last forty years, along with economic pressures that have forced a number of women into the marketplace, have led to increasing numbers of haredi women entering teaching. Although some of them teach in nonharedi state religious schools, quite a few others have become part of the network of haredi women's education.)

The facilities in the gan were minimal. Each of the three classrooms had a blackboard, a teacher's cabinet containing a few books, and seating for the children. In two of the rooms, the youngsters had small desks with two or three chairs at them, and in the third they were seated along several long, low tables. The teachers had larger tables, but more often than not these were pushed into a corner or shunted aside while the rebbe moved freely about the room. On the walls were pictures, often scenes of the holy days or drawings depicting tableaux from the Bible, some of them colored in by the children. And everywhere there were signs with words on them: words of blessing, scriptural quotations, or reminders of the season.

At first, I was struck by the presence of so much to read on the wall. After all, the youngest of the children here were between two and three years old and the eldest hardly more than four. What possible purpose was there in putting words on the wall that they could not read? I wondered. But I would discover that these children *could* read, and words were part of their earliest sensory experiences. And even those who could not yet read were being sensitized to an unstated aesthetic that conceived of words as articles with which walls are decorated. After all, the Satmar rebbe had once suggested only half in jest that the stone walls of nearby Mea Shearim were held together by posters and broadsides. As I looked around at these decorative verses on the wall, I got the feeling that for the haredim, in the beginning was the word.

Connecting the two classrooms in the first building was a combination teachers' room and supply closet. Here the teachers, or more frequently, one of the two *behelfers*, assistants, would occasionally take a break or meet briefly. But as the quarters were so close, the room could not really offer much privacy. Besides, the nature of the school was such that the teachers could and often did walk into one another's classes and chat even though their pupils were there. In fact, there was a kind of intimacy about the place that allowed people to move into and out of all sorts of activity throughout the day with only the most minimal of formal bracketing of their behavior.

This does not mean there were not rules about what was permissible and what forbidden. There were, and one of the behelfers, who in the course of my time there was let go because he had taken too many naps in the teachers' room and had not sufficiently become engaged by his work, had clearly breached these unspoken rules. Justifying the decision to let him go, the principal said simply, "He is not suited for the work." There was no need to specify why; anyone who needed to have it explained was by definition too much of an outsider to appreciate any explanation.

The second building held one classroom that was used for the youngest group. Unlike the case in the other building, in which the classrooms opened directly onto the courtyard, this one had a corridor just outside the door that could be and often was bolted to keep the little ones from wandering off on their own.

A small, unvented toilet was tucked in a corner of the larger building. The smell from the toilet invaded the nearby classrooms, especially during winter, when doors and windows were kept closed. But the smell from the toilet was inextinguishable. Behelfers were often mopping up accidents or changing some of the youngest children's trousers.

Outside in a corner of the courtyard was a small fenced-in playground containing a rather dilapidated jungle gym and a few shabby toys, including a broken wagon and a battered tricycle. There were also some old painted barrels equipped with what looked like a steering wheel and meant to give the impression of a tractor. For these city kids who had probably never been to either a kibbutz or a farm, the contraption probably had other associations. A bare sandbox under a half-dead tree and three or four steps of a staircase that went to nowhere completed the layout.

Like so many of the black and white photos that were all the visual record that remained of east European Jewry, the tableaux that opened before my eyes in each classroom were at first glance a picture of yesterday. But unlike the pictures of their fathers, who were in black and white only, these boys were tinted in the hues of today. They wore colors and plaids. Later in life they would remove their colors in favor of the darker tones meant to mourn the destroyed Holy Temple and mark them as haredim.

In the third classroom quite a few boys had long uncut hair, sometimes hanging loose and other times tied into a pony tail. These were children under three years of age who had not yet gone through the traditional first shearing on Lag b'Omer. Originally limited to hasidim, this custom was increasingly becoming an accepted practice among many haredi families, including many of those of the Lithuanian approach to Judaism whose children attended this school. There was no mistaking even the hairiest ones here for girls since each child—like all other haredi boys—wore a little velvet skullcap or cappeleh, as their teachers called it in Yiddish.

The Teachers

A teacher was assigned for the approximately thirty-five boys in each room. In addition, there were two behelfers who floated about. For the youngest children there was Reb Avrohom, a third-generation Jerusalemite who had once been one of the Reb Arelach hasidim but who was now affiliated with a smaller hasidic sect, the Shomrei Hachomos, who had broken with the Reb Arelach after the death of the previous rebbe. A ruddy man in his fifties and the father of twelve, Reb Avrohom wore the distinctive white bulky-knit cap of the Reb Arelach under his hat.

As a young man, he had been a scribe, writing the parchments inside mezuzahs, tefillin, or a megillah, as did many other haredi young men in the yeshiva. Later, although he did not give up scribal arts, when his growing family required more money, and after he decided that "he did not find a place for himself in the kollel," meaning that he was not cut out to be a full-time scholar, he entered teaching. At the start, he was a first-grade teacher. Like all haredi teachers, he had received no formal training for the job. Rather what had qualified him to be hired—at least as far as his first employers, the local group of Satmar hasidim, were concerned—was his obvious experience with children as a father of twelve, and the patience, tenderness, and control he had exhibited in the first weeks on the job. Whatever Reb Avrohom knew about primary education, then, he had learned on the job.

There was something else Reb Avrohom and all the other teachers had to have in order to be hired: *yiras shomayim*, the fear of Heaven, the piety and anxiety that made them true haredim. Proving one had this was not always easy; it was a matter of reputation. Teachers had to be known in the community; outsiders were never trusted with the job of melamed.

In the haredi world the salary a teacher in gan received was as high as that earned by a rosh yeshiva, higher than what an elementary-school instructor made. In part, this was because this sort of work required a singular set of talents and exquisite patience, including an ability to help a youngster make the first important transition from childhood into a sense of Jewish peoplehood. Although they would not put it in these terms, haredim recognized the consequence and significance of this first transition and the character formation and process of personification that it included. The increased salary was an unmistakable sign of the high value placed on the position.

Avrohom had an aptitude and liking for the work with these little ones, and so after a few years in first grade he had grabbed the opportunity to become a kindergarten teacher when it became available at this school. To be sure, the approximately $350 he made a month, while more than he had earned before, still was insufficient to meet his financial needs; and so in the afternoons Avrohom found other work, sometimes collecting for the poor (and taking a percentage of his collection) and other times still doing some work as a scribe. But, he added, were it not for the assistance he received from the government's welfare fund, he would probably not be able to make it. The ideologues of the hasidim he belonged to were virulently anti-Zionist and antistate, but he still took the welfare money. Like other haredim, he occasionally dabbled in black-market currency exchange. It was good money, a portable business with flexible hours, and ideologically correct; anti-Zionists need have no compunctions about engaging in dealings the state of Israel prohibited.

Reb Yecheskel had the three-and-a-half-year-olds. A rotund, dark-haired man in his late thirties, he was a Sanzer hasid who was born in Rumania but had spent over ten years living in America near his rebbe, who at the time was headquartered in Union City, New Jersey. Although Yecheskel's father had also been a hasid, he had affiliated with a different rebbe; the son had shifted loyalties. After the war and the social upheaval it had caused in the hasidic world, such switches were by no means unusual. A deck depleted by firestorms and reshuffled by the whirlwind, Hasidism was stacking its cards in all sorts of new ways and with new players in the 1950s. Horizontal mobility was common as various groups competed, sometimes intensively, for members.

In America, Yecheskel had worked in a variety of businesses—"I worked heavy work," he said simply. But since coming to Jerusalem, he had abandoned such profane labor and returned to the field in which he had begun his work career: a teacher of the tinokos shel bais rabban. Although he and his wife had no children—something that normally disqualified haredim from teaching the young, to say nothing of stigmatizing them in the community—he had been given this job, in which he was only in his second year.

Asked if the financial benefits of the position were what had attracted him, he evaded the question. In the United States, Yecheskel explained, he had lived under far better conditions, both physical and financial. But he added sardonically, "Sometimes a Judaism that emerges out of poverty is a stronger one." In a kind of mild homage to asceticism, he suggested that if doing too well was not altogether sinful, it was at the very least impious—it was a theme repeated in diverse ways among many Israeli haredim, especially when they wanted to distinguish themselves from their American counterparts.

Yecheskel was very much a believer, and he was filled with stories, fables, and hasidic aphorisms. They punctuated almost everything he said and were a prominent feature of his teaching. For him life seemed to be a series of allegories, and our task as Jews was very simply to decipher the sometimes hidden and other times manifest lessons it taught. We put ourselves into stories and put stories into ourselves. This sort of storytelling was characteristically hasidic.[3]

The last teacher, Reb Yitzhak, was nominally the head teacher and responsible for the oldest group, those near four years old. Like Avrohom and Yecheskel, he too was a hasid, in his case part of the Rachmastrivka group which was an affiliate of the larger Skver hasidim. Like the others, he too had switched his hasidic loyalties, having grown up as a Bialer hasid. For twelve years Yitzhak served the Bialer rebbe as a gabbai. For him this had been a position of honor, a brush with greatness. But when the rebbe died, arguments began about who should be the next rebbe, and Yitzhak found himself on the wrong side. "What bothered me," he explained, "was that beforehand we had all lived together, but now there were different groups, some supporting one son and others supporting another." Feeling brushed off, Yitzhak voted with his feet and left to join the Rachmastrivka at that time. Still, he admitted, "I haven't really found my niche." Already his children were moving into the orbits of other rebbes: one son to Lalov and another to Karlin-Stolin.

In the modern marketplace of ideas and social movements, even the hasidim were touched, and the competition for adherents remained very fierce in many quarters. In all three cases—Avrohom, Yecheskel, and Yitzhak—hasidim had moved from one group to another in the aftermath of a dynastic transition. When one rebbe died and his crown was handed over to another, in that transitional period before the new incumbent fully filled the position of his predecessor, old scores were settled, rivalries erupted, and changes happened. Outsiders who saw only undifferentiated hasidim were wrong. Change masqueraded as continuity. The dynasty might go on, but these days nothing remained quite the same.

"I won't say that now I have what I had at the Bialer," Yitzhak concluded, "but it's alright."

It really wasn't. To be a teacher in a gan, even a head teacher, after having been the right hand to the rebbe was not exactly advancement, especially since this institution was not even a hasidic one. In a little over a year, Yitzhak would leave this kindergarten and find work in a hasidic gan closer to home at slightly better pay.

And yet in spite of everything, this rumpled-looking man, with a wisp of a black beard and a round black hat worn at a jaunty angle, wearing a threadbare frock coat that was always unbuttoned and looking as if he were running into the wind, was good at the work. When he told a story to the children or repeated the alphabet with them or even when he reviewed some apparently dry point of law, he seemed to hold them in rapt attention. His peers respected him, and the behelfers were wary of him. More than anyone else, Yitzhak organized the teaching here.

The Teaching

In the most general way, that teaching prepared the boys to be at home in the haredi world. Concretely, these men were instructing these children how to read, imparting information about Jewish ritual and heritage, introducing them to scripture and other sacred texts. Specifically, they were telling stories, singing songs, and performing certain basic Jewish rituals according to haredi norms. But they were doing more. By emphasizing tales, songs, and certain notions of piety, while sharing attitudes that stressed religious emotion or spiritual empathy, they were also subtly instilling in their pupils a hasidic ethos. When I asked them if they meant to do this, they all smiled and a couple shrugged their shoulders. My question seemed to make them conscious of something they had not thought about. But no one denied that this was possible.

Before looking at how this all happened, however, it is useful to think about what can be expected with children this age. As psychiatrist Harry Stack Sullivan suggests, children this age have an inner organization of experience that is still rather fragmentary and only partially rooted in reality.[4] For such youngsters, stories and fantasies can be as real as actuality and experience. The lines blur. If indeed all is possible to those who believe, then these children are among those most ready to believe, particularly if they find themselves in a setting and environment—like the rebbe's *cheder* (classroom)—they have been taught to trust.

This time of life, when experience has not yet had a chance to undermine ideals, is an especially auspicious time to instill moral order and introduce cultural prescriptions. Indeed, the argument has been made, by Emile Durkheim and many others, that if before the period of full-blown childhood—before primary school—"the foundations of morality have not been laid, they never will be."[5]

One of the most common and perhaps oldest techniques used by teachers to accomplish all this has been through the telling of stories. These stories "are in general of two types: They may be socially approved moral tales which have become ingrained in the culture because they set forth complex ethical ideals in a fashion that can be grasped by a child. Or they are inventions of the authority figure," such as a rebbe.[6] In either case the stories transmit "certain of the cultural prescriptions to the child," leading to a "more rapid transition in the personifications of the child than would occur simply from play and maturation, and so on."[7] As they help him grow into a person in tune with his culture, the stories also allow a child "to deepen his under-standing of human nature and the human situation; his moral sense is deepened also." Finally, at a more advanced stage these stories give children "the impression that they should be governed by certain influences which we call social values, or judgments, or the ethical worth of certain types of behavior."[8]

Such stories leave a profound impact. As Sullivan reports, "Their influence on the young, early in childhood, or perhaps all through childhood, often appears in personality studies which are made many, many years later."[9] In a sense, subsequent moral life can become an endless reverberation of these first childhood stories for "any story has a propensity to generate another story in the mind of its reader (or hearer), to repeat or displace some prior story."[10]

And what sorts of stories are these? They are what have been called "master stories," tales "by which we interpret and respond to events which impinge on our lives."[11] They are "basic faith understandings of reality and value by which we . . . shape basic approaches to the world."[12] In the case of haredim, these sorts of master stories are commonly Bible stories, frequently augmented by tales of sages and religious heroes as well as midrashic or talmudic elaborations of sacred texts. This means that the moral direction and cultural conception imparted in these stories, repeated by a teacher who is presented and perceived as God's stand-in, have a theological importance as well as a moral and cultural one.

This is not true just for the youngsters who listen to the tales. It is true as well for the narrators who as believers consider these stories as part of a single strand that ties together life and text. For the haredi, life as perceived in sacred texts and life as it is lived are presumed to be interchangeable. There can be nothing in one domain that does not somehow have its referent in the other. Torah and life are in principle one long articulation and elaboration of each other. And nowhere is this made more manifest than in such master stories.

To the question "Where did you get that story?" I would almost always be given the answer: "It's in the midrash," or some other textual reference.[13]

"Exactly as you put it?"

"Well, it's translated and improved," Yecheskel once said. As the teachers saw it, the narratives were changed only to make them com-prehensible to the children, but in their essence they remained rooted in the sacred canon. As I saw them, they were much more. But all this is better understood by taking a look into the classroom.

The Rebbe and the Rod

Next door to a home for the aged and across the street from a school for young girls, from eight in the morning until a few minutes before one each afternoon, for six days a week, during almost eleven months, the gan is filled with about a hundred little boys. They arrive each morning, little pouches filled with lunch hanging from their necks. Most come in yellow vans from a variety of haredi neighborhoods throughout Jerusalem. Some arrive hand in hand with their big sisters, girls in long dresses, who bring them into the school and then quietly slip away to their own classes in another building on a different block. Still others are brought by mothers or just as often by fathers, many of whom are on their way to spend the day studying in a kollel.

Were these little ones to be able to reflect on all this, they might be struck by the fact that in coming to gan they have joined in an activity that they share in common with almost everyone else in their family while also entering into a routine of Jewish study that stretches back for thousands of years. These are their first steps into a "society of scholars." [14]

But of course they do not see things that way. They are simply separating from home—some for the first time in their lives—and coming to cheder, a place to which, they have been told, their short lives have all along been leading them.

There to greet them is the rebbe, the new man in their lives whom they have somewhat anxiously anticipated meeting. He is, on the one hand, slightly familiar—living in the same neighborhood as at least some of them, dressing and grooming himself like their fathers, and speaking their language and all that connotes. That familiarity inspires confidence. On the other hand, what elicits apprehension is that he is also slightly strange—an adult other than their parents who has exalted authority over them and who tells them all sorts of new things that everyone assures them are important to know. Like him or not, he is their rebbe. In his hand he holds a rod.

All three of the teachers, Avrohom, Yitzhak, and Yecheskel, made use of a rod to help make little haredim out of these boys. Yecheskel's was a plain stick and Avrohom's a ruler. Yitzhak's rod was shaped like the staff on which the Torah scroll is rolled, a cane called an *etz hayim*, a tree of life, for from this "tree" all Jewish life grows, at least according to the tradition celebrated in these rooms. All three used their rods for pointing or occasionally for rapping an errant hand or an inattentive youngster. They did not use it to intimidate. More often than not, the rebbe was ready to "spare the rod." Like the shepherd who now and then uses his staff to collect his errant sheep, knowing that if he strikes them too hard they will run away or, worse, be wounded, and who therefore gently prods them in the direction he wants them to go, the rebbe would use his rod to underscore gently but firmly what he wanted. In a sense, this cane was less a tool and more a symbol of authority, a physical reminder of the rebbe's right to corral the consciousness of his pupils. Mostly, the rebbes held the boys' attention with what they said.

This capacity to be charmed by words did not mean that the boys were altogether tame and well-behaved. On the contrary, whenever one of the teachers left the room or turned his attention away, the boys erupted, many of them wildly running around the room or climbing on desks. They did it in gan, first grade, second, right up into seventh and eighth.

Yet when the rebbe came back or when he raised the rod or his voice, they stopped. Even the little ones knew how to control themselves in the face of authority. It was a weak control, always on the verge of crumbling, a control not fully internalized but dependent upon some external presence. It was as if the boys allowed themselves moments of complete abandon, a frenzy in the midst of order, because they knew there would always be someone of authority outside them who would come back and hold them in place.

This combination of frenzy and order occurred repeatedly during my time among the haredim. Beneath it was the idea that, left unsupervised, man had a natural inclination to run wild. That, after all, was a fundamental theme of haredi existence: not only the world out there can undermine their way of life, its controls, its order, but they themselves, their inner feelings, motivations, curiosities, and moods, their lusts, could also drive them wild.

The Stories

One day in the spring, during the Jerusalem sun of the *hamsin*, the fifty blistering days between the holy days of Passover and Shavuot, the little rooms of the gan became oppressively hot, and in the half hour before the end of the school day, Reb Yecheskel took his boys out to the playground. Thirty-six of them sat along the walls watching him pacing back and forth across the yard, his rod in hand. They sat quietly, listening to him tell the story of the giving of the Torah, the epochal event that according to tradition had taken place at Sinai, an event that Jews would celebrate on the holy day of Shavuot in a few weeks time.

The story Yecheskel told is perhaps one of the best known from the midrash, part of biblical lore with which countless generations of Jews have been introduced to this formative event of Jewish history. For some, perhaps, this was the first time in their lives they were hearing this founding myth.[15] Others might know the story, and this would be one of their first opportunities to repeat it, to demonstrate that they shared in the narrative heritage.

The teacher paced about rapidly, using different voices for the various speakers in the story, and the boys followed his every move and hung on his every word. Every so often, some of them echoed or cued a key word of the story, sharing in its telling. And thus they reflected and perpetuated "the pattern of meanings and inherited conceptions" embedded in the midrash.[16] If the boys were slow in responding to his prompting and questions, Yecheskel would wave his rod in the air as if conducting a chorus. And then, if that was not enough, he would bang it against something hard; and then just as Moses brought water from the stone, Yecheskel would get the boys to flow with the story.

Yecheskel used a lot of Yiddish. In spite of the fact that this was his language of choice, Hebrew had become his pupils' mother tongue. But as Yidn they would have to learn Yiddish, the counterlanguage of haredim, in which all later learning would take place. So while he told his story, he also subtly taught his wards Yiddish words.

In the tale God on high was seeking a mountain on which to present the holy Torah. Making their cases before the divine throne, several mountains vied for the honor of having this historic event take place upon them; they sang their own praises. "Choose me, I am the one worthy of such a great honor." But God ignored them and chose one mountain, far smaller than the others—"He was no show-off," the rebbe explained. Surrounded by smoke and enveloped in glory, this would be the one upon whom Heaven would descend. Here God would meet man and give him the Torah, the heritage by which the two would be forever bonded. This was Sinai, the little mountain that had been humble and said nothing about how wonderful it was.

"*Der Abishter* [the Lord] loves someone who makes himself small," Yecheskel explained in his combined Yiddish and Hebrew. This was the first moral lesson of his story: "Whoever is not a *baal gaiveh* [someone haughty], to him Hashem [God] gives the Toyreh."

Yecheskel silently let the point sink in. But he could not pause too long without losing the all-too-volatile attention of his audience. He rapped the rod on the jungle gym, pivoted around, and continued: "Now who's not listening?" Was this God addressing the people or Yecheskel talking to the boys? This was the first of many expressions that could have been part of the story just as easily as an aside. But then that was the nature of the moment, a time when now and then as well as inside and outside blurred. Stories like these came from the zone of the double entendre.

"After that, Hashem went to find who among the goyim [nations of the earth] would accept the Toyreh." Already at this early age, these children knew that goyim represented the absolute other of Yidn—the counterworld. The relation between the two was clear: "No ideas or institutions that held in the one were valid in the other." There was something elementary—even primitive—about this attitude. "Primitive man never looked out over the world and saw 'mankind' as a group and felt his common cause with his species. From the beginning he was a provincial who raised the barriers high."[17]

The boys might not yet know all the nuances of this antagonism, but they knew the basic "fact": goyim were not Yidn, and as long as they remained goyim, they could not share the essence of Judaism, the Torah. So from the outset of this story, whether they had heard it before or not, the boys knew how it would have to end. The goyim would never get the Torah. "Israel and the Torah are one," as the Zohar put it.[18]

"Hashem went to all the goyim and asked them: 'Do you want the Toyreh? Do you love the Toyreh?' "

This was no theoretical or philosophical question. It had all the immediacy of the present moment. Yecheskel had switched to the present tense. He looked straight into the boys' eyes now. His voice was the voice of God asking the nations, at this moment in the story, if they wanted the Torah. But he was now also asking each one of them this question, no less than it had been asked of their forebears.

The playground was again silent, save for the "voice of God" and the chirping of birds. The boys' faces looked rapt with attention; they ignored the noon sun. If the boys and Yecheskel were not aware of their replaying this paradigmatic moment of Jewish history, I could not help but sense it, especially afterward as I played the tape of the event over and over.

Yecheskel continued at last: "So the goyim said, 'Eh! Tell us what's in it.' " The tone was skeptical, impertinent.

Yecheskel deepened his voice again, intoning the words of der Abishter. He repeated a refrain everyone should know: "In the Torah it is written, 'Thou shalt not steal.' "

"No, no. This is not for us. No thanks."

The children smiled; a few giggled. Of course, how foolish to offer the Torah to the goyim! It was well known that goyim like to steal. The teacher told them so. Everyone knew it. Only the Yidn were worthy to receive the Torah.

Maybe "goyim" was too abstract a concept for youngsters who have been born into and lived their entire lives in a state largely populated by Jews. Yecheskel offered a gloss on the story.

"So Hashem went to America!" So many others were going to America, why not God too? Yecheskel made the phrase sound like the expression accompanying the frequent good-byes heard everywhere these days: "So I'm going to America!"

In this "overdrawn antithesis" Yecheskel was providing a symbolic frame to help the story ring with something the boys could understand.[19] In an aside he turned and with his back to the boys whispered to me: "See, I have to give them *mussar* [moral teaching]." But of course the moral teaching, extended meaning, and symbolic reframing of the story was as much for me, the American, as for the boys. One had to know that America embodied goyim; Yecheskel had learned that in his own life. Now that moral lesson was being passed on, all in the framework of this midrash that hyperbolically jumped through time so that America could come into the story.

"And he asked the American goyim, 'Do you want the Toyreh?' "

They too replied that they needed to know first what it contained. This time Yecheskel cited another of the Ten Commandments, again declaiming it in the same voice: "In the Toyreh is written, 'Honor thy Father and thy Mother.' "

What did this mean? How did erlicher Yidn honor their parents? Yecheskel offered clarification with a series of questions to which the students as one shouted answers. It was almost like a hymn with a repeated refrain, as Yecheskel beat his rod rhythmically against the jungle gym with each word.

"Is it permissible to tell a father and mother, 'I don't want'?"

"No!"

"Is it permissible to sit in Papa's or Mama's seat?"

Without missing a beat, again everyone cried, "No!"

"Is it permissible to awaken them when they are sleeping?" **Bang, bang, bang.**

"No! No! No!"

The reference was to a story they had heard before, about a boy who withstood all temptation, who refused offers of gold and jewels rather than awaken his resting father. Here was a chance to show they

absorbed that lesson, that they had the moral competence to understand the point of this narrative. With these three questions Yecheskel
gave concrete meaning to the notion of honoring one's father and
mother. And he indirectly reenforced a basic moral orientation of the
world these boys were to inhabit.

"But these goyim answer, 'No. We don't want to honor fathers and
mothers.' " This is America, a place where there is no honor for elders, a place where the young run amok, as Yecheskel saw it.

In the distance another sound trickled into the air. It came from
Yitzhak's class, where the boys were singing songs, repeating the
words and melodies that ring through hasidic life, tunes of the holy
days. Still inside their classroom, their voices were muffled by the
walls. In the minutes that followed, as the class moved outside too,
they would become louder and louder, until Yitzhak marched them
out into the courtyard in a line, where they too would enter the drama
that Yecheskel was building in the playground.

For now, that drama was not yet complete. Perhaps Americans
were also too distant an image for these little boys. Who are the goyim
they knew best?

"So Hashem went to the silly Arabs." In Yecheskel's version of
this master story, the Arabs—the local Gentiles—also were asked if
they wanted the Torah. More children laughed at this reference.
"Silly," or *kishkushi*, the Hebrew the teacher used, was one of those
words little children employed to make fun of each other. But was that
the only reason they laughed, hearing their teacher use a "kid's word?"
They were also laughing—as they had before—at the idea of giving
the Torah to the Arabs, the quintessential aliens. This was an attitude
that these haredim—even at such an early age—shared with many
others in Israeli society. The Zionists might think what the Arabs did
not deserve was the land, and the haredim thought that Arabs did not
deserve the Torah, but both shared the notion that Arabs were people
of a wholly other moral order, not deserving what the Jews treasured
most.

Like all the other goyim in this story, the Arabs also want to know
the Torah's requirements before making any commitments. Again Yecheskel began banging his rod against the jungle gym as he spoke: "In
the Toyreh is written: 'Thou shalt not kill,' bang 'thou shalt not steal,'
bang 'thou shalt not bear false witness,' bang 'thou shalt not covet.'

"You're not allowed to envy what your friend has," Yecheskel
added, bringing these lofty principles down into a form the boys could
comprehend. He pointed his rod at two boys.

"No, no," the Arabs answer in Yecheskel's voice, accompanied by a contorted face and wrinkled nose, a visual replay of how they responded. "Ooh! We don't want the Toyreh.

"This is not for us. We don't like a Toyreh like this. We want to kill and steal, to be false, to covet."

Are these not the very accusations that so many Israelis have made against the Arabs? The Arabs who would murder, steal Jewish land and heritage, bear false witness in the assembly of nations, and claim that the Jews are the ones who have displaced them when all believers know that this land was promised by God to the Jews. Are the Arabs not the ones who covet all we have? In Yecheskel's narrative the Arabs respond in the character assigned to them by this Jewish worldview.

"No, we don't want that sort of Toyreh," Yecheskel has them repeat.

However insulated haredim may claim to be from Israel, its attitudes, and the realities confronting it, these children and their teacher have obviously absorbed a great deal of the national enmity to Arabs. How else could this have become part of their midrash?

So what have we all learned so far, we who sit and listen to Yecheskel's retelling of this midrash? Goyim personify stealing. American goyim do not honor or respect their parents, and Arabs kill, steal, lie, and covet what is their neighbor's. In just a few moments and terms a three-and-a-half-year-old haredi-to-be can understand, the teacher has passed as God's truth the image of the non-Jew. It is a haredi message (resonating with many of the cultural inflections of Israeli society) that reinforces a distance from chukos ha goyim. The articulation of their version of Jewish culture required the abiding presence of a counter-culture that confronted them in all things.

"Well," Yecheskel continued, once again speaking in the voice of God, "if you don't want this, then you won't get the Toyreh."

"So God went to Israel [Yisroel]," then in Yiddish—*Der Abishter hot gegangen tsu di Yidn.*" The translation makes a subtle shift; what in Hebrew was "Israel" in Yiddish has become "Yidn." This affirms the notion that there is an equivalence between the two. And of course, these children and the teacher know that haredim are the real Yidn.

"And *der Abishter hot gefregt di Yidn,* he asked them: 'Yidn, Yisroel, do you want the Toyreh?'" The equivalences are repeated, as if to make them sink in; and the question is the question that every youngster is effectively asked when he comes to a cheder: Do you want the learning, the laws, the way of life that is all subsumed in what Jews call simply "Torah"?

"And they answered . . ."

At last, the celebrated answer with which the Israelites accepted their gift from God, the Torah, which would make them what they are and have become, was recited. This is the climax of the story, both in its plot and the retelling. In this little playground, narrative and performance become one.

But instead of the rebbe reciting this key line by himself, the children spontaneously join him in declaiming the words, some singing at the top of their voices. In a single utterance and moment of high drama, the boys and the rebbe rhythmically affirm and repeat the ancient Jewish acceptance of the Torah: *"Na'aseh ve nishma"* (We shall do and we shall hear). First comes the acceptance of the Torah, and only later an explanation of what its demands are. That is the only right response. Again and again they sing the words *"Na'aseh ve nishma."*

In this little drama, are these little boys playing the role of the Yidn in the story or, by repeating these words, are they accepting their destiny as Jews here and now? At some level they seem to be doing both. And that, after all, is the point of such master stories.

To be sure, on its face, there might seem to be nothing particularly wrong about asking to see a contract's demands before making a commitment. But as the children are learning and relearning, for the truly faithful this is not the way to respond to a gift from the Lord. Only goyim ask questions first. Yidn start on faith with observances and not with questions; first they do, asking questions only after the basic commitments have been made. Later in life, perhaps, these youngsters will assimilate this principle in many other ways. For now, they can simply declare it as part of their understanding of this story.

Having declared their acceptance of their heritage, they now can learn what they have received. "Oh, you want to hear the Toyreh?" the teacher asked in the name of God.

Blurring even further the lines between story and reality, the rest of the story consists of a series of lessons of how to behave as Yidn. Telling them that these events took place during the "Days of *Hagbalah*," the three days preceding the receiving of the Torah, days soon to be upon us again, Yecheskel framed his narrative in terms the children could understand.

"Now, Hashem said, 'Wash nicely and for three days be clean and pure.' "

At that very moment the teacher snapped his rod hard against a bar and called to one of the boys, "Don't touch your [bare] legs!"

The command only seems to be an aside, a demand unrelated to the story. After all, just yesterday I saw him flick the rod at a child who rested his hand on his bare thigh. The child cried, but Yecheskel explained that the parts of the body below the waist are the sites of impurity. He had told them many times that by touching their bare body parts there they befouled themselves, and Jews should remain pure and beautiful. Hands that wandered down there could only come to no good.

These are children then who will thus grow up with a concrete meaning to what purity means; it means, among other things, being careful about how and where they touch themselves and others. Purity is not an abstract concept; it is part of their experiential lexicon. And now during this story, hearing that the Israelites had to remain "pure," the children can dip into that lexicon and pull out an experience to give meaning to the commandment that the teacher has just told them that God gave to the Israelites on the eve of the giving of the Torah.

And just to make sure, at the moment that he repeats the story of the Israelites' purifying themselves, Yecheskel subliminally calls up the notion that they, the children here, also could be impure if they touched their bare legs. These boys know pure and impure, at least in a very instrumental and perhaps rudimentary way. Perhaps this is what some imagine the Israelites were doing in keeping themselves pure: they took care about what they touched.

"And God told the people that they must not touch the Mountain. They should be pure and beautiful."

Just then, into the courtyard came the boys from Yitzhak's class. Singing and dancing, each child's hands on the shoulders of the one in front of him, their earlocks swinging, they marched toward Yecheskel's group. The sight was a choreographed tableau of festivity and celebration. As Yecheskel recited the Ten Commandments, the content of the received law, the children of Israel listened, danced, and sang.

Of course, it would be wrong to suggest that this exquisite timing was carefully planned and perfectly executed. It is not in the nature of the cheder or even this gan to plan such elaborate pageants. Yet there is a kind of internal timing, a sense of when things are right, that informs the action here. For Yitzhak's class too this is the climax of the morning. They also have been sharing an experience that leads to this celebration of the giving of the Torah, which everyone will celebrate in three days' time. That their commemoration coincides with Yecheskel's class is only because all of the children are part of the same world, a world in which the most important reality is the upcoming celebration of a founding event, a celebration that in the haredi world is shaped by a common cultural consciousness.

"Purify our hearts to serve you truly," the boys and Yitzhak sang.

"I am the Lord your God," Yecheskel thundered.

As Yitzhak's class moved off to another corner of the courtyard, Yecheskel asked a series of questions that gave actuality to the first commandment. Striking a tree with his rod, he asked: "Is it permissible to say that a tree is God?" He struck the jungle gym: "That a piece of metal is God?"

Each time the children shouted replies with increasing vigor: "No!" Could one not say that with each shouted reply they were assuming the yoke of these commandments, right here and now, insofar as they comprehended them?

"To serve you truly, to serve you truly," Yitzhak's class sang again and again.

Yecheskel sniffed the air. "Ah," he cried with a show of bliss. "After the Torah was given, there was a sweet smell in the air. No one could quite tell what it was."

Captivating his boys one last time, he had them whiffing the air, as if they too were at Sinai and could smell the sweetness. Seeing some boys look toward me, I did it too. The air here was indeed redolent with the sweet smell of the jasmine trees that shaded the yard.

We had dipped into the midrash without leaving the here and now. Each Jew must see himself as if he too were at Sinai, as if he personally received the Torah—thus have the rabbis explained what is essential to Jewish collective memory. Again, the teacher sniffed the air. And when was this, he asked them?

"Shavuot," they answered in unison. "Shavuot," Yecheskel replied, the day after tomorrow. And with that the story ended.

"This is why," Yecheskel went on, "we decorate our homes with sweet-smelling plants and flowers on Shavuot. This reminds us of the sweet smell after we received the Torah. And we are happy, and sing.

"And what else do we do on Shavuot? Shall I tell you?" There is one more lesson to be learned, one more connection to be made between these stories and the order of life as the boys know it. The boys nod yes; they want more.

On the night of the holy day, Yecheskel tells them, Papa will not go to sleep.

"Oh, he may take a little nap in the afternoon, but in the evening, after dinner, Papa and all of the older boys will go back to *shul* (the synagogue), the yeshiva, the bes medrash."

In the haredi world, that is not altogether unusual, for all paths for men seem to lead at least in the first instance to these places. But on this night their fathers and older brothers will stay and study Torah the whole night. This, Yecheskel explains, is how they will prepare for *kaboles ha-Toyreh* (receiving the Torah). Just as they have prepared themselves for that here in the gan, reviewing this story, so too their fathers will prepare with review of the Torah. School and community experiences are part of a single fabric of experience.

Their teacher knows the order of life at their home not only because he is the "wise teacher" but also because he shares a common culture with his pupils. Without that, the preparation and enculturation that goes on in the school would be meaningless at best and culturally dissonant at worst, frustrating and disorienting those meant to be instructed.

"People who decide to send their children to our schools," the rosh yeshiva explained to me, "know who we are. They send them here because they want what we give, because we are all one community."

Yitzhak's class came back again and together with Yecheskel's they sang " *'Na'aseh v'nishma' omru k'echad,*" the song that repeats and celebrates the unquestioning acceptance of Jewish obligation: " 'We shall do and we shall listen,' they said as one."

Us versus Them

"The distinction between any closed group and outside peoples becomes in terms of religion that between the true believers and the heathen." [20] The theme of us-versus-them, so much a part of haredi consciousness, came up often even in this gan. For Yecheskel, the archetype of "them," the heathens, was often America, a world ruled by base appetite and immorality, the place he had fled for Jerusalem, where his Judaism could be "stronger." To bring it up, however, he had to read it into and out of the sacred canon.

The occasion was a review of the portion of the Torah read in the synagogue that week. Such Bible passages were often the unifying theme for many weeks' stories. The stories were actually haredi glosses on a narrative which itself, like the midrash of Sinai, was an elaboration or interpretation of Scripture. In that, narrated stories like these were part of the oral tradition of commentary that was part of Jewish history. The interpretations might be haredi, but the technique and approach was classically Jewish.

In today's elaboration on the text, Yecheskel began by reviewing the account in Numbers of the twelve spies whom Moses, "our teacher," sent to the Promised Land to scout what was there and report back to the Israelites in the desert. As the Bible tells it, ten of them returned with reports that described the land in bleak terms, an act for which they and the generation that believed them were punished by not being allowed to enter into that land. Only two spies, Caleb and Joshua, who saw the promise of the land and retained a faith in God's promise that He would bring His people into it, offered a different verdict. In return, they, alone of the generation who left Egypt, were allowed to settle in it. That is the basic story. And here is what Yecheskel did with it.

"I'll tell you what," he began, "the spies came to the Land of Israel and saw giants."

He played out the text in a series of dialogues. He became the spies and his pupils the Israelites who listened as he reported, in a variety of voices, what had been seen.

"The giants were so tall that we seemed like ants," said one spy.

"They will swallow us up," said another.

"And how was it you were able to see so much without them swallowing you up," the people asked, and the children wondered.

"Everywhere the spies went," Yecheskel continued, drawing from the midrash, "the giants were burying their dead. Hashem made a miracle; the giants were too busy with their dead to notice the spies.

"And then the spies went home and took with them the dates, grapes, and pomegranates of the land. And they returned to Moses, our teacher.

" 'Hey! *Shalom aleichem*, what's doing?' "

The teacher's dialogue was in the language of everyday life; everyone around here greeted one another this way. This helped collapse the temporal and cultural distance between the narrative text and the life of the listeners; they could imagine the scene.

"Yecheskel continued: " 'Where were you?' "

" 'Were you in Israel?' "

" 'Was it nice?' "

Yecheskel made faces, scrunching up his features as if to say, "Well, yes, it was nice, but . . ." He shrugged his shoulders and tilted his head to the side.

"They took out the fruits. Wow, they were like bombs!

" 'Look how big these grapes are! Like a house! Look at these big pomegranates!' The spies displayed the fruits of their excursion to everyone; the harvest was impressive. But that was not what overwhelmed the spies.

" 'But look, there are people over there with such big mouths to eat these things that with one gulp they could swallow you as well. They are such huge people. Aren't you afraid to go there?' "

One boy particularly caught up in the story called out, "No!" This was not simply the cry of a believer; it was the outcry of the heroic Israeli. This boy was in today's Israel, no longer afraid of giants, ready to live in the Promised Land in spite of all the risks. Although they do not serve in the army and despite the nominal scorn they have for the Zionist army, many haredim—perhaps including this boy—have absorbed the Israeli confidence that their little nation is strong enough to conquer giants. "We are not afraid," says another next to him. They are no longer the cowering Jews of the exile, haredi ideology notwithstanding.

Smiling at the boys' response and momentarily diverted from the flow of his tale, Yecheskel looked at them and said: "Wait, no, they did not answer that. *Halevai* [would] they had said no. Instead, they said [and he spoke now in Yiddish, so that the speakers sounded like locals], 'Moses, our teacher, we told you to send the spies; now look what they tell us.'

"And all the people began to cry."

"Why?" asked a child.

"Because they were afraid of the big people." Saying this in Yiddish, he made it sound almost as if he were speaking about fears that the children themselves might have about people outside their own neighborhood—the police, the Zionists, the big people out there.

"But Caleb and Joshua said, 'Sh! What are you saying? Be quiet! You will see, we can certainly go there! *Hashem* will help us get there in peace!' "

In Yecheskel's version of the story, success in conquering the land comes through God's efforts and not man's. And it comes with faith and "peace."

"But the people began to cry and they wanted to stone Caleb and Joshua. And do you know what night that was?' "

A boy called out the answer: "Tisha b'Av." This is the Ninth of Av, a day anchored to sadness and Jewish suffering. In the tradition, this day has become the repository for all that is evil in Jewish history. And the first of its evils was this. Either the boy knows the story or else he is already so attuned to the meaning Tisha b'Av has for Yidn that he knows it must be the day.

"That's right."

"They were all sitting low on the ground," a boy added in Yiddish, recalling the way Jews traditionally sit in mourning on this day of the Temple's destruction. He had gone right into the present, describing the manner in which Tisha b'Av is now commemorated.

Answering him in Yiddish, Yecheskel said, "In those days they were not yet sitting low on the ground because there had not yet been a Holy Temple."

The children's conception of time and history is of course still not developed. Yet what they have here—precisely in their mix of time and history—is the basic structure of the haredi collective memory that blends together all the tragedies of Jewish life and thus sees Jewish life as an endless repetition of the same themes.

Yecheskel corrected their history even as he confirmed the ahistorical view: "Seeing them cry, *Hashem* decreed that this would be a night of weeping for generations—*lo aleinu* [may we be spared]—a time of crying until the Messiah will come. Year after year we cry. And those who were spying in the Land of Israel—except for Caleb and Joshua, who didn't say *lashon hara* [slander] about the land of Israel—do you know what happened to them?"

"I know," says one boy. "Their tongue went out and on their tongue there were ants." Yecheskel concluded: "And these ants wounded them and they died, because they spoke lashon hara." [21]

Wrote the Hafetz Hayim, whose concern with slander was one of the major themes of his thought, "If a person hears that his little son or daughter is uttering lashon hara, he is commanded to rebuke them and separate them from it." What is true for the parents is likewise an obligation for the teachers, for otherwise the young "will become used to it," and then "it will be difficult to break them of the habit." [22]

"About whom did they say this lashon hara?" the teacher asked.

"About the Land of Israel!" The children cried out.

"And is one allowed to speak badly of the Land of Israel?"

"No!" a few children replied.

Yecheskel repeated the question louder. More children shouted, "*No!*"

The teacher's voice and the repetition signal that this is an important point. This is the Land of Israel, the Holy Land, the Promised Land, the place that Yecheskel has returned to from America, that other, counterfeit Land of Promise. This is the place he has sacrificed for, the place where people become stronger, more haredi, in their Judaism.

And now Yecheskel added a little question, as if to express all he knows and give these little boys a bit more of a haredi orientation: "About America is it permitted to speak lashon hara?"

The boys seemed momentarily confused—where did this question come from? One or two answered no as they did before. Yecheskel chuckled.

"About America?!" he repeated, incredulously. Quickly, a few of

Above: Little boys in kindergarten, or gan. (Courtesy of Moshe Kahan)
Below: In the playground of the kindergarten.

Above: Studying Talmud in the primary school. (Courtesy of Moshe Kahan)

Below: Recess at the yeshiva: teachers confer as the students play.

Yeshiva students standing under a redrawn globe.

Above: Posters of warning and instruction are plastered on walls of the neighborhood. Right: Children in Purim costumes in Mea Shearim. Below: Purchasing lulavim (palm branches) for the holiday of Sukkot.

Above: Three generations celebrate at the Belzer bar mitzvah. (Courtesy of Belz Archives, Jerusalem)

Below: The festival of Lag b'Omer is celebrated with dancing outside the tomb of Shimon bar Yochai.

Left: Using a quill on parchment, a scribe completes a Torah scroll.

Right: A Lithuanian-style kollel—
an academy of Torah learning for adult (married) men. Below: Young men reviewing Talmud in the yeshiva.

Above: At the funeral of Rabbi Weiss, women gather behind the men in the procession to hear the eulogy. Right: A father gives his three-year-old son his first haircut. (Photograph by Menachem Friedman) Below: The Belzer rebbe lights the Chanukah candles. (Courtesy of Belz Archives, Jerusalem)

Above: Hasidim at the Western Wall in Sabbath shtreimels (*fur-trimmed hats*).

Below: A hasid in the courtyard of the Hungarian Houses, a haredi neighborhood.

the boys picked up the message; America is that evil empire, and one can speak evil about it. "Yes, yes!" they said.

But just to make sure they understand the boundaries of the antagonism, a little boy added: "But about B'nai B'rak it is forbidden to speak lashon hara."

B'nai B'rak, that other capital of haredi life in Israel, the sister city that is at the other end of the direct taxi link from their neighborhood, where so many of the important yeshivas are, where the streets are filled with black and white counterparts of their Jerusalem, cannot be anything but part of the holy Promised Land. B'nai B'rak is haredi and the haredi one does not slander.

Yecheskel affirmed the youngster's conclusion with a smile: "Yes, about B'nai B'rak it is forbidden."

And now another boy, jumping on the bandwagon, continued: "And about Jerusalem, which is the best of all places, we can say nothing bad."

The children have a very clear theologically and ideologically framed geography. Some places are good and one must speak only well of them—these are holy places where people are holy—Jerusalem and B'nai B'rak—but of other places like America where iniquity rules there is no problem in speaking ill of them and no punishment for such actions. After all, don't their elders constantly speak ill of the nonharedi precincts and must it not be with the sanction of the Torah and the sages—the melamed being the first of these—so it must be alright. The teacher here at this early age already confirms something they have already apparently absorbed: We know who is us and who is them. We know who are blessed and of whom we may speak ill.

Then and Now: Connecting with the Jewish Past and Relating to God

In a community that gives the highest value to yesterday and sees tradition as the great teacher, the need to repeatedly demonstrate that there is nothing so ancient and archaic in the Jewish past that it does not have its place in the Jewish present is constant. I call this process "traditioning."[23] It means never seeing the past as beyond retrieval but rather experiencing it as an ongoing reverberation in the present.

In a sense, traditioning was embedded in everything the children learned about the past, and especially about the Bible. For them there really was no history, for history sees the past as discrete but ultimately not recoverable, while the haredim were always dipping into the past as if it were still present. To them the Bible was not just an account of the dawn of Israelite peoplehood but a code book for Jewish behavior. The lives of its heroes were not simply the stuff of stories but archetypes for contemporary behavior. Similarly, the rabbis were not simply ancient lawmakers, figures of Jewish history; they were living mentors for contemporary existence. The stories and lessons teachers repeated were thus not just moral tales or archaic codes; they were the necessary ingredients of recipe knowledge, the information needed for everyday life as a Jew. In short, there was nothing so old that it was meaningless today. As if to hammer this home, haredim often stressed precisely those elements of Jewish life that seemed to be most out of tune with the times. They reveled in anachronism, asserting its timeliness. This was of course the polar opposite of the modern attitude that valued novelty above all.

In the gan, the teachers seemed determined to give special attention to those sorts of matters that might to others seem beyond contemporary relevance. Two examples will suffice.

One came in Yitzhak's lesson on the matter of tithing and the other in his review of the laws of the Nazarite. Both seemed at first blush to be concerns that were part of another time and another place. But Yitzhak and the boys would bring them into the present.

"What is ma'aser?" Yitzhak began by asking one morning. He rushed about the room waving his rod: "And to whom do we give it?"

The children shouted the answers that almost all of them seemed to know. Tithes are given to the priest, the Levite, and the poor. Did this mean that these children knew about tithing in all its complexity? Of course not. They knew about tithing the way children might know that a sales tax was collected when they bought something in the store. It was the stuff of everyday knowledge in a world where the everyday included codes of the past.

The reference to tithing (ma'aser) was from the Bible portion of that week, but Yitzhak described it as part of contemporary Jewish life. He pointed to a drawing on the wall of a produce market like the one in the neighborhood outside the schoolroom. In the picture the boys could see a greengrocer handing over some fruits and vegetables to a bearded haredi. "He's collecting ma'aser," Yitzhak explained. To the boys who passed such vegetable stalls on their way to or from school, the scene was familiar. In many stores and stalls they could see signs that said TITHES HAVE BEEN TAKEN. They had learned to buy only from a grocer who gave ma'aser.

In the mornings many boys had probably seen the legion of men and yeshiva boys who made the rounds of synagogues, gathering coins and charity from worshipers. That too was a kind of tithing. Perhaps some of them were even the beneficiaries of tithes.

But Yitzhak was not only interested in giving them a chance to exhibit their knowledge of tithing. He wanted them to build this knowledge into a theodicy. He wanted it to be connected to their understanding of how the world worked, an understanding that placed a relationship to God at its core.

"*Kinderlach* [children]," Yitzhak said, addressing them in Yiddish, "do you know what Hashem promised us if we give tithes?

"Hashem promised us that if we have crops that are scanty or grapes that are not too sweet, then if we give tithes, we shall have far more crops and sweeter grapes. And then we will be able to succeed in selling our produce in the market.

"But if, *chas v'shalom* [Heaven forbid], a person does not tithe, nothing will remain for him of his crops."

In the world that the teacher constructed for his students, tithing was a reflection of a fixed moral order, an acknowledgment of a necessary submission to divine will and commandment. It helped set the moral compass. The relationship with God was not abstract; observance brought reward and sins retribution. This simple message had to be stamped into the children's consciousness. Like Yecheskel, Yitzhak used narrative to drive his points home. "I'll tell you a story that is written in the midrash," he continued. "Once there was a man—I don't know what his name was," Yitzhak began.

That the man had a name was important; for children, a *"ma'aseh she-haya,"* a story that really happened (and that is what children like to demand of tales), requires characters who have real names. Yet to give them names is also to particularize the events. Yitzhak knew this too. He found a solution, which he used often. Saying the man had a name signaled the verity of the story, while not knowing what it was allowed the same story to provide a universal message, beyond the specific man whose name need not be known. "Once there was a man —I don't know what his name was."

What was, however, important to know was that "this man was a zaddik," a righteous Jew, and so his actions were a lesson to all of us. "He had a small field." As a zaddik, the first thing he always did was to "take off the tree a tithe that he would send to the priest" and then the "tithe to the poor of Jerusalem. And God blessed him so that the next year the field gave forth even more fruit."

All was right with the world; here was a universe in good moral order, where virtue is rewarded: *zaddik v'tov lo,* the righteous are blessed for their good deeds. The rewards for observing the command-

ments are prompt. This is a God the young can understand. He is
unambiguously just.

"So the man continued all his life to give ma'aser." Always scrupulous about tithing, he found his yield growing from year to year.

"And all his children ate from this harvest, and then they sold the
extra fruit in the market, so that this man and his family became very
rich.

"But one day the papa died."

A few of the boys smacked their faces, mimicking adult reactions
they had seen to news of misfortune. "*Oy vey,*" said one. "What
happened?" asked another. If all was right with the world, how could
this tragedy of death occur? Why was the zaddik punished by death?

"He was very old and went up in the heavens to Eden," Yitzhak
explained. Death was not always a punishment; it was an extension of
the good man's life, a time of reward for virtue, an everlasting life in
the world to come. Now, as on many occasions, the teacher helped his
students discover "the metaphysical environment" of "other-worldly
forces and unexplained natural and supernatural phenomena."[24] Yitzhak continued.

"After their father died, his children took over the field and saw to
it that everything would grow. They harvested all the fruit from the
trees. And then do you know what they said?" Yitzhak paused. "They
said, 'Why should we give ten portions to the priest? We'll give just
eight.' " The children are reminded how much a tithe is.

The decision to skimp on the tithe was a fateful error. If the children in the gan understand this, it is because their moral compass has
been properly set; but the greedy children of the zaddik, clouded in
their moral vision, could not see the truth. That would prove to be
their undoing.

"So the next year there was a smaller harvest, and do you know
what? When the harvest was smaller, these children wanted to give
even less because they thought, 'We have less for ourselves this year
so we can give away even less.' They gave even less to the priest and
the poor."

So it went—each year less was given and a smaller bounty received.
The children in the story foolishly thought the tithe was dependent on
their wealth; they did not see that it was really the tithing, the observance of God's commandments, that accounted for their wealth. They
did not understand where everything begins. Their punishment was
direct and just; they became poor. Yitzhak concluded with the moral
of the story: "So it is beneficial to observe and carry out all the laws of
tithing." It was so then, and it remains so today. The boys nodded
solemnly.

To Be a Child of God

If one of the lessons of this story was that laws have their reasons and that nothing in Jewish tradition is out of date for those who would be erlicher yidn, Yitzhak's class on the Nazarite expressed this even more. Nazarites, always an exceptional category of people, even in biblical times, are those who take upon themselves additional strictures and religious obligations beyond those demanded by the letter of the religious law. In these days they are a rarity—some might argue an impossibility. To integrate the matter of the Nazarite into the child's world is thus a challenge of the highest order, for it demonstrates how something apparently most archaic is not. If even the Nazarite can be part of life, then in a sense potentially no element of the tradition is out of reach or irrelevant.

Yitzhak reviewed the laws, showing the children that God concerns Himself with even the smallest details—but this sort of concern was something they already learned to take for granted. Even at this early age they could see that their lives—saturated with religious ritual— were preoccupied with detail. The challenge was to make the specific details of the Nazarite fit into this life experience.

In terms comprehensible to his pupils, Yitzhak introduced the concept of the Nazarite by explaining that such a person is someone who wants to be a "child of God [yeled shel hashem]." This provided a first important link; the Nazarite was also a "child," in some respects like them, for they too are children. Yitzhak said nothing about the rarity of Nazarites nor did he emphasize the fact that they are not part of contemporary Jewish life. On the contrary, much of what he described —at least at the outset—could easily sound like someone likely to be found in the neighborhood; haredim too thought of themselves as having a special relationship to God and were willing to fulfill religious obligations beyond those demanded by the letter of religious law.

Now came the details. "The Nazarite may not cut his hair, and he may not even comb it, for if he does, one strand may be pulled out by accident, and he has taken an oath not to cut his hair."

This is of no small interest to these children. Hair plays an important role in their lives. It serves in a very real way to identify and distinguish haredim from others in their environment. Not only do their fathers and all adult males around them have beards and earlocks that frame their faces, but their mothers have their hair covered— either with a kerchief or with a wig. More important still, many have just had or know someone who has had their first haircut on Lag b'Omer following their third birthday. If the Nazarite is a child of God by virtue of his unshorn hair, perhaps they were as well. Certainly, a great deal was made of that first traumatic haircut. And even those who have had their heads clipped still have long unshorn earlocks that they are learning to twirl, curl, and groom. So while they are not Nazarites, this obscure character about whom they are hearing for the first time in their short lives is after all not so distant as he might seem at first.

"Well," Yitzhak continues, "the Nazarite is forbidden to comb his hair, to make his earlocks nice." The teacher makes the connection they might only have been imagining. He runs his fingers along his scrawny earlocks as he talks.

Now there is nothing in the text about Nazarites having earlocks. But in the world that Yitzhak conjures up for his pupils, there can be no question that they surely have them. All those venerated from the Jewish past are presented in the image of the haredi of today.

Removing his glasses and mussing up his hair to depict what he describes, Yitzhak continues: "The Nazarite's hair becomes wild."

The children giggle and few murmur, *"Iksa"* (Phooey).

"And the Nazarite is prohibited from drinking wine—so on what will he make Kiddush?" As the boys know from their experience, Kiddush, the sanctification and blessing over wine, is an essential of all Sabbath and holy day meals. Yitzhak understands that his pupils know this; he can take this basic cultural and ritual competence as a given. Like them, a Nazarite is an observant Jew, so certainly he, like them, also must recite Kiddush. But he has a religious problem: Kiddush is recited over wine, and he may not drink wine. What happens? This is a riddle—to be sure, one that only makes sense to someone who shares this basic knowledge—that holds Yitzhak's listeners and captures their attention.

Legal riddles like this one will be part of these boys' pattern of learning throughout their intellectual lives. Whether the question is how a Nazarite can make Kiddush or whether the prophet Elijah's appeal to God to heal a dead boy was a vain and therefore improper prayer, these Jews will be exploring such conundrums as they make their way into the society of scholars, the only legitimate avenue of intellectual life ahead of them. Here in kindergarten, under their rebbe's guidance, they hear their first such riddles.

Already, they know some answers are to be found on another plane of logic, a plane that is theologic. "He's the child of Hashem," one boy guesses and therefore, as God's ward, has different obligations. "Maybe he doesn't have to say Kiddush," another boy speculates. But these are not the answers.

"No," Yitzhak explains, "he has to make Kiddush on challahs." Instead of making the benediction over wine, he will make it over loaves. Even these youngsters know that at every Kiddush over wine there are also loaves. They have seen this as long as they remember. Now they learn about the connection. What was part of an inchoate and not altogether coherent order, is integrated correctly and becomes part of the syntax of Jewish experience, where everything seems to fit together in a coherent whole. The answer to this riddle provides them with a fact that they can put into place: Kiddush is not just wine; it can be loaves as well—and that is why the loaves are there during the recitation.

Yitzhak takes this opportunity to give the children time to show they know what the different blessings are on wine and bread. This allows them to hear themselves once again make the blessings that they and the Nazarite would recite at Kiddush time. It brings the moment to life. It reminds them of what they do in fact already know and also reinforces their knowledge of the details around which their lives will revolve. Of course, not every child will put this fact into place; many will miss it. But in time, practices, rules, theologies, texts, and life will progressively fall into place.

In his account Yitzhak listed the various grape-related foods the Nazarite may not eat: grapes, grape juice, raisins. Paying special attention to what passes one's lips is something the boys have also already learned to do. They know that meat and dairy foods may not be mixed; they know to eat fruits from which tithes have been taken; they know that what some permit to be eaten, others prohibit. The situation of the Nazarite is thus not qualitatively different from their own; only the details are different.

Now Yitzhak asked the children to repeat aloud after him the two prohibitions: "The Nazarite must not cut or comb his hair; the Nazarite may not eat anything having to do with grapes." Echoing is a common pedagogic device in the haredi schools. Oral traditions of learning are maintained.

"And you know what else? Should I tell you what else?"

"Yes, tell us, tell us," some of the children said while others nodded.

"So, I'll tell you something else. The Nazarite must not go, chas v'shalom, to a *levia* [funeral], or he will be not kosher. And he is not allowed to be not kosher."

To toddlers who know nothing of funerals, this statement would be perhaps most obscure and meaningless. But the haredi child has referents for it. The cars coming through the neighborhood with loudspeakers announcing a death and funeral, the community gatherings for such events, and even the pilgrimages to the tombs of saintly rabbis are part of haredi life that even the very young witness. As if to signal this to be the case, one boy announces: "I know that a *cohen* [member of a priestly family] is not supposed to go to a funeral." This extraordinary piece of legal knowledge—ritually related to the case of the Nazarite—is absolutely unimaginable in the intellectual repertoire of most kindergarteners, but among haredim knowing this is no more exceptional than an American youngster knowing that the Red Sox play in Boston.

"And a goy cannot go to a funeral," another boy called out.

"No, no," Yitzhak said, "a goy can never go with us to a funeral."

Now the teacher does not quite explain the reasoning for this but the idea that a Gentile is excluded from such an event is not puzzling. Different cultures have different sets of facts that are accepted on their face. Among the haredim, rules such as these are obvious and taken for granted. A goy is a being of another order. The next words Yitzhak spoke implied as much: "Regular people may go to funerals," he explained. "But a Nazarite may not, because he is a child of God." This also raises no objections from the children. "He may not go to a funeral; he must stand far, far, far away."

Again Yitzhak reviewed the lesson, asking the children along with him to adumbrate with their fingers the prohibitions that mark the Nazarite's existence. By now the boys were no longer passive listeners; they were shouting the answers out ahead of him. One child enthusiastically began: "He is forbidden to cut his hair." Everyone repeated this. They ran through the other details in the same way.

"And he does this all?" asked Yitzhak.

"Because he is a child of God," they all answered as one. *To be a child of God is to be marked by restrictions.* This they shall learn again and again.

"And he goes about with long hair and others ask him, 'Why do you go about with such wild hair?'" Yitzhak took on various voices, acting out the imaginary dialogue. The lesson became a narrative.

" 'Curl your earlocks,' people say to the Nazarite. But he does not even curl them, because . . ."

". . . because he's a Nazarite of Hashem," a child breaks in. He has learned the expression. Yitzhak wanted more detail.

"Because if he curls or combs his hair and even a single hair falls, he will be doing something forbidden and he'll have to give up being a Nazarite, Heaven forbid, and that will be a big mess."

The breach of a rule is, "Heaven forbid," something that would become "a big mess." What does this mean? For all people the breach of norm is associated with anxiety about the consequences. The more mysterious the consequences, the less likely are we to risk the breach. Intuitively, perhaps, Yitzhak played this out. There was no need to tell the boys what would happen to the Nazarite who breaks the rules. Suffice it to say, there will be a big mess. And what of us, the boys might think, what if we too break the rules? A big mess.

"And what happens when he ends his time of being a Nazarite?"

So there is an end to being a Nazarite—just as there was an end to having one's hair uncut, just as there is an end to everything.

A young boy with a newly shorn head calls out an answer: "He makes a Kiddush!" When his hair was cut, his family celebrated by lifting a glass and making Kiddush. Wasn't that what they did on Lag b'Omer at Meron? The child's answer integrates this story into his world of experience. Surely for this child of Hashem the same must happen.

"No, no, he doesn't make Kiddush," the teacher replies, winking at me. "This is not a wedding."

And now, speaking in the present tense, he tells what does happen. "He goes to the tent of meeting in the Holy Temple [but of course there is no such place these days], and he brings with him a little pigeon, a little sheep, and a little goat."

The Nazarite will offer a sacrifice. The theology here is too complex for a child to integrate, and so Yitzhak presented only its instrumental details. People used to bring sacrifices to the Temple. We no longer do. This is a routine fact, completely integrated into the haredi conception of the world. Even at this age, it is beyond questioning.

But Yitzhak helped them glide by these details. "You want to know what he does with his hair, right? He also brings a basket of matzahs and comes to the priest. And he says to the priest, 'I'm finished being a Nazarite. I said I would be one for a month and now the month is over; I said I'd do it for a year and now the year is over.' So the priest takes all these animals"—the teacher listed them but missed one: the goat, as one of the children reminded him—"and then he takes a thigh."

"I like the thigh; I always eat it," one boy yelled with enthusiasm. "I like the leg too."

"So they cook the thigh; they put it on a fire, and they cook this as a sacrifice.

"And then right there by the fire, he shaves all his hair off, even here"—Yitzhak pointed to the top of his head. "And do you know where he puts it? Under the sacrifice and burns it there, all those wild hairs. Afterward the priest takes the sacrifice, the thigh, and the basket of matzahs and he lifts them." The teacher lifted his hands up and some of the children mimicked him, as if reenacting the scene.

"Who lifts it?"

"The priest," some of the children answer. They have kept up with the story.

"This is a *tenufa* [wave offering] before Hashem," the teacher concludes. "And he's no longer a Nazarite and he can . . ."

". . . cut his hair," one of the boys broke in.

"And he can . . ." Yitzhak continued.

". . . eat grapes." This time several boys offered the answer.

"And he can . . ."

". . . comb his earlocks nicely."

"And he can make Kiddush . . ."

". . . on wine."

In the melody of its rising and falling cadences and the rhythm of replies and responses, this was a chanted drama come vividly to life, a performance not only of what the children had learned but of an order of existence they had assimilated. At last, it ended with a litany of all the blessings the Nazarite would make. The children said them all. Now both children and teacher began to sing together. It was a familiar Jewish song from Scripture: "I will bring you blessings overflowing." Again and again they repeated the last words as their teacher led them: "Blessings overflowing, overflowing, overflowing," as if this were a benediction they offered themselves, a blessing for having held on to the past by making it part of their present. It was a play filled with all the passion they could muster.

How different this story and its implications were from what I might find in kindergartens elsewhere. How exquisite the drama. This dilapidated three-room school was not the sort of place I had expected to see dramas of such a high order. But here they were: some of the most profound passions of haredi Judaism I had yet seen, played out as little haredim were being fashioned. "Passion and passion in its profoundest, is not a thing demanding a palatial stage whereon to play its part," Herman Melville once wrote.[25] No better proof could I find than in the dramas I found played out in this school for little haredim. I was so deeply impressed with what I had seen in these elementary forms of the haredi life that I became enormously curious about what I might find in the higher grades and in the yeshiva itself.

13

Primary School

"Every child, school, group, aims at a common goal: to raise a generation that will continue, that will be one more link in the chain of generations of the original Judaism, as it was—something closer to what was," said a Belzer hasid to me once. This was an expression of what Margaret Mead once called "postfigurative culture." Postfigurative culture, as she explained, was a way of life in which the present was made to appear as part of an "unchanging continuity" with the past.[1] Haredi society was very much a postfigurative culture. In some ways the primary school was a key instrument in this process.

The trip from the gan to the primary school was a walk of a few minutes. On a quiet street, barely wide enough for two cars to pass each other, in a house faced with rough-cut Jerusalem stone, its golden blocks covering a drab interior, I found grades one through five. There was no sign on the building, which was really little more than two stories of rooms, a long veranda, and a courtyard. Only the sound of the chanting voices of the boys helped me find it on my first visit. Opening the closed but unlocked iron gate, I climbed the stairs to the upper floor and, walking along the veranda, peeked hesitantly through the partially open doors to see which room I might go into first. I knew that word of my arrival had preceded me so that the teacher would know who this obvious stranger coming into his classroom was, but slipping past the half-open door, I felt all the reticence of a newcomer to school coupled with the discomfiture of an interloper. Nevertheless —and perhaps this is what my anthropological discipline had done for me—I endured these qualms and quietly sat down to watch. I was greeted with sidelong glances, nods, children pinching and signaling each other to look at the stranger, and a hand gesture by the teacher motioning me to sit down.

Books and Jews

Again, days stretched into weeks as I spent time in the various classrooms. Gradually, a sense of the primary school took shape in my mind. If the gan had been a place of songs and stories, the yeshiva— into whose first tier I had now entered—was a place where everything went on over, around, and through the pages of an open book. Fastening the boys to the books and in turn to the world inside the texts in them, and finally to the tradition that tied text to peoplehood and Jewish ways and values became the primary concern here.

In the youngest grades this meant harnessing the boys' attention, still very much unbridled and childishly untamed, and nurturing their sense of restraint. Practically, it meant getting them to know all the letters of the alphabet and how to read the Bible and other sacred volumes, to be comfortable for long hours over an open book that had no pictures, and then making them believe that the book and the tradition that stood behind it were the best places to express and preserve themselves.

This is perhaps what is embedded in a comment by one of the Lubavitcher rebbes, Yitzhak Yosef Schneerson (1880–1950), which articulates the relationship between the book and the essentials of faith: "Fortification through the study of the pure Torah routs and breaks all obstacles and impediments, and the crux [of this] is teaching tinokos shel bais rabban . . . who must know the shape of each letter and its sound, which was given at Sinai, and [who] thereby will be fortified and implanted with an internal essence that is [none other than] the essence of Judaism, so that their heart will be loyal to God and his Torah forever." [2]

Over the course of their lives, books would not only become objects of veneration and study, they would also become a cultural and moral preserve. In the years ahead it would be over books that they would spend time with their peers, the *chavruse,* or learning partners. When they passed through the outside world, while sitting on a public bus or when waiting for customers in a shop, the book would serve as an "involvement shield," a barrier against the temptations and invasions of a foreign culture.[3] The book would be a guide to, and an instrument of, piety. Hymnals, prayer books, Psalters, Bibles, volumes of the Talmud, and other sacred books were always at or in hand.

By itself, literacy has no value. Haredim do not learn to read so that they can explore the beauty of writing or revel in the pleasure house of literature. For these Yidn, literacy is an expression of, and a medium for, Jewish fidelity, a means of Jewish learning, a vehicle for plumbing texts and getting at the essence of what God has revealed in the Torah, a ticket for entry into the house of study. It is a matter of faith. "The letters of the Torah are the names of God."[4]

Learning about the letters begins early. According to rabbinic tradition, a five-year-old must be taught to read. For many haredim, learning the sounds of letters may come even earlier. But only in the first grade can reading begin in earnest for, as Talmud puts it, and as the haredim who go by the book believe, "whoever tries to teach a youngster below the age of six to read Torah, runs after him but can never reach him."[5]

From the start, reading—like prayer—is oral recitation. One does not begin reading sacred texts only with the eyes—at least not at first. Nor does one read alone. At the outset it is rather a kind of group chant. The text is externalized rather than internalized. Perhaps this sounds like rote learning—and to an extent it is. But as I listened to these chants day after day, I sensed there was something else at stake here, something social. The child who could not read the letters or whose attention wandered was carried by those who could and remained focused on the page. A child found his voice first in the chorus of others. Even before they realized it, the way they learned to read made them dependent upon and part of a *group* experience. It might begin as echoing and joining in with others, but later it could become something one could do alone. Yet even then the echoes of the group, though silent, forever reverberated in the mind's ear. And even solitary reading, particularly of sacred texts, which were the only books studied with any serious attention in the haredi school, was commonly intoned, as I would see even more dramatically in the yeshiva later. The solitary voice was a chorus of one rather than a solo.

While haredim teach their children to read words at about five or six years, by about age seven, they begin them on Bible texts. Along with prayer, this confirms reading as a sacred act, freighted with all sorts of symbolic meaning. The portion of the Bible they read first is not Genesis. Although by virtue of their review of each week's synagogue Torah reading and stories their rebbe told them in kindergarten, the youngsters—as I had just seen—already knew the major narratives and characters of the entire Bible; when they began to review the text, it was at Leviticus, what is called *Torat Kohanim*, the priestly teachings and laws having to do with sacrifices and tributes brought as sin offerings.

While there are a variety of explanations that have been given to this traditional practice, including the one that occurred to me in the lesson about the Nazarites, one cited in the midrash is frequently offered in haredi circles. "Why do we begin to teach the young Torat Kohanim and not Genesis? As the young signify purity, so do the sacrifices signify purity; thus the pure come and deal in matters of purity."[6] The connection is metaphoric, coupling mystical notions of childhood purity with the purity that is supposed to emerge out of the bringing of the sacrificial lamb.

Religious purity is a theme that underlies haredi education. While at one time purity may have had to do only with matters of ritual, today it has a broadened meaning that connotes shelter from the "abominations and impurities" of contemporary nonharedi culture. Parent-teacher organizations here were "committees for the purity of our camp."

Undoubtedly, the choice of Leviticus and its concerns with matters of purity is not only symbolic; there is also an element of intellectual discipline involved here as well. To review the complex regulations of sacrifices and priestly codes, to know what is pure and what defiled, requires a capacity to memorize and to think logically, for in the final analysis these laws, though based on certain enigmatic values, are relatively systematic.

Finally, there is another reason to begin with Leviticus. The stories in Genesis, when examined carefully as texts, are filled with awkward ambiguities, breaches of norm, and revolutionary models who are, ironically, not always appropriate for the young haredi who is in school to learn how to be restrained by the demands of his culture. Genesis is, after all, replete with accounts of intermarriage, incest, rebellion, murder, theft, family rivalries, unexplained tests of character, and a host of other matters that only the person who is already firmly rooted in his faith and way of life dares examine closely. As oral tales, these stories can be "translated and improved." But on a printed page they are far more striking. Young minds are better structured by the concreteness of Leviticus, however dull much of its narrative may be.

After the Bible comes the study of Mishna, the core text of the Talmud. Only later, in the upper grades, do the boys begin to study the more complex and intricate logic of the Gemara, the talmudic elaborations of the Mishnah. But by then, they take for granted the notion that the study of books is their life. And at least for the scholars among them, enthusiasm comes from getting into ever-more-recondite texts and finding their meanings and significance. And perhaps most importantly they have been stamped with values and perspectives that allow them to overlook everything deviant. By then they have entered the domains of postfigurative culture.

Into the Classroom

"When one is faced with a society which is still alive and faithful to its traditions, the impact is so powerful that one is quite taken aback," Lévi-Strauss writes upon his encounter with the Bororo, deep in the Brazilian jungle.[7] For me, walking through the door and then watching from a corner as the man I will call Reb Moishe Palefsky took his fourth-grade class through its lessons engendered many of the same feelings. Even more than what I had witnessed in the gan, this room seemed to be the incarnation of the east European Jewish past I had seen only in photographs. At first, it was easy to forget that I was in Jerusalem in the late 1980s and to imagine that I was sitting in a Polish or Lithuanian cheder. The walls were quite bare, except for a poster in the rear that listed the biblical judges of Israel and the length of their reign. No more pretty pictures as in the kindergarten. The only review here was from the pages of a book. Thirty-five boys sat around worn tables on long benches that filled and framed the room. They leaned against each other. At the front center was the teacher and his large table. On each table there were open books side by side. Some boys held their fingers in them to mark a spot, others draped their arms across them. And the language of instruction was Yiddish.

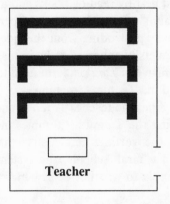

Teacher

This configuration was far from random. It was a smaller version of the arrangement in the main study hall of the yeshiva: long tables and benches facing a smaller teacher's table. In the structure of its space, fourth grade was a prefiguration of the years ahead. If they learned to be at home in this environment, they would feel familiar in a yeshiva ambience later on.

Along the back wall, piled on the corner of a shelf, were the boys' satchels, filled with books. On another nearby shelf on the right wall were prayer books, their bindings worn, their ragged pages disintegrating from continuing use. They had titles such as *The Old Vilna Prayer Book, The New Prayer Book for All Lips,* or *The New All-Inclusive Prayer Book.* Whatever else one could say about all these editions was that, old, new, or all-inclusive, the prayers in them were all the same and none of them contained benedictions for the State of Israel or its defense forces such as might be found in prayer books in nonharedi religious schools. Such invocations on behalf of the welfare of the secular Zionist state and all it symbolized had no place in a haredi school. They might bless the queen of England, the United States government, or other foreign powers, as they sometimes did in the exile—that, after all, was necessary if Jews wanted to remain in the good graces of Gentile protectorates. But to pray for the welfare of the Jewish heretics who set up the secular and sinful Israeli way of life was unnecessary—or so the established thinking in haredi circles went. Of course, the fact that they felt sufficiently secure here not to *have* to insert prayers for the well-being and support of the State of Israel suggested that they felt certain their fellow Jews—no matter how sacrilegious—would suffer their presence, even if, as Yisrael Eichler of the Belz believed, they did so grudgingly.

Along a third wall of the classroom was a line of dirty windows that looked out on the nondescript stone courtyard. These schools did not need views of Jerusalem beyond the courtyard; the world they wanted to see was visualized best by reading books and imagining other times.

A tall, rather gaunt man with a salt-and-pepper beard and wiry, tightly curled earlocks protruding from the side of his head like tiny antennae, Moishe Palefsky appeared to be in his sixties. He described himself as a Lithuanian *ben Torah,* a term used to distinguish haredim who were not hasidim. To him, teaching was an awesome religious responsibility: "Anyone who teaches Torah to one who is not worthy," he explained, quoting the Talmud, "tumbles into hell."[8] For eleven years he had taught the worthies here. Before that, for many years, he taught at the Torah v'Yirah schools, the system associated with the Neturei Karta. In reply to whether he saw many differences between this school and the other, which I presumed to be far more extreme in its haredi character, he scratched his head through his large black skullcap, tilted it slightly, and, pulling on his beard, replied that there was only one difference he could think of: the color of the clothes the boys wore. At the Torah v'Yirah the dominant colors were black trousers and white shirts, whereas here the boys put on all sorts of colors. Did brighter colors reflect less piety, I asked? Perhaps, he answered, it might be a sign, but he was not certain how significant it was. At this age—seven to nine years old—the differences were nearly imperceptible.

Palefsky was a teacher caught up in his material more than in his students. More than he loved teaching, he loved learning. In action he reminded me at times of a concert pianist who plays mostly for himself and forgets all about the audience. For the already inspired in the audience, nothing is so engrossing, but for those not yet fully initiated, such a teacher or performer remains a distant presence. Perhaps he might have been better appreciated in a higher grade.

Palefsky seemed to know all the boys by name. At first, I thought he had the attention of only a minimum of them and addressed himself only to those, but he always surprised me (and them) when he turned to those who appeared inattentive and asked them a question. With gentle questions or an occasional pinch or slap, he managed to bring them toward the text from their orbits somewhere in outer space. He did manage to absorb a number of boys in his own enthusiasm.

Not that this class was a picture of cooperation and involvement— far from it. Much of the time it was rather more like a three-ring circus, always on the edge of chaos. While Moishe went on with his lesson, a series of questions and answers punctuated by recitation of the text, followed by a formalized explication of it in Yiddish, students at various tables went on simultaneously with their own activities of talking, hitting each other, pushing and pulling on their common desk, or imitating the movements of the teacher—often in bold mimicry.

One boy in particular imitated the teacher almost constantly, at times coming perilously close to getting caught but always managing to look involved just when the teacher turned toward him. This cat-and-mouse game absorbed many of the boys around him, who tittered with muffled excitement at the risk of the game. Occasionally, the teacher caught a boy either misbehaving or not listening. This would bring a rap of the rod or a box on the ears. Yet while corporal punishment was frequent—pinches on the ears were common—it did not seem to trouble any of the boys. They took it as part of the normal routine. "One should love admonitions," wrote Rabbi Yoelish Teitelbaum, the rebbe of Satmar.[9] If they did not necessarily love admonitions, these boys were at the very least accustomed to them. Perhaps they took for granted that life consisted of outbursts for which there was swift and sure retribution.

Patterned Thinking

For all the fooling around, more often than not when Moishe called on a boy, even one who seemed to me to be totally detached from the proceedings, the boy—to my amazement—managed to come up with an answer or comment the teacher found satisfactory. Either the questions were too easy and obvious, or the answers—no matter what they were—were sufficient to satisfy the teacher (though my knowledge of the text belied both possibilities). There was a third possibility: these boys early on had learned patterned responses to the kinds of questions their teacher might ask. This capacity would epitomize haredi consciousness: a kind of consciousness that allowed one's mind to wander in the secure knowledge that it had a kind of ingrained capacity always to return to the straight and narrow, as if thought patterns as well as replies and responses were so ritualized that they were on a kind of automatic pilot. One might call this "patterned thinking," a mind set by cultural norms that went along prefigured lines of review and repetition.

For all their fooling around, by fourth grade these boys had already learned more Talmud than most other Jews would know in a lifetime. Not that they were scholars. But compared with the talmudic illiteracy of contemporary Jewry, these fourth-graders were masters. They were familiar with legal concepts and talmudic terms that few of their peers outside the haredi world were likely to know. They knew, for example, the length of the daily term of the Sanhedrin, the supreme rabbinical court, and when ripe wheat had to be eaten according to Jewish ritual law, the matter the Sanhedrin was considering in a case before it. They knew many of the laws that distinguish between commandments contingent to performance within the boundaries of Biblical Israel and those possible beyond those boundaries. They knew a variety of laws pertaining to service in the Holy Temple, destroyed more than two millennia before. They knew how to find parallels in scriptural texts based upon principles of exegesis set out in the Talmud. This knowledge, even in its rudimentary fourth-grade form, served as a way of separating them from secular Jews. "Chiloinim are boors," as one boy put it.

Moishe did more than just recite the words and review the laws with the boys; he bracketed the recitation with questions that required them to elaborate or explicate the Mishnah so that the principles emerged from it. It was a method aimed at getting them to learn not only the simple text (which they would have to learn by heart) but to embed the passages along with their patterned explanations into memory. Only when this last step was complete and the boys could reiterate the text along with the explication and discussion would the teacher move on to something else. That at least was what was supposed to happen.

The musicality of the process was striking. They would read text, sing explication, and then repeat it all over again. The rise-and-fall sounds of text and explanation had a kind of chant quality to it.

But while fifth-graders, as I would see later, did this smoothly, these boys, still new at it, had not yet perfectly learned the connections between the text and its explications. Postfiguratively, they knew where they should end up, but they could not always get there easily. To deal with these gaps in their knowledge, they would handle troublesome passages by slurring or swallowing their explications in the singsong that made up their recitations. The trick was just to get the cadences of the refrain right.

A few giggled when they met my eyes and saw that I noticed they were faking it. Absorbed in his own thoughts or else not wanting to examine his students too closely, their teacher seemed satisfied with the sound of things. Seeing this, some of the students settled into their chants. Occasionally, there were one or two who broke out of this chant by asking direct questions.

Although most of these boys spoke Hebrew at home and among themselves—something more and more of the young haredim, particularly those associated with the Lithuanian yeshiva world, were doing —Yiddish remained the predominant language here, unlike in the gan. Yiddish would separate them from other Israelis.

Learning to Pray

Teaching children how to pray is a central concern in traditional Jewish life. The Talmud and codes are filled with charges to initiate the young into worship.[10] Most haredi parents, whom their children commonly see at prayer, instruct their young in some liturgy as well as in basic blessings over food. Haredi neighborhoods are dotted with synagogues, and the day is often oriented around morning and evening trips to them so that children grow up with the sights and sounds of prayer surrounding them. Nevertheless, increasingly, the actual task of training the young in the techniques and conscious practice of prayer goes on in the schools.

"The teacher must be present during the time of the pupils' prayers," decreed Rabbi Yoelish Teitelbaum, the Satmar rebbe, in a dictum that expresses the haredi stand on these matters. At the very least, "he must monitor them to hear their pronunciation to see that it does not become spoiled and to rehearse them in the [proper] order of the prayers." [11] But there is more. "One must be meticulous in seeing to it that children pray properly," writes Avraham Kahan of the Reb Arelach hasidim. Of late, this task has become more difficult. "In previous generations when people prayed with devotion, naturally this influenced their children so that they would also pray properly, and one did not have to monitor them so closely. But this is not true today *when, because of our many sins, prayer is among the things men trample upon.*" [12]

As Rabbi Kahan saw it, prayer had become routine and uninspired, lacking the driving devotion that all true worship must have. "Today, therefore, if we do not monitor the children, they will often not pray at all." Indeed, so devoid of feeling were many, even among the haredim, that "in many places when at the time of praying the children are not watched, practically none of them pray, except for a few of those who on their own tend towards the good. But most of the youngsters do not pray, and naturally when they mature they also often forgo prayer." The consequence of this was that they would never get used to praying. And then, "Heaven help us, this causes children to follow in the ways of the evil culture." [13]

Under such circumstances, teaching the young to pray is especially crucial. In third grade, the teacher I shall call Akiva Damsker was particularly concerned with these matters. As he inaugurated his students into worship, he began by chanting the prayers himself. Then he offered a commentary on their meaning, or some words of spiritual encouragement. Most of what he did, however, was to display devotion as he prayed: swaying, singing, and sometimes even clapping his hands together in a kind of ecstatic gesture.

At one level the boys seemed to pick up quickly what to do. From the open prayer books in front of them, they knew the right words to say; and watching him, they knew how to recite them. Some did this better than others. Pointing to several youngsters who, with screwed-up faces, eyes closed, bodies shaking back and forth, hands moving imploringly, and voices loudly intoning the words, seemed to put on especially notable shows of devotion, Akiva whispered to me, "They have learned to imitate their fathers." These boys, I was told, had fathers eminent in the community for their piety; their demeanor reflected their parentage. Watching these peers would help the others.

But was this really prayer, or was it simply a display? Children, especially third- and fourth-graders, could hardly be expected to know about spirituality. But they could acquire the techniques of davenen, as haredim refer to prayer in Yiddish. Perhaps what I was witnessing was what could be called *imitatio fidei*, an emulation of fidelity to prayer more than actual and deeply felt worship?[14]

On the other hand, even if this was nothing more than a show, this was a show that most other children their age did not feel a need, or have any idea how, to put on. And so even if what I saw was less than full-blown prayer, it was still an exhibition particular to haredim. When other kids their age were trying to show how good they were at other things, these boys were trying to show they were caught up in the throes of praying to God—that was striking.

More than that, the particular davenen style they exhibited was haredi. It was characterized by an Ashkenazic, sometimes even a particularly Lithuanian, accenting of the words, echoing a sound associated with a Jewish past in eastern Europe, and an exuberant swaying characteristic of hasidim (even though this was a misnagdic school), along with faces meant to show they were imploring someone for help, blessing, and grace. All this was what haredim normally did when they prayed. But it was particularly impressive to see in a little child. Undoubtedly, haredi adults were as impressed with it as I was—which was probably why they put so much effort into getting their youngsters to pray. Put simply, a child at prayer could stimulate the adult to doing no less. So here again was a case of the little child leading them.

Learning Creeds

Although textual study in these grades was focused on Talmud and the codes, the teachers still spent time orally reviewing the biblical passages of the week. Where the emphasis in the gan had been on narrative—even when the concern was with law and practice—stress in the upper grades was put increasingly on the matter of creed.

Reading through the final chapters of the book of Numbers, the fifth grade reviewed the encounters between the Israelites and the tribes on the east bank of the Jordan River. Among these were the Moabites, whose refusal to allow the ancient Israelites to pass through their territory on their way to the Promised Land resulted, according to the text and tradition, in an eternal enmity between Moab and Israel. Moabites were forever after to be considered *personae non gratae*, marked off by a divine prohibition on marrying them.

In the review of the verses, a boy asked a question: why, in order to cross into the Promised Land, did the Jews not just kill every last Moabite? Although ostensibly a query concerned only with the text, this question carried an undertone that anyone living in contemporary Israel could not fail to miss. Moab is in what is today the nearby Kingdom of Jordan, a nation in perpetual conflict with Israel. Today's Moabites are Arabs. That the Arab-Israeli conflict is part of haredi consciousness is already clear from what we have seen in the gan. Coupled with the general attitude of disdain for non-Jews, these children who asked why the Moabites were not all killed were also asking another question: why did our ancestors not solve for us the problem of an enemy who is still with us?

Was this an explicit and conscious element in the question? Did the children think about the Arabs beyond their neighborhood or about the hostilities that today infect much of Israeli life? Did they know where they were? One could not help suspecting that they did, that even in the midst of a consideration of an ancient biblical story, contemporary external realities intruded at some level. I would see the limits of this very soon when I examined their geographic consciousness, as I shall detail in the next chapter.

In his answer the teacher turned in another direction. Holding his students in the grip of traditional exegesis, he explained that had all Moabites been destroyed, then Ruth would not have been born and the entire chain of Jewish existence would have been broken. A Moabite who married Boaz the Israelite, Ruth became the great-grandmother of King David, the greatest of kings, forebear of the Messiah. The boys knew about Ruth. This conundrum of her Moabite origins was one of the puzzles for which traditional biblical interpreters offered a variety of explanations. Although only fifth-graders, the boys were already aware of the enigma. Here in class they were provided an explanation: the idea of divine providence. That idea suggested that hidden motives and implications lay beyond immediate realities. Providence was the religious dimension of postfigurative culture.

A fully developed sense of providence, however, requires the believer not only to know that there is a "divine plan"; it also calls for a shaped belief that places limits on itself. It means knowing what not to ask. This does not come naturally in the fifth grade. Another boy stood up and asked, "If God can do everything, why could he not allow Ruth's family to survive an Israelite attack on the Moabites?"— a tough, subtly heretical question.

"Yes, of course the Almighty could do anything He wanted. He could make a young girl come out of Moab. But a young girl needs a mother, and the mother needs a husband. And the husband has to make a living, and they have to have a house. And if they need a house, they need someone who will be a carpenter. And of course they will need someone who makes clothes, and so on." The teacher paused and gazed around the classroom to see if the boys looked convinced. "So you see for Ruth to be born, they needed a whole community of people, because no single person can exist alone. Only Adam could be alone, and even he needed a helpmate."

It was a message crafted to explain the complexity of a divine master plan; it was also a way of reminding the boys of another principle by which they lived: no single person can exist alone. All of us are part of a community. Watch out not to ask an outsider's question.

For these youngsters and their teacher Bible lessons were clearly far more than a literary foray into a text or a recitation of a narrative. They were pretexts for passing along values, tools for deflecting heresies, and, perhaps most importantly, means for helping give substance to what it meant to be a Jew in the world they inhabited.

14

Where Are We?

On my way to observe the upper school, I met Rabbi Jeremiah Horne, as I shall call him, an immigrant from Chicago. He came to Jerusalem for the first time in his twenties, in order to study in a yeshiva. That experience moved him to settle here, and so after a brief return to America, he came back and made his home in Jerusalem. That had been about forty years ago.

"I came here to learn at Hebron," he explained about his early years in the famous yeshiva that had relocated from Lithuania to Hebron in the Holy Land and then later, after the Arab riots of 1929 and 1936 in which a number of yeshiva students were murdered, to Jerusalem. "I was at Hebron for two years and then moved to Mir [Yeshiva] after I was married. Since then I have had a special feeling for Eretz Yisrael." He spoke about "Eretz Yisrael," the Land of Israel, not the state. Haredim could and did feel attachments to the God-given Land of Israel, but not to the secular state.

But was Horne haredi? In his gray suit, trimmed beard, and combed earlocks neatly tucked behind his ears, he was the picture of a modernized yeshiva man. Horne parried my question. We spoke in English.

"I know I am haredi. I live in a neighborhood with other haredim; I teach in a haredi yeshiva, and my children are all haredim; but I don't think only in those terms," he said. "I prefer to think of myself as a *ben yeshiva* or *ben Torah*." A ben (son of the) yeshiva was a person who had gone through the Lithuanian-style nonhasidic yeshiva system and who, because he had assimilated its values and worldview, continued throughout his life to draw his Jewish identity from that experience. Sometimes when he graduated, he called himself a ben Torah. He was someone steeped in Jewish tradition and the details of Jewish law. He was not simply governing his behavior according to the norms of the street—even if that street was a Jewishly observant one. He was part of a rabbinic elite. Thinking of himself in these terms allowed Horne to distinguish himself from other haredim and observant Jews. Not every haredi man could call himself a ben yeshiva.

Because he was thinking in his observance, as he explained, Horne considered himself, as many misnagdim still did, years after the battles with the hasidim, as part of the Torah elite. He therefore did not feel a need to dress exactly like all other haredim. He could be in gray where they were all black. Still, he was no less rigorous in his attachment to the law.

Horne elaborated: "I would define myself in terms of *dikduk* [scrupulousness] in *mitzvahs* [religious commandments and observances]. That would be the main thing." That scrupulousness emerged from his education in the yeshiva. He was not one of those boors—many of them haredim—who lived only by custom and blind habit; the ben Torah knew what the Torah expected of him and lived up to it. "We look to be *machmir* where we can," he continued, using the Hebrew word to describe a lifestyle of greater stringency and restriction. He offered examples. "We eat *shmura* matzah when our parents just ate regular matzah. We eat *glatt* kosher when in the old days they were happy to eat any kosher." Unlike the regular unleavened bread, shmura matzah was watched from the time of the wheat's harvesting to make certain that it was absolutely unleavened. Glatt kosher referred to meat specially inspected to make certain that the cow from which it came did not have any lesions on its lungs (that they were smooth or, in Yiddish, glatt) and therefore the cow died not from disease but only from the ritual slaughter. Both terms today had come to connote an attachment to higher and more punctilious standards of ritual observance. "We have principles and fight for them. We don't have to make compromises anymore."

Farhern

I found Horne sitting in the yeshiva office. For many years he had been associated with the school as a parent. During the last year and a half, however, he had joined the staff. His job was *farhern,* to probe, the boys.

To understand farhern (Yiddish for "listening"), one needs to realize that all formal learning in the yeshiva does not take place only in classes. Some goes on in a format that combines examination with tutoring. In groups of two or three, and sometimes even solo, boys in the upper primary grades are sent out of class to sit with a special rebbe before whom they must demonstrate the extent of their knowledge. This demonstration is facilitated by a series of probing questions the teacher asks. At their best these questions are meant not only to check what the students know but also to focus their thinking and learning, a form of individualized attention that will alert them to what they need to concentrate on more intently.

Normally, farhern is carried on orally. In their responses the students explicate a text, usually talmudic but at times also scriptural, or else they explain some laws from codes. In practice, the recitation commonly consists of a kind of desultory, almost liturgical, repetition of an excerpt along with a set series of explanations, the kind of sing-song review that the boys were beginning to learn in fourth grade. It means moving between the language of the text and its Yiddish translation and elaboration. Often the process is almost automatic and routine. Even the way the boys sway or twirl their earlocks as they go through the motions of examination looks as if the whole exercise is part of a scripted piece. One has only to observe several dozen of these performances to see how much is standardized, if not formally then by custom.

Still, for all their routine and ritualized quality, these performances, when carried on under the close scrutiny of a sharp examiner, can at times allow the students genuinely to distinguish themselves. Those who falter in the flow of their recitation are probed further by unexpected questions that either further fluster the unprepared, intensifying the feeling of being inadequate to the task, or they give the good student a chance to show that his was simply a momentary lapse.

In search of a satisfactory and even impressive performance, students often present set pieces they have memorized. Given that the examiner listens to dozens of students each day, a good job of memorization and a formulaic review is the best way of avoiding a too-careful scrutiny and grilling. Of course, like countless generations of students, these boys too have learned how to fake it.

To think of these sessions of farhern as essentially oral exams or as an exercise in impression management, however, would be to miss some of the appeal of their ritual nature. Here as always in the yeshiva, the questions to be asked are the timeless ones and the answers to be given are those that generations of scholars and sages have already given. For years yeshiva boys have reviewed these same texts and codes in answer to generations of teachers. In a sense, farhern is a kind of synthesis of ritual and learning, precisely the mix characteristic of the review of sacred texts which is at the heart of yeshiva learning.[1] Learning is more of an initiation than an inquiry here. And that is the safest sort of education for haredim.

Results of farhern are shared with the classroom teachers and parents, serving as a guide for the child's progress in school. In a sense, the rebbe who does the farhern is a kind of surrogate for both parents and teachers in that he is the one before whom progress and understanding must be displayed. If he is satisfied, everyone is satisfied. This is probably why, as a former parent who is also a rabbi, Horne was considered an appropriate candidate for the position.

Sitting in the small anteroom to the principal's office, Horne was filling out little yellow cards that would be distributed to those youngsters who had successfully recited and explained passages from the Mishnah by heart. These merit slips were the "report cards" that the school sent home. Quite a few of the boys had gotten into a fierce competition to see who would get more Mishnahs listed on his card. Some had memorized ten, others thirty. One eighth-grader had learned nearly two hundred, a substantial accomplishment considering that some Mishnahs can run to over a page in length.

The enthusiasm for learning was not necessarily driven only by a desire to impress their parents and teachers but also stimulated at least in part by the peer rivalry that was a component of the yeshiva atmosphere. Getting A's was not the goal here; that sort of grading was not even used. Learning a list of Mishnahs—that was something.

There were no standard kinds of grades at all here. Nor, for the most part, did parents have organized conferences with the teachers. They simply wanted to know if the rebbe was satisfied with the progress their child had made. An affirmative reply was sufficient, an enthusiastic one was superior. But in all events it was the rebbe's judgments that were key.

Between filling out his cards, Horne was examining the sixth-grade boys in Talmud. Every ten to fifteen minutes another two or three were sent in by their teacher. They sat down side by side across the table from Horne. Except for their reading of text, the entire conversation was carried on in Yiddish.

While the boys were being tested in this room that also served as something of a teachers' lounge, various people came in to make telephone calls, drink coffee, or wash their hands. There were occasions when the rosh yeshiva and the principal walked by, causing the boys to stand up in a traditional display of respect. And of course there was me, the observing stranger. Yet in spite of all the distractions, the boys seemed to have an ability to ignore most of the surrounding disturbances. They made a kind of mental space for themselves amid a plethora of noise and activity, something they probably had learned to do in their crowded classrooms and homes. It was a sort of concentration hard to imagine among many youngsters their age, but here it was the norm.

The text the boys reviewed came from a chapter in the tractate Baba Metzia entitled "Ha-Mafkid" (He Who Entrusts). It dealt with the responsibilities incumbent upon someone who becomes a trustee or caretaker for another's personal property. The specific passage in question focused on the liabilities attendant to a voluntary as opposed to a paid caretaker of an object, plant, or animal that was stolen or died during the period of caretaking. In another culture these matters might have been more appropriate to a first-year law-school class; here this was introductory Talmud for the sixth grade.

Horne began by asking one boy to open the large volume to a particular page. Then he pointed to a place on it: "Begin here." Without hesitation, the boy started to rock back and forth on his chair and vocalized the text in rhythmic accompaniment to his movements. Every so often, Horne broke the rhythm with questions.

"So how is a living object different from an inanimate one for the trustee?" he asked. The boy listed several essential legal differences.

"What constitutes legal possession?" he asked. The boy reviewed the laws, summarizing the text. Most of the time, however, Horne let the boys go on uninterrupted. Then he would switch from one boy to the other and ask the second one to continue. When one was on, the other sat still.

"Where are we?" he would ask all of a sudden. This abrupt query of course necessitated each boy's listening and following along carefully to everything his chavruse said so that he would not miss a beat. I could see quite a few silently mouthe the words along with their partners. Occasionally, a boy would nudge another with his leg under the desk, either to keep the other on guard or else throw him off it. At a certain point Horne closed the book (sometimes he carried on the entire farhern with no text open) and asked the students to continue by heart. They repeated the often tortuous path of the Talmud's digressions and its stream of arguments and logic.

The entire process normally took between ten and fifteen minutes. Now and then, if one got stuck, his partner would offer a hint. This was not discouraged. While there was some competition in chavruse, there was also a sense of camaraderie that would after all be nurtured throughout their years as students in a yeshiva. Besides, helping a partner was the easiest way to subtly but unmistakably establish one's superiority.

A Test of Another Kind

While I could see that the boys examined were oriented to their texts, I wanted to see if they were oriented in other directions as well.

"Would you let me ask them a few questions too?" I asked Horne one day. "I see they know Talmud, but I want to get some idea about their knowledge in other areas as well."

Horne asked what I had in mind.

"Geography," I replied. This was a subject that would not bring in the forbidden matters of secular learning. It seemed innocuous enough. "I want to see what they know about the place where they are located."

That was no problem, he said. I would discover, he assured me with some pride, that a ben yeshiva was no less informed on this matter than any other of his age.

As the boys came in, Horne explained that he had some work to complete but that I had a couple of questions they could answer in the meantime. With this tacit approval, the boys seemed to take enthusiastically to the idea. After all, they were curious about me, and my questions might serve as much to reveal information about me as to query them. Any such questions I would ask might be a welcome break in school routine. These were boys eleven and twelve years old, and the questions I asked them were ones that I had informally tested on some of their nonharedi peers. Admittedly not a scientific pretest, I was, however, satisfied that the answers to my simple geography questions were the sort of information other Israeli youngsters of a similar age would know.

To begin with, I asked each boy to sketch the outlines of a map of Israel. None could. They had never seen maps. Some did not even know what I meant. Horne's face expressed surprise. With growing frustration, he at last assured me that certainly one of the boys, slightly older than the others, would be able to make the map. We called him in and asked him to draw the map. At first, he was startled by the question. I explained more precisely that I wanted him to draw a picture on a piece of paper that would represent the shape and borders of the country. "Ah, I know," he said at last, smiling. Now he understood what I wanted and that was easy. I handed him a pencil and a plain piece of paper, and he took both with a display of confidence. Biting on his folded tongue, he drew a series of lines carefully and deliberately. Horne smiled with an I-told-you-so expression as we waited for the finished product. At last, with a look of satisfaction and pride, the boy handed the paper to me and without a word I glanced at it and passed it on to Rabbi Horne. He stared incredulously at it for a moment and then at the proud face of the young boy.

"He's not serious," he said to me in English sotto voce as he stared at the nonsensical intersecting lines.

But it was clear to me that the boy was indeed quite serious, for he was already explaining to his fellow students who had been unable to do this great thing how he had long ago learned how to draw maps. Horne was in shock.

But I had not only asked the boys to draw a map. When they could not, I sketched the outlines of their country. Then I asked each boy if he could tell what lay to the east, the south, the north, and the west, each time pointing my pencil to the area in case they did not know the bearings of the compass. Again, no one knew. I laid aside the map. Quite a number of the boys asked if they could keep the little drawings. This was not the sort of paper they normally got to collect at school.

Next, I asked each boy to tell me the names of the surrounding countries, without necessarily specifying where they were in relation to Israel. In response, one boy began to list cities in Israel. Impatiently, Horne stopped him and told him that these were cities, and I had asked for *countries*. Ah, said one boy's partner, Israel was bordered by England.

"No, no!" shouted an obviously frustrated Horne. "England is far away." One after another failed this little geography test. Perhaps the most revealing answer came from one youngster who, in reply to the question of what bordered on Israel, confidently answered that Israel was surrounded by *"chutz la'aretz."* "Chutz la'aretz" is the Hebrew expression that most Israelis use to refer to the rest of the world. Literally, it means "outside of the Land (of Israel)," abroad. In this boy's mind the world was neatly divided. Just as there were goyim and Jews, so similarly there was Israel and chutz la'aretz. Hearing this, Horne looked as if he would explode either with exasperation or laughter.

On the map of Israel that I sketched, I now drew the only two large bodies of water within the boundaries of the country, the Sea of Galilee and the Dead Sea. In a country with so little water, I was certain the boys would at least recognize these two large bodies of water, one in the north from which the Jordan flowed and the other the salty lake in the arid area of the Negev, as the southland is called. To most Israelis this basic geographic knowledge is obvious. None of the boys could fill in the names of these bodies of water for me.

I asked them specifically where Jordan, Syria, Lebanon, and Egypt were. More than half the boys could not locate them. None of the boys had ever heard of Saudi Arabia (this was before the Gulf war), nor did they have any idea where it might be.

As I reflected on this ignorance in the days that followed, it struck me that in the world they inhabited, the information I had asked them was simply not important. They had a different map of the world. I had seen this most dramatically in a stained-glass globe hanging in the vestibule of the Zvil yeshiva. Here what looked at first glance like a map of the world, and in particular Europe, had been redrawn by the Zviler hasidim. On their globe a whole different geography existed. The large territories were not Russia, Germany, or Poland. They were named after cities of importance to the hasidim of Zvil: Apta, Lublin, Mezerich, Berdichev, Chernobyl. Cities had become countries. And at the center of the world was Zvil itself, "the abode of our glory." With its imaginary hasidic, Zvil-centered map of the world, this globe was, perhaps, the most graphic and symbolic illustration of the haredi alternative world. For Zvil hasidim, Zvil was indeed the center of the world; other maps were less important, indeed less correct.

Perhaps like the Zviler hasidim, these boys did not need to know where Jordan, Syria, Egypt, or Saudi Arabia were or what was beyond their boundaries because the Israel they inhabited was not the modern state. That state, its boundaries, and its neighboring states were ephemeral realities. There was little need to know about them. And certainly one needed to know little if anything about the geography of the rest of the world. If Horne was surprised by these results, maybe it was because he was not quite as haredi as the generation of youngsters that would be his grandchildren. He knew that was the case, but he was especially struck when he saw it in this way.

Perhaps the fact that the boys were unfamiliar with the geography so familiar to me was yet another way they demonstrated that they were haredim. Maybe this was the way they showed that they looked out upon another world than the one I saw.

And what was the geography they did know? I had one more series of questions to ask in order to get an answer. I recalled that in answer to my question about the countries neighboring Israel, one of the boys had mentioned the Philistines as neighbors; his Israel and the biblical one were the same, and he had no sense that today there were no more Philistines. Maybe that was a clue. Instead of asking the boys about today's map, I would ask them about a biblical one. This time I asked them if they knew where Mount Moriah was. All of them knew it was traditionally believed to be the place on which Abraham had bound Isaac in response to God's wishes and stood ready to sacrifice him. Several knew too that it had been the site of the Holy Temple in Jerusalem. Where did Abraham live when he made the trip to Mount Moriah? They all knew the answer: Beersheba. I asked them how long it had taken Abraham to travel from Beersheba to Mount Moriah; they all knew it had taken three days. Their knowledge of this biblical geography was clearly superior.

Now I tried to make a leap. I asked if it had taken Abraham three days to make the trip so long ago, how long it would take to make the trip between Beersheba and Jerusalem today? I knew it was about a two-hour drive, but the answers the boys gave were striking. One boy said the trip today would last eleven days; another said seven days. All of them gave me numbers that were greater than the three days of Abraham's journey. How could that be, I asked? Were the cities not in the same locations today as in the past?

While a few boys said something about the roads today having to go around more houses than they did in biblical times, it was one sixth-grader who seemed to put the answer best. "Abraham was a zaddik," he said. God had given him the power to jump through space. It was inconceivable that we today could do anything better or even as well as he did. We were pygmies to the giant who was our forefather Abraham. In the haredi view of world order, the ancients were always superior to contemporaries. So of course the trip would take the little men of today far longer. The notion that we necessarily do things—all things—better today than they were done in the past had no place here. In the haredi perspective, there was no geography that was not endowed with cultural significance. "Where are we?" was a question for which the answers very much depended upon whom one asked.

The contrast was remarkable. These were boys who knew the legalism of the Talmud and could find their way in that ancient text easily, even by memory, but they had no idea where they were in relation to a map. The ben Torah lived in an alternative world. For the rabbi's questions he had all the right answers; for me, none.

15

The Yeshiva:
Mussar Shmues

Although my time in the kindergarten and the primary school was beginning to give me a sense of what it meant to be haredi, no full understanding of the relationship between education and culture, of how the school acted as a medium for making and sustaining haredim, was possible without going to the *yeshiva gedola*, the upper school. Here, I already knew, was the vessel in which the men completed themselves, where they spent hours of every day and many of the best years of their lives.[1] For the mature haredi male—whether hasidic or misnagdic—the yeshiva gedola and particularly its main study hall, the bes medrash, had over the years become the only legitimate place to be. To spend time anywhere else was tantamount to *bitul Torah*, dissipation. So the place to go to see the mature expression of haredi culture seemed to be the yeshiva gedola.

For the haredi, particularly in Israel where most males spend forty years and sometimes more in school, the yeshiva gedola was far more than a place of simple instruction. To many it was the last true preserve of Judaism, a link to the past and a promise of the future in which all life would be Torah. It was perhaps one of the most important locations of Jewish collective experience. Instead of preparing one for life, the yeshiva became a kind of counterlife, a way of entering an alternative world that emerges from books. This education does not necessarily provide its students with "street smarts," knowledge necessary for navigating through the complexities of contemporary society. On the contrary, it refashions the world so that it is not like the street. Here where life goes by the book, a countervailing moral order can be constructed and maintained. And that life is viewed as ontologically superior.

Yeshiva and Youth

Who was in the yeshiva? Above all others, it was the bastion of the young, boys from the ages of approximately sixteen or seventeen to those who were in their very early twenties. A few of those who were older and married—avrechim, as haredim called these young men who studied in a kollel—would also come to the yeshiva for gatherings and particularly for important classes or discourses, shiurim and shmuesn. These young men had become the foot soldiers, the lifeblood, the future of the haredi world.

The haredi world might be visualized as a series of concentric circles. In the innermost circles, protected by everyone, were the youngest children, the tinokos shel bais rabban. Then came the sages, the admor (an acronym for "our master, teacher, and rabbi"), the rosh yeshiva, and the rebbe. And surrounding them, confronting and contending with the outside world (but figuratively with their backs to it) were the avrechim. Girls and women played similar roles in the female haredi world, although for the most part they stood in the shadow of men. What was crucial, however, was the emphasis on the youth.

There were a variety of reasons for this emphasis. The fact that haredim found themselves surrounded by societies that emphasized youth—both in modern Israel with its idealized image of the young sabra and in America with its youth culture—undoubtedly had something to do with it. Even though they remained formally separate, as we have already seen, haredim were subtly molded by the general society much more so than might appear on the surface. To be sure, they absorbed and transformed the elements of that surrounding culture. Thus, the haredi incarnation of youth culture, even as it betrayed certain parallels with all young, was, as I found it, significantly different from the children elsewhere.

Perhaps the rising role of youth in haredi society was the result of haredim being essentially members of immigrant societies. In immigrant societies the advantage is always to the young, who are less bonded to the Old World and most adaptable to the change that immigration necessitates. While young haredim certainly changed and adapted themselves to the new environment, they were also ideologically bonded to the Old World—or at least to traditions they associated with it. Hence, the haredi variant of this immigrant culture was to tie the young to the aged sage, while making the vitality of the latter's authority dependent on the enthusiastic support of these young. Sages like the Hazon Ish, Rabbis Joseph Kahaneman and Eliezer Schach of the Ponovezh Yeshiva, and Rabbis Aaron Kotler in Lakewood and Moshe Feinstein in New York, or the various hasidic rebbes who understood this and surrounded themselves with young followers accordingly became the paramount leaders of this new immigrant haredi society.

Perhaps the emphasis on youth was a by-product of the tragedy of the Holocaust. In that tragedy the old order of aged leaders who had warned their followers not to leave the European ghettos or change their ways had made it easier for the Nazis to capture and identify their obedient followers. These aged sages had not succeeded in saving very much.[2] This failure had perhaps led after the war to a subtle repudiation by the survivors and their offspring of the domination of these elders. Yet, since the traditional authority in yeshivas was always in the hands of elders, it was not possible for this repudiation to be open and radical. It therefore could only take a more oblique form of making the elders become somehow dependent upon the following of the young. After the Holocaust, the approval and adulation of the young was the crucial seal of success for the aged sage.

Finally, the emphasis on the young was also a consequence of the realization that only they could act as a bridge between a past embedded in nostalgia and memory and a future filled with promise. A living image of the past in the present, the young who looked and acted enough like their elders even as they radicalized and subtly adapted many of their practices seemed to bring yesterday, today, and tomorrow together.

Particularism

As already noted, yeshivas were not all alike. Some followed the misnagdic, Lithuanian tradition and others expressed a variety of hasidic outlooks. Among hasidim the pivotal and communal importance of the yeshiva was a relatively recent phenomenon, beginning in the years after the First World War when Hasidism started emphasizing the study of Torah over mysticism and iconoclastic exercises in piety, thereby becoming less radical and more religiously conservative.[3] In the years after the Second World War, the yeshiva became increasingly a fortress of tradition holding off the corrosive forces of modern secularity.

While all these institutions emphasized the study of Talmud above other texts, hasidic institutions offered talks on *hasidus*, the special spiritual recipes of Hasidism, while misnagdic ones provided mussar, discourses and devout exercises aimed at bolstering ethical morale. In practice, both hasidus and mussar aimed at the heart more than the mind and drew moral lessons from sacred texts. Although both hasidus and mussar had similar aims, there were variations in emphasis in each, of which insiders remained acutely aware.

Some of these differences were part of the special historical heritage of hasidic and misnagdic Judaism. Softened for a time when circumstances of galloping assimilation blurred the distinctions between various hasidic sects or between them and the Lithuanian misnagdim, they were once again emphasized in the waxing particularism of haredi life. That particularism had intensified for several reasons. First, by the mid twentieth century, many Orthodox Jews felt that at least within their ranks they had stemmed the tide of assimilation; their young were not dropping out of the tradition. There was therefore less reason to downplay the differences among the various strains of Orthodox Judaism. Second, because by the late twentieth century they were no longer significantly separated geographically from one another—as they had been in prewar Europe—but were rather all concentrated more or less in the same areas and because the overall number of Orthodox Jews had diminished in this century, they were now involved in a far more intense competition for adherents. The competition for loyalties was no longer with those who advocated assimilation to secular culture as much as it was with other Orthodox groups. In reaction to the perception that all Orthodox Jews and haredim were alike, these groups needed to emphasize their differences lest they lose a sense of their particular identity. Such a loss of clear identity would mean a loss of members and possible oblivion, and that was anathema. This particularism, occasionally restrained by a sense of a common enemy in the secular world, allowed these groups to maintain an independent existence. For many the yeshiva became the vehicle as well as the emblem of a particular and definite identity.

Not all distinctions were ones of content. Just as an outsider to the world of American universities might not be able to fully appreciate the distinctions among schools of the Ivy League—a distinction without a difference, as some might argue—that insiders considered important, so too outsiders could fail to recognize the distinctions among yeshivas that insiders saw as significant. And just as an American might, for example, choose to go to the University of Pennsylvania over Princeton because members of his family had for generations gone there and yet at the same time say that his choice was based on its superiority as a place of learning, so similar explanations might be offered to account for attendance at a particular yeshiva or kollel. Thus, a student might say he likes the Kaminetz way or the Ponovezh approach to Torah study or prefers the mussar in one over another or that he is convinced that the Ger yeshiva is where he can learn more hasidus than at Belz, often these decisions are based at least as much if not more on the fact that his family is tied to the communities linked to these yeshivas.[4]

As for yeshivas like Or Ha-Chaim or Aish Ha-Torah that exclusively serve the newly religious *(ba'aley t'shuvah)* decisions about where to attend are often a matter of the circumstances under which the person's religious "conversion" occurred. If someone from a particular institution has been instrumental in bringing about the religious awakening, the neophyte will naturally move into that yeshiva's orbit. In general, the case of neophyte haredim is a separate story and needs its own discussions.[5]

More than simply variations in educational philosophy, yeshivas could be differentiated according to the worldview from which they sprung and the communities with which they were affiliated. Often talks on hasidus and mussar were the medium through which these distinctions became visible.

Mussar

As an effort to instill a certain moral order and to shape character, the constancy and habituation of Talmud study carried on with a chavruse, a fixed partner in study, is probably most important. In this ongoing meditation on texts, ideas are tried out, truths imparted, worldviews fashioned, culture established, and personalities completed all around the study tables. But for one who would explore "learning as a moral enterprise" and articulate the essence of this enterprise, who would like to examine the moments when moral right and wrong are made manifest, the mussar shmues is an even better event to witness.[6] Unlike Talmud, which is transmitted in a shiur, mussar is passed on in what is more intimately called a shmues, a chat or conversation. In a way, the mussar shmues might be seen as the yeshiva gedola counterpart to the story in the cheder.

Mussar—literally, "moral teaching"—was a kind of ethical instruction that arose in Jewish Europe during the nineteenth century and became most popular among the Lithuanian yeshivas. As a movement, it was founded by Lithuanian Rabbi Israel Lipkin Salanter (1810–1883). As an idea, mussar articulated an alternative to the threatening attractions of the Haskalah and an antidote to the dangers of religious complacency. It taught that even those who scrupulously observed Jewish ritual and followed the dictates of Jewish law—as did those of the Lithuanian yeshiva world—could make their Judaism "a matter of habit and convention," and once it was mechanical and perfunctory, "it would therefore fail to bring about the truly perfect service of God."[7] It taught that "the power of man's natural instincts" was such that it always jeopardized the pure service of God, even making piety "a source of spiritual pride, Torah-study a quest for scholarly prestige, and Law-observance a matter of showing off"; natural instincts could transform a visit to the synagogue into little more than "a social event," and charity into "a tool of social ambition."[8] Mussar aimed at raising the level of Torah observance by bolstering the moral and spiritual dimensions of that observance. It advocated the strict adherence to halacha, while enhancing spirituality. In its essence, mussar suggested that Jewish law was not simply a legal system but also something that enhanced moral standing for those who scrupulously followed its dictates.[9]

In all this, mussar also presented an alternative to Hasidism, especially for the Lithuanian Jews who could not accept what they viewed as excesses in early Hasidism. Salanter pointed out that in its enthusiasms, "hasidic teachings could turn even the drinking of whiskey into an act of divine service," and indeed there were early hasidic efforts to enter the realm of the forbidden in order to do battle with evil inclination—efforts that appeared to Lithuanian misnagdim as nothing short of blasphemy.[10] Often, almost in contrast to what misnagdim considered the impetuous tendencies in early Hasidism, mussar stressed the disciplined abnegation of selfish instincts through meditation, exhortation, study, spiritual exercise, and attachment to the dictates of law "until the teachings of the Torah would become . . . second nature." If not asceticism, this often meant embracing austerity, in emulation of Salanter's "rejection of material comforts and possessions."[11]

At first, mussar often depended primarily on the pensively melodic "reading of ethical works, of isolated sayings from the Midrash and Talmud, and of verses from the Bible [which] served as vehicles for creating a certain mood and for implanting certain feelings." [12] Over time a *mashgiach ruchani*, a spiritual mentor whose primary office was to initiate and guide students in the ways of mussar, to teach them religious mores, became a mainstay of many yeshivas. He offered weekly or even daily shmuesn, discourses heavily punctuated with stories and scriptural quotations and often inflected with the cadences of mussar chant. Although resisted in some quarters of the yeshiva world at the outset, mussar—or at the very least, shmuesn, which expressed its perspectives—were by the beginning of the twentieth century "becoming the prevailing trend in the Lithuanian" yeshivas. [13]

Often, they stressed the insidious nature of sin or emphasized the moral profundities of the law or the value of austerity. Reflections of these differences were found in yeshivas in places like Slobodka, Kelm, Telshe, Radun, Novaredok, and other Jewish centers of eastern Europe where mussar became an integral part of the curriculum.

Over time, as hasidic and misnagdic distinctions often blurred, mussar shmuesn and talks on hasidus that hasidic masters offered their disciples also became similar. Even later, both became more like rabbinic sermons and less like spiritual exercises. But whatever else they became, they remained an important part of the sentimental and moral education of the Orthodox world. Still today they play an important role inside the yeshiva, for they focus attention on the moral essence of what it means to be a ben Torah or an erlicher Yid.

In the yeshiva, these shmuesn, perhaps more than anything else I witnessed, shaped or at least marked the shape of the haredi character of the people I observed. A summary or even a composite of all the shmuesn I listened to in all the yeshivas I visited is neither possible nor necessarily useful. Instead, I have chosen to review a typical example of such a talk at one such yeshiva.

The Shmues

As on nearly every Monday evening in the bes medrash of the Kaminetz Yeshiva, [14] an institution with origins in Lithuania, Rabbi Moshe Aharon Stern, the mashgiach ruchani, was scheduled to give what was loosely called a mussar shmues. "Loosely" because this was not a classic discourse complying with the traditional guidelines that the fathers of the mussar movement had set forth for those who wanted to carry out the spiritual exercises and development that they called by that name. Yet, if it was not exactly a perfectly formed mussar shmues, it nevertheless aimed to arouse and morally fortify those to whom it was addressed. In these times it served as mussar.

A tall, slightly hunched-over man in his sixties, with a wiry but bushy gray beard and one eye that always seemed to focus on some middle distance and another that looked directly at those he addressed, Stern squinted as he spoke. Removing the glasses that held his gray earlocks in place and tilting his head upward, he would rub his eyes. Then squinting, he appeared to look past the faces of his audience and turn his sights inward. It was as if he could see these matters more clearly without his spectacles on. And we, his listeners, would only see them too if we followed what he had to tell us.

Moshe Aharon Stern was an immigrant from America, "a Yankee," he once said with a giggle and in an English resonating with the cadences of Brooklyn. He and his parents were born in the United States and both his grandparents were married there. His maternal grandfather was well known as the author of an inspirational book, *All for the Boss* (the "Boss" being the Almighty), which in its time had been very popular among Orthodox Jews in America and, when translated into Hebrew, was even more widely read in Israel. His paternal grandfather, an only child born ten years after his parents' marriage, was renowned as a young Torah genius, an *ilui*. Studying with great rabbis and even with his mother, who taught him all the Scriptures, the ilui memorized the entire Mishnah, with its volumes of words, and several tractates of the Talmud. And he studied mussar. This was Rabbi Stern's family heritage, his *yichus*.

In the mid nineteenth century this grandfather left Lithuania for America. His famous teacher, the great Hafetz Hayim, Stern explained, said to him: "*You* can go to America. *You* will not get spoiled; America will not have any influence on you." Stern smiled as he recounted the story. This was a point of great pride for him: to be in America but not to be part of it. To be a Yankee, but not be "spoiled" by what America was—this was the idealized haredi experience of America, as indeed of the modern world. And it was the story of his paternal grandfather.

In America, like many other children of immigrants, Moshe Aharon's father entered into the mainstreams of the culture: he attended Columbia University and became a successful accountant ("He was Lou Gehrig's private accountant," Stern explained with a proud smile). But at the same time he also attended yeshivas so that even when he entered a career, he remained a *marbitz Torah*, a man who spent hours studying sacred books.

"The rabbi in our shul used to say of my father, 'He's our rebbe.' " Obviously, even though his father had left the world of the yeshiva, he too had not been spoiled by America. Yet this man who was successful in being a marbitz Torah even as he became Lou Gehrig's accountant was not the model haredi whom his son would emulate. The son, Moshe Aharon Stern, would be a haredi who returned to a life within the protective custody of the yeshiva, and not a yeshiva in America but one in "Jerusalem, the Holy City."

Born on Division Street on New York City's Lower East Side and moving between there and Brownsville in Brooklyn, Moshe Aharon grew up in a world that was already becoming far more bounded by the yeshivas. As he put it, his teachers who came to New York from Europe on the eve of the Holocaust "turned us over." Paths his father had followed from yeshiva to Columbia University and back again were becoming less traveled. Although once a New York Yankees fan ("I still know the names of all the good players when I was a boy"), Moshe Aharon would not ensconce himself in American high culture. He would not go to Columbia University like his father. His yeshiva teachers, many of them from the great centers of learning in Jewish Lithuania, forswore the idea of university education. What was possible for earlier generations, a capacity to surmount the corruptions of the university world and remain loyal to Torah, was no longer conceivable for this more haredi one. Stern would not pursue a career that led to the American definition of success. His was not the American dream. "It became my dream to go to *lern* in one of the European yeshivas."

But when his time came, after graduating from Torah Ve Da'as Yeshiva High School in New York, it was World War Two and too late to go to Europe. To escape America and its culture, he would have to go instead to the Holy Land. In May 1946, he did, coming to Jerusalem as a student in the Kaminetz Kollel. Here the "Yankee" married a fourth-generation Jerusalemite, and here he continued to live for over forty years. When he left the kollel, he became teacher of the oldest boys in the *yeshiva katanah*, the primary school. Later he was assigned responsibility for the high-school boys, and at last he became mashgiach ruchani for the yeshiva gedola, a position he has held for over seventeen years.

On the job Moshe Aharon developed a kind of eclectic approach to mussar that drew from several traditions—Novaredok, Slobodka, and Kelm. And of course he drew from his teachers in America who brought a variety of traditions together. At Kaminetz he also acted as an adviser on all sorts of matters. Boys came to him for guidance, and his discourses about the basic elements of husband-wife relations were an important prologue to many marriages. His seminars for bridegrooms were given in three languages: Yiddish, English, and Hebrew. But his Monday night mussar shmuesn in the yeshiva were meant as basic moral lessons, fundamental directions for the students in their spiritual growth. Stern had a collection of over two hundred different such discourses that he had given throughout the years in all sorts of institutions.

The Monday night audience at Kaminetz commonly consisted of slightly more than fifty people, which included the students of the yeshiva as well as the roshei yeshiva and number of laymen who considered themselves to be *b'nai Torah* and who came for this once-a-week experience to be Jewishly revitalized. Stern sat at the front of the large room, behind a table piled high with all sorts of books. Although he only occasionally needed to open them during his talk, he would quote liberally from them, as if routing his own thoughts through the sacred tradition and hence giving them an authority and voice beyond the immediate.

In the world of the yeshiva, the ideal was always to demonstrate that one was an heir of the ancients, an interpreter who could penetrate their superior comprehension of the sacred texts. Anything else was revolutionary and, as such, out of place in the traditionalist atmosphere that permeated the place.

Seforim, holy books, were everywhere around the room: on shelves against the walls, atop the tables, or in people's hands. In a room with white walls, no pictures whatsoever, and no apparent aesthetic dimension, the books, with their gold embossed letters and leatherlike bindings in various hues of blue, black, and brown, added color and character. The other elements of the room that might have been regarded as once having been motivated by an aesthetic sense— a podium and table on which the Torah scrolls are placed for reading and a pulpit from which most prayers are led, in front of which were hand-painted letters spelling the name of God and a seven-day candle and eternal lamp—were either in disrepair or appeared neglected. A dusty camp lamp to be used at times of electrical blackouts lay on top of the pulpit. A number of burned-out or empty light fixtures were distributed throughout the room. In short, everything about the room seemed to say, "Do not look at the physical plant here; the beauty we see cannot be seen except in the pages of these books."

Neither neatly stacked nor catalogued, they were for the most part oversized volumes of the Babylonian Talmud, lying about as if they had just been or were about to be perused. There were also prayer books, some texts dealing with moral guidance (*The Path of the Righteous* [*Messilat Yesharim*] and *How to Repent* [*Al Ha-T'shuvah*] two were entitled), and a few Bibles. Most had frayed pages, their bindings either crumbling or obviously repaired. Lying on every table, worn in appearance, they gave off the unmistakable message: "We are used here."

"Even before a child learns to speak, he should be taught to kiss seforim, and thus he will become accustomed to honoring seforim."[15] On those rare occasions when the books were dropped or put away on a shelf, they were often kissed. It is in this sense that one may consider these books not just items of study but objects of reverence, icons of the yeshiva.

So when Stern sat himself down behind the stack of books that he did not actually open in the course of his talk, he was as much as saying that whatever else he did that evening, he was displaying his homage to these icons.

The shmues began a little after eight. There would be no give-and-take with the students, no questions or interruptions, as there were during a Talmud shiur. Instead, everyone sat transfixed, though here and there someone would whisper a comment or translation of the Yiddish to his neighbor or someone would nod in agreement or cock his head in a show of admiration.

Because much of the talk's impact was not simply in what was said but in how it was expressed, this record is necessarily wanting. Stern exuded a passion and conviction. He communicated this in his vocal inflections, gestures, and even in the silences between some of his words—all of which often reminded one of prayer. As that was a religious act, so too was this. As that was a spiritual experience, so too was this.

Yet if the reader can only imagine, on the basis of his or her own experiences of spirituality, the expressive character of Stern's performance, a performance restrained in its passion by the fact that this was a Lithuanian-style yeshiva where, unlike the case in a hasidic rebbe's talk, such displays were secondary to the content of the Torah taught, some review of the topics covered is possible.

Learning from Samson

Stern began with a lesson from Samson, who, blinded, shackled, and near the end of his life, was brought in by his enemies the Philistines for sport to the great feast they were having. This was not the all-powerful Samson with great hubris of the early chapters of the story in the Book of Judges. This was a Samson who via his suffering and blinding had experienced spiritual growth. This was the man who was about to live his greatest hour and make the supreme sacrifice. This Samson was not the Jewish Hercules as much as the weakened and tormented Jew who begs God to allow him to avenge the injustices he has suffered. This was a Samson far more at home in the post-Holocaust haredi world, a Samson with whom the haredi yeshiva world could identify.

Stern described the majestic character of the Philistine gathering into which the sightless and fettered Samson, once a great judge of Israel, was brought. This was a den of iniquity, a place rampant with lust and sin, a Philistine pleasure palace. As he described Samson, Stern elicited familiar images of the great sages who also throughout Jewish history had been brought weakened and hobbled before their tormentors for perverse sport. It was a story that now echoed with other events in Jewish collective memory. Images of the Nazis and before them the Romans were undeniable.

As I listened to the story, I could not help recalling the gan. Once again it was stories that acted to organize the experience. Here the narrative had far more nuances and the moral messages were more complex, but the basic nature of the experience was really the same: character was being formed through the medium of an interpreted narrative.

Stern repeated the part of the story that described how Samson asked the lad who brought him into the hall to place him near the supporting columns of the building. As Stern quoted the text, Samson made his requests in a Lithuanian-accented and -inflected Hebrew. And then as he elaborated the speech, Samson spoke in Yiddish. Suddenly, Samson sounded like a Lithuanian Jew with whom the listeners could conceivably identify.

Stern repeated the text: "And Samson called unto the Lord, and said, O Lord God, remember me, I pray thee, and strengthen me, I pray thee, only this once, O God, that I may have one vengeance of the Philistines for my two eyes" (Judges 17:28). As he spoke Samson's words, Stern squinted blindly, and one almost had the feeling that it was for himself that he was speaking. Maybe this was because the words were not read but rather emerged out of the narrative with a natural ease that made them sound like a request coming straight from him.

Stern focused on the phrase upon which the midrash itself elaborated: "one vengeance . . . for my two eyes [*n'kam achas mi shtay einay*]." Why *one* vengeance for *two* eyes, he asked?

To answer this question he proceeded to quote a variety of scriptural sources via the rabbis. While it was an impressive display of erudition, something valued in the yeshiva environment, that was not all it was. It was also high drama. Reviewing each explanation, Stern took on a different literary style. It was not that he changed the sound of his voice but that he went into each interpretation making it sound as if it were the authentic word of the rabbis. And each time he left one exegesis and moved on to another, he showed how easy it was to expand the understanding of the text.

Most of the commentaries he quoted in his exploration of the question were in Hebrew, yet after each quotation, Stern offered a Yiddish translation. Why, I thought to myself, is this man translating Hebrew texts into Yiddish for an audience that speaks Hebrew and needs no translation? By putting these texts into Yiddish, he was putting them into the framework of the world that this audience inhabited (or at least the world they sought to inhabit)—the world of the Lithuanian yeshiva. Making Hebrew into Yiddish made the speakers of the words into Yidn. This was not just translation; it was transformation and transference.

But wasn't that precisely the purpose of a mussar shmues: to translate, transform, and transfer the text and its message to the world of the listeners in such a way that they became attached to it. Of course, everything had to be repeated in Yiddish. Everything had to be put into the yeshiva's own language.

At last, Stern reached the point of the midrash. Samson asked for only *one* vengeance, the one he would take in this world. But he did not want to take his full measure of revenge, for he did not want to use up completely the credit for all his good deeds that awaited him in the world to come. Payment for the other eye would wait.

In a number of additional commentaries, Stern repeated this essential message, his mussar for the evening: there were rewards that awaited one in the world to come and therefore one should not take all one's pleasures in this world. Even the great Samson, who once so relished his worldly pleasures, learned this by the end of his life, when he became like a haredi.

Deferring Pleasure

Stern turned next to the Book of Ruth—Ruth who married the rich Boaz and who, according to the midrash, was privileged to live to see her great-great-grandson King Solomon ascend to the throne, Ruth who enjoyed many rewards in this world. He cited the verse in which Boaz tells her to eat at mealtime in the fields. ". . . and she did eat, and was sufficed, and left" (Ruth 2:14). According to the Talmud in tractate Shabbat, as Stern explained, the verse is to be understood as follows: she did eat in this world, and she was sufficed until the days of the Messiah, and she left some for the future, for the world to come.

He elaborated the lesson, telling his listeners that they should not consider their rewards in this world as a measure of who they are and what they merit. There was no point in becoming attracted to the fleeting, empty, and meaningless pleasures of this world. This was a message of austerity. Surrounded by a society and living in times that demanded instant gratification, that emphasized the importance of having it all here and now, he urged his audience to identify themselves with those who put off pleasures for a later time, who looked forward to the world to come rather than this-worldly pleasures. It meant embracing an alternative set of values.

There was something here that made me think of the Protestant ethic, at least as Max Weber had defined it.[16] This was an ethic that celebrated not only austerity in the here and now but also implicitly urged people to worry, to be anxious, to tremble, to be haredim, about what awaited them in the hereafter. Whether or not all of Stern's listeners truly believed his message, I cannot say, but they were seriously attentive to it.

Embracing austerity and restraining the pursuit of this-worldly pleasures was difficult. Those who made their Torah study peripheral and their work primary were in the greatest risk of jeopardizing their true rewards for fleeting pleasures; that was obvious to the people of the yeshiva. Stern offered clear warning to those who had left the protective environment of the yeshiva and were already out in the world making money. Although he did not mention them by name, this included the American Jews—even the haredim among them—who were making their fortunes, living in worldly luxury and smothered in self-indulgence. He paused, and the silence was telling.

Stern continued. The yeshiva was the only refuge for the pure. But even the yeshiva people were in danger from their own smugness and hubris. This was a lesson that needed repeating.

I spoke with Stern about this later. Was it true that America suffered from too much wealth and therefore even the erlicher Yidn there experienced this? Did this mean that their salvation was endangered?

In reply, he repeated one of the many parables that seemed to shape his thoughts. "I visited someone in the United States a few years ago, a ben Torah." Stern nodded as he spoke, as if to imply that I had caught the drift of his message. "We got into his car, a beautiful car." He said "beautiful" as if it were two words: "beauty full." "The car had everything. Beautiful thick velvet seats, beautiful radio, lots of room, even a telephone—this was before so many people had telephones in their cars. So I said to him—we'll call him 'Reb Shmuel'— 'Reb Shmuel, this is a beautiful car.'

"And you know what he said to me? He said to me: 'Reb Moshe, *bist a na'ar* [you're naive]. This is last year's model; I've already ordered next year's model.'

" 'Why?' I asked him. 'This is a wonderful car; you could keep it still for years.' You know, it was one of those big Lincolns, a really gorgeous car.

"And he said to me: 'Reb Moshe, my neighbor already has a new model and it's eating me up.'

"So what can you say to him? But it's not just in America. It's coming here too, and it's making it harder and harder here."

The world of comforts was undermining the world of religion. If America was not mentioned in Stern's talk in the yeshiva, it was certainly in his mind—no less than it was in the minds of many of these haredim, from Yecheskel in the gan to Yisrael Eichler at Belz, who once said to me: "This is the problem with America. In America people allow themselves all sorts of liberties in order to earn a livelihood. We here have shown our American brothers what it requires to be haredi. But I have to admit, they have also aroused in us a desire for the material benefits. And we must wonder who will triumph, who will convince the other. Will we show them the way to be haredi or will they lead us to their ways?"

Everyone knew that the antipode of the righteous son was, as Stern explained, the son who was a *zollel v'soveh*, a glutton. Gluttony was not just for food; it was also a hedonistic voraciousness for pleasures of this world. Carried away by his appetites and unbridled desires, he could by his example lead others to *tarbut ra'ah*, evil ways (literally, "a bad culture"). "Life is too easy now," Stern asserted. "When I was a yeshiva boy, the breakfasts were meager: a piece of bread, a piece of herring, and tea, and then we sat for six hours and learned steadily. No breaks, no chances to go out to see what's doing and feel the breezes and air of Jerusalem." This was true learning without the comforts and this-worldliness of today. It was the environment in which Yidn were properly forged.

We are asked, Stern reminded his listeners, to know God in all His ways, but he who is too much in this world cannot, does not, have the capacity to know the ways of God because he becomes too caught up in the concerns of this world. Those from the yeshiva in Novaredok, Stern later told me, were famous for stressing this message, always on the lookout for some way of humbling themselves and wiping away excessive enjoyment and pride.

"The great sage Rabbi Shimon Bar Yochai had two disciples. One went abroad and left the Land of Israel. There he became a wealthy man. When the other student saw this, he became envious of him." When the rabbi saw this envy, he said to the student who remained, "If this is what you want, take yourself away to it and leave the Torah." As had been the case in the kindergarten, the words of the teacher blended with those in his story: Rabbi Moshe Aharon Stern and Rabbi Shimon Bar Yochai were speaking together. The students of one were the students of the other. The message was the same: there is no way to be a true ben Torah and also become a wealthy man. Those who thought making money was primary and learning secondary were deeply mistaken.

Stern, who had left America, who had given up the possibilities for personal wealth, saw the parallels today. As a collector of funds for the yeshiva, something he regularly did, he often came face-to-face with wealth and saw how corrupting it was, even among those who gave some of their money to the yeshiva. They thought him naive, but they were naive, fools who sold their souls for money. They tried to make up for it sometimes by supporting the yeshiva.

"Rejoice Zebulun in thy going out and Issachar in thy tents," as Scripture put it (Deuteronomy 23:18). They all of course knew the comments on this verse by Rashi, the great medieval exegete: "Zebulun and Issachar formed a partnership. Zebulun dwelt by the sea ports and went for trade in ships; and when he earned a profit, he provided food for Issachar while the latter sat and studied Torah. . . . The Torah of Issachar was made possible by Zebulun." [17]

But Stern reminded his listeners that if Zebulun's soul was at risk, Issachar was not without sin; he too had to be morally vigilant. Evil was sometimes hard to recognize; it had subtle ways of clothing itself in what appeared to be righteousness. There were those who were "zollel v'soveh with a hechsher [seal of approval] from the Badatz [the rabbinic religious courts]." They appeared to be doing everything the law required, but in a pernicious way remained fundamentally corrupt and immoral. The very fact that they believed they were without sin or at the very least were self-righteous and self-satisfied was their greatest sin. This alone would diminish the reward awaiting them in the world to come. Being haredi was not simply a matter of actions; it was a state of mind.

To Be Haredi

"What shall I answer to the Lord?" Stern called out in a quavering voice quoting the famous line from Psalms. Rhythmically, he repeated it several times until its cadences echoed in everyone's head. He wanted it to become everyone's own question of how he would answer his maker at the end of his days. "There will come a time when we shall have to give an accounting of ourselves," he added at last. "Then what will we say?" It was an answer each listener would have to provide for himself. But if Stern had succeeded, he had implanted in his listeners a sense that they needed to worry about that day of reckoning, that they had to be "haredim."

At last, he ended the shmues with one more story. It was about a scholar who kept a notebook in which he recorded all of his sins from the age of thirteen until his present age of ninety.

"Imagine, one notebook for all those sins. Were it me, I'd have had shelves full. But this man had but one notebook. One day he forgot the notebook on the table in the yeshiva. A few of the yeshiva boys ran over to see what were the sins their great rabbi had committed and recorded in the notebook. When they opened the cover, they were stunned by what they saw: the first page had not yet been completely filled up!

"If we all had to write down our sins after we committed them, perhaps we would be more careful about making those sins. We sin without thinking about it."

Those who remained aware of their own failings were those who would have the fewest of them. That was the way to be haredi.

The talk was over. Everyone stood up for the evening prayers, which were recited slowly. The worshipers were careful, perhaps even obsessive, about enunciating each and every syllable of the prayer properly so that none of the words slurred into the others. No one wanted to commit a sin now. They were praying not just for this world but for the next. "Safeguard our going and our coming—for life and for peace from now and to eternity," they prayed.

Deliverance from Temptation

As I reviewed the many mussar talks I listened to in the yeshiva and how they tried to fashion a haredi protective barrier around those to whom they were addressed, I could not help realizing that at the same time that they were trying to warn of the evils and temptations of the world, they were paradoxically revivifying them. In a negational way the outside world was finding its way into the yeshiva, dressed in mussar's admonitions and warnings. Psychoanalysts long ago taught us that what were once subject to veneration can "turn into objects of horror." [18] But the opposite could also happen: objects of horror, the forbidden can, and often does, become fascinating and venerated. Describing ancient taboos, Freud writes: "These prohibitions must have concerned activities toward which there was a strong inclination." [19] Whenever Stern or any other mashgiach ruchani told haredim to be wary of this or that, whenever he invoked ethical taboos or encouraged positive behavior and observance, he at the very least necessarily reminded his listeners not only of the taboo but also of how attractive the breaking of these taboos was. And if Freud and the psychoanalysts were right, then "in their unconscious there is nothing they would like more than to violate them." [20]

Stern, and the supporters of mussar, remained convinced that they could successfully do battle with the evil inclinations, with hubris, with sin, with the pleasures of this world. They knew that the words of mussar were a strong weapon against impulse and temptation. They knew that the feelings evoked by their mussar would make religious anxiety and fear, being haredi, triumph over the pleasures of sin, the attractions of being like the other nations. But of course, if they knew this and were so sure of it, why then was the mussar shmues repeated so regularly? Clearly, the temptations remained active.

The surrounding civilization, with its abiding examples of other ways of being a Jew, could not help but, at the very least unconsciously, tempt the haredim "to do the same." Mussar, and the kind of life it encouraged, while appearing to foster "renunciation of something desirable," was in effect a form of atonement for the "most powerful longings," which it could not help but sustain. [21] As such, it repeatedly brought hidden images of contemporary nonharedi life into the yeshiva.

No one better exemplified this than Stern himself. Did he not gather experiences from the outside world as he traveled around raising funds on behalf of the yeshiva? Like other meshulachim, emissaries in quest of money, he came face to face with creature comforts, conceit, selfishness, and all the temptations. He knew them well. And as mashgiach ruchani he even saw the insidious influences of vanity and hubris in the hallowed halls of the yeshiva. If it was his great talent to see all this and turn it into mussar, it was still true that he represented a brush with the other, impure ways.

Maybe mussar was like medicine. If you were sick and took it, it could make you well. But if you were well and took it, it could make you sick. The crucial thing was to take only what you needed—no more and no less.

16

The Yeshiva: Shiur and Chavruse

In the world of the yeshiva a place at the top is reserved for the rosh yeshiva. In its narrowest meaning the term "rosh yeshiva" denotes simply "head of the yeshiva." But there is an exquisite ambiguity in the phrase, for in Hebrew the word "rosh," as in English the expression "head," resonates with all sorts of meanings. Most simply, it may refer to an administrative position at the head of a complex organization, the dean of an educational organization. Alternatively, it can refer to someone who is a leader, a chief, whose authority is charismatic or at the very least political. "Rosh" and "head," however, can also be synonymous with intellect. In this sense, having read and comprehended so many holy books, the rosh yeshiva becomes the embodiment of those books—wisdom, scholarship, and da'as Torah. By virtue of this, he can offer true guidance.[1]

In contrast to the rosh yeshiva, the hasidic rebbe, as already noted, based his authority foremost on his charisma. But as Hasidism diminished its radicalism and became part of a more conservative trend aimed at preserving an Orthodox form of Judaism and emphasized the yeshiva and Jewish learning as the primary medium for that effort, and as hasidic groups grew in size, the rebbe who started as the master of the ineffable name of God (Baal Shem Tov) also became more of a yeshiva head, both by virtue of his followers' emphasis on his scholarship and in his need to be head of a large and complex organization. To be sure, not all hasidic rebbes placed equal emphasis on scholarship, and even those who did often appointed a disciple to actually head their yeshiva. In addition, many rebbes continued to emphasize piety and spirituality at least as much as scholarship, if not more so. But none could ignore the yeshiva.

On the other side, with the rise of established yeshivas with their own traditions and defined approaches to Judaism, the rosh yeshiva took on numerous of the characteristics of a rebbe. He too became associated with miracle tales and charisma. Although renowned for superior erudition, many yeshiva heads often found that their charisma eclipsed the substance of their scholarship. In addition, a rosh yeshiva often held his position by virtue of familial ties with other yeshiva heads or other scholars.[2] And thus, just as hasidic dynasties evolved, so in parallel fashion dynasties of roshei yeshiva also evolved. In the end, each leader became an admor—master, teacher, and rabbi.

This process of "admorization" turned both rebbes and roshei yeshiva into religious guides for those who would swim against the tide of contemporary secular culture. Their pronouncements became more than simple interpretations of what the law or piety demanded; they were recipes for how to live a proper Jewish life, how to avoid the evils of secularity, or even what to do about some particular decision that might seem to be beyond the scope of Torah. As the reach of the Torah could in principle have no bounds since the Torah's claim was over all conduct, so the admor possessing da'as Torah, "a degree of divine guidance," gained a boundless authority.[3]

In some senses the admor played a role roughly analogous to the prophet of old. While seldom claiming to have spoken with God, he nevertheless claimed to be able to fathom His will through an understanding of His Torah.

The educational impact of the rosh yeshiva is undeniable. Sometimes this is achieved by the selections he makes of those who will teach in his institution. Other times it is by dint of his own teaching and the style or outlook he displays which serves as a model for others to emulate. In either case he fashions the school in his image. But it is the Talmud class, or shiur, that he gives that is in many ways the ultimate representation of who he is and what he would have his students become. These classes are expected to be the most advanced and challenging, demanding pyrotechnic displays of erudition as well as a capacity to bring together often diverse and digressive themes into a single text. A lively shiur will allow the students and the rosh yeshiva to test one another, though often these challenges are quiet and subtle. A seemingly innocent comment about an apparent contradiction, a passing gloss on a text, a perplexing question, or an unexpected parallel can throw down a challenge as dramatically as a lively debate or repartee of questions and answers.[4]

Typically, during the shiur the rosh yeshiva stands in the front of the room, leaning against a lectern or *shtender*, his volume of Talmud open before him. The students sit or stand next to similar shtenders or sit on pews around long tables, their books open to the same page. They follow along in the text as he recites, explores, and interprets the text. He also draws upon auxiliary texts, which have been posted on the bulletin board in advance. The assumption is that the students will have reviewed the text and all the auxiliary sources so that they can more easily follow his line of thought. Here, as in general in the Talmud, the goal in the world where tradition reigns supreme is to go over paths already beaten by previous generations of scholars. Thus, the idea that the students will know or be able to figure out in advance where and how their teacher will get from the Talmud to his exegesis does not portend an empty exercise in review. On the contrary, it offers an opportunity to make the old ways one's own.

Sometimes the preparation is so complete as to obviate the need to actually recite the text. Instead, the teacher and students can move directly to a discussion of it, almost as if they were picking up on a conversation already begun long before the actual beginning of the shiur. And indeed, to the many traditionalist students of the text, it has. They are joining a discussion that is part of a great chain of interpretation that begins in the oral tradition of the Mishnah and the Talmud and moves through medieval exegetes such as Rabbi Shlomo ben Yitzhak (Rashi) and Rabbenu Tam, Rabbi Shmuel ben Meir (Rashbam), Rabbi Meir of Rothenburg (Maharam), Rabbi Yitzhak Alfasi (Rif), and on to later commentators like the fourteenth century's Rabbenu Nissim (HaRan), the sixteenth century's Rabbi Shlomo Luria (Maharshal) and Rabbi Shmuel Eliezer Edels (Maharsha), the seventeenth century's Rabbi Yoel Sirkes (Bakh) or later Rabbi Bezalel Ronsburg—and even into contemporary commentators.[5] And they, in the shiur, are the last links in that long chain.

Sometimes the debates are carried on in a kind of talmudic shorthand in which complex passages or arguments are referred to in a brief Aramaic phrase. Nothing so much serves to exclude the unschooled and uninitiated or those who are not sufficiently erudite than a discussion such as this. And nothing so well serves to affirm the rosh yeshiva's superiority than his ability to reply to and dispose of a question with a brief reference like this. Listening to a learned jurist presenting a brief based on cited legal precedents before an inquiring court can give some idea of what these exchanges are like.

Students do not face the teacher alone. Rather, they are organized in a chavruse. While a duo is the most common arrangement for this, situations with three or even more people studying together are not unheard of. Thus, most of the review of text becomes a sort of "dialogue and debate."[6] The partners are not necessarily equals in scholarship nor in their capacities to learn the texts. "For some students equal ability makes for a productive relationship, but others may find it necessary to study with someone either more or less capable than themselves. One . . . may need to feel that he is 'teaching' the other."[7]

A chavruse offers a medium in which the participants can grow. But these partnerships often go beyond being only about Talmud study and evolve into a relationship in which the other becomes more than a fellow student but also a confidant, alter ego, confederate, a partner in life. In time, an intimacy characterizes the chavruse relationship—with all the ups and downs of any intimate bond.

When I first began attending and observing the shiur, I assumed that this lesson was what gave substance to the chavruse learning. I imagined that what happened was that the students spent the time either preparing for or intellectually digesting and reviewing the insights and instruction gleaned from the class. But the more I watched what actually went on within yeshivas, the more it became apparent that chavruse learning and not the rosh yeshiva's shiur was at the heart of yeshiva life. The give-and-take over the text along with one's partner was what made up the warp and woof of yeshiva activity. The shiur had to be integrated and absorbed into that reality.

The rosh yeshiva must know his students well enough to help them find the right chavruse. And when he succeeds, he has helped bring to life a new being. Undoubtedly, this helps nurture in some students a feeling that makes the rosh yeshiva seem like a parent, an ultimate source of life. As the student matures, his rosh yeshiva's influence is integrated into his consciousness. A ben yeshiva always remains linked to his rosh yeshiva, no less than a hasid is tied to his rebbe.

What could enhance that influence? Surely a haredi frame of mind, an abiding anxiety about the proper way to be a Jew, an insecurity that did not allow one to break new ground but threw one back on the past. As this sort of backward look in human development would amplify and reassert the role of the parent, so in learning it would enhance the importance of the rosh yeshiva, making him forever master, teacher, and rabbi. And so while the yeshiva chavruse allowed the young a sense of independence and intellectual autonomy, the condition of being a haredi ben yeshiva counterbalanced that.

17

⚜

Rosh Yeshiva

At the age of sixty-seven, when many others were slowing down their activities and thinking about retiring, or had already done so, the Rosh Yeshiva[1] was still a busy man. He took the time to see to it that his students received proper instruction and that they were exposed to what he considered appropriate influences. He had the final word in selecting teachers and admitting students. His home was always open to those who needed his counsel, which he gave at all hours of the day and night. He even played a role in *shiduchim*, matchmaking, seeing to it that his students were suitably married off when the time came. And all the while, he dedicated himself to hours of Torah study, and in particular the Talmud, the core of his identity as a leading scholar at the yeshiva. For many people he was the crown of glory of his institution, a living symbol of it. In every sense, his life was the yeshiva.

He was willing to meet with me and talk because, as he explained, he thought it might help the yeshiva in some way. We met in late afternoon in his modest three-room apartment on the second floor of a small stone building in a neighborhood not far from the school.

Climbing to the top of an exterior flight of stone steps at the end of a narrow alley along the side of the building, I was greeted at the door by a tall, gray-haired, slightly stooped man with puffy eyes who shook my hand and with a "Shalom aleichem" ushered me into a room that was a combination study and dining room. Because he was from Pittsburgh, Pennsylvania, originally, we were able to talk in English. But his was an English heavily punctuated with Hebrew and Yiddish words, a kind of interlanguage in which he always switched to Jewish phrases when he talked about concepts that came from his Jewish consciousness. It was a language that never let me forget that I was talking to a man who was *from* a land of English speakers but not truly *of* it.

We sat at a large table in the center of the room. This seemed to be the standard place for meetings: Eichler, Stern, and now the Rosh Yeshiva all took me to the same sort of setting. Around us the walls were lined with cases bursting with papers and books; more were piled in cardboard boxes that filled each corner. And even the table had several stacks of folders and large volumes of Talmud and other seforim all over it. On the floor, hidden somewhere among a sheaf of papers, was a telephone. He had to follow the wire to find it when it rang.

Through a portal along an inner wall I could see some of the bedroom, which looked much like the room we were in, except where there was a table squeezed in among the papers and books here, there two small beds and a chair were squeezed in among the books and papers. At one point during our time together he excused himself and went into the bedroom with a physician who came to take his blood pressure. The two sat on one of the beds—the chair was heaped with books. Out of sight was the kitchen where, from the smell of things, the Rosh Yeshiva's wife, who never came into our room, was busy cooking. Like Eichler's and Stern's wives, she stayed out of the room when I was there. From where she was, however, she would occasionally send in some messenger who would bring the rabbi and his guests a glass of dark, sweet tea. On the walls of the dining room there were two pictures: a rather dull painting of Rachel's Tomb and a photograph of an elderly bearded man whom I recognized to be one of the Lithuanian rabbinic founders of the yeshiva.

While the setting was hardly Spartan—indeed, it had a comfortable, overstuffed, lived-in feel to it—it was certainly not luxurious. If anything, his home, like the disheveled man himself who seemed to give little attention to his appearance, seemed the embodiment of modesty. It was as if he had taken to heart the cautions of mussar that warned against too much comfort.

Not that all prominent rabbis were so simple in their comforts. There were quite a few haredim who luxuriated in possessions. Among hasidim, for example, a rebbe who was bedecked in a coat with a mink collar or whose home was a large mansion, whose car was luxurious, equipped with the most sophisticated equipment, including even a cellular telephone, was not unusual. But the rebbe was a symbol of the success of his disciples. With a rosh yeshiva, that was not always the case. Besides, the yeshiva this man headed was a relatively small one, often struggling for its financial survival. Extravagances here would have been wanton, taken at the expense of Torah.

How did he get to be a rosh yeshiva? From his beginnings in Pittsburgh, where he was one of a small number of Orthodox Jews, he had gone for two years to New York's Yeshiva University, an institution whose motto was "Science and Torah" and which offered secular studies along with religious ones. The science part was irrelevant to him. "But," as he explained, "when I got there, I discovered that the other students did not take Torah learning as seriously as I wanted to or as seriously as some of the *rabbaim* [rabbis] wanted them to, so I left." Leaving meant going to a more traditional yeshiva, where the emphasis on long hours of Talmud study was hardly, if at all, diluted by other concerns, and where science and secular studies were not even taught.

In 1947 he came to Jerusalem for a visit and by 1949 he had moved here to study in this yeshiva. He was a serious student, distinguishing himself by his scholarship, something that led to his marriage to one of the two daughters of the rosh yeshiva. That marriage virtually guaranteed that he would become the next rosh yeshiva, a post he now shared with his brother-in-law, the husband of his wife's sister.

In the warmth of a May Monday, he had taken off his long black frock coat and hung it over his chair. On his head was a large black yarmulke. Hanging on a hook in the wall, his black hat looked down on us like a saucer suspended in space. He sat in shirtsleeves, atop of which he wore a black-striped *tallit katan*, the fringed garment meant to remind all Jews of their obligations to God ("And it shall be unto you for a fringe," as the Bible instructed, "that you may look upon it and remember all the commandments of the Lord and do them, and that you not seek after your own heart and your own eyes, which you used to go whoring.")[2] The black stripe, something haredim were scrupulous about, was a reminder to mourn for the Holy Temple the Romans had destroyed.

Perhaps it was his English, whose syntax and cadences were so familiar to me, or maybe it was the fact that he began our conversation with a series of questions about myself so as to locate me in the Jewish universe, but as we spoke I heard echoes of rabbis among whom I had grown up, the teachers in the yeshiva katana I once attended. His perceptions, values, and worldview were not that different from theirs, which once touched the perimeter of my Orthodox Jewish upbringing. This was something he perceived as well, for when at last he began to answer my questions, he spoke to me as if I were an insider, talking in allusions, shorthand terms, and polyglot that only natives would understand. If my yarmulke was smaller than his, my clothes more colorful, my social circle wider, I was in the final analysis someone who prayed as he did and who understood the sanctity of the texts and the sacred responsibility of studying them. As he saw it, I came from where he came; I had simply not yet gone the full distance.

Our conversation was formally about haredi education, although I was searching here, as I had with Eichler, for some expression of creed. We spoke for several hours.

The Call to Scholarship

What, I wondered, were the goals of the yeshiva and its education? The Rosh Yeshiva looked at me with consternation; his expression seemed to say, "You know better than that."

"Our way is not a goal-oriented education. We learn Toyreh, period. It's a mitzvah to learn Toyreh, and that's what we do." He paused a moment and scratched his head through his yarmulke. If I was asking about goals, maybe he could give me something. "It may not be incorrect to say that there's a goal to become an erlicher Yid, a *yiray shomayim* [God-fearing person], a *talmid chacham* [scholar]."

But not everyone can become a scholar, I protested. Some might not have the requisite intellectual foundation.

"But that's the goal." He smiled and pointed to the wall behind me at a picture of the founder of the Yeshiva. "He used to say that the mitzvah of Talmud Toyreh is not that you should learn or even that you should *koveya itim le Toyreh* [set specific times to review Torah].[3] The mitzvah is that everybody should become a *gaon* [master of the texts] if he has the power to be one. Nobody knows if he is capable of becoming one. So on the one hand it is not goal-oriented education; in another respect it's the most powerfully motivated education possible. Everybody is supposed to use all the *koichos* [might] that he has to become the biggest talmid chacham that he can. Reb Boruch Ber Leibowitz [1866–1939], head of the Knesset Bet Yitzhak Yeshiva in

Slobodka, used to say that if someone had the koichos to become a Rabbi Akiva Eger and he only became a Boruch Ber, so he killed a Rabbi Akiva Eger." Akiva ben Moshe Eger (1761–1837) established a famous yeshiva in Posen and was well known for his talmudic scholarship. He was especially revered by Boruch Ber Leibowitz, who upon seeing a newly published copy of Eger's commentary on the Talmud was reported to have "excitedly pronounced the Shehechiyanu blessing [reserved for special, first-time experiences]."[4]

"Everyone," the Rosh Yeshiva continued, "is duty-bound to become the greatest possible talmid chacham that he has in his koichos to become."

This was a message of the primacy of scholarship. In a place like the yeshiva a person had to think of himself as striving to be a scholar. But this was not scholarship for its own sake alone, as I had already discovered from my observations. The scholarship he was talking about was a means of bringing about a religious transformation. One studied the wisdom of the sages of the ages so as to become like them. That was why the Rosh Yeshiva could parallel becoming a talmid chacham with being an erlicher Yid.

So Many Customs and Traditions

"Our children begin at the age of two. I don't know why at that age." He shrugged his shoulders. "We didn't originate anything here. That's just the way it's always been done. When a child is capable of keeping himself clean, a mother sends him to learn Toyreh." He paused for a moment and then added, "It's possible that in different places there were different *minhagim* [customs]. I'm not aware of all the minhagim. We have so many here now."

Later, as I reviewed my tape of the conversation, I reflected on the meaning of this last comment. Of course, there was the reference to the authority of tradition, affirming an order in which yesterday fashioned today and tomorrow: "That's just the way it's always been done." Then there were the facts: children began at the age of two; before that they belonged to their mothers. But he added two important commentaries on these facts. First was "we didn't originate anything here." Later, in a subsequent conversation, he would say, "We are a very conservative group." And then he added the point about minhagim, customs.

In these days, after what had been called by many the "ingathering of the exiles," observant Jews arrived in Israel carrying with them a large variety of religious customs. "I'm not aware of all the min-hagim," said the Rosh Yeshiva. "There were so many, one could not keep track of them all." Now these keepers of the tradition suddenly found themselves in a situation in which they came face-to-face with others who, like them, claimed to be true to the Jewish past (and who appeared to be) but whose past was quite different. There were not only the Jews of the Middle East who came into contact with European ones. There were also Lithuanians and various hasidim who came face-to-face in the same place.

To be sure, traditional Jewry had always been aware of a variety of traditions and customs, and it had by and large tolerated these variations. However, when those who maintained another tradition were in another community, even if only in another village, and far away, these differences were theoretical rather than real. The present circumstances were different. Historical realities had concentrated these bearers of various customs and traditions in a single class of people, locating them in greater propinquity to one another than ever before. Now the other ways were no longer far away; they could not be ignored. Alternative traditions and customs competed in an immediate and sometimes uncomfortable way with one another. One group's old ways were new to another. And all this went on under the banner of preserving or being true to the past. So there they were: committed to old ways and surrounded by new ones, all of which claimed to be the old way.

Sometimes tension erupted among these competitors for the authority of the past; different groups argued that only they were really being true to and upholding the tradition. Others were branded fools or heretics. But many times, and especially because of the overwhelming numbers and contrast of the non-Orthodox world, it was hard to dismiss the traditionalism of others. The various traditionalist Jews became allies in spite of themselves. They became "haredim." "Haredi" became a confluence of customs, a pluralistic identity in which differences of customs had become tacitly tolerated.

"I'm not aware of all the minhagim," the Rosh Yeshiva said. "We have so many here now." "We" included all the haredim.

Limits

During our conversation, a doctor came in to examine the Rosh Yeshiva. He had been feeling dizzy lately and was having his blood pressure monitored. Like other haredim, he was comfortable with the idea of having his body examined by a physician, knew about and wanted the best medical care, and was prepared to follow faithfully the advice and counsel of this healer, although he, like most haredim, was certain that in the final analysis it was, as Orthodox Jews repeated in their thrice-daily prayers, "God, the King, who is the faithful healer."

After the doctor finished with him, he went into the kitchen to examine one of the women there. The normal reticence about contact between married women and men other than their husbands that is part of the standards of behavior of haredi Judaism had no place where the doctor-patient relationship was concerned. To be sure, physicians had to be sensitive to these issues, often having separate office hours for men and women or examining women at times with a female chaperon in the room. (I saw and heard of no cases of female physicians, although I have heard of American haredi women being attended to by some female gynecologists.) Some male doctors left the examining room door very slightly ajar so as, strictly speaking, not to transgress the prohibition of being alone in a closed room with a woman other than their wife. These qualifications notwithstanding, haredi women, like the men, used doctors.

But was this dependence on physicians not problematic, I asked the Rosh Yeshiva when he returned to the room? Leaving aside the fact that it demonstrated that far from being inextricably wedded to the past, haredim were attached to modern science, at the very least in the form of medicine, it also raised another issue: "This doctor whose skills you value and whose advice you follow is a product of another world. Without that world and all it has achieved, you would be at a loss. Doesn't this mean that the haredi world is dependent on the 'sins' of others? You need someone to learn science, even though you don't want to be the ones to do so."

I had already explored this question at Belz. In a sense, I had puzzled over it through much of my own life as an Orthodox Jew. Like all other such Jews, I had long ago learned about what we Jews called the Shabbes goy.[5] This was the Gentile who enabled the observant Jew to fulfill his own obligations to the laws and prohibitions of the Sabbath by performing for him the necessary tasks that the Jew himself could not do. Thus if, for example, the Jew was forbidden to kindle fire on the Sabbath by biblical injunction, he could nevertheless find a Gentile, a Shabbes goy, who could light a fire or a lamp for himself which the Jew could then also use. There were many such tasks crucial to allowing the Orthodox Jew to maintain the integrity of his religious observances that depended on some outsider—the goy— doing the prohibited. That always bothered me. Did it mean that there could not be a place or community made up only of Jews who all observed every jot and tittle of the Torah's laws? Did that mean that the religious system that I had been taught covered all of life's eventualities was not self-sustaining?

It seemed to me that the haredim found themselves in the same quandary—only more so. They, after all, were even more restricted in what they allowed themselves to do. Jews in my modern Orthodox world became scientists, physicians, and in general shared in the secular world without necessarily losing their attachments to Judaism (although haredim did not agree with this optimistic assessment) and so there were fewer things they needed outsiders to do for them. But the haredim were far more dependent on outsiders. I wanted to see how the Rosh Yeshiva answered it.

"This is a well-known question. A rabbi was once asked for permission by a man who wanted to send his son to become a doctor. 'After all, we need doctors,' the man argued. He was answered by the rabbi as follows: 'The world requires shoemakers. Do you want your son to be a shoemaker? No, you depend on others to be shoemakers.' So I say the same thing. Yes, we depend that others are doctors. So what?"

"Doesn't this create a situation in which haredim could not exist alone?" I asked, pressing my question. And then just to make sure that we stayed with the specifics as well, I added: "And how would you react if one of your students came in and told you that he had decided to go to the university to become a doctor? Would this square with the way of life you want him to live?"

At first, he answered in a strictly legalistic way, citing chapter and verse of a responsum by a famous rabbi that argued that in certain circumstances it was permissible for Jews to go to university. Of course, I thought to myself, the Rosh Yeshiva himself had done so for two years (albeit at a place that called itself Yeshiva University).

I said I was less interested in the legal issues of whether or not someone could go to the university but more interested in the social and cultural implications of haredi existence.

"It's very far-fetched that one of our boys would want to do this, and it's never happened," he answered, still skirting the question.

"Well, if it's not likely to happen that one of your students would become a physician, then it seems that the community *is* dependent on outsiders."

A smile played across his features as if to suggest that if I insisted on pursuing a silly question—one which true insiders had no need to pose—he would give me an answer that would set me straight.

"Right, for doctors we're dependent on outsiders. For cobblers and lawyers and tailors as well."

"Does that present a problem?"

"Does it present a problem for other communities that they don't have tailors?"

I tried to suggest there was a difference here because in other communities virtually anyone could be anything. There was no a priori exclusion.

"I imagine in most cases people don't aim to be anything," he countered. "There are quite a few professions which are limited. Today in Israel ninety percent of the construction workers are Arabs. Potentially anyone could be anything, but that's not the way it is."

He was eluding the theoretical and ideological matter and focusing instead on the practical realities. I tried one last time. "But isn't the haredi world dependent on the nonharedi world for some of its most basic needs?"

"We plead guilty. There's no community that's not dependent on other communities for its needs. I don't think we're exclusive in that respect, that we're dependent on others." He was implying that in effect there was no essential difference between haredim and others because in reality there were always practical interdependencies among people. There was no need to see ontological significance in these matters. Every community had its own limitations.

It was the path that had to be followed to become a doctor that constituted the great danger, not medicine itself. That path led through the spiritual minefield that was the contemporary university. The Rosh Yeshiva quoted a verse from Psalms to which he gave his own twist: "God looked down from heaven upon the children of men to see if there was a maskil that did seek the Lord (53:3)." The so-called wisdom of the university was poison, and so was the social atmosphere in it.

"Today's universities are a far cry from universities of former times. Today the university is as far from Toyreh as can possibly be. First of all, immorality is a normal way of life there. In my time maybe it was fifty percent [who engaged in nonmarital sex] in the university. Today they say it's eighty or ninety percent, who knows? An erlicher Yid, a yiray shomayim, naturally can't condone this. A person who will become a university student today will completely leave the way of life of Toyreh."

"But is there not the possibility," I asked, "that there are some erlicher Yidn in the universities? From my own experience, I think there are," I could not help adding.

He smiled at me.

"Would you consider that information dangerous because it would tempt your students to go to the university, because it would suggest the possibility that one could do both?" I continued.

"Right. I wouldn't want my students to be tempted to go because the chances are that they would go away from Toyreh. I wouldn't want a child of mine to go.

"I had a friend in America. He was a rabbi, and his children went to university and terrible things happened to them. They totally left Yiddishkeit. This, after everything their family had tried to implant in them. And this is a common occurrence in America. So yes, there may be erlicher Yidn in the university. But the dangers are so great there, the risks so tremendous . . . " His voice trailed off.

There was an echo here of an attitude with a long history in the haredi world. If the surrounding society glorified the university and new secular learning, haredim turned their backs on this sort of knowledge and exalted not only the time-honored wisdom of the Torah and tradition but even the grace of blind faith: "And we understand nothing, and still we believe. . . . And everyone must believe in God with a simple and complete faith and not be among the philosophical investigators."[6] A good Jew was expected to "annul his reason and to surrender completely to the wisdom of the Torah," for "even a minor departure from the enclosure of the Torah is prohibited."[7] As Rabbi Yitzhak Yaakov, the Bialer rebbe, put it in 1906, at a time when Jews were beginning their intellectual love affair with the university and secular learning: "Although in this generation they want to learn the alien wisdom and *their* crafts so that they will be able to make a living, this is absolutely prohibited."[8] As there could be "no mixing the impure with the pure, profane with the sacred," so there could be no blending of Torah with other wisdom.

And what of the Rosh Yeshiva's physician? Although haredi in appearance, he was, as I now learned, not always what he seemed. Like most other haredi doctors—and there were not that many—he had become attracted to a haredi way of life after completing his training. Had this happened earlier, he would probably not have chosen to pursue medicine as a profession, the Rosh Yeshiva explained.

"There was a doctor who lived in Nahariyya who became a haredi." Nahariyya was a city in the North, along the coast. There were very few Orthodox Jews there. "And he asked if, now that he had changed, he should move to the holy city of Jerusalem. And he was told: 'Now you live in Nahariyya, the citizens of Nahariyya see that a doctor also can be a Jew. If you live in Jerusalem, the Jews will see that also a Jew can be a doctor. It is better that you remain—for now—in Nahariyya.' "

"What about the modern Orthodox?" I asked, referring to those Jews who believed they could be observant in the most Orthodox way yet still go to the university and enter into the mainstreams of modern culture.

"Look, let me explain it this way," he continued after a moment. "If it were a question of someone's child drinking a liquid that was possibly poison, say like drinking water from one of the wells up north —where the risk of drinking poison is less than the risk we would incur were one of our children to go to the university—then the modern parent would not let the child drink the water, even where the risk was very small. Better to be safe.

"But on matters of the life and death of the Yiddishkeit of their children, they take the unnecessary risks." He sighed. "The Yiddishkeit of the modern Orthodox is very superficial."

In my conversation with Yisrael Eichler I had heard a similar argument: "If you once saw someone cross a deep ravine while walking on a tightrope, would you or any of the many people watching him think to cross the high wire on your own because the tightrope walker is doing it?"

How was it possible that some people did go to college without getting their Judaism undermined?

"If you take a sterile object and put it in a place filled with germs, it will immediately be harmed. But if you take a nail, a regular nail covered with germs, and put it into the same environment, it will not be harmed. This is so with us. We are the sterile objects and so we are more harmed by being put in that atmosphere. Those who go to college with their Judaism and come out with it are nails. Their Judaism was contaminated in the first place.

"Some people say that the people you call the modern Orthodox are worse than the secular Jews. A secular Jew knows he is secular, but a modern Orthodox thinks he is religious and can do all sorts of things and not lose faith—and that is the error." He smiled at me and scratched his head through his yarmulke.

Defenders of the Faith

Dependence on others for medicine was one thing, but there were other dependencies that were not quite as benign. One in particular that served to estrange many in Israel from the haredim was the fact that they did not subject themselves to the universal draft. Along with Arabs, haredim were the only class of citizens who systematically refused to serve in the Israel Defense Forces. I put the question to the Rosh Yeshiva.

"What do you say to a father whose son went to the Israeli army, one whose son was killed or wounded who comes and asks why should his son risk, lose, or ruin his life while your son sits secure in the yeshiva and learns?" This question seemed the epitome of the moral challenge. But the Rosh Yeshiva had an answer.

"I would tell him what I really believe: my son sitting and learning Toyreh is the reason his son wasn't killed. And if his son was killed, then my son sitting and learning was the reason that other sons weren't killed."

"But aren't the risks very different?"

"Who knows what risks we incur? Do you know how many poison gases are going to be thrown at all of us here? We're all in a risky business. And as far as pleasures in this world, his son has more than my son. Our children have very little time to take out for the many pleasures in this world because they have dedicated their lives to Toyreh. So you see it's a trade-off. They defend the land and we defend the faith.

"But we have something to offer which is not so common. We aim to have *midos tovos* [good qualities]. We offer yiras shomayim [the fear of Heaven]. Whether we always succeed is another matter."

I thought for a moment about the famous midrash of the Lamed Vov, the legend of the thirty-six just men whose purity and righteousness protect the world. According to the legend, no one knew who they were, but there were always those thirty-six (*lamed vov* in Hebrew) without whom the world should have been destroyed long ago. That they should be observant of God's laws and commandments had always been assumed by the tradition.

The Rosh Yeshiva insinuated that the ben yeshiva served this same function. But he added an element not in the midrash: the notion of a quid pro quo. Since the people in the yeshiva were defending the faith for their fellow Jews, they had a right in turn to depend on those others for certain physical defenses. Physical protection and spiritual protection—which was more important?

This at last *was* the ontological explanation. Of course, this was true only when the haredim succeeded in truly being God-fearing—something the Rosh Yeshiva tacitly admitted was not always the case.

"The grandchildren of Rabbi Akiva Eger once asked him how come that he had such a fantastic knowledge of Toyreh, that what he learned he never forgot? There were other gaonim [Torah scholarly geniuses] who also had good heads but did not have this knowledge. Is it true that his head was so much greater than the other's?

"So he answered, 'No.' But his strength was not his head. The difference between him and the others was yiras shomayim. Rabbi Akiva Eger believed with every iota of his soul, that every word of Toyreh is for him a question of life and death. Somebody who needs a medicine on which his life depends will never forget the name of the medicine, because if your life depends on it, you can't forget it. For Rabbi Akiva Eger, with every word of Toyreh, he felt that his life depended on it and so he did not forget it.

"Now I will admit that the haredim of today are ten miles further from yiras shomayim than even the other haredim of Rabbi Akiva Eger's day, who were haredim to a much greater extent than we are talking about here. And still haredim today—compared to all the other kinds of Jews you could mention—believe that the Toyreh is their life.

"By the way, that's one of the big differences between the haredi world and the modern world. Modern people—probably including the modern Orthodox—believe that today we're much more advanced, superior human beings than they were in Moshe Rabeinu's [Moses, our teacher's] time. And we haredim believe we're going downhill since Moshe Rabeinu's time.

"You talk about these modern Orthodox. They're a hundred and fifty light years from Moshe Rabeinu and Rabbi Akiva Eger. Their belief is very pliable. Do they believe in *Toyreh min hashomayim?*"

"Toyreh min hashomayim" was a phrase that asserted that the Torah, in all its complexity, was divinely revealed to Moses at Sinai and that it was therefore inviolate. This is one of the fundamental principles of Jewish faith, which according to traditional Jewish doctrine (asserted by the medieval Jewish philosopher and rabbi, Moses Maimonides, among others) a Jew must believe if he is to be fully a Jew. For the Orthodox, this dogma—running so much counter to the norms of contemporary rationalist modernity—has become a kind of litmus test of faith. Those who genuinely believe it are counted by many as among the truly "religious." Those who do not may call themselves religious, Orthodox, or any other kind of faithful Jew, but to the traditionalists they are really not.

"For the modern Orthodox, Toyreh is not a matter of life or death. They're not sure if they believe it's min hashomayim. To them what's more important is that their son makes a good living.

"If their son will become a great college professor and he'll be a little less *frum* [religiously observant] or he'll be a *mechallel Shabbes* [desecrator of the Sabbath] once in a while, or maybe he'll forget [to pray] a Mincha once in a while, so *nisht gefarlach* [not so terrible]. It's not a matter of life or death."

The Rosh Yeshiva looked at me as if I were the college professor he had in mind. "If that happened to my sons," I responded, "I would consider it a real tragedy."

"If it would truly be a real tragedy for you," he shot back, "you wouldn't under any circumstances send your sons to college, because there's a good possibility that if they go to college then they might not eat kosher. I know people whose children go, and not only is it that they forget Mincha; they become *frei* [free] altogether. For you it is not a question of life and death; it's not a great tragedy for you if he'll be a great professor, and he'll forget a Mincha once in a while."

"If someone thought that his Yiddishkeit was a matter of life or death," I replied, trying one last time to make my point, "I would think that nothing could harm him, and yet it's precisely those people who are most afraid to venture into the university and the world it represents."

The Rosh Yeshiva was not impressed. "Do I know that my children can't be led astray? Who can say that?"

Wasn't there a danger that someone can go astray from reading the Jewish mystical texts? Hadn't Kabbalah produced heretics as well? Didn't the Talmud tell of the great rabbi Elisha ben Abuya who became a heretic? Didn't many yeshivas turn out rebels?

The Rosh Yeshiva had no patience for these casuistic arguments; they seemed to him to miss the point. Yes, of course there were dangers everywhere; that was the nature of the religious life. But there was no need to take "unnecessary" risks.

"We are far less exposed to the outside world, to its mores. Look, your children will be taught that it's normal to be immoral. They will be taught that it's abnormal to be moral. From a psychological point of view, it's normal to be like modern people are. The question is what is more important for you. You won't let your child go to drink from the wells because one of three wells there is poisoned. But still you would let your child go to the university where there are more than one in three chances that he will be poisoned, thinking it's abnormal to be a good Jew."

"He'll know what to drink and what not to drink. I will have prepared him in advance."

"You know that with all your preparation there is still statistically a one in three chance that he will go away from Yiddishkeit."

"Are the only people who have not gone away from Yiddishkeit in the haredi world?"

"I'm saying haredim believe that Yiddishkeit for them is a matter of life or death. They worry over it all the time. I suppose at the heart of it all is what I said before: yiras shomayim. They are *afraid* of doing an *avera* [sin], afraid to go away from the path of Hashem."

Giving Advice

"We have certain principles and *darchay chaim* [ways of life] which we were taught by our rebbes and which we perpetuate."

The teacher and not the parent was the ultimate guide in life's ways. Indeed, as I would later discover, even in matters of the intimacies between husband and wife, the teacher, the rabbi, was the ultimate authority. For haredim, moral guidance came from parents only insofar as they acted in accord with the rabbis' orders. And that order was the interpretation of the sacred order, rooted in Torah scholarship.

As if to illustrate that haredim turned to their rabbis for guidance on the paths of life, the Rosh Yeshiva took a phone call from a man inquiring about the suitability of a match, a shiduch, he was considering for his son. The caller wanted to check with the Rosh Yeshiva before making any final decisions. He wanted more than a character reference (though that was the ostensible question); he wanted approval. Was the father of the future bride really haredi? the caller wanted to know. He had heard that somewhere in the family there was someone who served as a consul for the State of Israel. If so, this would diminish the yichus, the symbolic family estate and worth, of the bride. Did the Rosh Yeshiva know if this was true?

No, there was no truth to this, the rabbi assured his caller. And what was more, the father-in-law to be was, "for a *ba'al ha bayis* [layman]⁹ the biggest talmid chacham in Europe that I know of."

It was an obvious inversion of the values of the nonharedi world. Whereas people of that world might have been thrilled at the possibility of some official of the foreign ministry, someone who had succeeded in the great world, coming into the family and might have considered his Torah scholarship at best intriguing and at worst irrelevant, among the haredim exactly the opposite was the case. Involvement with the state and its world was anathema, and Torah scholarship was all that counted.

And then, the Rosh Yeshiva added a personal element to close the conversation: "Whenever I went through Switzerland, I stayed in their house." That he would trust these people to that extent was a tribute. Then he reviewed the family tree of the wife.

This call was a reminder that while the modern made his personal decisions alone or with a small circle of his family and intimates, the haredi made his decisions in the community, with his rabbi.

"The truth is that we are a very obedient society to the people we consider *g'doilim* [eminences], people like the Hazon Ish, the Brisker Rav, or today Rav Schach and Rav Elyashiv[10]; we do what they tell us. For example, if we had a question of whether to send a child to the university, we wouldn't consider all the pros and cons that we've been talking about. We would go directly to Rav Schach.

"In my time, whenever I had any important question in life, I went to the Brisker Rav [Reb Velvele Soloveitchik], and I stood in line with hundreds of others. He was my rebbe. Whatever they told us to do, we would do. Whenever you came to him, you always went away with an answer."

All that there was for the individual to choose was which rabbinic authority to make his own.

"Is it that they are afraid of committing a sin or that they are afraid of the social consequences, the stigma and exclusion they would suffer in their tightly knit communities if they deviated from norms?"

"Sure, no one wants to be different. But ask yourself why the communities maintain these standards, why they would make someone who deviates feel bad. The answer is obvious. The community as a whole has a sense of yiras shomayim. And so anyone who counts himself in it—even if in a particular instance he doesn't exactly feel *ol malchus shomayim* [the yoke of the Kingdom of Heaven]—is still part of the community of yiray shomayim."

Other Jews

After this, we talked more about a whole range of other topics. About whom he considered his authorities and who were his allies and opponents. Beyond the specifics, the Rosh Yeshiva made it clear that he was at best ambivalent about all of them. There were rabbis he called his own, others whom he saw as having legitimate authority but who were nevertheless "not my g'doilim," and still others like the official chief rabbis of the state whose authority was somehow tarnished though still recognizable.

As for opponents: "If a person is for himself a Reform or assimilated Jew, I can only have *rachmonos* [pity] for him. But those who stir up hatred are another thing; they stir up the whole society. And those who are brought up and educated to hate the black Jews . . . ." He used the term that many nonharedi Jews used as a shorthand for those who wore the black hats and coats, the haredim. "For them I have no sympathy."

And yet, even among them there were those one could turn around. "We are very interested in making ba'aley t'shuvah [those who return to the observances], in bringing people to Yiddishkeit. We like to bring back Jews."

And what of those who seem beyond reach?

"There is no such thing." He looked at me and smiled the biggest smile of the afternoon.

The afternoon was fading into twilight and the time had come to say the evening prayers. The Rosh Yeshiva stood to put on his black frock coat and hat, and we walked together to the yeshiva chapel. Secure in his world, certain of what he believed, he maintained a dignity and authority that was impressive in its conviction. I had seen all I could see in the yeshiva. It was time to return to the community.

18

Passages: Matchmaking, Betrothal, and Wedding

"The life of an individual in any society is a series of passages from one age to another," wrote Arnold van Gennep in his classic essay *The Rites of Passage*.[1] The key passages in our lives are all marked publicly because all communities exercise their power to define and ratify changes in individual status. Indeed, one of the best ways to understand the relationship between a community and the individuals in it is to look at the rites of passage. Among the two most important of these are marriage and death. In both cases, persons are "captured," separated from a group to which they have belonged for a long time, and thus they implicitly call into question the capacity of those groups to hold on to their own.[2] They are thus not simply matters that concern the individuals undergoing the experience.

To deal with the loss and change that marriage and death represent, societies of all sorts have instituted weddings and funerals. These ceremonies essentially reassert the group's control over the passage. They demonstrate that there can be no marriage without our formally marking it; and death is not final until we have said our final farewells. Neither love nor death is more powerful than the community. Weddings and funerals are demonstrations of this and therefore especially good occasions to observe and examine the community in action. I turned my attention to them now.

There were several other good reasons to go to weddings and funerals to uncover the haredi community. Just as I had discovered that haredim broke the routine of their lives and found ways of leaving their neighborhoods without leaving their communities with group outings like pilgrimages, so I had already begun to realize that the ubiquitous weddings and funerals were also examples of protected mass diversions. A haredi, after all, did not generally go for a night out; he did not go to a movie or a show, a café or a restaurant. To do this would not only bring him into contact with dangerous influences, it would also be *bitul zman, bitul Torah,* a waste of time more appropriately given over to sacred pursuits.

But weddings and funerals were legitimate times out—proper diversions. According to Jewish law, *mesameach chasan v'kallah,* to give joy to the groom and bride, was a divinely ordained good deed that the sages listed among those whose reward one reaped in this world and the next. To be sure, the pleasure of a wedding, with its dancing and singing, festive meal and gathering, was a reward in itself. As for funerals, taking time off for *levias ha-mes,* accompanying the dead to their final resting place, was an equally important religious obligation. It too was listed as a deed for which one was doubly rewarded. And if it seemed that funerals could hardly be described as events that were fun, the most important of them, those that drew the entire community, were—as anyone who carefully observed them soon discovered—notable occasions of diversion from the everyday patterns of life activity. And both were protected diversions, occasions when the gathering was of insiders, with the perils of contact with outsiders greatly diminished.

Betrothals and Weddings

Why so many weddings? To the haredim, those who view themselves as the true Jews, life does not become complete without marriage. "Any Jew who does not have a wife is not a man," the Talmud declares.[3] "A man may not live without a wife and a woman without a husband," adds the Tosefta.[4] And when must marriage occur? "A man who is twenty years old and has not yet wed is spending all his days in sin," warn the rabbis.[5] Ideally, as they explain, "Eighteen is the time for marriage,"[6] As for women, the Jewish sources are equally unambiguous: "When your daughter matures, go get her married right away."[7]

There are many reasons for this endorsement of early marriage. Certainly, among the central ones is that it provides a way of satisfying and at the same time institutionally controlling the vigorous and disruptive sexual appetites that reach a feverish pitch during these post-pubescent years of life. Second, although most important from the tradition's point of view, marriage facilitates the fulfillment of the biblical prime directive to "be fruitful and multiply." And even though according to Jewish law "only the male is required to fulfill the commandment to be fruitful and multiply," he may not marry a woman whom he knows to be barren.[8] Having children, the creation of a family, is thus a crucial aim of marriage.

But having a family is more than a ritual obligation. For erlicher Yidn it is the essential way of finding their niche in the society. The single adult is an anomaly; the couple without children is considered afflicted, the childless woman deficient. Marriage is the first corrective step, the way to move properly from childhood to adulthood and from thence into the community. Where does the whole process begin?

Making the Match

"A man and a woman. A meeting between the two sexes. A first contact. Marriage. Matchmaking. A deal. Formally, we are speaking essentially about a deal. Two sides that want to come to an agreement for a common goal."[9] Among haredim, love—if it comes—comes after marriage, for matrimony is not simply the concern of the couple; it is the affair of the community. And even before the wedding regulates change, matchmaking controls it. Finding a mate is far too important to be left to the caprice of love; it is best handled in a reasonable, planned, and logical way so as to minimize the disruptions that passions could cause. "Much effort is expended by haredi society in order to nullify the personal, intimate, romantic in the process of finding a partner."[10]

"This is how it is and how it has always been," said one haredi to me. To be sure, there have been some adjustments to contemporary realities. Nowadays, the couple are consulted before the match and given an opportunity to approve or reject a potential mate. How does it work? Two cases: a girl and a boy.

Moshe's Daughter

A hasid from Mea Shearim whom I shall call Moshe told me how his sixteen-year-old daughter became bethrothed. Deeply concerned about her future and in light of the fact that all her classmates were getting matches, she was particularly nervous about her prospects for marriage. Although a good student—certainly important—her family lacked yichus. "Yichus" means having the right family and community connections. It means being related to someone important—a scholar, a famous rabbi—or having a family known for its piety. "Yichus" means not having skeletons in the closet—skeletons like a family member who has left the world of religious observance.

Even if one has yichus, there are other matters that can somehow disqualify or at least diminish one's chances for finding a good match. Being too different is dangerous in a community that prides itself on its Ashkenazic black and white uniformity. The person who is too dark-skinned or with unusual features may be in trouble. Even having hair that is the wrong color can be a problem. "I had a hard time finding a wife because my hair was red," one hasid told me. "They thought I looked too much like a goy."

Psychological or emotional problems—anywhere in the family—can also reduce a person's value on the marriage market. Here it is not just the stigma that is avoided; there is also a fear that somehow these problems will be passed along.

Moshe's daughter was worried that in the tightly networked haredi world she would be found wanting. First, her parents are both first-generation haredim, newly Orthodox, and therefore rootless in haredi society, bringing little or no yichus to a marriage. Second, to make matters even worse, they were in the midst of a divorce, after over twenty years of marriage and five children. Third, not only was her father not a scholar, her mother was not Ashkenazic. All these givens, the daughter feared—not without reason—made her a hard match.

Indeed, when her father walked out on her mother, the girl was in anguish not only because of the breakup of her family but also because she feared this would foreclose any possibility she had for an acceptable marriage. Her past was after all key to her future. She sensed that her prospects for marriage were not dependent on anything over which she had control. Totally powerless, she felt her destiny to be completely in the hands of others.

The girl ran away from home and spent time with a Neturei Karta family whose daughter was her school friend. Her parents let her stay and the friend's family provided shelter; she was after all part of the community. Taking over the task of finding her a mate, while her own family dealt with its turmoil, these neighbors also sent out word through the community that she was still eligible and should be married off as quickly as possible.

Even before this turn of events, *shadchanim,* matchmakers, had already begun soliciting her parents, as they had those of other girls in her class. This was natural. In the haredi community the shadchan is like the college or army recruiter. He or she comes near graduation time and knows exactly where and when to find prospects. Several of the first suggestions for a match were rejected out of hand by the parents—in particular, Moshe. They were from families who were newly Orthodox or else in turmoil like themselves. Whatever troubles there were in the family, both mother and father knew that their daughter's future would only be assured if she married into a "good" family. They wanted her to marry "up," which meant moving into a family with roots and respect in the community.

At last, the shadchan found her a match the parents considered acceptable, a brother of her teacher's husband, a Sanzer hasid who was studying in a Lithuanian yeshiva. Although Moshe was a Lubavitcher hasid, he was ready for his daughter to marry into a different group. "He's a fine boy, a hasid from a fine family," Moshe explained. The proposed bridegroom was twenty-four years old, advanced in age by haredi standards. He "looked a little bit funny," Moshe explained; he had been born with a cleft palate. Although surgically repaired, this had apparently made it hard for him to find a match. In spite of the drawbacks to Moshe's daughter, the boy's parents had consented to the proposal. At first, Moshe was not sure the deal was struck. In a previous case where both parents had agreed to move forward, the boy had at last refused to accept the marriage when he discovered that the girl's parents were separated.

Moshe made inquiries about this family and was told by those who knew them or who knew someone who knew them that they were warm and close. They also had some yichus, a cousin who was a brother-in-law of a well-known scholar. Then Moshe met the boy briefly, and he liked him. He thought he would be good to his daughter, or at the very least good *for* her. Like Moshe himself, the boy's father was not a scholar. And while Moshe worked for a yeshiva, the boy's father worked as a clerk. Neither of them made very much money.

It was time to arrange a formal meeting between the families and the couple. But first there would have to be an understanding of the financial arrangements. This was something the parents alone would work out; it was too important to be left to the children. (Indeed, nearly everything about the marriage was too important to leave to the children.) What was the nature of the financial arrangements?

For every couple the first question is, Where will they live? The accepted formula in most cases is that both parents pay half of the price for the new couple's apartment and share the cost of the wedding. From the outset Moshe told his *mechutan,* his daughter's future father-in-law, that he could not afford more than about $20,000 toward the apartment. In the current market, the least expensive apartment in a haredi neighborhood was running about $50,000 (and this in a marginal neighborhood in Ashdod, a city on the coast where haredim had begun to move); this meant that there were some financial issues still to be worked out. The wedding, even a most modest affair, would cost about $5,000, and the shadchan would walk away with about $500. With these sorts of expenses, these two families would obviously have to go to one of the many community funds for *hachnoses kallah,* monies collected for the bride's dowry. If there was not enough available, the boy might himself have to go around collecting money (or else someone would have to do it for him). This of course would take him from his studies, would make public his financial troubles, and would make the prospect of this particular marriage less attractive to him. In such a case, while his getting married would bolster his status, the search for funds would counterbalance much of this.

This was a time to search the family network for support. But with everyone having large families these resources were being constantly stretched. And all the while, a rising influx of Soviet Jewish immigrants was raising the cost of apartments. The government was threatening to give less support to yeshivas, who would in turn give lower stipends to their students. Money was getting tight. Marriages would become more difficult. Haredim would have to be particularly creative in finding resources.

At last, Moshe and his mechutan managed to put together what they thought was a workable package. There were loans, some creative financing, and hopes and prayers that in the time between betrothal and wedding, the housing market would not change too radically. Now if their children agreed, the marriage would be on.

At last, there was to be a meeting between the couple. Given the troubles between Moshe and his wife, the decision was made to have the meeting at the home of the boy's parents. As in several other hasidic groups, the Sanzer custom is not to serve any food in the house to the other family until and unless there is a betrothal. So when

Moshe and his wife brought their daughter, there was nothing on the table.

The boy and girl were allowed to meet for half an hour; they sat alone in another room, the door slightly ajar so that neither would be, strictly speaking, alone with a member of the opposite sex. The parents chatted outside.

At last, Moshe's daughter came out. Parents and daughter spoke privately while the boy's parents consulted in the other room with their son. She liked the boy. He made her laugh, and—even more important—he had quoted Torah thoughts to her. He must certainly be a scholar. And if she got a scholar, she would surely find a proper niche in society; her future would be assured, and she would not be shamed. Yes, she was certain he was the one for her.

She was sixteen. Did she understand what this meant? She would be seventeen when she was married. The boy would be eight years her senior. Moshe explained to her that this was for keeps; he did not want her to go through what he and her mother were experiencing. She was sure, she said, this was the one for her. Please, please, could she have this one?

The boy too had agreed to the match. The betrothal could now go ahead. Suddenly, the boy's parents brought out a big spread that they obviously had prepared in advance. Had either of the children not approved, the parents would have made some phone calls and started some further negotiations. But now that all were agreed, the betrothal contract was brought out and signed. In accordance with custom, dishes were broken as a sign of the betrothal. And though the hour was near midnight, a taxi was sent for Moshe's sons, to bring them to the celebration.

By the next day when the girl came to school, word of her engagement preceded her; signs of celebration were posted in her classroom. All the girls surrounded her and asked who the boy was and what she thought of him. At last, she was *in* again. The wedding would take place in a year, the following Adar (March). "When Adar comes in, happiness abounds," said the sages.

Moshe bought a set of the Talmud for the boy (as was expected) and his daughter received a watch in return. There was no point in giving seforim to girls; learning was for the men. In the course of the year, the girl would get other jewelry.

From now on Moshe and his family—but especially his daughter —would be invited to all the celebrations (mostly weddings) of her future husband's family. This would give her a chance to see him, as she peeked through to the rooms in which the men were gathered

(even at celebrations men and women remained separated). He, however, would seldom if ever see her. With her girlfriends she might find
excuses to sneak glances at him as she passed near his yeshiva and
waited for him to go by. But there would of course be no further
reserved meetings or private discussions. The deal was done. Both
could go back to their lives until the wedding. The girl felt far more
relaxed. Her future lay ahead of her and she had passed the first large
hurdle.

Yankel

"Yankel," a Nadvorner hasid, had troubles finding a bride. He was
a "fine yeshiva boy," but there were "troubles" in his family. His
father was dead and a brother had a nervous breakdown; a second
cousin was in the Israeli army. These were serious strikes against him.
Now nearly twenty-three, his future was in jeopardy; he wanted to
find a wife more than anything.

For a time, his desperation had driven him into negotiations for a
divorcée. Among haredim the divorced—especially women—were
spoiled goods. It did not matter whose fault, if anyone's, the divorce
was. In the end, Yankel decided this was not a desirable match. At
last, after many negotiations, he was presented with the choice of a
Tunisian girl. This was not ideal for an Ashkenazic Jew, one from
generations of east European hasidim like him, or so he believed. She
was darker-skinned than he was, and knew no Yiddish. She spoke
French but was learning Hebrew. Although her family was a pious
one, they were of Sephardic origins. They were not enthusiastic about
a daughter marrying an Ashkenazic hasid. Still, both sides agreed to a
meeting.

Yankel's aunt, the matchmaker, arranged for him to meet with the
girl at the home of a friend, a son of the admor, the leader of his
hasidic sect. This would put him in the best light; the location would
speak volumes about his yichus. Still, this would be just a preliminary
meeting to form some face-to-face impressions. The family flew in to
Israel from France where they were now living. For about a half hour
both families sat together. Her parents spoke only French—his aunt
translated.

Then Yankel's mother suggested they leave the couple alone for a
while. But, she added, there was no need for any hurried decision.
Better that her son sleep on it for the night. "Let him dream about
this, to see if he still likes her in the morning." Yankel's mother was

convinced that in dreams God's will could often be known. And matches needed such divine signs. Of course, Yankel's mother agreed, if the girl did not like *him*, that too would end the matter.

For half an hour the couple remained alone in the room, the door slightly ajar, while the parents sat outside discussing financial and other details. Yankel told his grandfather that he wanted only a half hour because sometimes "everything in the heart beats properly but there is still not much to say." He had little experience talking with women other than his sisters.

In their time together Yankel and his intended talked about where they had gone to school and where they might make their home. Was she prepared to move to Israel? Would her parents allow it? Would she miss them too much? Would he allow her to visit France?

After about a half hour, Yankel's grandfather asked if he could come in, but the boy asked for a bit more time. He discovered he had no trouble talking, nor did she. There were matters to settle. In the end, Yankel was satisfied and the girl, "Yehudit," willing. But there were still other matters that needed doing. Yankel asked everyone to wait while he paid a late-night visit to his rebbe. Without such a consultation, he would not move forward.

The Nadvorner rebbe made his inquiries. Who was the girl? Who was her family? What did the boy think?

"I don't know," he answered, but he was blushing. The rebbe was silent, waiting. And then Yankel said, "I think maybe yes." The rebbe smiled.

Yankel curled and uncurled his very long earlocks around his finger as he recounted the story. "What concerned me was 'honor,' for in the matter of a mixed marriage between hasidim and Sephardim, honor is at stake. And these matters of honor do disturb things."

The rebbe gave his blessing.

"For me, the rebbe's blessing absolutely sealed the matter. The rebbe would not bless a marriage that would bring me dishonor." The blessing tacitly told Yankel that his place in the community would not be harmed by such a marriage. After all, to anyone who would ask he could say, "The rebbe blessed the marriage." There remained no doubt whatsoever in his mind that this would be his wife. The admor always knew what was best. And everyone in the Nadvorner community knew the admor knew what was best.

Yankel came back to where they were waiting for him. "The rebbe gives his blessing." It remained for the families to agree. His mother still insisted on his sleeping on this matter. Yankel worried that the girl was too dark.

The next day the rebbe called one of his sons and asked him to gather information about Yehudit and her family. A rebbe must look after his hasidim like family. Then he asked his wife, who had seen the girl. "She's not so dark," she told him. The rebbe repeated this message to Yankel when he came later for one more word of reassurance. "My wife says it's not so noticeable; she's not dark at all. Your imagination is working a bit here. *Efshar ligmor* [complete the deal]," he said.

Yankel went to a second meeting with Yehudit's family. As an orphan and a mature young man, he was doing more of the negotiating than would normally be the case, and it made him more anxious and uncertain. "It was a bit hard," he recalled, "but I was calm since the rebbe had given me the blessing, and I said that I could now close the marriage even without seeing her again. For if the rebbe says that this is it, then I know that this is mine and I have nothing to fear, and I know that I shall have a good life."

There were no discussions of love, no expressions of passion. Before they were about to drink l'chaim to close the deal, Yankel wanted once more to check with the rebbe. He made a phone call. "The admor calmed me down with a few words on the telephone, and so I was calm and happy and I felt as if I was getting precisely what I was looking for." As he retold the story, he paused here. Then he smiled broadly and said, *"Boruch Hashem* [Praise the Lord], he was right."

Yankel concluded, "Now, when an unmarried avrech asks me advice, I tell him, anyone who has brains should get himself a sensitive and gentle European girl like mine [Yehudit's North African Sephardi background had been transformed in his mind to "European" since their marriage]—they are much better than the sabras [the Israeli-born]."

In both these cases, the marriage is a kind of *contractual* arrangement, a deal, with the couple having the right of refusal but little else. But more than that, it is also a *social* arrangement, a way to locate the couple in the community, a way of institutionalizing their passage into the next phases of their lives so that they may stay in that community. Where will they live? How will they live? These are the crucial questions to be asked and answered.

Misnagdic Matches

Even among the misnagdim, the young men of the Lithuanian yeshivas, matches are arranged. Here, however, more time is allowed for the couple to meet in advance of the wedding. Occasionally, they may even go out together for a walk. Compatibility is a greater concern. The misnagid yeshiva boy is somehow more independent. Yet he too, if he is to remain true to the haredi view of life, will check with his rosh yeshiva, his parents, his community, before making any decisions about marriage. And his female counterpart will hardly be more independent.

A Misnagid's Wedding

But what about the wedding itself? Again, a case history speaks volumes. The previous illustrations emphasized the world of the hasidim; this one comes from the misnagdim. The groom was a boy studying in the Mir Yeshiva, an institution founded in White Russia early in the nineteenth century and, after the Second World War, reestablished in Jerusalem. The bride came from a family of Hungarian Jewish origin that had lived in Jerusalem for three generations. They had met through a family matchmaker and after several rendezvous agreed to marry. For this couple, as is generally the case among young haredi misnagdim—perhaps more so than for hasidim—matters of personal compatibility were a major concern. Hence the greater number of meetings between the couple before any final decisions are made.

At last, the wedding was held at the Ramat Tamir Hotel in Ezras Torah. With its newer and somewhat larger apartments and parks, Ezras Torah is what one might call a haredi suburb. As for the Tamir Hotel, unlike many of the hotels in downtown Jerusalem, whose front desks were piled with brochures like *Hello Israel*, which listed restaurants, movies, and other sites of interest, the Tamir stocked a glossy circular that listed and described "The Yeshivas of Jerusalem." For its guests, this brochure contained the sites of greatest interest. On the Tamir's newspaper stand were none of the Israeli national papers, only haredi ones. And unlike the other hotels, there were no guests here who were not Orthodox Jews. So the Tamir was on the approved list of places that haredim used for weddings.

To be on the list a party hall must have a kitchen whose standards of kashrut observance are exacting, must cater only to a haredi clientele, and must abide by a sometimes shifting series of stringencies that haredim establish on an ongoing basis. Because the Tamir Hotel's catering was under the supervision of the Eda Haredis, all weddings within it had to have separate seating for men and women. The father of the bride, a somewhat liberal member of the haredi community, had wanted a modified version of this seating: a section in which men and women were allowed to sit together in addition to the two separated sections. The hotel refused because the community tightly controlled what went on here; any deviations and the owner risked losing his Eda Haredis kosher supervision and with it the many weddings that made up his business.

Like all other moderns, haredim had learned well how to use their considerable and growing economic clout. Those who did not meet their expectations or live up to their standards lost their business. And there were more and more who found themselves embracing the strictest standards to stay in operation. The liberal outlook of the host notwithstanding, as a member of the community, he was institutionally locked into its standards. The wedding was not exactly his to make just as he wanted it.

The *chuppah*, the actual taking of vows under the traditional wedding canopy, was scheduled for approximately eight-thirty in the evening. Beforehand, people would sit at tables—men in one room and women in the other—and nibble on food, chat, or sing songs. Quietly and unobtrusively, mendicants moved throughout the room. These alms collectors were a ubiquitous feature of many haredi weddings. They knew that if they were to be supported by the community, weddings were the place to solicit that support. Seeing them, the host quickly rushed over and handed each some shekels.

Men organized various congregations for reciting the evening prayers. Hallways, corners, and other function rooms were momentarily taken over for the purpose. Then, with the prayers completed, the groom would be danced in to place a veil over his bride. Accompanied by a phalanx of his friends and teachers from the yeshiva, he would behold her briefly and then be danced out again. Unlike the elaborate productions that many associate with the chuppah in the United States, with long marches down an aisle by endless lines of relatives and friends, parents, grandparents, bride and groom—a kind of Jewish version of the English royal wedding—the actual ceremony at this haredi wedding and many others like it was relatively brief and simple. Held outside under the stars, the canopy was surrounded mostly by men (women stayed inside since, with the men always in the front, they would never get close enough to see or hear anything anyway) and the bride, accompanied by her mother, circled the groom—dressed in white robe, or *kittel*—seven times before the seven blessings and vows that made up the ritual were read. A public reading of the *ketuba* (marriage contract), a sip of wine, the breaking of glass in mourning for the fallen Temple, and the ceremony was over. Now the crowd went back inside, where quite a few people had remained, never bothering to actually witness the ceremony.

In the meantime, the new couple were ushered away to a room by themselves. This isolation together—*yichud*, as it is called—was the first time they had ever been allowed to be completely alone together with a door closed. Originally meant to allow for the consummation of the marriage, yichud was today (when the bride's virginity is no longer attested) normally a chance for the couple simply to eat a bit—they had fasted all day, for the wedding day is by tradition a time when all their sins are washed clean and for Jews atonement is coupled with fasting.

In the meantime, the community—all those assembled—began the *seudas mitzvah*, the banquet. People continued to arrive and depart throughout the evening. They were from all walks of haredi life: the more liberal Lithuanians, heads of yeshivas, sectarian hasidim. The differences to insiders were clear. Among the men what to an outsider might appear to be just so many men in beards and black coats were to insiders a rainbow of differences. The length and shades of black of the frock coats, whether or not they had four buttons or two, the placement of a ribbon on a black hat, the cut (or lack of cut) of a beard, the curls and length of an earlock, the color of socks and the length of trousers or knickers, hats versus black-velvet yarmulkes, neckties or no ties, were all clear signs of who was who. A hasid from Ger had knickers and a high-brimmed hat, a Lithuanian ben yeshiva wore a double-breasted frock coat, Lubavitchers had fedoras, Breslov hasidim had gold-striped coats, and so on.

People watched to see who came and who went, who was seated where. And the host, the bride's father, above all others, had to keep his eye carefully focused on the door to make sure he caught all the comers and located them properly. There were no place cards and there was no preset program. Those were American innovations that had not yet made their way here.

And what of the women? They were in a separate room, doing much the same as the men—eating, talking, and dancing. They were clearly visible to anyone who walked out into the hallway and peeked inside, as I did. The hallway acted as a meeting place for the more liberal men and women.

The music came from a keyboard player, a drummer, and a clarinetist, along with a male singer (the sound of women singing is absolutely prohibited in haredi circles—too immodest). The instrumentalists were Lithuanian yeshiva men, while the singer, a Yemenite, had long earlocks and wore a hat. All the tunes—Ashkenazic melodies—were played in the same fast tempo. While they played and sang a host of favorites, at a couple of points during the proceedings the keyboard man played Bach and Mozart as background. No one seemed to notice, but there was no denying that at the very least, aurally, this world was not quite so closed. Indeed, even the treatment of the most traditional tunes was influenced by sounds from other domains. One song was introduced by what sounded like the opening bars of "Lady of Spain." The music at hasidic weddings was no different. At least musically, culture and counterculture came very close to each other.

At last, the new couple ended their yichud. Each went into a separate hall. When the groom came in among the men, he was greeted with song and dance, as was the bride in her parallel and simultaneous entry among the women. And as they were each surrounded by circles within circles until they could hardly be seen by anyone outside the ring, the imagery was unmistakable. At the very moment of their separation from their families of birth, as they entered into their new family that would be their own, after the briefest of time alone together, here was the community enclosing them, reminding them that they were inside it. The circles grew tighter and tighter; there was no getting out.

19

Passages: Funeral

While death undoubtedly remains a great puzzle to all people, its reality is a constant presence in haredi neighborhoods. The walls of their surroundings are always plastered with the black-on-white posters mourning the death of one or another citizen. The streets regularly echo with the clarion call of an impending funeral, as members of the *hevra kadisha*, the burial society, drive through with a loudspeaker atop a car from which they repeatedly blare the details of who has died and where and when the funeral will take place. Every zaddik wants to be buried in the Holy Land, where according to tradition the Messiah will come first and where the resurrection of the dead will begin. When important community figures die, the streets are choked with mourners, the funerals almost like neighborhood pageants. Bodies wrapped in shrouds, carried through the streets on their way to burial, and trailed by a procession of mourners are also common sights.

Less a celebration but no less a community gathering, the funeral is the time when people try "to face death, to conquer and master it, to come out of it alive."[1] Put differently, it is a time when haredi society celebrates its life. Nowhere did that become clearer than at the funeral of Rabbi Yitzhak Yaakov Weiss, Av Beit Din, chief of the religious court of the Eda Haredis.

Rabbi Weiss died on the eleventh of Sivan. (The only calendar that counted in the haredi world was the Jewish one; most people did not even know their birthdays on the Gregorian ["goyish"] calendar.) This was a day which, according to *Erev Shabbos,* one of the more prominent haredi newspapers, was heavy with mystical significance; it was exactly two years after he installed a new Torah scroll in the Zupnick Buildings, headquarters of the Eda Haredis.

From early morning people had plastered the walls with posters announcing the death and funeral, which was to begin at 3 P.M. (or 3:30, according to some) at the Zupnick Buildings. At first, before the body was even prepared for burial, there were only three posters. The largest was of course posted by the Eda Haredis itself, which both bemoaned the loss of their judge and announced that the funeral was declared by the court of Eda as a time of *bitul melacha,* an occasion to cease all work.

As the morning progressed, however, more and more posters of mourning appeared from a variety of other organizations, including all the major haredi political parties, yeshivas, and the girls' schools like Bais Yaakov. Even as the eulogies were being spoken and broadcast over loudspeakers mounted atop the buildings, new death notices were being affixed to the walls, including ones from the supporters of the Eda in America and Canada. Long after everyone knew of the death and the funeral, signs were still being put up.

The fact that there were so many posters announcing Weiss's death was significant. As every insider knew, the importance of a person was often measured in the number of posters announcing his passing. The walls around the Zupnick Buildings were now plastered with the black-on-white notices of Rabbi Weiss's death. As the time for the funeral approached, these posters began to eclipse all others on the streets around the buildings.

At first, those reading the signs did so to get the basic information and news. But by the end the posters became signs of affiliation and solidarity with the community. By then the reading of the posters began from the bottom. The last line was always the signature, and everyone wanted to know who was paying respects. To pay respects to Rabbi Weiss was also to pay respects to the community from which he came and whom he represented. There were differences between those who posted early and those who did so later. The latecomers' respects were not nearly as valued as those who were first to be posted. No one wanted to be the last one to add his poster to the wall.

But the posters did not simply allow a group to pay respects. They also provided a vehicle for it to advertise itself and its message in public. For those who wandered about at the margins of the crowds that collected for the funeral, reading these posters became an important occupation. People moved through the streets looking at the signs, reading out of them the messages that only insiders could catch. A group of young yeshiva boys read one broadside and chuckled among themselves over a signature from the "Holy Yeshiva" Such-and-Such. The readers knew this "holy yeshiva" had contested some of Rabbi Weiss's court decisions. Here in the death notice the "mourners" were having their last word; they were getting back; they were the "holy yeshiva."

A poster from the Satmar community appended its funeral announcement with a reminder that men and women should be careful in the crowd not to come into direct physical contact with one another. The message was clear: we at Satmar are scrupulous in our stringency on this matter of segregating the sexes.

By three-thirty the courtyard around the Zupnick Buildings was packed. Only a relatively few dignitaries and close family members would get inside where the body lay in a simple white shroud on a stretcher. From the moment of his death, Weiss's body had not been left alone. After being removed from nearby Bikur Cholim Hospital, where he died, it was ritually washed by the men of the hevra kadisha and purified in a time-honored ritual. Wrapped in a shroud, clothed in a *kittel* and in his black and white prayer shawl, its fringes ritually cut, the body had been escorted to the Zupnick Buildings. Now it lay there, watched over by young yeshiva boys reciting Psalms.

The nearby streets were fast filling up; it was still early. In the ninety-degree heat, mourners—almost all of whom were dressed in black, including black hats—tried to find some shade. Doorways were plugged with people; the sheltering shade from the few trees were quickly grabbed. Women congregated in a separate alley; some stood on rooftops or crammed onto verandas.

Who's Who?

For those outside waiting, perhaps the most interesting activity was keeping their eyes on the narrow path that snaked through the throng toward the door and along which dignitaries entered. Timing was important. Each "immortal" made sure to find his own good time for a funereal entrance. One or two could be seen sitting in their cars or otherwise waiting for a signal from a gabbai as to precisely when to enter.

With the arrival of each dignitary, a murmur spread through the crowd. "Who is it?" "Look, who is here?" "It's . . ." The more important the arrival, the larger the moving phalanx of black-hatted men who surrounded him, the more heads that turned and the wider the path became. Thus, the arrival of the most important people became palpable: if there was a lot of turning and pushing, someone of great eminence must have arrived. And when he was inside, the sounds of the commotion as he was seated came over the loudspeakers through the open microphone, confirming for the uninformed who went by. The *yunger leit*, someone announced suddenly, should remain out of doors. Apparently, there were a few overzealous youths who tried to push their way inside.

Why had so many come? Why had they heeded the call for *bitul melacha*? After all, funerals were common. Hardly a day went by without new memorial posters being affixed to the wall or a car with a loudspeaker driving through the neighborhood announcing a funeral. There were even many people from abroad whose death was announced with the words "his [or her] casket is coming." So why so much ado about Rabbi Weiss?

In life Yitzhak Yaakov Weiss was able to draw on ties that cut across the haredi community. First, as chief judge (Av Beit Din) of the Eda Haredis (for almost exactly nineteen years to the day that he died), he was himself an influential figure. Its decisions were after all law for many who considered themselves haredi. Second, born in Galicia nearly ninety years ago, he had married a daughter of an Av Beit Din from Hungary and had served as a judge there for many years— thus bridging these two domains of traditional Jewry. For a post-Holocaust generation in search of authorities after the decimation of their community, he was an important symbol of continuity with the sacred and martyred past. Third, he was a brother-in-law of the Viznitzer rebbe, himself a prominent figure in the haredi community, sitting as he does on the Council of Torah Sages and serving as leader of a large sect of hasidim. He had yichus. Fourth, Weiss was author of a significant series of contemporary code books known as the *Minchas Yitzhak*, the ten volumes of which were used by many haredim as a guide for how to behave according to the strictest interpretations of Jewish law. In this age of going by the book, Weiss had written *the* book, a sequel for many to the *Mishnah Berurah* of the Hafetz Hayim. Thus, he had ties in both the hasidic and the nonhasidic worlds. Weiss was remembered as one of the rabbis who after the Holocaust had solved many of the thorny legal problems of *agunot,* the "bound" women who by Jewish law could not remarry as long as their husbands had not officially been declared dead or judged divorced. After the war and its legacy of missing persons, agunot had abounded; through his scholarly and sensitive interpretations of Jewish codes, Weiss had legally freed many to start a new life. The community remembered him for this. Finally, although actual membership in the staunchly anti-Zionist Eda was relatively small, nearly everyone in the haredi world had in some way been affected by Rabbi Weiss. Not only did his judgments affect huge numbers of people who abided by the religious court he headed, but his supervision and certification of kashrut (religious dietary standards) at local hospitals and other public institutions had made these places accessible to many in the community.

He was, in short, not simply a local leader. So when the word went out that there were not only tens of busloads of mourners from all over Israel but ten planeloads from a yeshiva outside London to which the rabbi had connections, few if any were surprised.

There was probably one more reason people had for coming. The date was the twelfth of Sivan, a sweltering Thursday at the start of a long, hot summer with no holidays for a long time. Here, suddenly, was an extra holiday, a respite from the humdrum of everyday life. Under cover of the funeral, people could mass together—some had not seen one another since the last big wedding or funeral—and catch up on things. This unexpected break, this bitul melacha—all in the framework of a religious event—allowed one to take time off without feeling any sort of guilt or misgivings. This was not to be missed. The young threw their children into strollers and prams and went; the aged got up and out. Students used the time to get together with their friends. Children got off early from school and chased one another through the streets, barely hiding the joy on their faces as they rushed toward the Zupnick Buildings. What a challenge to squeeze through the crowd, trying to get toward the front. People were shtippen zoch all over the place. Amid all the formal mourning for a man who had died at a ripe old age, revered by all, there was thus a community exercising communion.

The funeral had a collective political and social importance, for it provided an unmistakable way for those gathered to demonstrate their collective size, strength, and presence to the world. The assembly took on a life of its own. It was not just Weiss they were all coming to honor. It was themselves, the spectacle of their existence, that was being celebrated. No one could fail to be impressed by the size of the crowds. Today photos were allowed, even encouraged. The secular press was there, and the haredim knew it; many were pleased. A few whispered when they recognized some of the prominent reporters. Participants reveled in the fact that the police had closed streets for them and had summoned a helicopter that hovered above them, a mark of pride for many who pointed to it again and again in the sky. Later, they proudly took part in a funeral cortege. This show of respect to the rabbi was a prominent display to the world that "We are still here and not to be ignored!" Haredim loved moving in waves, "making the streets black with our numbers," as one man put it.

Thousands marched in the massive silent parade through the city, past the Old City walls and Arab neighborhoods, with their residents staring in mesmerized silence, up to the ancient Jewish cemetery on the Mount of Olives. There they would lay the rabbi to rest.

Eulogy

A broiling June sun beat down upon us. Black hats and coats, kerchiefs and yarmulkes, absorbed the heat. An acrid odor of sweaty gabardine filled the air. People mopped their foreheads. A hose was dropped from the roof for those who wanted water and trucks moved through the streets distributing drinks. Now at last at four-thirty the formal proceedings were about to begin.

The basic structure of the funeral was simple. First, recitations of Psalms; second, eulogies and stylized entreaties addressed to the deceased for forgiveness for offenses committed by the living, importunings meant to enlist his aid as intermediary on high. Next came a recitation of Kaddish, the memorial prayer. Finally, the funeral ended with a mass procession to the cemetery, interment, and a final repetition of Kaddish. That was the elementary design, but each of these details was embellished with the particular mark of the community.

Thus, when someone inside began in a broken voice to recite Psalms aloud over the microphone, the crowd understood that they were not here simply to quietly listen but began to recite the words responsively. Most seemed to recognize the Psalm from the opening words, and many said it from memory while others pulled out small Psalters from which they read.

The recitations transformed the streets and squares into a kind of open-air chapel. It was as if this community had found a way to sanctify even the most profane of its places. This in itself was not unusual. They often found themselves in crowds on these streets reciting Psalms or praying. They did so whenever there was a mass protest—whether against the drafting of women to the army, archeological digs at sites considered too close to Jewish cemeteries, or any other practices they considered threatening to their way of life. At such times prayer was a form of public expression: a symbolic appeal to another order and a reminder that God was on their side. As such, it was an effort to overcome a sense of powerlessness. Some of that was going on here too, for nothing reminds people of the limits of power more than death, and funerals are protests against it.

One after another, the dignitaries began to offer their eulogies. Again and again, Weiss was praised for having been a defender of the faith, a champion of yesterday's ways of yisrael sabbah. Who was it they had lost? "The crown of our glory." Where was he going? "To the yeshiva on high." The afterlife was after all a mirror of the haredi world. The reward for being a scholar was to be able to sit in the yeshiva on high. Past and future were all part of a seamless whole.

But the eulogy was not just for the departed; it was also a way for each speaker to distinguish himself and make an impression on the crowd—if not upon Heaven. As they asked for pardon and described the holiness of the man, speakers screamed, their voices dramatically breaking with tears. "He who studies Torah has a soul from heaven though his body remains earthly, while he who does not learn has both a body and soul that rest in the ground."

"During his last night of life," one of the eulogizers, his voice breaking, told the crowd, "this holy spirit recited the *Shema* [Hear, O Israel], preparing himself for death."

Said another, "Who knows what the cause for this great man's death was?" The death of a holy man could not be viewed as simply the natural course of life, the consequence of an old man suffering several heart attacks. No, Weiss was a martyr in the haredi culture war against the outside world; Weiss had died because of the pritzos of Yerushalayim (whores of Jerusalem) who everywhere surround and defile the Holy City. Who were they? All the women who dressed immodestly, who lusted after men, whose lewd photos on bus shelters debased us. For months haredim had been fighting to remove the suggestive advertisements for swimsuits and other products in which pictures of scantily dressed women were displayed on bus shelters throughout the city. The funeral eulogy was a chance to launch yet another attack in this continuing battle. The implication was clear: the sages and holy men were endangered by these posters and by the world outside; the culture war was a battle of life and death.

As speakers begged the deceased to forgive them, the tenor of many eulogies took on the qualities of prayer. Amid the melodramatic wailing, the actual words were sometimes difficult, if not impossible, to understand, but their tone was unmistakable. One rosh yeshiva sang his oration to the tunes of the book of Lamentations; the melody was the same as that sung in mourning for the Temple on Tisha b'Av and the lines rhymed.

The eulogies painted the ideal model of a haredi Jew: humble, pious, a scholar, and willing to fight for the way of the Torah against those who do not keep its precepts. Whatever he was in life, in death Weiss was perfect.

As the afternoon and the speeches wore on, people, increasingly worn out by the heat, let their attention flag. A few started smoking and others collapsed wherever they could. Beggars weaved about, jingling change and asking for contributions.

"Charity will deliver us from death," they whispered.

Procession

At last, about two hours after the eulogies began, an announcement was made that there was a need to hurry to bury Weiss before sunset. The law is strict on this: the dead must be buried as quickly as possible, and after sunset a new day would have begun, too late for interment. All eyes turned toward the door of the Zupnick Buildings to watch for the body to be brought out. Suddenly, six young pallbearers carrying the enshrouded body on a stretcher rushed out, forming a human shield around the moving stretcher. For nearly three miles the body led a line of mourners ten or more abreast through the city, down into the Valley of Jehoshaphat and up to the Mount of Olives. They walked westward, but someday—so the tradition claimed—the footsteps would go the other way as the Messiah led the resurrected from the mountain back through the valley and into Jerusalem. Along the way, the pallbearers handed off their holy load to others without missing a step.

In a blitz the body was whisked past me, a wide phalanx of yunger leit sweeping the crowd to the side and behind them. So quickly did the mass of people move that parents and children were sometimes separated. Near me I heard a boy call to his mother to get going, and then I heard her reply that she could not move until all the men had passed by. A woman did not intrude herself into a swarm of men. Indeed, for the most part, women did not join the massive processional that oozed and flowed through alleys and narrow streets until it broke out onto the Kings of Israel Street and toward the Damascus Gate.

Many people strained to see the dashing pallbearers who burrowed through the crowd that sometimes swept out in front of the body. Like many others, I was simply swept along by the mass of people. Young and old followed along, one leaning upon the other. It seemed an apt metaphor for haredi life and what the funeral had made palpable: being haredi meant being *in* the community and being swept along with it wherever it went. There was little point to resisting its pull and push.

I walked along for a while. The parade passed many onlookers. The police closed the streets on the route of the march. The parade was a sea of black. People marched for the most part in silence. Occasionally, a car carrying an admor and his entourage would come honking through and this would cause some excitement and swarming in the crowd. As we passed through Arab East Jerusalem, through streets that normally saw few Jews on foot, one could not help realizing that once again, as on pilgrimage, the haredi community had found a way to move beyond its regular orbit only by moving en masse.

At the entrance to the valley of the shadow of death, quite a few stood on the precipice and stepped back to watch the sea of black flow into the canyon and up the mountain. "Look, look," a father said to his children. But it was not just the rabbi's body in white surrounded by the black of the mourners' coats that he pointed out. It was the sight of so many of their own that he showed his children. Out of death came a reminder of life. "Look how many people, look how many we are!"

20

Passing Signs:
The Writing on the Wall

In some places people say the "walls have ears." In the haredi neighborhoods, the walls have mouths. The posters on them are the words they speak. Few last more than a few days; like the daily newspaper, they have a quick rise and fall in people's attention. As they are plastered on—commonly by Arab day laborers working for the printers—people gather to read them, fresh off the press.

This emphasis on words and posters is by no means exclusive to haredim. Most of the towns of Israel have prominent billboards on which are affixed broadsides and handbills covered in words. Unlike Americans, for example, who will stop to look at a picture and read only the smallest number of words, Israelis commonly will stand for long periods of time reading every last syllable of a five-hundred-word poster. So too do haredim, and in this one might say that they were like other Israelis. It was the content of their posters, and their juxtaposition, which was unique. Reading them is a way to get a line on what exercises and concerns the community.[1]

What was on these posters? Already noted are the pervasive signs posted about the education and the cultural protection of children, warnings about how to act and where to go on Purim, and of course the ubiquitous announcements of death. But there was much more. There were posters that explained how to dress, where to pray, what to eat and to avoid eating. Others that advertised new books or places to shop for products of special need to the people who lived here. There were posters that offered moral guidance and political advice. Direction and counsel were everywhere, and one could use these broadsides as signs that marked the various directions to turn.

I saw ads for spas at the Dead Sea that claimed to scrupulously follow haredi standards of conduct, or announcements of special bus lines that offered direct service to the tomb of one or another zaddik, trips haredim often made. There were ads for face creams and soaps as well, especially those graced with the certification of the haredi rabbinic courts, which affirmed their ingredients to be unquestionably kosher. These simple commercials for places, products, and services were ways to demonstrate to and remind the community not only that it carries economic clout but also, as one haredi put it to me, "Whatever *you* have, *we* have too—but on our own terms." Yet these product advertisements served another function as well. They allowed competing certifications, products, and services along with the groups behind them to take their rivalry to the streets. For every new edition by one seller, there was a "better" or "newer" deal from another; one bus line competed with another, one group's kosher certification superseded another, one spa offered more than another, and so on. Indeed, rivalry was an important subtext of much of the poster culture—and not just in the commercial realm. There was also competition for the hearts and minds of the haredim. Broadsides became tools in this, articulations of points of view, public stances that either attract or repel followers. Reviewed carefully and often heatedly discussed among clusters of people reading a new one, they allowed readers to explore what being haredi means.

The following sign, affixed to a store window on Israeli Independence Day, told passersby that this store was not closed in order to *celebrate* the holiday of the Zionists, but to *protest* against it. It stood as a reminder that haredim contest the secular Zionist Jewish option, that they do not accept the idea that being a Jew means being a supporter of a secular state and its secular holiday. Independence was a sham; the true Jew was never independent but always in the service of God. Not only did the poster imply all this, but it invoked parallels and expressions—"Na-Zionists" and "may their name and memory be blotted out"—that associated the Zionist claimants on the Jewish culture with the greatest enemies of the Jewish people. The clear insinuation for the haredi reader was: if you are not with us, if you celebrate

With the help of Heaven

MY STORE IS CLOSED
AS A SIGN OF PROTEST!

Against **40** years of fluttering the flag of
rebellion against G-d and His holy Torah
and more in the name of "Israel" by the
Na-Zionist heretics, may their name and
memory be blotted out, and their
agudist and impure partners, may their
name and memory be blotted out.

[Signed]

HE WHO GRIEVES AND LAMENTS THE SIEGE OF THE *NA*-ZIONISTS,
MAY THEIR MEMORY AND NAME BE BLOTTED OUT.

THE STORE OWNER

their holiday, you are the enemy. Nevertheless, if an aim of the poster
was to mark the "boundaries between groups" and strengthen "group
consciousness and awareness of separateness," it also revealed that
Israeli Independence Day was on these people's minds.[2] Who could
miss the fact that this store, like those in the other parts of town that
did celebrate the day, *was* closed.

Not only were rivalries between insiders and outsiders expressed
on the signs; there were also ideological battles fought *within* the community reflected on these billboards. One of the most bitter of these
was—still in these days—the historical rivalry between hasidim and
misnagdim. This time it exploded in a feud between the hasidim of
Chabad, followers of the Lubavitcher rebbe, Menachem Mendel
Schneerson of Brooklyn, and the yeshiva people whose nominal leader
was Rabbi Eliezer Schach, head of B'nai B'rak's Ponovezh Yeshiva.
The immediate matter was messianism. Devoted to their rebbe's leadership, many of the Lubavitchers claimed to see in him and his messages glimmers of a messianic time. Signs proclaimed this everywhere.
To the misnagdim and Rabbi Schach, these suggestions were heresy.
The controversy, expressed on a variety of fronts, including rival political parties (Lubavitch aligning itself with Agudat Israel and Pono-

vezh with Degel Ha-Torah), spilled onto posters too. One such broadside began with the following huge headlines:

A SHOCKING REVELATION

In the words of Chabad themselves:

THE REBBE IS THE MESSIAH AND EVEN THE CREATOR OF THE WORLD HIMSELF

Beneath them was reproduced the masthead of the Lubavitcher newsletter, *K'far Chabad* and the following paragraph from an article in it, circled and enlarged:

> . . . the Messiah at the time of redemption will be revealed to all people to be made not of flesh and blood, not even flesh and blood like our great teacher Moses, but rather to be the Holy One, blessed be He, himself!

Juxtaposed to this was another quotation: "Soon indeed His Holiness, our master, teacher and rabbi, May He Live for Many Good Days, Amen—the King the Messiah, in all his glory and grandeur will reveal himself."

Were the Lubavitchers saying their rabbi was the Messiah, even God himself? Careful readers would see in the Hebrew letters for "indeed"— ש מ מ (English: M-M-S)—the initials of the Lubavitcher Rebbe's name. To opponents like Rabbi Schach even this was appalling. "THIS PAINS US VERY MUCH!" the poster concluded in giant letters. "But we cannot close our eyes to the facts."

Posters put the give-and-take on the walls:

OUR TEACHER THE GREAT RABBI SCHACH DENIES MALICIOUS DISTORTIONS:

With the help of Heaven, Friday, 25 Adar I 5749 B'nai B'rak
I have heard claims made in my name that at a gathering connected with the upcoming elections, I said the people of Chabad are not Jews. I publicly announce that in malice do they distort my words! I spoke in Hebrew, and this is what I said: what they [Chabad] do is not the "Jewish" way. They distorted my words on purpose to damage and libel me for they think that from this they will derive some benefit and gather more votes in these elections. And when they claimed that I called them the children of an impure woman, I testify before heaven and earth that I never said words such as these but only criticized their effort to build a ritual bath that was not in line with the standards of the Chazon Ish, may the memory of this righteous man be a blessing. For he alone is our teacher, and he too opposed their ritual baths with all his might. I do not forgive anyone who fabricates words on his own and then says that I said them.

And with this I request that each and every one will pass these words to his fellow.

Eliezer Menachem Schach

If the Lubavitchers claimed the rebbe as their Messiah, the followers of the Rabbi Schach publicly chose other paths. He was their leader but was no Messiah.

With the help of Heaven, 28 Adar 5749

VIGOROUS PROTEST AND TORAH WARNING

We the students of the holy grandfather, remnant of the Men of the Great Assembly and chamber of the Hewn Stones [where the ancient *sanhedrin* sat] of the previous generation, who illuminates the paths of hundreds of thousands of faithful believers of the house of Israel in our holy land and in the entire world: The awesome genius and gilding of the generation **Our teacher Eliezer Menachem Schach**, may he live many good days, amen, the head of the Ponovezh Yeshiva,

Obligate ourselves to vigorously protest the dishonor of the Torah, a sin that will not be forgiven, by the editors of the newspapers "Erev Shabbes" and "Yom HaShishi" [popular newspapers of the Haredi Press] that published announcements and interviews which grievously wounded the giant of our age, our rabbi and teacher. We proclaim, with all the strength of our holy Torah, a complete ban on all those who come in contact with or, heaven forbid, support those who perpetrated this.

We, believers and children of believers, affirm that this our Torah may not be changed and we will always follow and listen to the da'as Torah imparted to us from the lips of our great sage and singular teacher, may he live many good days, amen.

We shall continue to cleave to the line and path that our rabbis and teachers, may their souls be bound up in the paradise forged: [rabbis' names are listed]

By their light and as one blessed group shall we journey toward the true Messiah.

For insiders, posters like these were responses to ongoing exchanges. To outsiders they were mysteries. As each camp fired broadside after broadside, local readers checked the walls to see battle lines drawn and redrawn. For many haredim the posters were the box scores of a continuing contest. Who would have the last word? Whose argument was better? Whose broadside was more vitriolic? Who went beyond all boundaries? Who would have to apologize? What did the people on the street think?

There were other kinds of give-and-take on the walls. During the intermediate days of Passover, for example, days when schools were closed and children on holiday, a poster announced the arrival of an amusement park in town. To counter its appeal and its encouragement of lightheadedness, always a risk for those who were committed to the anxieties and stern character of haredi life, someone had affixed a poster next to it that advertised a new "Guess the Right Passover Laws" game for children. All over the neighborhoods, whenever the first sign went up, so too did the second. They offered alternative views of how to entertain the children. YOU CAN TAKE YOUR CHILDREN TO THE AMUSEMENT PARK FOR THE HOLIDAY, the first poster said, to which the second replied: NO, DON'T DO THAT; THERE ARE OTHER MORE HAREDI WAYS OF ENTERTAINING THEM. TRY A JEWISH LEARNING GAME INSTEAD."

With the help of Heaven

GIFTS TO THE POOR FOR THOSE WHO TAKE CARE

IT IS IN YOUR HANDS TO SAVE SOME JEWISH SOULS AND ALSO OBSERVE THE OBLIGATION OF GIVING GIFTS TO THE POOR WITH CARE.

In line with the instructions of our rabbi and teacher, the scholar and chief judge R' Moshe Aryeh Freund, may he live many days, funds will get to the poor on the very day you make your donations:

Send donations to . . . .

The community was not all rivalries. There were also signs that reminded people of their obligation to take care of one another. Many promoted philanthropy, reminding people of the abiding religious obligation of charity, the need to "strengthen, encourage, and lighten the heavy yoke of financial obligations put upon the poor so that they may continue to promote Torah and live according to its holy dictates."[3] Under the aegis of their rabbis and institutions, the community was always searching for ways to link giver and recipient. Posters described families in need and detailed how and where to give funds. The assumption was that the haredim had to take care of their own or no one else would.

There were also signs of the times that showed that while these people might be inside the ghetto, they knew what was going on outside too. When many Israelis demonstrated in the streets for more housing, haredim did too. Not only the chiloinim needed more houses:

DEMONSTRATION TODAY

Monday, the 1st of Av 5750, at 7:30

About the lack of housing in the haredi areas.

MEET IN KIKAR SHABBES

The Assembly of Haredim who lack housing

But perhaps the most pervasive signs of all had to do with the matter many haredim considered to be among the essentials that separated them from all others in the modern world: sex.

"I'll tell you something," one hasid once said to me, "the greatest dangers we face are mindlessness, materialism, and"—he paused for a moment and looked over at my tape recorder—"turn it off."

I pushed the button. "And?"

"Sex. These are matters that for you and people like you are not considered quite so dangerous but which for us are the drug of death. I can't easily speak about those matters that modesty prevents, but I will tell you there are lusts that draw from us all that is holy. This is something from which we must totally separate ourselves, and the first step is in the utter separation between men and women in the haredi world."

"No sex at all?"

"A clean house has to have a mop, a bucket, and a broom. Once a week you have to clean the house well and then put these items away for the next time. A house that does not have these items gets dirty, and where there is dirt, there is sickness as well.

"But a house in which they put the mop and the bucket on the table is also a dirty and sick house. So it is with sex. In the modern world the mop and bucket are on the table. Everything is sex.

"*Kedushat ha-yesod*"—he used the term for essential holiness— "requires you to put these matters off the table."

But when they put it off the table, they plastered it on the wall. Everywhere haredim went, they were reminded of sex. Haredim believed, perhaps no less than Freud, that "the sexual instincts . . . are conspicuous for their strength and savagery," and "Woe, if they should be set loose!"[4] They too were prompted to strictly regulate and control these passions, so constantly lurking beneath the surface. Signs were all over the place.

For haredim nothing so much embodied sexuality as a woman. Her hair, arms, legs, and voice were enough to arouse the basest instincts. Thus, in public, on the street, in the presence of men, women had to be properly covered. Signs proclaimed this message again and again. Indeed, among those posters with a life longer than a few days there was one that hung at the borders of the neighborhood, a marker that implied that beyond that point was another domain. No one could miss it, and no one did. It was even printed in English for those who were total outsiders and who might not otherwise get the message. And those who for one reason or another did not take note of it were reminded of the fact by the Modesty Patrol of the Eda Haredis or

---

DAUGHTER OF ISRAEL

The Torah requires you to go about in modest clothes that cover all parts of your body according to the law

A REQUEST TO WOMEN WHO PASS THROUGH AND VISIT

NOT TO PASS OUR NEIGHBORHOODS AND OPEN PLACES IN SHORT CLOTHES AND SHORT SLEEVES

The Residents

individuals who took upon themselves the role of "Guardians of the City," the Neturei Karta.

By no means was this the only such sign. There were others, like the one below, that addressed the young girls who might still be thinking about how to dress themselves. At an age when their secular counterparts know nothing of lewdness, prostitution, and immodesty, young haredi boys and girls already have working definitions of these. Mottoes, rhymes, and epigraphs are posted everywhere reminding them what they are. They list appropriate dress and behavior for those who would not be lewd or immodest. Even the littlest children had to be properly covered. Modesty had to be inculcated again and again, for sexual appetites were always lurking below cover, at all times and ages, ready to burst through and confound erlicher Yidn.

YOUNG GIRL

SHE WHO WEARS SHAMELESS CLOTHES,
WOEFUL ARE THE DAYS OF HER YOUTH.

HER SINS ARE MORE NUMEROUS THAN THE
STRANDS OF HER HAIR.

COVERED ARMS, COVERED LEGS,
NECK AND HEART COVERED—

THIS IS MODEST DRESS!

It was so important to keep the sexes from coming too close to one another that some stores had posted signs announcing that, in line with the recommendation of the court of the Eda Haredis, they would have separate shopping hours for men and women because otherwise in their cramped quarters prohibited physical contacts might occur. Among haredim, even the most apparently innocent brushes were fraught with danger.

Some were ready to be even more extreme on this matter. Thus, on the eve of the Days of Awe and Yom Kippur, the holiest of days, a time of atonement and repentance, one group of eight men in the Ezras Torah neighborhood published a proposal—they called it "a great repair," and duly posted a sign on walls and lampposts all over the affected streets.

A GREAT REPAIR

As we stand in the days of mercy and forgiveness, we come with a request to the dear residents of our neighborhood, the community of Israel.

Since on Sabbaths and holy days we thank G-d there are no cars that travel through our streets—these streets and sidewalks are filled with women and daughters of Israel, praise G-d, and there occurs on this account (not intentionally, heaven forbid) difficulties and disturbances in observing our accepted restraints of modesty.

THEREFORE WITH THIS WE TURN AND ASK FOR "A GREAT REPAIR" SO THAT THE SIDEWALK ON THE RIGHT, FROM THE DIRECTION OF MATTERSDORF AND KIRYAT SANZ, **WILL BE USED FOR THE PROMENADE OF MALES ONLY,** AND THE WOMEN SHOULD CONCENTRATE THEMSELVES PLEASE ON THE LEFT SIDE.

Similarly, the women should try to stop gathering in doorways and alleys on the paths leading to synagogues.

And through these restraints of modesty may we all merit on this judgment day to be inscribed in the book of life and for a year of redemption and salvation, speedily and in our time.

[signed]

Of course, few if any took the recommendation seriously, but the motives behind it, the desire to fix a defect in their lives, to better prevent contact between the sexes were, as many had to admit, admirable and entirely understandable. Things could happen when males and females were too close. Perhaps someday it would be possible to follow their proposal. Clearly, to many, rigorous separation represented an ideal. Out of sight, out of mind, beyond reach, beyond trouble—this was the way sex was to be handled.

There were also posters that were more subtle in their concern

A CALL TO THE DAUGHTERS OF ISRAEL

The sins of our generation have made it common lately to see MARRIED WOMEN WEARING A GENTILE WIG that is practically identical to their own hair, so that they appear to go about with—heaven forbid—uncovered heads. We consider ourselves obligated to inform everyone of our da'as Torah: **THIS IS ABSOLUTELY PROHIBITED.** And even in those places that permission was given to wear a wig, no one ever imagined that Gentile wigs such as these that make women look like free women, prostitutes, heaven forbid, would be permitted. With these wigs there is no obvious difference in the appearance between a woman who is married and one who is available. And one sin will elicit another, **AND THIS CERTAINLY CANNOT BE PERMITTED.**

And in our generation, when the separation between the vineyard of the house of Israel has been breached and the barricades of modesty have been destroyed in a frightening fashion, and each day our despoilment is worse than the day before by those who plow the fields of prostitution, the lowest of the low —our obligation must be redoubled to create a reserve and preserve that the destroyers cannot touch, to stand fast and fence in our faithful.

And therefore all G-d-fearing people who care about the honor of their maker and the honor of their holy Torah so desecrated, and whose heart aches and trembles [haredi] about its continued existence must be scrupulous not to go about with any wig but only with an appropriate head covering.

AND OF COURSE TO BE SCRUPULOUS IN ALL THE DETAILS OF DRESS, IN THE WAYS THAT OUR MOTHERS DID, so that they remain in line with the demands of modesty so as not to arouse attention and not, heaven forbid, excite the low-lifes.

And for this our sages of blessed memory promised that the kosher woman, whose modesty is her glory and grandeur, will merit upstanding children, loved on earth and on high. . . .

with sexuality. On the surface they seemed simply to be focusing on the matter of married women's hair. These were broadsides that periodically reminded women, who "naturally" seemed inclined to adorn themselves, that they had to be careful about what they did with their hair. For the haredim a woman's hair was a special problem. It was symbolic of her femininity, something to be hidden away once she married. Among the most scrupulous, it had to be shaved off completely, the shorn head then covered with a kerchief. But some women wore wigs over their own hair, wigs as attractive as their own hair (some might say more so). This seemed to abide by the letter of the law, but to many haredim it missed its spirit. The spirit was to keep married women obviously off-limits to all men except their husbands.

This poster was signed by twelve well-known leaders, including the rebbes of Ger, Lalov, Spinka, and Vizhnitz, as well as a number of yeshiva heads from B'nai B'rak. In its flowery language it touched many of the themes that were basic to haredi Judaism: the prohibition to be in any way like the Gentiles, the importance of keeping separated from those who did not share the same ways of life, the need to tremble and remain anxious about the future of Jewish existence, the importance of preserving the next generation pure, and the abiding presence of corrupting forces all around. The key to all this was the woman and her properly covering her hair—or more specifically, keeping her sexuality under wraps. If she let it all hang out, woe.

For all the public concern with sex, it was nevertheless one of the most secret matters of haredi life. What was on the signs on the walls was only one part of the story.

21

The Triumph of Sex

To the haredim I was a combination of opposites. If I was not a true insider, I was also not, strictly speaking, a complete outsider. Although I wore a yarmulke on my head and thereby identified myself, as several of them put it, "as a believer," I was clearly not one of them. I was something more ambiguous, standing at the intersection of closeness and distance. After all these months, my time in the yeshiva, visits to rebbes, pilgrimages, weddings, funerals, and so on, I shared some level of understanding of, and maybe even a degree of empathy with, their ways. But in spite of that, I was not going to share their way of life—and they knew that. That I wanted to learn more about them, and appeared to find all they told me interesting while seldom imposing my own opinions into the discussion, or at the very least muting them whenever I could, invested me with a kind of charisma. But the fact that I continued to embrace elements of the world that they continued to reject made me fundamentally repugnant. Most of the time I did not think about this—although it was certainly implicit in my role as anthropologist and participant observer. But when I began my search into the normally unspeakable region of sex, I found myself thinking about these matters. It was then that I discovered that for many of the haredim I was the perfect stranger to whom they could divulge these secrets.

In his now classic essay on the stranger, sociologist Georg Simmel articulated the special power of the stranger when it comes to secrets. As a stranger, especially one whom people expect ultimately to move on, he said, one "receives the most surprising openness—confidences which sometimes have the character of a confessional and which would be carefully withheld from a more closely related person."[1] I was enough of an outsider that they could talk with me about matters they would not easily talk about to one another, but also enough of an insider so that I could comprehend the meaning of these revelations.

Why talk about sex? For one thing, as the pervasive signs in the neighborhoods suggested, it really *was* on their minds; they saw it intruding itself everywhere. But because there was such a taboo against talking about it, they were deflected from discussing their concerns until someone like me—beyond the taboo but not beyond understanding—came along who was at once interested but not looking to criticize their concerns. For my part, to echo William F. Whyte in his study of Italian ethnics to whom he was likewise a stranger: "I was glad to accept the people and to be accepted by them," without either having to "argue with [them] or pass moral judgments upon them."[2]

In the close relationship that often develops between an anthropologist and the people with whom he shares a life, displays of closeness are often a necessary component of the experience. Somehow, by revealing and talking to me about these normally taboo matters, people signaled a special kind of intimacy and demonstrated their trust. To be sure, I was expected to reciprocate with understanding, fascination, and answers to questions they had about matters in my world—from the innocently naive to the penetrating—that they were also curious about and did not know how or whom to ask.

What was the difference between movies, theaters, and symphonies? What were "background music," "jazz," and "classical music?" Were hasidic songs classical music? Why did sons seem closer to their mothers and daughters to their fathers? Why do some men look more at women and others don't? In my classes where men and women learned together, which were smarter? Was there a lot of cheating among married couples where I lived?

And perhaps there was another reason. Matters of sex were bona fide secrets. Secrets weigh on people. Indeed, as Simmel suggested, secrets carry a tension that is only "dissolved in the moment of revelation. This moment constitutes the acme in the development of the secret; all of its charms are once more gathered in it and brought to a climax. . . . The secret . . . is full of the consciousness that it *can* be betrayed; that one holds the power of surprises. . . ."[3] Simmel calls this "the fascination of betrayal."[4] For many of the haredim to whom I talked, the disclosure of these secret matters was a moment of power, a chance to bowl me over with what they told me.

So when, tentatively at first, I began to ask some of the people with whom I had established relationships of trust to tell me about matters of sex, I found to my surprise that they were ready to talk to me about these matters. And often, after I was given some particularly private sort of information, there would be furtive glances and pregnant pauses during which my reactions were clearly being gauged. Some might have been there to shock me, to see if I would be repelled or attracted. But more often I felt that the fascination of the betrayal was a prideful act meant to teach and instruct me about their world. As one man put it: "You think you understand, Professor, you understand nothing—listen to this."

I suppose there was also another motivation—but this one was beyond reason. I discovered it when I once asked a hasid whose trust I had earned to reflect for a moment as to why he had shared such intimacies and confidences with me. He answered simply: "I believe that everything is preordained in heaven. Our conversations, your questions and my answers, all preordained, and therefore with the help of Heaven, it will all turn out for the best." His revelations were then nothing short of an expression of faith—not responses to my questions or interests.

At first, I was struck at how the disclosures seemed aimed at proving how different erlicher Yidn were from the chiloinim. The revelations were meant as critiques of the coarse lust and physical passions that haredim claimed obsessed others. Unlike them, erlicher Yidn had sex lives that were refined reflections of the demands of religion. Attitudes toward, and practices of, sex were simply one more element in the contest of cultures: *they* do it their way, and *we* do it ours; *ours* is better, finer. Later, however, as haredim began to talk about details, about how they perceive and relate to the body, about how they are initiated into the knowledge and practice of sex, about their notions of masculinity and femininity, about the relationships between men and women, far more came into the picture.

But all this I know only now, in retrospect. At the outset I was not certain what—if anything—I could learn. In preparation, I read all the books dealing with the subject I could get hold of, including ethical tracts, educational guides, and finally—although they were hard to procure by outsiders like me—sex primers, especially those given to those about to be married. These were books that mixed citations from the sacred literature and ethical tracts with counsel and advice about how to deal with matters of the body and coupling. While many of the hasidic groups and a few of the misnagdic yeshiva students had their particular manuals, there was much that was repeated in all the handbooks. Fundamentally, they were all built on the same premise: sex was blessed and divinely ordained, but it was up to God's creatures to strictly regulate it according to the dictates of religion. And restraint was always in order.

While these books gave me insights into the formal aspects of haredi sex life, asking for them and getting advice from my informants about what to read also served as a means of raising and exploring the subject in conversation. After being turned toward a particular book, I would read the tract, ask for clarifications, get new recommendations for reading, and finally be given extensive explanations and confidences. It was these last that enabled me to get beyond the books and learn what happened in real life.

A Haredi View of the Body

This account, however, should not begin with a discussion of sexual relations or even a general view of sexuality, but rather with the haredi conception of the human body. To the haredi, and in line with the opinion of the sages, the body is to be a temple of God: "If a person sanctifies his body by his behavior, then the Holy One, blessed be He, dwells within it."[5] Properly, all one's bodily pleasures "should be in the service of the Creator."[6] Perhaps that is why the Seer of Lublin, one of Hasidism's early founders, declared: "When the body enjoys plenty the soul too enjoys spiritual richness."[7] Nevertheless, physical pleasures always run the risk of overwhelming the spiritual. At best, they can become a "drug of death."

And yet there are bodily pleasures that all people inevitably experience. Eating, sleeping, and the pleasures of sex are among the most prominent. To the contemporary haredi, one of the most difficult struggles of life is not to be overcome by the charm and seduction of these pleasures. "With trembling ["haredi-ness"]," wrote Rabbi Eliezer Papo, the nineteenth-century Bosnian author of *Pele Yo'etz*, an ethical tract much studied by haredim, "must a person approach his food and the rest of his pleasures."[8] All of these must be sanctified with benedictions, both before and after.

Eating must not be considered an end in itself. Rather, "a person must conduct his eating only to enable him to be healthy and strong enough to serve God, may His name be blessed."[9] Every morsel devoured offers a chance to utter a blessing. Nor must one be a glutton and exceed his basic needs of nourishment.[10] When a person turns his full attention to God, it is often with fasting that this is done. Many haredim engage in regular fasts for the repair of their spirit.

As for sleep, said the sages, "The beginning of one's decline and fall is sleep," for "when he sleeps, he does not busy himself with Torah nor with the service of his Maker."[11] Following kabbalistic custom, many hasidim began to rise at midnight to recite prayers and engage in study, while other haredim—particularly those of the yeshiva world —studied until late at night and then made certain to rise at dawn's earliest light in line with the rabbinic warning that "morning sleep drives a man from this world" because it makes him miss his morning prayers.[12] Ideally, a person should "habituate himself to a minimum of sleep" and even that minimum "should not be for the pleasure of his body, but only to fortify his body for the service of God."[13]

And what of sex? Among the haredim, as I would discover, sex "is not perceived as a personal matter, an intimacy that occurs between a man and woman."[14] It is a religious obligation. "A man shall leave his father and mother and cleave to his wife, and they shall be one flesh," says chapter 2 of Genesis. And why? Because they must "be fruitful and multiply" as God commanded the first couple. The Talmud and later the Code of Jewish Law elaborated the point: "Anyone who does not procreate has as much as spilled blood and diminished the image in which he was created, causing the Holy Presence to remove itself from the people of Israel."[15]

Even when one had children, the obligation to engage in sexual intercourse did not end. "Even though a person fulfilled the obligation to be fruitful and multiply," Maimonides, the great medieval philosopher and Jewish codifier ruled, "our sages obligated us not to cease from further procreation as long as we have the strength, for anyone who adds even a single soul to the House of Israel has as much as built the entire world."[16] The more children the better; birth control was shunned.

And what about those who could no longer have children or who engaged in sex at times when conception was impossible, for example during pregnancy? Here there were two good reasons for continuing. First, as it is written in Exodus (21:10), conjugal pleasures are one of a Jew's fundamental religious obligations. The sages always interpreted this verse as a mandate for a husband to satisfy his wife's sexual needs, whether or not these could lead to procreation. As for his needs, these were the second reason for engaging in sex. Since a male's sexual cravings were a constant irritant, something that would take him away from his obligation to study and serve God, he should fulfill them so that he would be able to return undisturbed to his true calling. To be sure, these urges were constant reminders of human weakness, and therefore it was best to learn to minimize them lest they become over-powering. Marriage was the sanctuary within which these urges could be controlled.[17]

Beryl and Breindel

Sociologist Howard S. Becker has argued that stories are "an effective, maybe the most effective way of transmitting an abstract point."[18] Throughout these pages, I have followed this approach and I continue to here. Rather than summarizing what I learned from the many people I talked to about all this, I shall focus on two people whom I'll call Beryl and Breindel. Their story contains in it some of the essential points of what I have learned about sex and the haredim. They were members of the Reb Arelach hasidim.*

While the matter of sexuality is of concern to all haredim, no group is more concerned with controlling these bodily pleasures than the Reb Arelach. Soldiers in the Modesty Patrol, the self-organized group of young avrechim who took it upon themselves to root out all signs and hints of sexuality, prowled about the community to see to it that no breaches of the strictest standards occurred. They were the ones who spit at the women who passed through their neighborhoods in attire they considered too revealing. They were the ones who created "committees for the purity of our camp." They had rules about all physical pleasures, including exercises for eating, such as taking their food slowly to the mouth and then putting food back when they felt they wanted it too much. They even had a prayer to be recited prior to taking food, the first words of which are "This is not for the pleasure of my body." Enclosing themselves behind a linked fence of stringencies and observances, they seldom left the domains of their neighborhood. While I had found breaches in their barriers at their Sabbath shalosh seudos, to me the Reb Arelach hasidim still seemed to represent the furthest reaches of the haredi world I could explore. Unquestionably, there were others known for certain extremes. Ger hasidim

---

* I have altered some minor facts here to protect anonymity. The essential elements of the narrative are all true.

prohibited unmarried boys from going to weddings so they would not look at the bride and have their passions aroused. Nadvorner hasidim were always trying to purify themselves. Yet I suppose in the black and white haredi world, I still thought of the Reb Arelach as being at the furthest extreme, the heart of darkness.

Like other haredim, the Reb Arelach watch their children and monitor their encounters with their bodies. But they were thought by many to be the most scrupulous about it. Both girls and boys were never allowed to touch themselves in their private parts, however innocently. Boys in particular were warned not to move their hands to the lower parts of their body. What they were supposed to be particularly careful about was not to "harden themselves." An erection was a prologue to the even greater transgression: masturbation.

Teachers and parents were always on the lookout for signs that boys were involved in such private bodily excesses. So much was this the case that as a teenager and during a doctor's examination, when asked to report when he first noticed the growth of his pubic hair, Beryl had answered that he did not know as he never looked at this area of his body. Was this really true, I asked? Not really. He knew, but he was afraid the doctor would tell his mother and then she might suspect he had masturbated. Since before he could remember, he had been warned away from his penis. He would never forget getting a good whack for having been caught probing himself through his trousers.

Of course, he admitted, all boys touched their penises and knew about erections and sometimes even talked about them, but it was not something they did gladly. It was a horrible sin, and he felt abominable afterward. The body was—as he put it—"an awful burden." Only when he was about to marry did he begin to discover that this body could be a source of pleasure and that this pleasure would have a religious reward.

And what about girls? As Breindel explained, they were taught their bodies could be the source of a male's undoing, a menace that had to be all covered up, from the earliest age. Indeed, as she and other women would tell me, it was best if they stayed away from boys and kept only with their own. For the most part, girls played with other girls—and even after marriage they tended to spend more time with other women even than with their husbands, who could often be a distant presence. It was only through sons—which they all were supposed to want—that females could really get to spend extended time with males. Some did manage to establish close relationships with brothers, but these were expressed primarily in the shelter of their homes. As for fathers, they tended to focus on their sons, and when they did establish a relationship with a daughter it was often awkward or remote at worst or downplayed at best.

For girls, however, the body impinged itself upon them as much as, if not more than, on the males. While boys might not be alerted to the full role of their bodies in their lives until just before marriage, girls had to learn about physical matters at the onset of their menstruation. The general tendency was to talk only minimally about these matters. Important details were often left out. What *was* said was commonly in the nature of informing the girl that her body was preparing itself for childbirth, her true bodily mission. Few other details were provided. But what she did know was that it was her responsibility to sanctify and protect the palace of her body from the corruption of all other lustful passions.

So the haredi girl grew up with a twofold view of her body: first, it would only fulfill itself when she married and had children; and second, it could be a palace of holiness, but if she was not careful, it could also be the source of sin and a place of profanity, a hazard to herself and others.[19]

During her period, a woman's body was rendered impure, for it had missed the opportunity to conceive. Instead of being associated with life, it was now a painful reminder of mortality. As long as she was unwed, this did not matter—though the onset of her menses was a sign that she should get married as soon as practical. But once married, a woman who was impure could not have sexual relations with her husband. To change her status, she had to immerse her body in the mikveh on the seventh day after the end of her period before she could resume sexual relations with her husband. Only by virtue of this immersion in the waters of life and a subsequent ascent to purity could she once again sanctify herself and feel pleasure in her body.

In the still of the night, the married woman slips into the mikveh, dips her naked body in the water, making certain with the assistance of a "mikveh lady" who attends her that there are no loose hairs or other foreign objects on her that will separate any part of her body from direct contact with these purifying waters, which symbolize her return to fertility and the orbit of life. And then, purified, she goes home to have intercourse with her husband. Thus, for generations, have all women who abide by the Jewish laws practiced what the rabbis called "family purity."

For males, however, there are far more opportunities for their bodies to become impure. A wet dream, impure thoughts, improper touching—the list seems endless, with some groups stressing more items and others fewer—can bring about defilement. In each case, the mikveh remains the first remedy. From just about the time he is toilet-trained and can walk until his death, the haredi male learns that a visit to the mikveh is part of the routine of his life. Although stressed more by hasidim than their misnagdic counterparts, who tend to downplay the efficacy of acts beyond reason, a weekly, if not daily, immersion in the mikveh is part of the ongoing haredi relationship to the body. Some dip twice a day.

Not that the visit to the mikveh is all swathed in religion. As Israeli journalist Amnon Levy, whose beat includes haredim, correctly notes, and as I discovered from my first visit on the eve of Yom Kippur, it is a "social gathering-place of the first order. A place to while away time. A place to exchange opinions and information." [20] As they dress and undress, clean themselves in the steam room (which a few of the larger mikvehs have put in), wait in line to get a shower or to descend the few steps into the small indoor pool, or on their way in and out, the men and boys often concern themselves with far more mundane mat-ters. Indeed, as they remove the layers that cover their body, the black frock coats and trousers, the black and white fringes, the white shirts, the long bloomers and white stockings, haredim seem sometimes to remove their inhibitions as well. In this naked state, when sacred matters cannot be discussed, when all that still marks a man is his circumcision and his beard or earlocks, the body and all its corruptions can and sometimes do take over. Gossip abounds, and there have been rare incidents when prohibited sexual activities such as pedophilia or homosexuality occur under the cover of the mikveh as well.

This does not happen with women, for although they have the accompaniment of an attendant who stands at the edge of the pool with towel in hand, they each immerse in the pool alone. But with men their fellows are always around. There is no busier place for men to meet on a Friday afternoon, an hour or so before the onset of the Sabbath, than in the mikveh.

If the mikveh is there to purify the body, all of life, with its mun-dane realities and physical desires, stands as a counterforce able to defile it all over again. "You have to keep going to the mikveh," Beryl explained, "that's the way it is." But why must the body be pure? In part, it is to enable it to engage in sexual intercourse. For while sex can defile a body, it can and also does redeem it. To learn how that is possible, however, an initiation is required.

The Initiation into Matters of Sex

Among most haredim—and certainly among the Reb Arelach—
knowledge about sexual matters, and even the basic facts of life are
limited until just before marriage. Until then sex is only a source of
corruption. Then, commonly a day or two before the wedding, both
the future bridegroom and the bride are separately initiated into its
redeeming features. Too important a task to be left just to parents,
sexual initiation is something haredim have assigned to special counselors. Men for men and women for women. How does it work? We
can follow Beryl and Breindel to find out.

Coming from a family of twelve, Beryl was a young member of the
Reb Arelach. Already in his twenties and still not an outstanding
scholar, he nevertheless maintained his status as a yeshiva student
because, like other haredim, he did not want to be drafted into the
Israeli army. Later, after his heavy weight and other health problems
secured a permanent deferment for him, he still wanted to stay in the
yeshiva because he knew that as such he would have a far better chance
of finding a match. "Women want a scholar," he explained.

Yet while the yeshiva nominally kept him on its rolls, everyone in
the community knew that Beryl was not a scholar and so the rosh
yeshiva turned a blind eye when he stopped coming regularly to study
in the bes medrash and found work in a tefillin factory, helping to tan
the cowhide from which were made the little black boxes that every
observant Jewish male wore during his weekday morning prayers.
It was not a very prestigious position—tanners smelled bad and
they worked with their hands—but Beryl was known to be a sweet-
tempered young man. Still, in the scheme of values of haredi matrimony, his personal qualities were not that important. He was a
difficult match.

In general, finding women willing to marry Reb Arelach hasidim
was difficult because the sect's demands were extremely strict. They
were also known to be among those given the least freedom and leeway
to live their lives. While the women who grew up among them might
be prepared to completely shave their heads upon marrying, don the
black kerchiefs and black stockings that were their distinctive mark,
and stay within the four cubits of their community, few other haredi
girls were enthusiastic about this way of life.

No one among the Reb Arelach women had been ready to marry
Beryl. After much searching, the matchmaker managed to find Breindel. Coming from another group of hasidim, she had a brother who
was negotiating to marry Beryl's sister. The haggling over that match

had become linked to this one. When the dust of all the give-and-take had settled, Breindel and Beryl had been coupled as a kind of bonus to the other match. The two had met for fifteen minutes one year before their wedding and approved of each other. It was an awkward beginning, neither of them knowing exactly what to do. Breindel had studied in a girls' seminary the Reb Arelach thought a bit too modern. Beryl wanted to make certain she was not tainted by the experience. She in turn told him that the idea of completely shaving her head and wearing black was daunting; she did not think she could do it. She wanted simply to cut her hair short and then wear a wig like her mother.

"My mother shaves her head," Beryl explained. "I could not imagine my wife not doing this." The thought of a woman with hair repelled him. But a woman with a shaved head was something familiar, a reminder of his mother, someone he could get close to, and if they were to be close, she would have to shave too. Besides, like all other Reb Arelach hasidim, he had signed the yearly agreement on the anniversary of the death of the Maggid of Mezerich, one of the founding fathers of Hasidism, to abide by the group's customs, which included a commitment to have his wife dress like other Reb Arelach women.

At her wedding Breindel would be dressed in all white, her face and still-uncut hair to be covered by a thick veil which Beryl, as part of the ceremony, would ritually place upon her. According to custom, only on the next morning would her hair be shaved. Then, like her mother-in-law, she could save one of her long braids and put it away as a keepsake.

Breindel might agree to shave, she replied, but the black kerchief and stockings were too much. At the very least, a colored head covering and brown stockings were the compromise she demanded. The Reb Arelach were very strict about these matters, and those who did not abide by all the group's rules ran the risk of banishment—something Beryl did not want, for he had nowhere else to belong. Still, he would talk to his rebbe about the matter. Fortunately, as Beryl saw it, the rebbe agreed to Breindel's compromise, as he had for several other couples as well. The alliance was set and both Beryl and Breindel could go back to their lives for the next year.

Now after a year, on the eve of the nuptials, it was time for Beryl to receive the last-minute instructions before his marriage. Neither of his parents felt a need to talk to him about these matters. This was not their responsibility; the community through the counselor had taken that away from them—and, Beryl concluded in retrospect, they were just as glad.

Not that Beryl knew nothing about matters of sex. Growing up, he had his suspicions. But he was never certain. For example, although he read in the Bible about Jacob "knowing" Rachel or Abraham "knowing" Sarah and he knew that a man was supposed to "come" to a woman, he was not really sure what these words meant. He knew little of sexual functioning. Even as a boy he had not talked about these matters. When he had nocturnal emissions, he said nothing, but rather secretly believed that he had a problem of bed-wetting and chose rather to leave the matter unspoken. When he asked his father what was the meaning of those penances which, because they had "spilled their seed," men were supposed to recite before going to the mikveh, his father brushed aside the questions and said these were matters of Kabbalah that he would learn about later. As a good son, he had never pursued the matter nor had he discussed it with his friends. He was too embarrassed.

Of course, in school he had learned the portion of the Talmud that repeated the account of Rabbi Kahana who had hidden under his teacher's bed to learn from his master how to properly perform sex—but like so many things that he knew the ancients did that were different from us, he supposed this one was too.[21] Students certainly did not hide in their rabbis' bedrooms today to find out what goes on between husband and wife. Besides, the text offered no details. He had heard vaguely about sexual intercourse but "I was sure that it was something that goyim [and people who wanted to be like goyim] did. I could never imagine that something so animal-like and coarse would be done by erlicher Yidn."

And then he went to the counselor.

"And what did he say to you?"

"He began by telling me that what he was about to describe was going to shock me, but nevertheless I should not be frightened because it was not at all something bad—if I learned what to do. He told me that what he would tell me to do was something that I was not the first to do. Before me, Adam, the first man, had done it. He told me that our patriarch Abraham did it, and so too Isaac and Jacob. He told me that all the virtuous and pure zaddikim did it. He told me my father did it and that he himself did it. And then he told me that even the rebbe, may he live many long years, amen, did it.

"And when he said this I knew I too would have to do it. Still, I wasn't really sure what it was. But I'll tell you, when he finally told me what it was that I would have to do, I was in shock."

Beryl's consternation was not simply over the fact that suddenly all those parts of his body that had once been taboo and about which he had not been allowed even to think, let alone touch, would now become the center of his concern. The unthinkable was suddenly expected. And as if that was not enough, he would, unbelievably, have to do all this with a woman he barely knew—a woman with whom before this he had not even been allowed to be alone in a closed room.

Yet perhaps what shocked him most of all was the discovery that he would have to perform this act of coitus—*tashmish ha-mitah*, it was called—which he had no idea how to do, not after a month or even a week, when he and his bride would have had a chance to get to know each other, but rather that first night. Could this be true?

There was a joke about this, he told me now that he could laugh about these things. Upon learning about these marital responsibilities, a young hasid had like him been appalled to learn what would happen on his marriage night.

"Why so shocked?" the counselor had asked him. "After all, your father did this as well."

"Yes, of course," replied the stunned bridegroom, "but *he* did it with my *mother*. But me, *I'm* going to have to do it with some woman I don't even *know*!"

Again and again, haredi men told me how stunned they were when they were told about the marriage-night responsibilities. "Until they come to the moment of truth, they know nothing," said one Sanzer hasid. "Until he comes to the actual act, the boy who sits in the yeshiva knows nothing. Those who know something are *prostakim* [louts]. Look, when I was a *bochur* [boy], I also knew that we had these desires. I controlled them, buried them. But when they sat with me a few hours before my wedding and told me everything, I thought they were taking a knife to me and cutting off my legs. I was in total shock. Tomorrow night with a stranger? It couldn't be!"

Breindel had been no less frightened. Although for years she had some inkling about what lay in store for her, this did not make the prospect any less worrisome. She too had not expected matters to have to move so swiftly, to be confronted by a stranger and not be aware of exactly what to do. No man had ever come so close to her. Few besides her father had even touched her. Now this? She was lucky. There were girls who received no counseling, the thought being that the husband should control matters. They were completely unprepared for that first night or the ones that followed it Many were staggered by the experience.

"I was not in shock," Breindel explained, "because I knew something. I talked with my girlfriends. But I had a girlfriend who knew nothing and went to a counselor who told her everything. And in the middle of it she couldn't stand it and ran away and came home and told her mother that she could not believe that the woman whom she had always respected could say such 'foolish' things."

Breindel's experience turned out to be fortunate; she had a husband who was no less frightened than she was and who did not force her to do anything she could not do. Still, there were quite a number of newlyweds who came out of these first experiences deeply shaken. Surprisingly, most marriages seemed able to survive the trauma.

Why was the preparation so sudden? Why not soften the blow? As one counselor explained: "Yes, so some of them go into shock. But don't worry; they are freed of it very fast. Believe me, this little jolt is not too high a price to pay for the way of life we lead. Better they should have one moment of shock and years of protection than they should wallow in impurity before marriage as the chiloinim and goyim do."

Given that most people did manage to get past those first encounters—marriages tended to last and families were large—perhaps there was enough about the experience of intercourse that provided pleasure to offset the surprise and embarrassment. With the exception of a few lay therapists who had to deal with the failures in the process, and therefore thought modifications would be in order, most people seemed ready to leave things as they were. Even here the haredi prime directive stood: change was not in order.

Although coitus was an important element of the traditional consummation of the marriage—which was why it had to be performed as soon as possible after the ceremony—if a bride was having her period, she remained off-limits from her husband. In the atmosphere of anxiety that many young haredim experienced in anticipation of their wedding night, such a sudden onset of menstruation was not uncommon. While the strictest ideals of the law considered this turn of events undesirable—unconsummated marriages were a curse, some said— many young marrieds were relieved to discover that their new spouses were forbidden to them for several weeks. This would give them some time to marshal the mettle necessary for engaging in intercourse.

Others, however, believed that if the sexual encounter did not occur right away, the pressure would build up as they moved toward the day when sex was again permissible. They wanted to get the mitzvah (as they called it) over with quickly.

What were the details of the counselor's initiation? Each one had his or her own style. By and large, the hasidim seemed to stress mystical and ethical matters and gave very little in the way of practical instruction. The misnagdic b'nai yeshiva, on the other hand, had guides who told them not only what to do specifically but also offered advice and counsel about how to make one's partner happy and relaxed. All counselors had books for their initiates to study.

Here is how it went with Beryl. After he had been told how this was something that others had done before him, the rabbi talked to him about the sanctity of marriage and procreation. The two were one. It was through these that he would rid himself of sinful desires and thereby be cleansed of an evil inclination. He spoke about that small limb Jews often called their bris, the sign of the covenant between Abraham and God.

"This bris," the counselor told him, "which can draw us to God, is also the place where our evil inclination struggles with us most mightily. A man's true strength is recognized by the extent to which he conquers these urges. Although it is just a small limb, its hunger is great and its power to deflect the mighty from the true course of their lives is awesome. One needs great inner strength and many barriers in order to escape from it. But one who decreases its physical satisfactions, who focuses only on the sanctity of the act, who performs it once a week on the Sabbath, and only then, as an act of sanctification, can sap the strength of his evil inclinations. In time, the physical side will be weakened so that its cravings will cease to chase after you."

There were risks. As another hasid explained: "There are certain matters—like sex—that once we have had them, rather than being satisfied, our hunger grows. If you think that after a person marries, his desire no longer burns, you are wrong. To our regret, there are many stories now and in the past of married men going to Gentile women."

"Is this common?" I wondered aloud. "Don't some say this is permitted?" I had many times heard the dictum that "the stirrings of sin are worse than sin itself" as an explanation for why sometimes going to a prostitute—something a significant number of haredim were known to do late at night—was better than thinking lustful thoughts all the time.

"Heaven forbid. This is absolutely prohibited. There is no permission! A person has to know he has desires and guard them. That is why we make fences around him to protect him. That is our work as Jews."

Of course, Beryl also knew about these barriers. The counselor told him about the times that he must stay away from his wife. During her days of impurity, her menstruation, she was to be out of bounds. Any discharge of blood, for example after the breach of her virginity or during and after childbirth, made her prohibited to him. And both had to be careful to count the right number of days after the end of the period. Mistakes were unforgivable. But he need not worry, the rabbi assured him, these absences would only kindle their longing for each other, for they would approach their union afterward with all the freshness of their original coming together.

"I didn't really understand what he was talking about then," Beryl said, "but now it makes sense to me."

His obligations toward his wife and to the goal of having children went beyond that first night. Although he was not to become consumed by this activity, he was expected to "do the mitzvah" each Friday evening at midnight during those weeks of the month when his wife was not menstruating—"the days of her purity," the counselor called them. And on that night once a month when she returned from the mikveh after her immersion, he was also to perform his obligations.

While giving his wife children was his paramount obligation, he could also try to give her pleasure. "Our sages of blessed memory interpreted the verse in which God said 'It is not good that man should be alone, I shall make him a *counterpart*' to mean that if he succeeds in making his wife happy she will be a help, take his *part*, but if he fails, she will *counter* him in everything, battle against him." Beryl was to keep his wife happy so that she might not oppose him.

But that pleasure was for her and not him. The rabbi told him that any bodily pleasures he might have should be accompanied by the thought that their purpose was to serve his Maker—and even when he gave his wife pleasure, this too was in order to perform God's will and not to fulfill his animal passions. Only when he acted in God's image was he rising above his animal nature.

"A man must fulfill all God's commandments not only because they give him pleasure—even if they do—but because God commanded him to do them," he told Beryl in words that the young man still recalled. He had read them over and over in the volume he received at the time and which he studied all day before his wedding, as if preparing for an examination that he would have to pass that night.

To Beryl all this seemed fine, for he could not imagine any pleasure in all the counselor described. Since then, however, he had discovered how devious the evil inclination was, and he knew that he could sometimes be trapped by these physical pleasures. "When you begin to feel them," his counselor had explained when several months after the wedding, Beryl had called upon him for more guidance, "think of the sanctity of what you are doing and repeat quietly to yourself, 'Happy are the limbs that are sanctified during the act.'" Whispering this paternoster again and again, he was assured, would prevent his being carried away by his lusts. "I'm still working on it," he confided to me.

Beryl listened carefully to all the guide told him, not certain he would be able to remember all the particulars. "It's all in the book," the teacher told him, handing him the slim volume entitled *Holiness and Modesty*. There were just a few more points that he wanted to stress. Before beginning there were certain prayers to be recited. These begged their Maker that any child that might come of this union— preferably a boy—would be "worthy of existence." It was a long invocation, but if he could not recite it all then at least he should have in mind this thought: "Master of the Universe, this droplet, what shall it be, mighty or weak, wise or foolish, rich or poor? May it be Thy will that what I am about to do is for the sake of Heaven." And for those times that he was performing purely for his wife's pleasure, he should say: "I hereby prepare and ready myself to fulfill the commandment [mitzvah] of conjugal union, as it is written in the Torah, 'and her conjugal rights shalt thou not diminish,' and fulfill the commandment to make my wife happy and sanctify myself with what is permitted me, as it is written 'thou shalt be holy.'"

There should be nothing under their conjugal bed, no shoes and nothing foul-smelling that could somehow harm the spirit of the child. There were various customs that some practiced but others did not. These were in the book. Mimicking ancient mystical rituals of affection, some men repeated the traditional signs that Jacob had given Rachel: grasping first the right thumb, then the toe and earlobe. Others surrounded their bed with a white powder, enabling them to see later if the evil spirits had surrounded the bed; if so, their birdlike footprints would be visible in the powder. Not everyone did this, but the rabbi recommended it. Water sprinkled around the bed was another way to guard against such demons.

It was good to confess one's sins—certainly on the day before the wedding night—but in any case, penitence was the best preparation for this act of sanctification. And of course, if he had any quarrels with his wife, this was the time to make up. Certainly, they should be clean, for if they were not, this might harm their children. Lovemaking on a full bladder led to children who were bed wetters. It was Beryl's responsibility to explain to his wife that she too should clear her thoughts, for in every marriage bed there are three partners: husband, wife, and their Creator.

When at last they were ready to begin, in the stillness of the night, the room should be darkened. Neither was to see the other naked— for to do so would make them no different than dogs. In this sacred moment, each had to guard the modesty of the other. Special garments should be set aside for the purpose. Then, under the blankets, they would slowly raise these pajamas—no more than necessary—and in silence complete their holy coming together.

During that moment there were lots of things they could think about, but it was best to concentrate on the patriarchs and zaddikim, for in this way they could see to it that whatever would come of this union was not defiled by impure thoughts. Under no circumstances should Beryl ever visualize another woman while making love to his wife. "He who makes changes below runs the risk that changes will be made on high," the rabbi had warned. One tampered with the mystical order this way. Changelings came from such unions and sometimes even death. Such activities were no better than onanism, a killing of seed that was a sin for which the punishment was severe. If he could, he should recite the names of the generations from Adam through the twelve sons of Jacob while he was moving toward climax. This might become difficult, but Beryl should persevere, for it was a good way of disciplining his passions.

Beryl should not think there was no room for feeling here. "There is no joining together of a man and woman that is not preceded by hugging and kissing," but certainly the kisses should "only be on the lips or face, and not, Heaven forbid, anywhere else." Such displays were meant to make his wife feel good and arouse the love between them. But of course there was no doubt that too much of this was not good, for it diminished their sense of the sanctity of the act.

When they were finished, the woman should turn toward the left, and then after about half an hour, he could leave her and return to his own bed, but not before they had each ritually washed their hands. The Zohar suggested, and the Reb Arelach followed the advice, that after the union, a small amount of pure water should be sprinkled around the bed, for this, like the water on their hands, would purify their act. It was also advisable to rinse themselves, but on the Sabbaths this had to be done with care lest some prohibitions be transgressed, and so not everyone followed this practice. Still, if Beryl could, he should immerse himself in the mikveh the next morning. And if he could do this in cold waters, he would be especially blessed.

"Remember," the counselor concluded, "in these moments with

your wife there are two possibilities facing you. One is the possibility of immediate but fleeting pleasure. It may be intense, but when it is over, there is nothing left. But on the other side stand children who will be scholars and zaddikim, servants of God, pure of mind and faithful, and that is a pleasure that is the greatest in the world, and far more lasting."

The implication was clear. Beryl could let himself go and seek only the pleasure of passion or he could religiously follow all the advice, take each ritual seriously, and he would then have righteous children and a far greater reward.

Breindel too had been given some preliminary counsel about these matters. Far briefer than what her husband received, her session focused on her obligations as a wife. First and foremost, Breindel was reminded that her responsibility was to have children. These would complete her as a woman. For Breindel, who when I spoke with her still had no children after more than a year of marriage, this obligation weighed heavily upon her. "'A woman who has no children," she said to me, her face a mask of pain, "is like someone who is dead." Breindel's voice grew very quiet as she said these words. "I don't know what such a woman does. I know many such. They have no joy in life. In our society everyone has children and she does not. She is nobody with nothing to do and nothing to live for." Breindel was taking certain herbal medicines recommended by someone among the Reb Arelach whom she and Beryl had consulted about having children. So far, no results.

Although in his middle twenties, Beryl still had practically no beard and when I asked him about it, he told me some doctors had directed him to get his hormones checked. He had not yet gone for this examination. Did he know what hormones were? I asked. Yes, he knew they had something to do with fertility.

"But do you realize," I said at last, knowing that with this comment I was overstepping one of the cardinal rules of anthropology—I was actively affecting the situation I was supposed only to observe, "that if you have hormonal problems your wife's taking herbs or any other remedies to have children will make no difference because the problem may be in you."

Beryl laughed. Of course he knew that. "But Breindel wants to take the herbs. She wants to exhaust all her remedies as a wife, to fulfill her responsibility. And I will let her do her part. Then I'll do mine."

Within a month of this conversation, Beryl reported to me that he had gone to the rebbe's assistant on these matters and the man had given him pills (ginseng root—it was the rebbe's standard medicine for fertility). If these did not help, he would go next to a doctor—but only when the rebbe so decided.

As a wife, Breindel had other responsibilities as well. She listed them for me: "A woman has to honor her mother-in-law, father-in-law, and her husband." In an earlier conversation about the role of the haredi wife, Beryl had read to me from *Rabbi Frisch's Marriage Manual:* "Even though the woman is a man's partner, she should not think of her husband as a comrade but rather as a master. And the woman should love her husband and he shall rule over her as it is said: 'And thy desire shall be to thy husband, and he shall rule over thee.' "[22] Now as I listened to Breindel, I took note of the fact that she did not elaborate on the point as her husband had. Instead, she continued: "A woman is supposed to make it possible for her husband to study Torah. She should encourage him to go to the yeshiva and not make too many demands on him for her private needs. She should prepare the house, make the meals, see to it that everything is in order. Of course, she should also not spend time alone with other men."

Her counseling session was not so much on techniques of intercourse as on how to make certain she was observing the laws of ritual immersion and on ways of developing a lasting relationship with this strange person who would be her husband.

Because as a haredi woman Breindel could not be alone with a man who was not her husband, Beryl was our constant companion throughout our conversations, although to give his wife some freedom he had sometimes gone to another room or when he was with us immersed himself in a book. Indeed, during all my conversations with haredi women, their husbands were within sight as we spoke, a fact that undoubtedly played a part in all I heard.

"I was told not to talk to anyone about our private moments," Breindel continued. She was referring to the very matters I was here to talk to her about.

Much of the counseling session was devoted to reminding her of the need for modesty. She repeated what she was told: "A woman must be careful not to arouse the men in the street or other public places. I know not to be too interested in matters that don't concern me, not to go to places I should not go and to dress modestly." Although the words were never spoken, the counselor was reminding her that her body had a power to attract men far beyond anything she might realize. Only if she restrained it from doing so, however, was she fulfilling her responsibilities as a woman, for the honor of a woman was within. But he implied something else too: "Men are likely to think impure thoughts," Breindel explained, "and we must be careful not to inspire these."

"I was taught about the laws of mikveh, which I already had heard about," Breindel continued. She learned how to check her body to determine when she was "pure," how to count the days after the end of her period, and that she was to be with her husband after her ritual immersion. These were not matters she and her husband should talk about. "When you are unclean," the counselor told her, referring to the days of her menstruation and the week afterward, "leave a special handkerchief as a sign near your bed so that your husband will know he must not come near you." But when she had purified herself, she put the handkerchief away. Then she had a right to expect her husband to satisfy her needs, whatever they might be.

Restraint, modesty, responsibility, and expectations—these were the substance of her counseling in the brief session before her wedding. Had it not been for the fact that her older sister told her some of the physical elements of intercourse—though in a very telegraphic fashion—she would have had to discover them on her own.

There were some who, in spite of counseling, did *not* get those details straight the first time. One to whom this happened was a Nadvorner hasid I'll call Shimon.

Shimon's bride was in the midst of her period when the day of their wedding arrived. The counselor was told, and knowing they would not consummate the marriage right away, accordingly gave Shimon an abbreviated lesson. He could be with his bride at the wedding, the rabbi told him, but they were prohibited from having sexual contact until her immersion in the mikveh. He was not to worry about this: "This is not a bad sign," the counselor told him. "Forget what you have heard about curses." Shimon was relieved; the thought of intercourse had made him very anxious, so anxious that he had hardly heard what the counselor said to him after learning that this was an expected feature of his marriage night.

About two weeks later Shimon's first efforts at intercourse were not altogether successful. Neither he nor his wife knew exactly what to do. She had come from Europe and either she had not been properly instructed or else assumed that modesty required her remaining largely passive during the encounter. For over a month and a half they failed to consummate their marriage.

As time went by and Shimon's wife "Ruth" failed to get pregnant as expected, this caused the couple and their parents considerable consternation. Maybe they were indeed cursed. After all, a union that does not yield children is a failure. Not only the couple is implicated in that failure—the parents are too, for they were the ones who contracted it. Even the matchmaker may get concerned.

Anxiety and guilt began to color the relationship, and this in itself, as all concerned realized, could compound the problems. Shimon called on his counselor. Several times at night—in the midst of his lovemaking—he would telephone and ask for guidance. Counselors were used to such calls. For all their archaic and mystical customs, haredim are becoming increasingly sophisticated psychologically. Each time Shimon was told to relax, to take his time, not to rush but to lie with his wife all night if necessary. But Shimon was finding this difficult. He felt self-conscious, and he did not know what to do as he lay there. Even the preparations for sex were proving to be anxiety-provoking. His custom—like that of all other Nadvorner hasidim—was to sleep with his wife twice a week when she was clean: Tuesday and Friday nights. He was finding the buildup exhausting. He was finding it particularly difficult to master his passions and lusts. These were being aroused in ways that he had not expected, and he had learned that they were improper except at the moment of coitus. He was apparently also having trouble preventing erections at the times when they were not supposed to occur, which seemed to him to be almost perpetually. Even extra immersions in the mikveh were not helping.

He had spoken to the rebbe about his difficulties in consummating his marriage, and the rebbe had given him special herbs to take. The rebbe was able to accomplish great miracles in this area, and Shimon told me of several instances when he successfully predicted the birth of a child to a barren couple. One was a scribe whose wife gave birth to a daughter immediately after he completed the writing of a Torah scroll that the rebbe had asked him to carry out. The miraculous powers of the rebbe were beyond question; he had "the keys to healing that are in heaven."

Still, there seemed no helping Shimon and so his parents decided that he ought to see another counselor. This time he went to a Lithuanian one. The Lithuanian guides were known to give different sorts of advice than the hasidim. Perhaps he might learn something he did not know. The couple was desperate, for soon the entire community would be whispering—and without a child the pressure would build for him to divorce. And divorced people were very hard to marry off.

The Lithuanian adviser was indeed far more open in what he had to say. Because he knew that Shimon was already married and was coming to him with a problem based on experience, he went directly to the heart of the matter. He provided graphic technical advice, illustrating the coital positions with his fingers for the boy. He told Shimon to lie naked with his wife, rather than wearing the long nightshirts they commonly used. If that was too anxiety-provoking, they could even take off all their clothes under the blanket and caress each other. He talked about techniques of arousal. He talked about mutuality, about encouraging his wife to tell him what she wanted. He told him to hug and kiss and get very close to her. But he also gave the boy a detail that his earlier adviser had not emphasized enough: he told him that an erection was insufficient unless one alternately inserted the penis into and extracted it from the woman's vagina. Simply stated, he told the boy to stroke his wife's sexual organs with his own and that would lead to ejaculation.

Shimon returned from this adviser wiser but somewhat revolted by what he had heard. He found the advice "coarse," lacking a tone of "holiness and purity and modesty" that he felt characterized his first initiation. He did not need all the talk of foreplay, he explained, for this would happen "by nature" and need not be discussed. Still, he had learned something he did not know: the essentiality of penetration.

"And now," Shimon said at last, as he ended his narrative and called Ruth in from the next room, "the problems are solved." She brought in their new baby boy, living proof that they had mastered the lesson.

The Implications of Initiation

The view of the relationship between husband and wife and the sense of what sexual relations were supposed to be certainly described an alternative order of life from the one dominant in contemporary secular society. Haredim downplayed love and passion and emphasized religion and a spirituality that transformed sex into a ritual aimed at diminishing physicality and controlling appetite. This was precisely the opposite of a culture that saw sex as a chance to express inner feeling and let everything hang out. Even the canons of taste were different here: bald heads on married women appealed to their husbands; long hair repelled them. Sex was to occur almost as if the body was not there.

What happened in the bedroom was also a way of enacting and affirming the character of relationship between haredi husband and wife. She was to show him respect; he in turn owed her pleasure and was to think of no one else when making love to her. The woman was to be subservient; the man had to control the encounter. Together, they were not simply husband and wife; they were people on the road to becoming parents. Their bodies were not governing them; endowed with a religious spirit, they were something higher.

For the haredim, however, sex also had the dangerous potential to corrupt, to make human beings act in ways that were animal. If they followed the guidelines of their religion, they would avoid that, transform the meaning of their action, and make the human in the image of the divine. All this was possible if they were not carried away by their passions and instead directed by their ritual responsibilities, carrying out mystical acts of union. A husband and wife in their darkened bedroom did not see each other; they were not obsessed by their bodies. Instead, they saw Jacob and Rachel and felt the gaze of Heaven. Sex for them was not immediate bodily gratification; it was a chance to play their part in the great drama of Jewish life, to serve their people and their Creator. It was a mitzvah, a stark contrast to what it seemed to be among the chiloinim—purely a pleasure—or so the haredim claimed.

"If you want to compare this with what goes on in the secular world," Beryl concluded, "there is absolutely no comparison."

Real Life

Beryl talked to me about the beginnings of his relationship with his wife. It developed slowly, each of them moving tentatively toward the other. While both had studied their guidebooks and recalled some of the words of counsel, instinct seemed to direct them a good part of the time. "We have followed our own ways," he summed up.

Anxious about their first night together, Beryl and Breindel entered their home without much conversation. Before their wedding, each, accompanied by his or her mother, had already visited their plain three-room apartment near the Toldos Aharon Yeshiva. The rooms had cost Breindel's parents about $60,000. Looking around the largely empty reception hall, they now saw a bare square room with only a phone on the floor. Furniture had already been arranged. In what they called the "salon" were a large table, a simple blue sofa, a breakfront displaying a few items of Judaica, and a large bookshelf packed with holy books. In addition to a tiny kitchen, there was also a bedroom with two beds in it, and a spare room that they hoped would someday be for the children but for now was treated as storage space. A few square feet of balcony—hardly more than a window bay—were enclosed by wrought iron. However modest it was, the place was now their own, and they were alone in it for the first time.

Although it was past midnight, Breindel fussed with some curtains; Beryl asked if she wanted some assistance. She did. Then she asked him to help her hang a picture in the bedroom. Slowly, they edged closer to each other. With trepidation, Beryl tried to remember what he'd read that morning in his handbook and learned the night before in the counseling session. But his mind was a swirl. Mostly, he remembered the parting advice his parents had given him—since his session with the counselor, they had offered him their own brief words of wisdom.

"Do not rush her," his mother told him. "Keep her calm and do not frighten her with sudden movements or shrieks. Be tender and thoughtful."

"Do what you feel is natural," said his father. "You'll know what to do." They said nothing about ritual and religion.

As Breindel and Beryl got into bed to "do the mitzvah," they recited their prayers, each one keeping eyes glued to the prayer book. This surely would stimulate thoughts of holiness. And it helped avoid the awkwardness of the moment and kept them from staring at each other. Praying seemed the most natural of preliminaries; all sorts of mitzvahs were initiated this way. So now this new one was too.

At last, they turned off the lights. Without a word—he wanted no interruptions between the blessing and the mitzvah—Beryl donned a special white yarmulke he'd set aside for the purpose, but he had no special pajamas. While he tried to concentrate on the names of the holy ones—Abraham, Isaac, and so on—during the moment of their coming together, he was too nervous to recite their names aloud. After Jacob he lost track of the names he knew so well. Breindel remained very still. Neither of them tried the various opening rituals of touching earlobes or toes. It all went very quickly. They did wash their hands before and after; and when they were finished, Beryl sprinkled water around the bed to ward off any evil spirits.

His father had been right. He had simply done what came naturally. He knew he had to build a family and a life with this woman. And she knew it too. They were determined to succeed.

Since that night he had learned quite well how to handle himself. Not that everything went without complications. He still could not

control his erections as the book advised him; they came upon him
when he least expected them. He still felt uncontrollable desires. He
did not know where to draw the line between restraint and giving his
wife pleasure. He could not always tell what she felt, but they never
talked about these matters—to do so would be inexcusably coarse.
Chiloinim did that, not erlicher Yidn.

There were problems in the relationship, especially because they
still had no children. Lately, Breindel demanded more sex than once a
week; she wanted children. As they were for her married friends,
children were for Breindel the measure of her coming of age. Not only
were they her ticket of admission to the status of adulthood in haredi
society, they would also give her something to orient her life around
and become the focus of a developing relationship with her husband.
Having children gave a husband and wife something tangible that
bonded them together. Without them, her marriage was nothing. For
now, all they had in common was their home.

For his part, Beryl admitted to me that he sometimes still felt closer
to his sister, with whom there were none of these tensions about sex
and children, and with whom be believed he could talk more openly.
Breindel sensed this and resented it. But what could she do? Without
children, she had little self-confidence and less justification to make
demands of her husband. Small things began to bother her, like the
time Beryl hung a picture on the wall at a place his sister had suggested. Breindel took it down. She, and she alone, wanted to decide
about how the house was to be decorated. Just because she had no
children did not mean that she was not the *baal ha-bosteh*, the mistress
of the house.

Although his mother generally kept quiet about his marriage, as
long as there were no children, she knew it was fragile and so she
worried about it. She supported Breindel, trying to boost her confidence, and tried to teach Beryl that he owed greater allegiance to his
wife than to his sister. Like many haredi mothers, she too lived for (or
perhaps through) her children. Even now, making certain their marriage worked was a part of her job. She was still reminding him to be
tender.

"In her way, she keeps me on the right road," Beryl admitted with
a sheepish smile. According to the book, the male might be the master,
but in real life Beryl was still buffeted between mother and wife.

Gradually, Breindel built up her confidence. In her year and a half
of marriage, she had come a long way from the unsteady teenager she
was in those first days and night with Beryl. Although still childless,
she was far from completely submitting to her husband's mastery. She

was beginning to shape their home and family life in very distinct ways. Not only where a picture was hung was on her mind and under her control; she had other, more fundamental concerns. Never all that comfortable with and still somewhat estranged from the Reb Arelach hasidim, she began urging her husband to go to other tishes, to see if perhaps he could find his way to a different rebbe and community. "I told him to look into Karliner hasidim or maybe Lalov. His sister was already in Karlin, so why not?" This was not the self-effacing haredi woman the guidebooks and counselors depicted.

It was Breindel who managed the budget, which sometimes included the disbursements they received from the G'Mach, the free loan society into which as an avrech Beryl had once put about a thousand dollars and from which he could, as a married man, take out interest-free loans. And of course, she was in charge of managing the household.

Even the idea of my interviews with her came from her new confidence. Hearing from Beryl about our conversations, she told him she also wanted to talk with me. Why shouldn't she get a chance to meet "the professor"? Accompanied by Beryl, I met with her at their apartment for the first of several talks we had.

Before I came in, Beryl yelled up to the window to announce our arrival. Unseen, the queen of the castle signaled her permission from the balcony of their top-floor apartment. We climbed the four flights of the narrow staircase and were greeted at the door by a pale-skinned, slightly cross-eyed, slim woman of just over twenty. She invited me to sit at the table in the salon and then sat on the other side of the room on the couch. My eyes jumped immediately to her kerchief. It was checkered blue and red; Breindel seemed to wear its bright colors like a proud banner, a symbol of her triumph over the black kerchief and all it signified. Following my eyes, she pulled it tightly over her clipped hair, which was short but not totally razed. During our conversation, she often played with the corner of the kerchief much as she might once have toyed with the ends of her braids. Although her ears were pierced, she wore no earrings now nor any makeup that I could see. Her patterned dress—she sewed it herself, as did many haredi women —went up to her neck, down to her wrists, and reached below her knees. Yet with all this covering on, she occasionally hitched up her leg to tighten her thick brown stockings, which went up to her knees. I found this movement, which allowed me momentarily to see her bare legs, arresting—almost suggestive.

Certainly, it was not the shape or sight of her leg that attracted me. It was rather the thought of it. How ironic. Precisely because they so emphasized covering it up, haredim, far more than any other group I knew, had succeeded in transforming a woman's body into a sex object. A leg and gesture that would never have caught my attention was now gobbling it up. For a haredi woman to bare her leg, even offhandedly, was a far more provocative act than it might be in the society outside.

Was this inadvertent gesture Breindel's way of unconsciously demonstrating that she was not quite as inhibited and restrained as I believed? Or was this all in the eye of the beholder? After all, haredim always argued that those who were not part of their world were obsessed by sex. I did not think I was thus preoccupied, yet here I was helplessly but undeniably focusing upon what was probably an innocent gesture and seeing provocation. Here was proof that actions do not have independent meanings; cultural frameworks situate their meanings and they do so in ways that supersede the individual's power to determine them.

I thought about asking her if she realized what she was doing, but of course had I done so and thereby called it to her attention, she would probably have been embarrassed, and the slender bridge between us through which I hoped to reach an understanding would have been closed. My question would only have proved to her that I had a dirty mind like all the other chiloinim. There was no way to find out the meaning of the gesture. This was a question that could not be asked, for its very asking would have imposed meanings and made an answer impossible. I didn't know the right words to ask.

I turned away from my reverie. Did Breindel mind if I used a tape recorder with her as I had with Beryl? "No," she replied. Sending Beryl to get me a cold drink from the kitchen, she answered the questions she knew I had come to ask her and talked about the counseling session she had received before marriage. At first she seemed shy, looking away from me when we spoke (with her cross-eyed expression I could never be sure). But then I recalled that this was what she had been taught to do. Women did not look straight at men who were not their husbands. Such immodesty was improper. As time passed, she seemed to lose her reticence and began to speak with a calmer voice and offer longer answers, even volunteering information beyond what I asked. But she never looked directly into my eyes.

"You know I was not always from the Reb Arelach," she remarked when she finished talking about her experience with the counselor. And then with a hint of pride in her voice, she added: "I went to Bais Ya'akov."

Although historically linked to Agudat Israel,[23] the Bais Ya'akov women's seminary was today one of those institutions that in some hasidic opinion had become associated with the more liberal fringe of the haredi world. Girls from there were reputed to be independent-minded, not easily domesticated. Not that they were anything like secular women. Certainly, from an outsider's point of view their way of life would appear indistinguishable from other haredi women. They also wanted husbands who were scholars, expected to have lots of children and give their lives to raising them. But from the perspective of the Eda Haredis and the Reb Arelach, Bais Ya'akov women seemed too modern, a bit too free thinking. They were ready to work outside the house if necessary. They were not always ready to defer to their husband's judgment on matters they thought they knew about, and they thought they knew a great deal. Perilously close to being like the Lithuanians, they were independent and not prepared to be dominated by a rebbe.

Among haredim being "free" was no compliment; it was an epithet of contempt. *Freie Yidn* (free Jews) lacked the restraint that was an essential of erlicher haredi Yidn. Lithuanians moved dangerously close to being free; they went beyond the borders of their world. They were *me'urav be'anashim*, mixing with all sorts of people, Beryl put it.

"We do precisely the opposite of the Lithuanians," Beryl said. "But Breindel is not a Lithuanian," he quickly added; his wife was not tainted. "She is faithful to the ways of yisrael sabbah."

I focused on such traditions. Had she heard about and did she believe in the various customs of whispering special prayers, sprinkling waters around the bed, placing powder nearby, checking under the bed, and the other practices meant to ensure that her offspring would be blessed and righteous men?

"Of course, and we do many of them. They are part of our method, although we don't think about them that much." Ritual life was not always self-conscious; it was, in practice and perhaps even by intention, a kind of second nature. "We do what we have to do," as Breindel concluded.

And what was that, I asked?

"It's what the Torah tells us, what we have been taught. But we don't make so much of this as you think."

"You do what you want in the bedroom?"

"Yes."

"And the advice and the books?"

"These help us find our own way."

Here was an independence that was not so different from what I might have heard in talking to any contemporary woman. After all, haredim were not the only ones to receive advice and counseling about sexual matters, about the relationships between men and women, about their bodies. As for the guidebooks, sex manuals were among the best-sellers in contemporary society. People read them and then improvised. They found their own way. If the result of Breindel's and Beryl's counseling was that in the end they found their "own way," was that any different from the modern who emphasizes his personal autonomy to find his own way? And yet, the way that they found, the second nature they had evolved, was one colored by their traditions and rabbinic morals and ethics.

I jotted down some notes. The texts and counseling notwithstanding, in real-life sex, "religion . . . was taken for granted. . . . ritualistic gestures were performed with the same casualness as all the others, as if they were utilitarian actions intended to achieve a particular result."[24] There might be spirituality in all this, but it was far from being as self-conscious as the descriptions of the initiation had made it seem. Genuinely human life manages to exist beyond the book, even among haredim who were so bonded to holy texts.

Watching me write, Breindel added: "But just because we follow the customs of yisrael sabbah, we are not strange." She objected to people characterizing haredim as some sort of bizarre sect. "We are not that. We are no different from other regular people." She could not read my pad, but that was precisely what I was beginning to note.

The assertion that her people were no different from other "regular" ones was striking. After all, everything I had learned about their initiation into sex, their attitudes toward the body, and even some of the practices we were yet to discuss all suggested a very different order of life. Their schools tried to impress them with their differences (though the walls of separation were, I had seen, not impervious to outside influences). Their communities were closed, with clearly marked boundaries. They valued yesterday over today, even though they were part of today. Their style of life and their appearances were certainly different, and so were many of their expectations about sex. But here was Breindel, in the midst of a discussion about haredi matters that seemed the most different of all defiantly declaring her similarity to "regular people."

"If I were the ears of the secular world and you wanted to explain to me what you and your world really were, what would you say?" I asked her one afternoon.

"I would say," Breindel replied, "that we are not a cult. I would tell them that it is they who wish to impose their ways on us far more than we who want to impose our ways on them. I would tell them that we are not so strange and different. We live by the laws of the Torah, but we have the same thoughts as you." Where was this claim coming from?

Could it be that parallel with the war that haredim carried on against the dominant secular cultures around them there was simultaneously a countervailing attitude that was at the least ambivalent about the differences or, beyond that, expressing a desire to share a common culture, to be part of the contemporary world around them? Certainly, I saw that tendency among American ultra-Orthodox all the time. In New York even the bearded Satmar hasid who sought to live undisturbed in his Jewish ghetto had become a part of New York and its social life and politics like all other ethnics in the city. And at his electronics business in midtown Manhattan, he could sound like any other American businessman, saluting customers and closing transactions with the vapid but quintessentially American "Have a nice day." But here, in a corner of one of Jerusalem's oldest neighborhoods, was a Reb Arelach hasidic woman who no less than the Americans was telling me she was a regular girl. She had her traditions, which framed her behavior, but inside that frame she claimed not to be so different.

Part of it, I suppose, was a matter of being politically equal. Non-haredim held most of the power in society, and the approximately quarter of a million Israeli haredim, by and large poorer and more dependent, resented that. More and more, they were asserting political power, first in competition with one another and then with the larger parties that represented mainstream Israel. Coalition politics and block voting had given them powers greater than ever before; they were part of the political process, no less than anyone else now. Breindel's comments undoubtedly came against this background. But what was at stake in this political contest was not just a quest for votes; it was a desire to assert haredi inclusion in the body politic, the society, the civilization of the times. And that too was embedded in Breindel's remarks.

"We are not second-class," she defiantly declared in fluent and colloquial Hebrew. Beryl nodded his agreement. It was not enough to make claims, however implicitly, of sharing a common culture, of social parity, of not being second-class. One could go further and assert superiority.

Triumphalism

"Is it true that for the haredi woman the husband is the master and the wife must do all he wants?" I asked.

"Not at all true," Breindel shot back. "This depends on the type of person. There are those who are more dominant and those who are less."

But what about the guidebooks that said that the woman must—I picked out the page and read—"honor her husband and she must fear him and conduct herself according to what he says, and in her eyes he should appear like a king?"

"Of course, I am supposed to honor my husband, but he too is to honor the wife. If he is a king, I am a queen."

Beryl nodded his agreement: "A husband should not treat his wife as a *tchachkeh* [doodad]."

"So the business about the mastery of the male—?"

"Not true at all," Breindel cut me short with emphasis. "You can tell that to everyone." Then she added, "And I walk side by side with my husband—not a few paces behind." Many haredi women did follow behind their husbands.

"Yes," Beryl nodded. "This is our way, next to each other."

"What do you think about a rule that prohibits a male from speaking too much to a woman because this will lower him?" I asked.

"Lower him? Where is that written?" Breindel asked. For her if something was written—in the holy books, of course—then it had authority. But if not, it was simply empty words.

"It's true," Beryl explained, taking a book from the shelf and reading aloud: "You shall not accustom your tongues to speak with women." He read from the great sage Rashi's commentary on a verse in Leviticus.

Breindel was silent for a moment, pondering how to assimilate this into her worldview. For her the words of the sages always had to be right, even when they seemed to go against her feelings. But by the same token she would find a way to fit the two together.

"Yes, I believe in this: when a man talks with a woman instead of studying, this is bitul Torah and so that necessarily lowers him. Of course, no one would say that if a man speaks once to a woman this lowers him. But if he does it continually, yes, he will become lowered.

"To tell you the truth, I feel more comfortable with women," she continued, taking the matter in a whole new direction. "Really, there is no need to speak to men most of the time. They are not comfortable doing it and neither are women. It's better to be with the women and not speak with the men." She paused before continuing, fluttering the edge of her kerchief between her thumb and forefinger.

"I don't think there are that many things to talk about with men. Business in the store, nothing more. It's enough for me that I talk to my husband and my father or brothers. Why should I talk to others?"

"Why do you think it is prohibited to talk to strange men?"

"Because he who speaks too much with women . . ."

She began to quote the text Beryl had just read.

"But you are quoting texts to me. Why do you personally think it is wrong?"

"That is why. I really don't know. Maybe it is not prohibited. Look, I am talking with you. I am not doing a sin, unless I do it too much."

We sat in silence.

"Besides your brothers, father, and husband, did you ever sit and talk with a male?" I asked.

"No."

"Am I then the first male outside of the family that you have ever talked to?"

Breindel tugged at her kerchief. "Could be. There are males in the stores. But an extended conversation? This could be the first." Her voice made it sound like no big thing.

Did she want to do the sorts of things that other young women her age might do were she not haredi?

"But I *do* what I want to do," she protested.

"What if you want to leave the neighborhood, go shopping downtown, are you free to do it?

"This does not appeal to me," she said with a snicker. "I have other interests."

"Would you want to drive a car?" Almost no haredi women drove cars. Having a license would require taking a course and a test that would put her in a car alone with a man not her husband. Besides, if she drove, she would be able to escape to far places. This was something pritzos (whores) did. A respectable haredi woman stayed away from the wheel.

"Maybe in America where you need to go great distances, but here no. It's not modest because when she drives, she will be all day on the streets, and a woman is supposed to be mostly at home. Who knows where else she will spend her time if she drives? This is not modest. Anyway, where would I drive to? We don't have a car. I would never even try it. Why should I? Everything I need is here."

"Would you run your own business?"

"This is an American thing, not for here."

"How about working outside the home?"

"I already do."

Although Beryl was not too keen on the idea of his wife working outside their home, she was spending about twenty hours a week in

the Raphael Free Clinic office. Raphael was the medical self-help organization haredim had set up, so, strictly speaking, Breindel was out
of the home but not out of the community home. But for her this sort
of autonomy was sufficient; it certainly distinguished her from most
other Reb Arelach women, as much as the colors of her colored kerchief and brown stockings.

Was she actually suggesting that she was like any other Israeli
woman, I asked on a subsequent visit?

"I am not that familiar with the secular woman, so I cannot really
answer that question," she responded. "But I am proud to be a haredi
woman. Those who think we are somehow inferior to men are wrong.
On the contrary, I feel more of a woman as a haredi, but it's difficult
for me to explain it."

Although she claimed not to be familiar with them, Breindel proceeded to offer her view of the differences between secular and haredi
women. It was a kind of attack.

"I am not so selfish as the secular woman; what *I* do is not just for
myself. Maybe they think that we're low on the floor. Not at all. Our
women know what their husbands want, and they know their role in
life." Her personal identity was absorbed in her sense of communal
belonging and collective consciousness. She was not simply a female,
but an important component of her culture, a player in a larger drama.
"Haredi women don't have to run around to try to be something else.
We know what we are, what we have to do, what God wants from us."

"I'll tell you how a haredi woman is better," Breindel said one day.
It was a matter that concerned her a great deal, and it was the reason
she claimed she was ready to keep talking to me. She focused on the
matters of sexuality that she knew I was particularly interested in. "A
haredi woman knows she has to hold herself back from her husband
when she is in an impure condition." Practicing sexual restraint was
crucial. "The chiloinim can never hold themselves back."

To Breindel the attitude of the secular woman was, as someone else
once put it, " 'use it or lose it'—in other words, make themselves
sexually available or else stand accused of abnormality."[25]

To illustrate her point she repeated an observation I heard many
times in the haredi community.

"One of my friends was in the hospital to have a baby," Breindel
began. Hospitals were among the relatively few places where haredim
came into very close contact with outsiders. Here, where the people
they normally saw only from a distance dropped their guard, haredim
believed they could catch a glimpse of the private and intimate world
of those strangers who did not share their culture. In the hospital the
haredim believed they got to see the private life of chiloinim.

"She told me what she saw among those goyim, those freie Yidn. She saw a woman who just had a baby, she's still tired, and what does her husband do? He comes rushing over to her and right away he hugs her and kisses her. They can't even wait to throw themselves at each other! It's disgusting. Right away they want to jump into bed together again."

"What is the matter with this?"

"It's lust. She's ritually impure now and he should stay away from her until she goes to the mikveh."

"Couldn't it be a show of tenderness or happiness?" I asked.

"No," she said. "They are uncontrolled. It's lust." This was an example of how culture determined perceptions. The haredim could see only what the ideology of their way of life permitted them to see.

"But with us it's better," Breindel continued. "We know there are limits, there are times for this kind of contact. When a woman comes back from the mikveh," Breindel concluded, her triumphant tone unmistakable, "then she can give herself to her husband, and each time it's like the first time. The secular women don't have this, so that's why they are always cheating on their husbands. Everything is permitted. Even in front of other people they jump into bed together!"

"What makes you say that they cheat on each other or permit everything?"

Breindel confided in me that occasionally late at night she listened to the call-in talk shows on the radio. It was not something her community encouraged. Television was off-limits because it showed abominations, and no haredi home had an antenna on the roof. But radio too was filled with impurity. Still, many like Breindel listened secretly, no rooftop antennas would give her away.

"I hear their problems. It's terrible. Abuse, cheating, lust—it's just terrible. But that is the way they live."

"Yes," Beryl added, "they live like all the goyim in the world."

"Is that what you think goes on all the time?"

"It's what we hear all the time. Why shouldn't we believe it?"

So there was the triumphalism. Of course, it's based on a caricature, no less than the counterview, which was just as skewed. If haredim thought their ways were best, they were in this no different from their secular Israeli counterparts who saw in the haredim the darkest side of human ignorance and primitivism. The two worlds that existed side by side looked at each other through the filter of their culture. Each saw the other in black and white terms. There were no nuances in the understanding. They understood the meaning of their actions in antithetical ways. To see it otherwise was a great risk. Understanding might lead to tolerance, tolerance to sympathy, sympathy to pluralism, and pluralism, the notion that there was more than one way to legitimately exist as a Jew, to an erosion of their own way of life. Erosion, of course, meant ultimate loss in the culture conflict. And that was anathema.

"It seems to me," Breindel continued, "that the secular woman tries harder to find favor in men's eyes. Everywhere she flaunts herself, she uncovers herself. But I don't have that problem. These women think they are free, but, as it is written, 'There is no one more free than someone who busies himself with the Torah.' I have none of their problems. Maybe the other women are jealous about their husbands, because they know what they see on the street, but I am not. I know that my husband is mine, that his desires are within the family."

"And do you busy yourself with Torah?"

"Men are obligated to study Torah, but a woman can also share in this. I know of a man who learned Torah, but not so hard as he could. And he wasn't always on time at his prayers either. Then he got married. After the wedding he began to be much more careful about getting to the synagogue on time. And in the morning, before his prayers, he was studying. At night, after a full and heavy day, he studied a couple of more hours. And people began to ask him what happened.

" 'My wife demands it.'

"She persuaded him, she was the influence on him. So a wife can learn Torah through her husband. So you see we get the credit for what our husbands learn."

I asked if she and her girlfriends compared husbands.

"We have been taught not to compare. This can damage a marriage."

In fact, from one of the lay therapists—they called themselves advisers—in the Satmar hasidic community, I heard that while the women did not explicitly compare husbands—that was considered coarse—they did use their conversations indirectly to learn what was expected of them, and what was normal.

Sometimes this silence did not always work to their benefit. One young woman who felt her sexual passions increasingly aroused for her husband was concerned that by having these feelings at times when her husband was not supposed to be with her, she was somehow dirty, sick, abnormal. Her husband was a "zaddik," never ready to deviate from the letter of the law and have sex except at the assigned times, so she could not talk to him about it; he would only see he was married to a sinner. Her friends never talked about such feelings; she assumed they never had them because they were wrong.

"Right or wrong," the adviser told her her feelings were "real."

"So help me get rid of them," she implored her, "before I become like the chiloinim."

Breindel expressed some of these opinions: "I believe that the craving and lusts of a person are so powerful that the moment she finds herself giving in to them, she is overpowered. I have learned how to control them. This is my superior strength as a haredi woman." If she was asking for more sex with her husband these days it was only in order to get pregnant; it was not out of lust.

What about free choice? I asked. In the secular world a person could choose his mate freely.

"But we have free choice too," she countered. "We meet before we marry." Without missing a beat, she added, "It's a fact that we have fewer divorces. The matchmaker is a help; the community helps. A person who goes to choose simply does not know what to choose. Freedom isn't necessarily happiness."

"And are you happy?"

"That is not the way we think about life. I get up at seven-thirty and make my husband breakfast, clean up a bit, and then go out to work and spend five or six hours, except on Friday. Then sometimes I go to my mother or I make lunch or clean up. Then I have to make the supper."

"And what about tomorrow?"

"A woman is in the house; she raises the children. The man has the role to study Torah and the woman raises the children."

"How many children would you like to have?"

"Ten."

"But you would not have room for them in this apartment!"

"So we will sell this one and get another with more room. God will help, *Hashem ya'azor*," she concluded.

"What does this mean?"

"It means you don't make preparations. If you have trust in God, you know He will help and you don't make plans until He makes plans. I know that chiloinim when they are pregnant go out and buy all the baby furniture. We don't do this. 'Hashem ya'azor' means that when everything goes in the right order, then we shall go out and get the baby furniture."

"There is no point to ask what will be tomorrow," Yisrael Eichler had written in his haredi paper, and then quoting the Psalmist, "Blessed is the man that maketh the Lord his trust." [26] Like other haredim, Breindel echoed this sentiment. "We're proud of our faith," she concluded, "not like the chiloinim."

Do you find your days boring?

"Not at all. What is better about a secular woman's day?" She paused for an answer, but I said nothing. I was not here to make the case for secular women's lifestyles. Perhaps she thought I would talk about their involvement in new technologies, their work in offices— she could see them in front of video display terminals at government offices, at the health service, in those encounters she had with the other Israel. For haredim this involvement in technology often represented what was best, perhaps all that was good, in the outside world. As if in response she continued: "I am learning to use computers." She was using a terminal at the Raphael office. "We are not so backward as you may think," she concluded at last.

The conversations that had begun with questions about sex had moved inexorably out of the bedroom. Intuitively, Breindel, who led me out, understood that it was what happened in the bedroom or more precisely the attitudes toward sexuality, that had made me, and people like me, think that she and her husband and other haredim lived so different a life that they were in another time and another order. But when she took me out of the bedroom and away from matters of sex, her message was that for all the differences I might imagine, there were plenty of similarities.

"There was a time," Lévi-Strauss has written, "when travelling brought the traveller into contact with civilizations which were radically different from his own and impressed him in the first place by their strangeness. During the last few centuries such instances have become increasingly rare." [27] What Lévi-Strauss had had to travel the rivers and jungles of Brazil to discover, I had found in this encounter and others like it. There was surely the strange here, and matters about which I could not ask, but there was also much that I could understand and even appreciate. With this realization my search for the essential haredi was nearly at an end.

22

Scribal Apotheosis

Inside their schools, where character is fashioned; on the streets and in the institutions of the community, where it is expressed; on pilgrimages, at bar mitzvahs, weddings, and funerals, where passages are marked; in the homes and minds of the insiders, past posters and into the bedroom, I had gone in search of the haredi. Now, as the time of my stay among them ebbed, I thought about what, beyond appearances, were the essential features of the haredim I had discovered. Were there common elements in all I had seen, something that would teach me not only about what these people were but what they taught me about culture and about the way that the past and present can coexist, or would I instead be left with a blur of images that amounted to little more than a scrapbook of memories? Reviewing my notes, as I now review the preceding pages, I find some answers to the questions with which I set out on my search.

My first question had been: were these people living embodiments of the past? While I did in fact find that haredim made a great deal of tradition, I also gradually realized that by expecting to find them untouched by the present or somehow sealed off from outside influences, I was "chasing after vestiges of a vanished reality," if ever such a reality existed.[1] In spite of their claims to be absolutely enclosed in the past, haredim were not. As an anthropologist, I should have known better, for, as Claude Lévi-Strauss admits: "It is in the nature of all societies to include a degree of impurity incompatible with the norms they proclaim."[2] In almost every place and situation I encountered, there was always a hint that the haredim were very much aware of and often touched by what went on beyond the borders of their world. The perfect reincarnation of the past that "I was looking for was already beyond my reach."[3] Time did not stop even in the precincts of tradition.

Yet "although I found them to be less unspoiled than I had hoped," I did discover, like Lévi-Strauss on his parallel journey before me, that among haredim, "ancient modes of life and traditional techniques re-emerged from a past, the still-living proximity of which it would have been a mistake to overlook."[4] If the past was not pure in the haredi world, it was still extraordinarily alive, and elements of it had found a way to coexist with the present. Much of yesterday was eternally being resurrected here. But these revitalized traditions were endowed with a new character that made them radically different from anything they had ever been in the past. To be haredi today, when most people were not, was not like being observant in days where few other alternatives were even imaginable. It was to take a stand, to create a new order under the cover of giving life to an old one, and to contend with all others.

Among today's haredim, I found two faces where I expected to find only one. One face expressed culture conflict and opposition, the abiding effort of haredim to separate themselves from and struggle against what they believed to be the corrosive influences of a contemporary secular society that dominated the world just beyond the borders of their own. From this aspect, everything was aimed to show that what they, the children of Jacob, the erlicher Yidn, did was right while what the others, the children of Esau, the goyim and chiloinim, did was wrong. It was all us-versus-them. For all of the internal competition among various haredi groups, the communal element, the sense of us-versus-them (even though the "us" and "them" in question varied at times) was something that all haredim appeared to share. If Esau tried to be up-to-date, Jacob remained bonded to tradition. If Esau wore colors, putting an end to mourning over the losses of the past, Jacob wore black and white, refusing to forget those bereavements. The destruction of the Holy Temple in Jerusalem, the Holocaust, and the loss of European Jewry remained enduring and defining collective memories. If Esau mixed with people, trying to assimilate, Jacob dwelt in his own tents, "a people who shall abide alone and not be counted among the goyim."[5] If Esau was a Hebrew-speaking Zionist, a soldier or a citizen of a secular state, Jacob remained a Yiddish-speaking anti-Zionist who stayed out of the army and retained a consciousness of abiding exile, still very much an east European Jew. If Esau wandered downtown to the cafés and movie houses, Jacob stayed in his narrow alleys and synagogues. If Esau was freethinking and willing to try anything to break old taboos, Jacob championed limits, restraint, and ritual. In personal relationships what Esau called love, Jacob knew to be really lust. Esau recognized few authorities; Jacob went to his rebbe and his rav. Esau attended the university, and Jacob learned in the yeshiva. Esau was a heretic, Jacob was a hasid, a ben Torah, a scholar. "We are not you" was the message coming out of this face of the haredi world.

But there was another haredi face, with exactly opposite features. Jacob and Esau, after all, were not only contenders; they were also twins. Here came the notion, as Breindel put it, that "we are not so strange and different." This other face appeared in Yisrael Eichler's collegial talk with me about word-processing programs and advice on car repairs. It showed up in the up-to-date political methods haredim used to achieve power. It was in their rabbis with cellular phones, yeshivas with fax machines, and haredi confidence in modern medicine and technology. It was, in fact, inherent in the nature of culture war: "Almost any contact between different cognitive systems leads to mutual contamination. The traditionalist defending himself against modernity almost inevitably incorporates elements of the latter within his own defense."[6] To contend with your enemy, you must think like him, anticipate his every move.

But then you become like him somewhat as well. Wherever haredim stressed how far apart *from* the contemporary world they were, they also betrayed evidence of how much a part *of* that very world had penetrated their own. Whenever I found a situation in which much was made of the contrasts between Jacob and Esau, I also found the correspondences. Inside Belz, within the haredi schools or the Lithuanian yeshiva, even among the fiercely sectarian Reb Arelach, there were reminders of the outside world.

While there remained riddles and occasions when I was not certain exactly what to make of what I saw, or found myself unable to articulate the right questions—as is always the case when a person from one world comes to explore another—the conclusion I drew from the fact of these two faces turned out to echo something Claude Lévi-Strauss discovered not at the end but at the outset of his journey. "It is an illusion," he said, in a remark that perfectly captures the features that faced me, "to suppose that the invasion of one element disencumbers another." There are occasions when "the end of one civilization," meets with "the beginning of another."[7] Culture is not always black or white. More often it is "the interweaving of cultural threads from different arenas."[8] As haredim demonstrated, people could maintain the old even as they absorbed the new.

In a way, the tension between being separate and traditionalist while struggling to convince themselves that they were also a part of the world, a dynamic and ever-precarious balance between essentially irreconcilable opposites, might have been the pulse of haredi life and the source of their vitality. These were not fossils; these were people struggling to keep their option on life, running as hard in their direction as people in contemporary secular society ran in theirs.

It was precisely in Israel, where an effort to create a contemporary, living Jewish culture out of an earlier religious heritage was the organizing principle, that this haredi culture could best be forged. Here, more ardently than anywhere else, the contest over what being a Jew today truly meant was being waged. It was the ultimate struggle over the question of who is a Jew. Whenever that issue came up, the haredim came out in force; their entire existence was bound up with determining who was a Jew.

This sense of who and what the haredim were did not come to me all in a flash; it emerged slowly and gradually, built up steadily of the evidence of history and my own observations. And yet, as I found so many times in the past, sometimes a culture emerges more clearly in a single instant than it does over an extensive period. A fleeting episode or overheard remark can crystallize complex realities in so striking a way that the image and the message it carries remain clearly emblazoned long after intricate theories are forgotten. I came upon such an image near the end of my days among the haredim.

One of the kindergarten teachers I interviewed and watched, Reb Avrohom, who was a scribe before he was a teacher and went back to being one again afterward, once told me he thought being a scribe was the best way to safeguard a haredi way of life. To copy or repair Torah scrolls, inscribe megillahs, write mezuzahs to be put on every Jew's doorposts, or prepare tefillin, inside which there were passages of scripture on parchment, was, he believed, to remain dedicated to religion and insulated from all that could corrode Jewish life. It was a profession in which haredim outnumbered all others.

As I thought about this observation, I began to be convinced. Alone in his room involved in such timeless Jewish occupations, the scribe with quill in hand seemed a genuine incarnation of the past, protected from the contaminations of the outside and the present. After all, the code was clear: scribes had to use parchment exactly as their forebears did. They had to write exactly the same words on the scrolls each and every time. Not a single stroke of their quill could be different. The placement of the words they copied or the shape of the tefillin could not deviate one jot from what it had always been. Even the thoughts that ran through the scribe's mind as he worked were governed by tradition—and he who let his mind wander would make errors, the fruits of his labor lacking in holiness.

In principle, then, Reb Avrohom seemed correct. To be a scribe was one of the best ways to be haredi, to remain apart, embedded in tradition, beyond the reach of the present. Maybe I should look at scribes—maybe they were the only true haredim.

The provinces of haredi life were dotted with scribes. Almost every yeshiva boy at some point made a few extra shekels by writing a mezuzah or a megillah in his spare time; the work was portable, the hours flexible, the pay more than decent—a mezuzah could fetch fifty dollars for less than an hour's work, a megillah could bring ten times that. A Torah scroll was never sold for less than twenty thousand dollars, and tefillin generally averaged about two hundred dollars a pair, with some costing as much as five or six hundred. And payment was often in cash, which meant even the taxes that the Zionists collected could be easily evaded.

Of all the scribes in Jerusalem, according to many haredim to whom I spoke, one man was the personification of the profession. His work was beyond question, as was his reputation for honesty and fairness. His name was Moshe Gershon Gottlieb, and he worked in a small room—hardly bigger than a closet—next to his apartment in the Hungarian Houses, just behind the headquarters of the Reb Arelach hasidim in Mea Shearim. An ageless man with white beard and matching wisps of hair around his ears, black-framed, yellowing glasses that slid down his nose, and fingers molded by the work he did with them, Moshe Gershon worked six days a week. His hours were organized around his religious needs. In the morning he was in his room after he finished his prayers. Afternoons he was closed while he sat in the bes medrash and learned Torah. Then, after dark, when he returned from the synagogue, he was back at his table, working until late at night.

There was always someone who needed new tefillin or another mezuzah. At Purim time countless people wanted a megillah. As for Torah scrolls, purchases of so momentous a character were made only from someone whose reputation was impeccable, and that put Moshe

Gershon on top of the list. But while he did all the things that scribes normally do, perhaps the largest proportion of his work was with tefillin. He not only inscribed the parchments in the boxes himself but also bought the work of younger, part-time scribes, which he then set into the tefillin. This was a painstaking task that required cutting and sewing the seams of the leather boxes, carving the corners so that they were perfect and in accord with the most stringent requirements, painting them with a special black lacquer, and binding the straps to them with the complicated knots that spelled out God's name.

As the traditional requirement is that tefillin should be checked at least twice every seven years, Moshe Gershon spent a good deal of his time opening the leather boxes to see to it that all the words on the parchment inside were still legible and not worn away by time. Or he would put on new tefillin straps, after the old ones became ragged or too short (a boy who got his first set of tefillin at the bar mitzvah age of thirteen often came back at seventeen for straps that could bind them on his longer arm and wider head). And nearly everyone found that with use tefillin got their corners shaved or lost their requisite veneer of black, blemishes the scribe could fix.

Moshe Gershon's workmanship was excellent. So even though he sat alone in his tiny workshop in a back alley, people from everywhere came to his door for his services. Not all of them were haredim. There were plenty of other Jews who used tefillin or mezuzahs and who wanted megillahs and Torah scrolls.

Long before this anthropological quest, I had come to Moshe Gershon's door. He was the one who sold me the tefillin I gave my son, Uri, on his bar mitzvah and checked the ones my father wore to see if they were still kosher. All the mezuzahs on my doors had come from his workshop. But for over a year I had not been to see him. Now, with anthropological rather than Jewish needs, I paid him a visit.

Past Toldos Aharon, I ascended two narrow outdoor staircases, entered a short tunnel, and found myself on a long veranda, redolent of boiled chicken soup. A few black-kerchiefed women were hanging up laundry, and little children played inside doorways, looking at me as if I came from another planet. It was a look I had long since gotten used to, though it recalled for me the first time I had come here only to encounter a little boy of about five who excitedly pointed at me and said in Yiddish to his slightly older sister, "Look! A goy!"

Moshe Gershon's door was in the middle of the building. When he was there, winter or summer, it was always open. I brought some tefillin for him to check. They needed some lacquer, and one of the edges of the box that went on the head was chipped. With this in hand

I would have a pretext for a conversation. As I approached, I saw there were already two people inside the small room. They wanted his advice about the parchments they intended to purchase and which, if they were deemed good enough, they would ask him to set into a pair of tefillin. To know how to evaluate work on parchment required a combination of erudition in matters of Jewish law, a sense of religious aesthetics, and a degree of self-confidence. A true haredi, however, worried over the decision. Was the line of this or that letter perfectly formed? Was there the proper symmetry in the writing? Haredim could find dozens of ways of grading such religious objects. The truly knowledgeable needed no advice from scribes; their lessers depended on them. But even the informed often looked for some confirmation from Moshe Gershon for their selections and evaluations.

The room held no more than three people at a time, so I watched silently from my place outside the door as he laconically took these customers through their purchase. He had seen it all so many times before. And then at last, the choice was made. "Be graced with mitzvahs," they said to him as they paid out the deposit and left. I came into the room.

"Shalom aleichem," we greeted each other. He recognized me. I pulled out the tefillin and told him what I wanted done. If I returned tomorrow after seven, he would have it ready. Now he was closing up; he had to hurry to the synagogue.

After seven the next day I returned, hoping I could spend a little more time with him. It was night now, and his little room glowed in the dark. Surrounded by little packets of parchment and tefillin, he was sitting, working at his table. In front of him were several quills. He picked up one. Had the light come from a kerosene lamp instead of a light bulb, I would not have been surprised, so much did the scene look to me like something out of yesterday. Here it was at last, a tableau of the past nearly perfectly preserved, everything done as it always had been, no changes, no disturbances, no contaminations. And the small room seemed the incarnation of the austerity and modesty that haredim claimed so much to value.

Moshe Gershon looked up when I came in, put down his quill, and turned to get the little velvet sack containing my tefillin. I took the opportunity to draw him out in conversation.

"You know I always wondered," I began, "about those old tefillin, the very big ones that my grandfather and people of his generation wore."

Moshe Gershon nodded; he knew all about these. "The ones from Poland, you mean," he said. "Yes, yes." They were twice the size of

the tefillin people wore these days and I thought to myself they were
symbolic of our relation to our forebears. If they were giants and we
pygmies, it stood to reason their tefillin were bigger than ours. I was
about to share this thought with Moshe Gershon, hoping it would
allow him to tell me about how much he thought of the past, how
wedded to it he was.

"They were not very good," he began before I could say anything.
"The leather was poor and the workmanship was crude. But what
could they do? They didn't really have the proper materials."

"You mean our tefillin are better?" I asked incredulously.

"Oh, much better. They had to make the tefillin big then because
they didn't have the necessities to make them smaller. We have much
better machines to shape them. Those old tefillin—of course, they
were kosher, but they weren't made from the fine hides we now have.
Now we can make them from a single skin, one piece, from fatty cows.
But they didn't do that. They didn't have the fattened cows; they were
too poor. Those old tefillin are not made from one piece; they were
separate sections stitched together."

The knowledgeable knew that tefillin made from a single piece of
hide from a fatty cow were the finest to be had. Moshe Gershon was
telling me that the tefillin of yesterday were superseded by newer
improved versions that only superficially kept the shape and color of
the old. In the ancient practice of making tefillin, where nothing was
supposed to change, there was indeed change. New was improved.
Today only looked like yesterday; it was in fact not the same—it was
better.

"Today, you could never sell anyone here those old big Polish
tefillin. They want something finer, the latest." He laughed. New
tefillin, new standards, a new day. And the haredim knew it. They
bought only the new, better brand. Those who wanted the old ones,
unchanged, were ignorants.

The phone rang. I had never noticed it before, but now the sound
called my attention to it. Moshe Gershon had installed it on the wall,
just above his quills. To answer the call he pushed a button on a piece
of expensive electronic gadgetry. A disembodied voice spoke from out
of the wall. It was a scribe calling from Tel Aviv with a question about
a Torah scroll he was repairing. The telephone linked this little se-
cluded room with the entire world. Moshe Gershon answered him
quickly before hanging up.

I burst into laughter. The austerity and isolation I had first seen in
this little workshop was not quite so perfect as I imagined. The phone
of tomorrow was there right above the quills of yesterday. Amid aus-

terity was luxury. The contrast was overwhelming. "I see that older is not always better." I said. "Not in tefillin and not in telephones."

He laughed too. "Lots of things are better now," he said.

"So why still use quills? Aren't there lots of better pens now?" I asked. He laughed at the silliness of my question. "For their purposes, they are still the best." Elements of the present did not totally dislodge the past.

The powerful image of the futuristic phone next to the traditional quill, the idea that ancient tefillin could be improved according to today's standards and yet still be embedded in tradition, seemed to me to capture much that I had learned among and about the haredim. And ultimately it answered the question with which I began. No less than their American counterparts, whom I had already discovered to be my contemporaries, these people were still around because they only appeared to belong to yesterday. Where others are absorbed by and celebrate the present, haredim may have found a way to absorb the present while celebrating the past.

Their extraordinary success in surviving and growing, in holding on to their children, must make the rest of us take notice. If the haredim are right, in the thick of the present, the best way to face may not always be toward the future. A look toward the past may be at least as good—or as the haredim might say, even better—to insure Jewish survival in the days ahead.

Epilogue:
Ethnographic Afterwords

I began this ethnographic account of life among the haredim with
Claude Lévi-Strauss's trip into the Brazilian jungles as my model.
Sometimes during the many months of my search for the essential
haredi, I worried that I might in the end find myself stymied by the
same paradox that confronted him during his quest for what he
thought was the definitive primitive, the Tupi-Kawahib. After a long
journey upriver to the heart of the Brazilian jungle, Lévi-Strauss at
last came face-to-face with the people for whom he had searched so
long:

> There they were, all ready to teach me their customs and beliefs,
> and I did not know their language. They were as close to me as a
> reflection in a mirror; I could touch them, but I could not under-
> stand them. [1]

I too had such awe-inspiring moments when I was overwhelmed by
the fact that the haredim were ready to talk to me and let me touch
them, but I was not always able to get close to what they meant or
were. Sometimes there were questions, like the meaning of Breindel's
hitching up her stockings, about which I could not ask. At other times

there were questions such as Yisrael Eichler's or the rosh yeshiva's about what limits I imposed on myself or what my Judaism meant to me that I could not answer. At times like these I confronted all the barriers that kept me a stranger.

To Lévi-Strauss, in such cases, there were only two possibilities: the strange could ultimately either remain altogether foreign or else it could be made all too familiar. At the outset I worried that I might do the same: either I would simply describe the haredim as exotic and leave them at that or dismissively reduce what I saw as another variation on modernity. At times, I probably did a little of both. But as it turned out, the people I saw were neither completely foreign nor all-too-familiar; they were both. Sometimes they remained quite out of range of my understanding, at the far reaches of Jewish life, and at other moments the same people seemed close, sufficiently familiar for me to be able to capture some of their essential qualities. I could be and was both insider and outsider, Jacob and Esau. Given that paradoxical double face, the best I could do was to be bricoleur and ethnographer.

Ethnographers see with a sort of deep vision, looking *at* but also *beneath* the surface. Rather like psychoanalysts, or interpreters of poems, beneath ordinary reality they find deeper meaning. "Ethnography," as James Clifford puts it, "decodes and recodes."[2] This means that the reality presented in the ethnographer's description is fashioned or distilled. It makes the exotic familiar and reframes the familiar so that it is seen in new and often unconventional ways. What emerges in an ethnographer's account is therefore not precisely what went on or even what was seen but rather a crafted interpretation of a particular experience. Turned on the haredim, this sort of vision and decoding compels the discovery that "beneath the dull veneer of the real [is] the possibility of another more miraculous world based on radically different principles of classification and order."[3] I have tried in some of this account to provide a hint of that other level of reality.

To see this way, the ethnographer must not only watch. He must also develop "what might be called epistemological empathy," an ability to understand the world in the way the insiders do without at the same time losing the objective distance that comes from his starting as an outsider and remaining committed to explaining matters so that an outsider can comprehend them.[4] That is why I chose not only to be bricoleur and ethnographer, but also participant observer. As such, I could also feel the charm of the haredi way of life, allowing myself to be caught up, for example, in a hasidic gathering, even as at times I could make out the dynamics and mechanisms that drove it. I could take part in a pilgrimage, pray, rejoice at a wedding, march in a mass funeral procession, share in a rebbe's tish, or absorb a rosh yeshiva's mussar—all without always having to fit it into a neat conceptual package.

To the pure scientist the explanations of the participant observer and bricoleur are often perceived as ingenuous, impressionistic, anecdotal, novelistic, unsystematic, lacking in structure, or ad hoc. And if the style of writing is meant to be engaging, rather than scientifically neutral, that is even worse. My stance and style place me in a precarious position. Bricoleurs as participant observers can get carried away. Distortions do occur; mistakes are made, perceptions can be wrong. The desire to make something read well can make it seem suspect. That is why I have always been careful to remind the reader that I used a tape recorder much of the time and where quotation marks are used, these are the words I heard (or my English translations of them). But context is what gives meaning to quotation and in this written account, as in all such documents, the author sets the context.

At some level of consciousness, I argue that the sorts of transcendent meanings I saw in the behavior or heard in the words of the people whose lives I shared and observed "are not abstractions or interpretations 'added' to the original 'simple' account. Rather they are conditions of its meaningfulness."[5]

Of course, the specific character of my description remains a translation, a recoding; such is the nature of making sense of one world in the terms of another. By making the exotic familiar or reframing the familiar so that it is seen in new and often unconventional ways, ethnography engages in alteration. Reality is never quite as pat as what is in the account. What emerges in the account is not precisely what went on or even what was seen but rather a crafted interpretation of a particular experience. "The text," as Clifford argues, "embalms the event as it extends its 'meaning.'"[6] There is no easy defense to such criticism, except to say that, in general, "understanding consists in reducing one type of reality to another," and "the true reality is never the most obvious."[7]

So did the people I watched see exactly what I saw? Would they agree completely with what I have written? Probably not. Did they mean their action to be what I saw or understand the words they spoke as I did? Not always. After all, they stand in a different relationship to what they did than I do. Where those being observed see action, the ethnographer also sees reactions. Where they see nothing special, he sees norms or values, patterns and effects. Where they mean one thing, the observer, who looks from another distance, sees other implications.

What about the particular settings and people I chose to illustrate and explain haredi life? Were they the best, the most revealing, typical? Those who imagine that practiced observers have worked out elaborate and scientific approaches to entering a field setting have probably not followed the anthropologist into the field. As often as not, decisions about how and where to go in are based on simple curiosity or determined by the path of least resistance. So it was for me. An open door, an available seat, a sense that my presence would be tolerated, a person willing to talk to me, and a notion that there was something here that I wanted to watch determined much of what I saw. Because I believe, as Ruth Benedict has argued, that "a culture, like an individual, is a more or less consistent pattern of thought and action," I trust that a look at one aspect of a culture can as likely as any other yield much the same information about what makes this people who they are.[8] And because I am a bricoleur, I can live with the sometimes serendipitous results of my wanderings. But I understand that for some readers only a more systematic approach would be satisfactory.

Some might argue that by its very character, an ethnographic account of a living community—particularly one as complex as the one I call "haredi"—is just a story. Perhaps so, but the ethnographer is still limited in the kind of story he can tell. Culture is not so malleable that we can impose shapes upon it that it is in no way ready to assume. As anthropologist Eric Wolf so succinctly put it: "The writer creates his work of art; the anthropologist, to the contrary, describes and analyzes a phenomenon he has done nothing to create. The work of art with which the anthropologist is concerned exists when he comes to it—it is culture wrought by Siuai or Tikopia or the people of Atimelang—all he can do is capture the phenomenon with fidelity and insight."[9] This is, however, easier said than done.

"The student who as an anthropologist has once fully participated in learning about another culture," Margaret Mead once observed, "is an altered instrument."[10] The anthropologist-ethnographer cannot go home again. The past of my grandfather, as I said at the outset, I did not find. But I did see a world striking in its cultural character. This is not a world for which I share an uncritical affection, nor is it one I am ready to condemn. But having looked at it through the medium of my discipline, I shall never see it the same way again. If I have accomplished anything in these pages, neither will you.

Afterword to the New Edition

While I hope that the people whose lives I have probed in these pages are now more easily discerned and their culture less opaque than might have been the case at the outset, there is perhaps more to say for those who want to know how the haredim of Jerusalem—my primary focus here—may be compared with those one discovers in America. Short of writing a second book, I shall take advantage of the publication of this new edition to outline some of the important parallels as well as some differences between the Israeli and American incarnations of ultra-Orthodoxy.

Both populations are composed of Jews who, in sharp contrast to most of their contemporary coreligionists, do not find living by the demands of Judaism or traditional Jewish life and custom uncomfortably narrow, unduly restrictive, or overly demanding. Nor do they look for values, ideals, or personal fulfilment beyond it. At a time when many if not most other Jews seek an escape from parochialism and anything that recalls the old ghetto, these Jews—both in America and Israel—are quite prepared to confine themselves to its domains and the dominion of those who share their point of view and way of life. In principle they consider the world beyond their insular enclaves, however apparently attractive and personally empowering, to be fraught with insidious temptation as well as moral and spiritual pollution. While they may make use of some of its products—particularly its technology, medical care, and creature comforts—and may try to adapt some of its procedures to their needs—particularly its political tactics and economics—they remain convinced that what is truly valuable and enduring is already within their grasp, handed down by tradition and custom and protected by their way of life. The sense of community, the almost obsessive concern with continuity and survival along with a strategic retrieval of traditions and customs to nurture it, the sense that history has a definite end and that they, the "true believers," know what it is, the perceived need to articulate a distinct Jewish identity along with its particular life passages, the powerful emphasis on the family and children and their role in assuring the Jewish future, the internal distinctions between hasidim and those haredim who identify with the world of the yeshivas, the opposition to change and willingness to fight back against the incursions of secular society, even the attitudes toward the strict regulation of sexuality are as true for haredim in Brooklyn as for those in Israel. In all these matters, there is no significant attitudinal difference between those who make their home in the promised Jewish homeland and those who have chosen to remain in the golden "Jewish exile" of the American land of promise.

Yet while haredim believe in the integrity and virtue of their Judaism and Jewish life, they nevertheless worry—ontologically tremble—over the possibility that modern society will try to erode that integrity and virtue. Propinquity is danger; the menacing precincts of modernity are just on the other side of their Jewish street, in the sin cities of America, especially New York, where many of them live, and in secular Israel, where the largest concentration of haredim can today be found. That uncomfortable proximity of the "threatening other" has transformed a quiescent haredi anxiety about safeguarding their way of life and ethos into a motive for defensive and at times offensive culture war. This war goes on all the time. Its battles are fought via the obdurate and deliberate commitment to a haredi lifestyle that is undeniably at odds with modernity. The black hats and coats, the Yiddish vernacular, the continuous concern with Jewish ritual and religion over all else, the increasing separation of the sexes, the turning away from primary secular education and the denial of any merit in university study in favor of Torah and its associated wisdom, the expressed trust that all comes with "God's help," the belief that human ability to control destiny or the future is limited, the supreme valuation of traditional family roles including having many children, the sense that history unfolds according to a divine master plan—all this and more throws down an implicit but unmistakable challenge to the values, beliefs, practices, and culture of modernity.

At other times, the haredi culture war becomes more active. The "others" are then attacked, either physically—when that is possible and not dangerous—or, more likely, in words and political or social action. In this more active phase, the haredim do more than offer the example of their Jewish alternative. They assail and de-legitimate those who do not share their ways, by exploiting their enemies' weaknesses, by using the tools of modernity against them, and in some cases by actively recruiting converts from among those Jews who seem safely ensconced in the life of the world outside. Indeed, in the most active phase of such a culture war, haredim seek in every way possible to undermine the world on the other side of the street. They fight it tooth and nail, using methods fair and foul to protect their way of life and institutions.

Yet active engagement with the other is—even in the form of conflict—always dangerous. The combatant who crosses over to do battle may be captured, brainwashed, and converted. Looking straight into the eyes of the enemy, moreover, can result in the unanticipated discovery of his humanity and similarity, weakening the resolve of those engaged in the battles. Converts and others who are "redeemed" from among the enemy, additionally, threaten to bring along with them some dangerous cultural baggage from their former lives that may be unpacked like a Trojan horse within the haredi enclave. And so unless there seems no alternative to active culture war because the other has crossed over and is now threatening to tear down the separation between his and the haredi domains, or unless the battle seems certain to be won, most haredim have and continue to prefer to remain quiescently inside their insular habitats and existence, to keep to themselves—secure in the belief that those outside who call themselves Jews will ultimately wither and disappear on their own via assimilation, and that they who remain safely within the Jewish cultural ghettoes will then inherit the only genuine Jewish future. Convinced that they are the true heirs of the ancients and that all other Jews who do not share their beliefs and practices are not, haredim therefore continue to embrace exclusivism, mistrust tolerance as a form of cultural suicide, and abhor pluralism. They believe that the survival of the Jewish people, of which they consider themselves to be the true representatives, depends on their own capacity to survive as haredim.

Nowhere are these feelings more intense than in Israel where the battle over the meaning and future of Judaism and Jewish life is contested continually, and where every non-haredi Jew represents an explicit and therefore dangerous alternative model of what Jews may be and how they may live their lives and still be called Jews. Here the dividing lines among the various contenders who seek to define what is genuinely Jewish are therefore most sharply drawn. Here the culture war over what is genuinely Jewish, over who most properly defends the faith, is more vivid than anywhere else. That is why I have chosen to draw my portrait of these Jews as they appear in Israel.

Indeed, the decision made at the dawn of Israeli statehood by the then new government to allow those who claim Orthodox commitments to avoid the universal army draft—for years the great melting pot of Israeli culture—has paradoxically helped make these lines even clearer. In order to stay out of the army and avoid its tacit socialization of adolescents into contemporary secular Israeli society, haredi men have chosen to remain longer than usual in the circumscribed world of Jewish religious study—the yeshiva—and the women have rushed to marry and have children. The consequence of this arrangement (unintended by the secular Zionist leaders who helped create this system now ruled illegal by the Israel's Supreme Court) has been ironically to help consolidate a haredi culture that continues to beget new generations that stand apart and outside the rest of the Israeli Jewish experience and society. It has reinforced the "us-versus-them" character of haredim in Israel.

America, like so much of the rest of the world, however, is different. It is the domain of strangers, of other nations—the "goyim," as haredim call them.[1] However much its new and open world beckons those who live within its surroundings, to the haredim its inhabitants—the goyim—do not represent conceivable or legitimate alternatives of what a Jew should be. On the contrary, they remain so far across the cultural divide from haredi life that it is paradoxically easier to live near them than to live in proximity to the non-Orthodox Jews who inhabit Israel. That a young haredi might see himself becoming an American non-Jew seems to the ultra-Orthodox community far less likely than that he might choose to become a secular Israeli. Thus, the American haredi can paradoxically allow himself to be in greater contact with America, go out to work in its domains, participate fully in its political life, and even brush close to its society because he remains convinced that the likelihood of his assimilation is small indeed. While he is culturally naive in this assumption—as some of his Israeli counterparts realize (the comments of Yisrael Eichler who in chapter seven acknowledges the differences between American and Israeli Belzer hasidim demonstrates this)—it nevertheless makes adult American haredim far less militant and scrupulous in their struggle to remain apart from the surrounding American culture. In a way, it is easier for American haredim to be both institutionally set apart from and instrumentally engaged by American life. (Of course, in the anonymity of a big America, it is also easier for haredim to stray temporarily with no one noticing.)

Israeli haredim, however, are far more active and engaged in their *kulturkampf* against the life outside their enclaves, going so far as to re-define Jewish Israelis as goyim. In a joke that captures this attitude, some Israeli haredim have taken a line from the liturgy that theologically explains the diaspora fate of the Jews—"*mipnay chato'enu galinu me'artzenu*," "because of our sins we have been exiled *from* our land," —and rephrased it as follows: "*mipnay chato'enu galinu be'artzenu*," "because of our sins we have been exiled *in* our land." To the haredim, this joke asserts, the modern state of Israel is not the end of the God-ordained diaspora; it is just a more pernicious form of it.

If the willingness and ability to engage in the culture war remains far more muted in Jewish diasporas like America, it does not, however, altogether disappear. While haredim here fall into the old pattern of dependent minorities, wary of their host society and seeking simply to live an unimpeded Jewish life, they remain careful about the temptations surrounding them. What efforts they do make to remain insular are most pronounced in the case of protecting their women and children—those they consider most vulnerable culturally—and in their relations with other Jews. American adult haredi males are thus commonly the ones most likely to sally into the outside. The young stay within the schools, the women within the community. While the young do not stay in the ivory tower of the yeshiva as long as their Israeli counterparts, thereby consolidating their attachment to haredi culture, they have borrowed from their Israeli counterparts by trying to extend the time they remain in this ultimate ghetto, taking a year or two after marriage before they go out to work. However, as they step at last into those work domains in even a limited fashion, they cannot help but adapt to the cultural and social demands of those environments.

Thus, haredim in Israel can and do demand that outsiders not violate their local Jewish codes of conduct when entering their shops or neighborhood, but those in America would, for example, not dream of making such demands in New York. In this new world they are not ready to fight the authorities, to stone cars that drive through their neighborhoods on the Sabbath, or to demand particular kinds of dress of those outsiders who visit the same; nor do they expect to demand government funding of their institutions—all in sharp contrast to their Israeli counterparts.

If either challenge the powers that be in America or conversely seek

their support, they must do so in subtle and sometimes even a subter-
ranean fashion. And when they fall afoul of the law—as some recently
have in their efforts to get federal funds for their schools and communities—they cannot expect to find an easy exit from their troubles, as
often becomes the case in Israel. The fight in America must be carried
on cautiously. Indeed, in the free and open political and social environment of America, the us-versus-them insular attitude of the haredim
gingerly tests the limits American tolerance and multi-culturalism.
And here sometimes the bounds of the permissible are crossed—most
visibly when haredim ignore or break what they believe are norms but
what government authorities say are laws. Missing is the willingness to
openly challenge those limits and the legitimacy of the laws that exist
among the more politically and socially powerful haredim of Israel (although America has surely given these Jews more latitude in disputing
the law and challenging its legitimacy than any other diaspora society
in history—which may be why they have flourished here almost as
much as in Israel).

There is a sense, particularly among Israeli haredim, that America's
permissive society has undermined their counterparts' cultural and social integrity. That is why the misfits and troublemakers of Israeli
haredi society, those whose behavior and beliefs seem beyond repair,
are often sent off to America—as if they could disappear here, find a
niche in which to locate themselves. But that is another story and far
too complex for review here.

All this being said, those who want to learn about haredim in general will find much in these pages that will provide the necessary background. They will also find much that is particular to the Israeli case.
And while there is undoubtedly much that could be added were the focus to be widened to include other haredim, I have avoided this temptation because of my belief that it is better to provide one clear albeit
limited picture than a kaleidoscope that, while colorful, loses the speci-
ficity that makes ethnography vital and illuminating. Let the reader
then know that my aim here is not to offer the last word on haredim;
rather, this is but a first word. For those who want to know more, there
is much still to be explored.

Notes

Prologue

1. See Moshe Samet, "The Beginnings of Orthodoxy," *Modern Judaism*, October 1988, pp. 249–267.
2. Clifford Geertz, *Works and Lives* (Stanford, Calif.: Stanford University Press, 1988), p. 16.
3. See James Clifford, "On Ethnographic Authority," in *The Predicament of Culture* (Cambridge: Harvard University Press, 1988), especially pp. 29–30, for why this sort of introduction does not work any longer.
4. James Clifford, "Introduction," in James Clifford and Géorge Marcus, eds., *Writing Culture* (Berkeley: University of California Press, 1986), p. 13.
5. Stanley Diamond in his introduction to Paul Radin, *The World of Primitive Man* (New York: Dutton, 1971), p. xxx.
6. Leo Jung, "What is Orthodox Judaism?" in Leo Jung, ed., *The Jewish Library*, 2nd series (New York: Bloch, 1930), p. 115.
7. Mary Pratt, "Fieldwork in Common Places," in Clifford and Marcus, eds., *Writing Culture*, p. 27.
8. Clifford, "Introduction," in Clifford and Marcus, eds., *Writing Culture*, p. 13.
9. Clifford Geertz, *The Interpretation of Cultures* (New York: Basic Books, 1973), p. 346.

10. Stanley Diamond, *In Search of the Primitive: A Critique of Civilization* (New Brunswick, N.J.: Transaction Publishers, 1975), p. 208.

11. Claude Lévi-Strauss, *Tristes Tropiques*, trans. John and Doreen Weightman (New York: Washington Square Press, 1973 [1955]), p. 19.

12. Geertz, *The Interpretation of Cultures*, p. 348. This is Clifford Geertz's characterization of the discovery.

13. Clifford Geertz, *Local Knowledge* (New York: Basic Books, 1983), p. 70.

14. Claude Lévi-Strauss, *The Savage Mind* (Chicago: University of Chicago Press, 1966), p. 17.

15. Emile Durkheim, *The Elementary Forms of the Religious Life*, trans. J.W. Swain (New York: Free Press, 1965 [1915]), p. 483.

16. William F. Whyte, *Street Corner Society* (Chicago: University of Chicago Press, 1955), p. 304.

17. Marvin Harris, *Cows, Pigs, Wars, and Witches: The Riddles of Culture* (New York: Vintage, 1989 [1974]), p. 5.

18. Clifford, "Introduction," in *Writing Culture*, p. 8.

Chapter 2. Who Are the Haredim?

1. I am indebted for many of the ideas here to Menachem Friedman. Our many conversations and my close reading of his work has been critical to my understanding. For a discussion of the character of contemporary American Orthodoxy, see Samuel Heilman and Steven M. Cohen, *Cosmopolitans and Parochials: Modern Orthodox Jews in America* (Chicago: University of Chicago Press, 1989).

2. Shimon Schwab, *Selected Writings* (Lakewood, N.J.: CIS Publications, 1988), p. 282.

3. The term originates in the Talmud but, toward the end of the nineteenth century in eastern Europe, became more widely used to refer to the way that traditional Jews would live their lives. (Menachem Friedman, personal communication.)

4. Margaret Mead, *Culture and Commitment* (Garden City, N.Y.: Doubleday, 1970), p. 1.

5. Ruth Benedict, *Patterns of Culture* (New York: Houghton Mifflin, 1934 [Mentor, 1946]), p. 49.

6. Walter Benjamin, *Illuminations*, ed. Hannah Arendt (New York: Schocken, 1969), p. 84.

7. Henry Sumner Maine, *Ancient Law* (New York: Henry Holt, 1885 [5th London ed.]), pp. 164–165.

8. See Jacob Katz, ed., *Toward Modernity: The European Jewish Model* (New Brunswick, N.J.: Transaction Publishers, 1987).

9. See Jacob Katz, *Out of the Ghetto: The Social Background of Jewish Emancipation 1770–1870* (New York: Schocken, 1973).

10. Katz, ed., *Toward Modernity*, p. 1.

11. Ibid., p. 2.

12. Cited in Horace Kallen, "The Bearing of Emancipation on Jewish Survival," YIVO Annual vol. 12 (1958), p. 9.

13. On assimilation, see Leonard W. Doob, *Becoming More Civilized* (New Haven: Yale University Press, 1960), p. 265.

14. Melville Herskovits, *Man and His Works* (New York: Knopf, 1949), p. ix.

15. J. L. Blau, *Modern Varieties of Judaism* (New York: Columbia University Press, 1966), p. 27

16. The phrase owes its origins to the late-eighteenth-century thinker Naftali Herz Wessely, but was later quoted and made well known again by the Hebrew essayist and poet Yehuda L. Gordon.

17. Abraham J. Karp, "Ideology and Identity in Jewish Group Survival in America," *American Jewish Historical Quarterly*, vol. 65 (June 1976), p. 312.

18. *Encyclopaedia Judaica* (Jerusalem: Keter Publishing House, 1972), vol. 6, p. 80; vol. 5, p. 901.

19. Herskovits, *Man and His Works*, p. 531.

20. Stephen Spender, *Eliot* (Glasgow: Collins, 1975), p. 9. Although Spender uses these words to describe the "ritualist sensibility" in T. S. Eliot's poetry, the phrase seems to capture an essential feature of the Jews in question.

21. While the use of the term "Orthodox" in connection with Jews has been traced back to 1795, perhaps the first major reference was in 1807 by Abraham Furtado, president of the Paris Sanhedrin called to endow certain basic laws of the state with the authority of Jewish law. The so-called Orthodox Jews resisted the effort because it seemed to them to subordinate Jewish law, or halacha, to state law.

22. Babylonian Talmud (hereafter BT), Sanhedrin 74b. In the words of the Lithuanian rabbinic leader, Chaim Ozer Grodzenski, "We must not yield one iota" (Leo Jung, *Jewish Leaders* [Jerusalem: Boys Town, 1953], p. 453).

23. Maimonides, *Mishneh Torah*, Hilchot Daot 6:1.

24. S. R. Hirsch, *Collected Writings*, vol. 1 (New York: Feldheim Publishers, 1990), trans. O. Furchheimer, "Religion Allied with Progress," p. 123.

25. "Why Do We Oppose," in *Ha-Chomah*, vol. 1 (June 1944), p. 2. See also Jeffrey Gurock, "Resisters and Accommodators: Varieties of Orthodox Rabbis in America, 1886–1983," *American Jewish Archives*, November 1983.

26. This prohibition has its sources in the rabbinic interpretation of Leviticus 18:3: "After the doings of the land of Egypt wherein you dwell, shall you not do; and after the doings of the land of Canaan, whither I bring you, shall you not do; neither shall you walk in their ordinances." Note that even the laws of the others are not to be obeyed.

27. The Will of Rabbi Naftali Yehuda Zvi Berlin, quoted in *Marbitzey Torah u Mussar* (Monsey, N.Y.: Sentry Press, 1977), p. 46.

28. Quoted in Mendel Piekarz, *Ideological Trends of Hasidism in Poland During the Interwar Period and the Holocaust* (Jerusalem: Bialik Institute, 1990), p. 99.

29. Ibid., p. 98.

30. Quoting Abraham Karelitz, the Hazon Ish (1878–1953), who became the voice of haredi Judaism in the post–World War II years, *Mussar Ha Torah*, vol. 2, no. 17 (22 Shevat, 5750 [February 1990]).

For a discussion of how the study of texts and code books served as a vehicle for conservatism, see Mendel Piekarz, *Ideological Trends*, pp. 50–51.

31. Menachem Friedman, "Life Tradition and Book Tradition in Ultra-orthodox Judaism," in H. Goldberg, ed., *Judaism Viewed from Within and from Without* (Albany, N.Y.: S.U.N.Y. Press, 1987), p. 247.

32. Wolf Zeev Rabinowitsch, *Lithuanian Hasidism*, trans. M. B. Dagut (New York: Schocken, 1971), p. 3.

33. Gershom Scholem, "The Neutralization of the Messianic Element in Early Hasidism," in *The Messianic Idea in Judaism and Other Essays on Jewish Spirituality* (New York: Schocken, 1971), p. 181. On the radicalism of early Hasidism, see Piekarz, *Ideological Trends*, pp. 37–50.

34. Quoted in Martin Buber's preface to *Tales of the Hasidim: The Early Masters* (New York: Schocken, 1947), p. v.

"It appears that the Hasidim, at the beginning, were not altogether sure whether to apply the doctrine [of tikkun] in all its implications to everyone or to limit it to the special category of the elect," Gershom Scholem notes, but concludes, "the original impulse tended toward the widest possible application of Hasidic principles and rules of behavior, but . . . in practice the leaders were quickly forced to restrict them to a narrower circle" (p. 192). Yet the notion that "every individual is the Redeemer, the Messiah of his own little world . . . is the essence of early Hasidism" (p. 202).

35. Piekarz, *Ideological Trends*, p. 45, quoting Isaiah Horowitz (d. 1630), one of the earliest voices of then radical hasidic ideas; and Rabinowitsch, *Lithuanian Hasidism*, p. 154.

36. Scholem, *The Messianic Idea*, p. 200.

37. Quoted in Piekarz, *Ideological Trends*, p. 48.

38. Rabinowitsch, *Lithuanian Hasidism*, p. 191.

39. Ibid, p. 16.

40. Ibid., pp. 9, 10.

41. Ibid., p. 85.

42. Quoted ibid., p. 148, n. 46.

43. Elya Svei, "Torah: A Source for Guidance in Every Phase of Jewish Activity," *Jewish Observer*, February 1982, p. 7.

44. The Maharal of Prague, quoted in Piekarz, *Ideological Trends*, p. 84.

45. *Collected Letters*, pp. 51–52, cited in Piekarz, *Ideological Trends*, p. 109.

46. Svei, "Torah: A Source," p. 9.

47. Rabinowitsch, *Lithuanian Hasidism*, p. 181.

48. Ibid., p. 218.

49. Quoted ibid., p. 142.

50. David Zvi of Neustadt, in Piekarz, *Ideological Trends*, pp. 56–57.

51. Schwab, *Selected Writings*, p. 313, remarks offered at the 63rd National Convention of Agudat Israel.

52. Menachem Friedman, "Agudat Israel," in *Encyclopaedia Judaica*, vol. 2, p. 422.

53. Schwab, *Selected Writings*, p. 273.

Ironically, Kagan's ability to settle local halachic disputes in his home community of Radun was limited. "When someone refused to accept his decision in a case of religious law, he resigned his position [as community rabbi]," ultimately dedicating himself purely to writing and heading his own yeshiva. (See Moses Yoshor in Jung, *Jewish Leaders*, p. 462.)

54. Playing on the Hebrew word for rabbis, *rabonim*, Chaim Ozer Grodzenski referred to the rabbis among the Reform as *ra bonim* literally "evil sons" (letter sent to Abraham Isaac Kook, cited in Daniel Schwartz and Christhard Hoffmann, "Early but Opposed, Supported but Late: Two Berlin Seminaries that Attempted to Move" [unpublished, n.p.]).

55. Cited in Jung, *Jewish Leaders*, p. 467.

56. See Irving Howe, *World of Our Fathers* (New York: Harcourt Brace Jovanovich, 1976) and Gershon Shaffir, *Land, Labor, and the Origins of the Israeli-Palestinian Conflict 1882–1914* (New York: Cambridge University Press, 1989).

57. Phillip Rieff, *The Triumph of the Therapeutic* (New York: Harper & Row, 1966), p. 41; cf. p. 27.

58. For a full discussion of these issues, see Menachem Friedman, *Hevra ve Dat* [Society and Religion: The Non-Zionist Orthodox in Eretz-Israel 1918–1936] (Jerusalem: Yad Ben Zvi Publications, 1977).

59. BT, Ketubot 111a, and also Shir ha Shirim Rabbah 2:7.

60. See the argument in BT, Sanhedrin 63b, which provides one of countless examples of how Jews are to be distinguished from all other nations.

61. Jung, *Jewish Leaders*, p. 468.

62. In time, the religious Zionists, drawing on the authority of Rabbi Abraham I. Kook, first chief rabbi of Palestine, evolved a theology that allowed for redemption brought about by such unbelievers. But the arguments on which this theology was based were never accepted by all Orthodox Jews.

63. Isaiah Margolis, *Kumi Ori* (Hebrew) (Jerusalem, 1925) cited in Friedman, *Hevra ve Dat*, p. 134.

64. Pierre Nora, "Between Memory and History," cited in Robert Paine, "The Law and the Land: Tensions of Time in Israel," in Henry Rutz, ed., *The Politics of Time*, vol. 4 (American Ethnological Society, forthcoming).

65. See Menachem Friedman, "The Haredim and the Holocaust," *Jerusalem Quarterly*, vol. 53 (Winter 1990); and "Les Haredim et la Shoa," *Penser Auschwitz*, pardes 9-10 (numéro special), pp. 148–177.

66. Friedman, "Life Tradition and Book Tradition," p. 244.

67. There are haredim in other places—western Europe, Australia, South Africa, and even South America and the Soviet Union—but these represent a very small proportion of the total.

68. Svei, "Torah: A Source," p. 8.

The notion of survivor guilt and of resurrecting the dead to greater power than they ever had in life is of course an old one, most dramatically elaborated in Freud's famous essay *Totem and Taboo* (London: Routledge & Kegan Paul, 1950).

69. Eliezer Schach, "On Jewish Survival," *Jewish Observer*, February 1982, p. 5.

70. Quoted in Rivka Shatz-Uffenheimer, "Confession on the Brink of the Crematoria," *Jerusalem Quarterly*, vol. 24 (Winter 1985).

71. Moshe Scheinfeld, "A Time of Assembly" (*Diglenu*, 1945), quoted in Friedman, "The Haredim and the Holocaust," pp. 95–96.

72. Rieff, *The Triumph of the Therapeutic*, p. 11.

73. Leon Festinger, Henry Riecken, and Stanley Schacter, *When Prophecy Fails* (New York: Harper & Row, 1956), p. 3.

74. The formation of the Bais Ya'akov schools for girls in Poland in 1923 by Sara Schenierer, a movement soon supported by Agudat Israel, marked the acceptance of the idea of the need to stimulate a self-conscious Jewishness in women via education. For more on the subject, see Deborah R. Weissman, *Bais Ya'akov, a Women's Educational Movement in the Polish Jewish Community: A Case Study in Tradition and Modernity* (M.A. thesis, New York University, 1977), and Judith Grunfeld-Rosenbaum, "Sara Schenierer," in Jung, *Jewish Leaders*.

75. Avraham Karelitz (Hazon Ish), letter to Y. Schnaidman in *Pe'er HaDor*, vol. 1 (B'nai B'rak: Netzach Publishers, 1966), p. 292.

Chapter 3. Community

1. Yosef Shilhav and Menachem Friedman, *Growth and Segregation: The Ultra-Orthodox Community of Jerusalem* (Jerusalem: Jerusalem Institute for Israeli Studies, 1986).

2. See Samuel C. Heilman and Menachem Friedman, "Religious Fundamentalism and Religious Jews: The Case of the Haredim," in Martin Marty and R. Scott Appleby, eds., *Fundamentalisms Observed* (Chicago: University of Chicago Press, 1991), pp. 197–264.

3. Haredim in B'nai B'rak quoted in *Ma'ariv*, November 3, 1988. See also Samuel C. Heilman, "Religious Jewry in the Secular Press," in Charles Liebman, ed., *Conflict and Accommodation Between Jews in Israel* (Jerusalem: Keter Publishing House, 1990), pp. 45–65.

4. See Samuel C. Heilman, "The Orthodox, the Ultra-Orthodox, and the Elections for the Twelfth Knesset," in Asher Arian and Michal Shamir, eds., *The Elections in Israel—1988* (Boulder, Colo.: Westview Press, 1990), pp. 135–153.

5. On the matter of cultural performance, see M. Singer, "The Cultural Pattern of Indian Civilization," *Far Eastern Quarterly*, vol. 15 (1955), pp.

23–26; Clifford Geertz, *The Interpretation of Cultures* (New York: Basic Books, 1973); and Samuel C. Heilman, *The People of the Book* (Chicago: University of Chicago Press, 1983), pp. 61–110.

Chapter 4. A Bar Mitzvah in Belz

1. The name is also sometimes spelled *Rokeach*, a name drawn from the famous commentary *Sefer Maaseh Rokeach*, written by one of the Belzer rebbe's ancestors, Rabbi Eleazar ben Samuel (1665–1742) of Amsterdam.
2. *Encyclopaedia Judaica*, vol. 4, p. 452. See also Yitzhak Alfassi, *Ha Chasidut*, 2nd ed. (Tel Aviv: Ma'ariv, 1977), p. 156.
3. Henry M. Rabinowicz, *Hasidism: The Movement and Its Masters* (Northvale, N.J.: Jason Aronson, 1988 [rev. ed.]), p. 161.
4. Israel Klapholtz, *Admorey Belz*, vol. 4, p. 167, cited in Mendel Piekarz, *Ideological Trends of Hasidism in Poland During the Interwar Period and the Holocaust* (Jerusalem: Bialik Institute, 1990), p. 111.
5. Rabinowicz, *Hasidism*, p. 164.
6. Issachar Dov Rokach, quoted in Piekarz, *Ideological Trends*, p. 111.
7. The term is Aramaic for "a young child." However, a talmudic reference (BT, Kiddushin 32b) associates this youth with wisdom (*yanik v'chakim*).
8. *Ha-Machaneh Ha-Haredi*, October 27, 1988, p. 13.
9. Pinchas Friedman in *Ha-Machaneh Ha-Haredi*, October 27, 1988, p. 14.
10. *Ha-Machaneh Ha-Haredi*, October 27, 1988, p. 9.
11. Ibid.
12. See Zechariah 3:2.
13. A. Y. Yabrov, "I Was Privileged," in *Ha-Machaneh Ha-Haredi*, October 27, 1988, p. 9.
14. *Ha-Machaneh Ha-Haredi*, October 27, 1988, p. 14.
15. Ibid.
16. BT, Sanhedrin 82b.
17. *Ha-Machaneh Ha-Haredi*, October 27, 1988, p. 14.
18. Friedman in *Ha-Machaneh Ha-Haredi*, October 27, 1988, p. 12.
19. Ibid.
20. Psalms 2:11.
21. Shalom Hayim Porush in *Ha-Machaneh Ha Haredi*, October 27, 1988, p. 15.
22. Y. Halberstam in *Ha-Machaneh Ha-Haredi*, October 27, 1988, p. 21.
23. L. A. Sussman in *Ha-Machaneh Ha-Haredi*, October 27, 1988, p. 22.
24. A reference to the stone in the *urim v'tumim*, the priestly breastplate, with which the High Priest looked into the future.

Chapter 5. Binding Ties

1. There is a remarkable parallel here to what Freud summarizes as the essence of the identification process: "First, identification is the original

form of emotional tie with an object; secondly, in a regressive way it becomes a substitute for a libidinal object-tie, as it were by means of introjection of the object into the ego; and thirdly, it may arise with any new perception of a common quality shared with some other person who is not an object of the sexual instinct" (Sigmund Freud, *Group Psychology and the Analysis of the Ego*, trans. James Strachey [New York: Bantam, 1960], pp. 49–50).

Chapter 6. At the Rebbe's Table

1. Leonard Meyer, *Emotion and Meaning in Music* (Chicago: University of Chicago Press, 1956), pp. 31–32.
2. "Meanings become objectified only under conditions of self-consciousness and when reflection takes place. . . . So long as behavior is automatic and habitual there is no urge for it to become self-conscious, though it may become so" (Meyer, *Emotion and Meaning in Music*, p. 39).

Chapter 7. This Is Who We Are

1. Claude Lévi-Strauss, *Tristes Tropiques*, trans. John and Doreen Weightman (New York: Washington Square Press, 1973 [1955]), p. 30.
2. Paul Radin, *Primitive Man as Philosopher* (New York: Dover, 1957 [1927]), p. xxi.
3. Amnon Levy, "The *Haredi* Press and Secular Society," in Charles Liebman, ed., *Conflict and Accommodation Between Jews in Israel* (Jerusalem: Keter Publishing House, 1990), p. 23.
4. Haredim see the secular Israeli press as hostile to them. See Samuel Heilman, "Religious Jewry in the Secular Press," in Liebman, *Conflict and Accommodation*, pp. 45–65.
5. Clifford Geertz, *The Interpretation of Cultures* (New York: Basic Books, 1973), p. 219.
6. Amnon Dankner, "A Black Israeli Week," *Davar*, November 4, 1988.
7. Peter Berger, *The Heretical Imperative* (New York: Anchor/Doubleday, 1979), p. 15.
8. *Ha-Machaneh Ha-Haredi*, February 8, 1990, p. 19.
9. Oswald Spengler, *The Decline of the West* (New York: Knopf, 1932).
10. Ruth Benedict, *Patterns of Culture* (New York: Houghton Mifflin, 1934 [Mentor, 1946]), pp. 48–49.

Chapter 8. Purim: This Is Who We Are Not

1. Peter L. Berger and Thomas Luckmann, *The Social Construction of Reality* (New York: Doubleday, 1966), p. 15.
2. Emile Durkheim, *The Elementary Forms of Religious Life*, trans. J. W. Swain (New York: Free Press, 1965 [1915]), p. 242; p. 240.

3. Much of what follows is drawn from Z. Ariel, ed., *Sefer Ha-Chag Ve Ha-Moed* (Tel Aviv: Am Oved, 1978 [1962], pp. 187–226.

4. The *Encyclopaedia Judaica*, vol. 13, pp. 1395–1399, lists many of these.

5. BT, *Megillah* 7a.

6. Zvi Singer traces the origins of this custom to Ashkenazic Jewry of the late seventeenth or early eighteenth century. (See Ariel, *Sefer Ha-Chag*, pp. 222–225).

7. Simcha Assaf, *Minhagey Chag Ha Purim B'Dor Dor*, in Ariel, *Sefer Ha-Chag*, pp. 211–212.

8. See Shifra Epstein, "Drama on a Table: The Bobover Hasidim Piremshpiyl," in Harvey Goldberg, *Judaism Viewed from Within and Without* (Albany, N.Y.: S.U.N.Y. Press, 1987), pp. 195–219.

9. See Sigmund Freud, *Jokes and Their Relation to the Unconscious* (London: Hogarth Press, 1953).

10. A copy of this poster is from the Menachem Friedman Collection.

11. On this subject, see Erik Erikson, *Childhood and Society*, 2nd ed. (New York: Norton, 1963), pp. 209–246.

12. Ibid., p. 212.

Chapter 9. Mass Pilgrimage

1. For a full discussion, see Z. Ariel, ed., *Sefer Ha-Chag Ve Ha-Moed* (Tel Aviv: Am Oved, 1978), pp. 284–302.

2. This essential text of Jewish mysticism is considered by most academic scholars to have been written in Spain during the years after 1275 by Moses de Leon (see Gershom Scholem, *Major Trends in Jewish Mysticism* [New York: Schocken, 1961], pp. 156–243), but in keeping with popular custom, the attribution of its authorship to a holy sage of an earlier period was what enshrined it in the sacred canon.

3. Ariel, *Sefer Ha-Chag*, p. 301.

4. Shifra Epstein, "Torah Mi Sinai and Reichberg Travel: Towards Understanding Pilgrimages to Saints Among Middle Eastern and Hasidic Jews" (unpublished paper), p. 2. See also *Toldot Ha-Nifla'ot* (1899:5) for a story about the hasidic Rabbi Elimelech of Lyzansk who appeared in a dream before Rabbi Kalonymus Epstein scolding him for telling a woman not to travel to his grave to pray (cited in Epstein, p. 11). See also Alex Weingrod, *The Saint of Beersheva* (Albany, N.Y.: S.U.N.Y. Press, 1990).

5. *Sefer Kavod Ha-M'lochim*, quoted in Ariel, *Sefer Ha-Chag*, p. 284.

6. *Shulhan Arukh*, Hilchot Kriyat Shema 75:2.

7. Claude Lévi-Strauss, *Tristes Tropiques*, trans. John and Doreen Weightman (New York: Washington Square, 1973), p. 186.

8. See Samuel Heilman, "Tzedakah: Orthodox Jews and Charitable Giving," in Barry A. Kosmin and Paul Ritterband, eds., *Contemporary Jewish Philanthropy in America* (Lanham, Md.: Rowman & Littlefield, 1991), pp. 133–144.

9. Peter Berger, *The Heretical Imperative* (New York: Anchor/Double-day, 1979), p. 17.

10. See Heilman, "The Gift of Alms: Face-to-Face Almsgiving Among Orthodox Jews," *Urban Life and Culture*, vol. 3, no. 4 (January 1975), pp. 371–395.

11. James Clifford, "Introduction," J. Clifford and G. E. Marcus, eds., in *Writing Culture* (Berkeley: University of California Press, 1986), p. 13.

Chapter 10. Third Meal

1. M. Singer, "The Cultural Pattern of Indian Civilization," in *Far Eastern Quarterly*, vol. 15 (1955), pp. 23–26.

2. Emile Durkheim, *The Elementary Forms of Religious Life*, trans. J. W. Swain (New York: Free Press, 1965 [1915]), p. 466.

3. Claude Lévi-Strauss, *Tristes Tropiques*, trans. John and Doreen Weightman (New York: Washington Square Press, 1973 [1955]), p. 38.

4. For a discussion of Jewish learning as worship, see Samuel Heilman, *The People of the Book* (Chicago: University of Chicago Press, 1987), pp. 239–260.

5. For a similar process of prayer and a more extended analysis, see Samuel C. Heilman, *Synagogue Life: A Study in Symbolic Interaction* (Chicago: University of Chicago Press, 1976), pp. 129–150. On the matter of varying approaches to time that organize activity differently, see Edward T. Hall, *The Dance of Life* (Garden City, N.Y.: Anchor/Doubleday, 1984), especially "Monochronic and Polychronic Time," pp. 44–58. Reb Arelach are polychronic, as evidenced in this example.

6. For the differences between *davenen*, a ritualized display of prayer, and *tefillah*, worshipful prayer, see Samuel Heilman, "Prayer and the Orthodox Synagogue: An Analysis of Ritual Display," *Contemporary Jewry*, vol. 6, no. 1 (1982), pp. 1–17.

7. On "tightness" and "looseness" in social situations, see Erving Goffman, *Encounters* (Indianapolis: Bobbs-Merrill, 1961), pp. 1–26.

8. Victor Turner, *Dramas, Fields, and Metaphors: Symbolic Action in Human Society* (Ithaca, N.Y.: Cornell University Press, 1974), p. 273.

9. On personal space, see Edward T. Hall, *The Hidden Dimension* (Garden City, N.Y.: Anchor/Doubleday, 1966), and Erving Goffman, *Behavior in Public Places* (New York: Free Press, 1963).

10. *Tanah D'Rabbi Eliahu Zuta* 12. The Will of the Great Rabbi Eliezer (Warsaw, 1912), p. 19.

11. Bronislaw Malinowski, "The Problem of Meaning in Primitive Languages," in C. K. Ogden and I. A. Richards, *The Meaning of Meaning* (New York: Harcourt, Brace & Co., 1952 [1923]), p. 315; p. 313.

12. Clifford Geertz, *The Interpretation of Cultures* (New York: Basic Books, 1973), pp. 216–219.

13. Herman Schmalenbach, "The Sociological Category of Commu-

nion," in T. Parsons et al., eds., *Theories of Society* (New York: Free Press, 1961), p. 337.

14. For a discussion of the implications of this sort of language shifting and maintenance, see Joshua Fishman, "Who Speaks What Language to Whom and When?" *La Linguistique*, vol. 2 (1965), pp. 67–88; Samuel C. Heilman, "Word Play and the Language of Lernen," in *The People of the Book* (Chicago: University of Chicago Press, 1983 (paperback 1987), pp. 161–202; and J. R. Rayfield, *The Languages of a Bilingual Community* (The Hague: Mouton, 1970).

Chapter 11. Education

1. Mendel Piekarz, *Ideological Trends of Hasidism in Poland During the Interwar Period and the Holocaust* (Jerusalem: Bialik Institute, 1990), p. 108.

2. Israel Meir Ha-Cohen [Kagan] (Hafetz Hayim), *Toras Ha-Bayis* (New York: Friedman Publishers, 1960), ch. 14, p. 27.

3. Speech at Yad Eliahu, March 27, 1990, published in *Ha'aretz*, March 28, 1990.

4. *Kitzur Shulhan Arukh* 165:1.

5. Israel Meir Ha-Cohen [Kagan] (Hafetz Hayim), *Davar B'It* (Warsaw: Baumriter Publishers, 1895), ch. 14, p. 32.

6. Rabbi Shmuel of Sochatchev, quoted in Piekarz, *Ideological Trends*, p. 58. Cf. the similar sentiments of Rabbi Menachem Mendel of Kotzk: "There are many ways to bring oneself closer to the blessed God, but excepting the Torah which is the certain way, all other ways are fraught with danger" (ibid.).

7. Speech, March 27, 1990.

8. Zvi Elimelech Blum, *Sefer Hanhagot Ha-Chinuch* (Jerusalem, 1981), p. 12.

9. Ibid., introduction.

10. "At five years the age is reached for the study of Scripture, at ten the study of Mishnah, at thirteen for the fulfillment of the commandments, at fifteen for the study of the Talmud" (Avot 5:23). Eliezer Papo in his *Pele Yo'etz*, a venerated moral guidebook, adds, "From the time a child is nursing, his father and mother must have in mind to raise him in the study of Torah" ([Jerusalem: Tushia, 1987], p. 284).

11. For a discussion of the growth of women's education among the Orthodox, see Deborah R. Weissman, "Bais Ya'akov, a Women's Educational Movement in the Polish Jewish Community: A Case Study in Tradition and Modernity" (M.A. thesis, New York University, 1977).

12. Speech, March 27, 1990.

13. Ibid.

14. Eliahu de Vidas, *Rashit Chochma* [The Beginning of Wisdom] (Jerusalem, 1972 [1580]), p. 246.

15. Rabbi Moshe ben Shlomo Eliezer of Vilna, cited in Blum, p. 5.

16. Nachmanides on Genesis 12:6.

17. BT, Shabbat 119b, and Judah Loew, *Netivot Olam: Netiv Ha-Torah* (New York: Hebraica Press, 1969), ch. 10, p. 44.

18. BT, Shabbat 119b.

19. Rabbi Moses Sofer, *Drashot Hatam Sofer* (Klausenburg, 1929), p. 327, cited in Blum, p. 227.

20. Eliezer David Greenwald, quoted in Blum, p. 108.

21. *Chanoch L'Naar: The Testament of Shalom Dov Baer Schneerson* (Lubavitcher Rebbe) (Brooklyn, 1943).

22. Yaakov Dadavski, *Kiyum Ha-Torah* (Jerusalem, 1921).

23. Psalms 111:10.

24. Papo, *Pele Yo'etz*, p. 1.

25. Abraham Isaac Kahn, *Maamar Chinuch Ha-Banim* (Jerusalem, 1967), p. 5.

26. *The Testament of Abraham Baruch Rosenberg, the Rebbe of Sziget*, part 4, p. 28, cited in Blum, p. 243.

27. Kahn, *Maamar Chinuch Ha-Banim*, p. 2.

28. BT, Sanhedrin 19b.

29. Avot 4:15, and BT, Baba Metzia 85a.

30. Cited in Aaron Roth, *Iggrot Shomrei Emunim* (Jerusalem, 1942).

31. See Erik Erikson, *Childhood and Society*, 2nd ed. (New York: Norton, 1963), pp. 255–58, in his description of children in toilet training.

32. Quoting from ads like these, Amnon Levy (*The Haredim* [Jerusalem: Keter Publishing House, 1989], p. 12) calls the language in them an example of haredi "exaggeration." Yet a close reading of haredi life will, I believe, reveal that from their point of view the need for teachers and other school support staff is in fact a matter of cultural life and death.

33. Clifford Geertz, *The Interpretation of Cultures* (New York: Basic Books, 1973), p. 367.

Chapter 12. A School for Little Haredim

1. One of the stipulations of my access to certain institutions and places was that they remain anonymous in my written account. Others did not demand such anonymity. This place did.

2. Georg Simmel, "The Stranger," in *The Sociology of Georg Simmel*, trans. Kurt Wolff (New York: Free Press, 1950), p. 407; p. 402.

3. "Storytelling won an established place in the life of the earliest hasidim. . . . The Rebbes often wove their teachings into an extended metaphor or parable or told an illustrative tale. . . . To a great extent storytelling continues . . . because it has remained part of the integral structure of hasidic religious and social life. Tales are exchanged casually at the besmedresh or in any social situation" (Jerome Mintz, *Legends of the Hasidim* [Chicago: University of Chicago Press, 1968], p. 4).

4. Harry Stack Sullivan, *The Interpersonal Theory of Psychiatry* (New York: Norton, 1953), esp. pp. 28–29, 36, and 217–226.

5. Emile Durkheim, *Moral Education,* trans. Everett K. Wilson and Herman Schnurer (New York: Free Press, 1961), p. 18.

6. Sullivan, *The Interpersonal Theory,* pp. 119–120.

7. Ibid.

8. Selma H. Fraiberg, *The Magic Years: Understanding and Handling the Problems of Early Childhood* (New York: Scribner's, 1959), p. 270.

9. Sullivan, *The Interpersonal Theory,* p. 120.

10. James Clifford, "On Ethnographic Allegory," in James Clifford and George Marcus, *Writing Culture* (Berkeley: University of California Press, 1986), p. 100.

11. James W. Fowler, *Stages of Faith: The Psychology of Human Development and the Quest for Meaning* (San Francisco: Harper & Row, 1976), p. 277.

12. Michael Rosenak, *Commandments and Concerns: Jewish Religious Education in a Secular Society* (Philadelphia: Jewish Publication Society, 1987), p. 108.

13. Capturing this style, Shalom Aleichem would often have Tevye preface every one of his parables with "As the Holy Book tells us . . ." See, e.g., *Tevye's Daughters,* trans. F. Butwin (New York: Crown, 1949), p. 30.

14. Samuel Heilman and Menachem Friedman, "Religious Fundamentalism and Religious Jews," in Martin Marty and R. Scott Appleby, eds., *Fundamentalisms Observed* (Chicago: University of Chicago Press, 1991).

15. I say "myth" here not to judge the verity of this story but because it clearly belongs in the genre of stories that anthropologists call "founding myths," accounts groups use to explain to themselves how they came to be or how their fundamental character was shaped.

16. Samuel Heilman, *The People of the Book* (Chicago: University of Chicago Press, 1986), p. 61. The relationship between Jewish study and recitation (echoing and cuing) and the process of cultural performance is discussed and elaborated on pp. 61–112.

17. Ruth Benedict, *Patterns of Culture* (New York: Houghton Mifflin 1934 [Mentor, 1946]), p. 7.

18. *Yisrael V'Oraita Chad hu* (Zohar, Vayikara 73).

19. Clifford Geertz, *The Interpretation of Cultures* (New York: Basic Books, 1973), p. 220.

20. Benedict, *Patterns of Culture,* p. 7.

21. The Hebrew word for "tongue," *lashon,* and the word for "slander," *lashon hara,* are related. "Slander" is literally "an evil tongue." The spies' tongues went bad because they spoke slander.

22. Israel Meir Ha-Cohen Kagan, *Hilchot Lashon Hara* 68.

23. Heilman, *The People of the Book,* pp. 62–67.

24. Brian Bullivant, *The Way of Tradition: Life in an Orthodox Jewish School* (Melbourne: Australian Council for Educational Research, 1978), p. xvi.

25. Herman Melville, *Billy Budd* (New York: Washington Square Press, 1948), p. 39.

Chapter 13. Primary School

1. Margaret Mead, *Culture and Commitment* (Garden City, N.Y.: Doubleday, 1970), p. 1.
2. Yitzhak Yosef Schneerson, *Sefer Maamarim* (Brooklyn: Mercaz L'Inyani Chinuch, 1972), p. 66.
3. On "involvement shields," see Erving Goffman, *Behavior in Public Places* (New York: Free Press, 1963), pp. 38–42.
4. Maharsha on BT, Shabbat 104a.
5. BT, Ketubot 3a.
6. Midrash Rabbah Leviticus 7:4.
7. Claude Lévi-Strauss, *Tristes Tropiques*, trans. John and Doreen Weightman (New York: Washington Square Press, 1973 [1955]), p. 234.
8. BT, Chulin 133a.
9. Quoted in Hayim Shlomo Rotenberg, *Hanhagot Zaddikim* (Jerusalem, 1988), p. 742.
10. BT, Sanhedrin 110b, and *Shulhan Arukh Or Ha-Chaim* 106, for example.
11. Letters cited in Rotenberg, *Hanhagot Zaddikim*, pp. 742–750.
12. Avraham Yitzhak Kahan, *Divrei Emunah* (Jerusalem, 1967), p. 59, italics added.
13. Ibid.
14. For the term *imitatio fidei* I thank Moshe Idel.

Chapter 14. Where Are We?

1. See Samuel C. Heilman, *The People of the Book* (Chicago: University of Chicago Press, 1986); and William Helmreich, *The World of the Yeshiva* (New York: Free Press, 1982).

Chapter 15. The Yeshiva: Mussar Shmues

1. See Menachem Friedman, "Life Tradition and Book Tradition in the Development of Ultra-Orthodox Judaism," in H. E. Goldberg, ed., *Judaism Viewed from Within and from Without: Anthropological Studies* (Albany, N.Y.: S.U.N.Y. Press, 1986); and Friedman, "Haredim Confront the Modern City," in P. Medding, ed., *Studies in Contemporary Jewry*, *Vol. 2* (Bloomington: University of Indiana Press, 1986). On the yeshiva, see William Helmreich, *The World of the Yeshiva* (New York: Free Press, 1982).
2. See Menachem Friedman, "The Haredim and the Holocaust," *Jerusalem Quarterly*, vol. 53 (Winter 1990), pp. 36–114.
3. See Mendel Piekarz, *Ideological Trends of Hasidism in Poland During the Interwar Period and the Holocaust* (Jerusalem: Bialik Institute, 1990).
4. See Friedman, "Haredim Confront the Modern City," and "Yeshivot of the Old Yishuv at the Close of the Ottoman Period: 'Institutions' or

NOTES 385

Seminars?" in E. Etkes and Y. Salmon, eds., *Studies in the History of Jewish Society* (Hebrew) (Jerusalem: Magnes, 1980), pp. 369–379.

5. See, for example, Janet Aviad, *Return to Judaism* (Chicago: University of Chicago Press, 1983); and Herbert Danzger, *Returning to Tradition: A Study of the Contemporary Revival in Orthodox Judaism* (New Haven: Yale University Press, 1989).

6. Stanley Diamond in the introduction to Paul Radin, *The World of Primitive Man* (New York: Dutton, 1971), p. xv, calls learning "a moral enterprise."

7. Joseph Elias, "Israel Salanter," in Leo Jung, ed., *Jewish Leaders* (Jerusalem: Boys Town Press, 1953), pp. 199–200.

8. Ibid., p. 200.

9. See D. Katz, *Tenu'at ha-Musar*, 5 vol.; H. H. Ben-Sasson, "Musar Movement," in *Encyclopedia Judaica*, vol. 12, pp. 534–537; and Aharon Sursky, *Marbitsay Torah U'Mussar* (New York: Sentry Press), 1977.

10. Elias, "Israel Salanter," p. 201, and Piekarz, *Ideological Trends*, pp. 41–43.

11. Elias, "Israel Salanter," pp. 203, 208.

12. Ben-Sasson, "Musar Movement," p. 537.

13. Ibid.

14. See Chaim Shapiro, "The Kaminetzer Partnership," *Jewish Observer*, October 1980, pp. 15–24.

15. Yitzhak ben Eliakim, *Lev Tov* 9 (Prague, 1920).

16. Max Weber, *The Protestant Ethic and the Spirit of Capitalism* (New York: Scribner's, 1958).

17. Translation by Abraham Ben Isaiah and Benjamin Sharfman (New York: S.S. & R. Publishing, 1949).

18. Elaborating on Wilhelm Wundt, *Mythus und Religion*, Teil II *Völkerpsychologie*, Band II (Leipzig, 1906), p. 312, see Sigmund Freud, *Totem and Taboo*, trans. James Strachey (New York: Norton, 1960 [1950]), p. 225.

19. Freud, *Totem and Taboo*, p. 31.

20. Ibid., p. 31.

21. Ibid., pp. 34–35.

Chapter 16. The Yeshiva: Shiur and Chavruse

1. William Helmreich, *The World of the Yeshiva* (New York: Free Press, 1982), p. 65.

2. See ibid., p. 67.

3. Ibid., p. 69.

4. See, for example, Samuel C. Heilman, *The People of the Book* (Chicago: University of Chicago Press, 1986), pp. 29–60.

5. Adin Steinsaltz, *The Talmud: The Steinsaltz Edition Reference Guide*, ed. Israel Berman (New York: Random House, 1989), p. 4. The names in parentheses are the acronyms by which many of these exegetes have become known among students of Talmud.

6. Helmreich, *The World of the Yeshiva*, p. 110.
7. Ibid., p. 111.

Chapter 17. Rosh Yeshiva

1. Whenever I refer to this man, I shall call him the Rosh Yeshiva to protect his anonymity.
2. Numbers 16:39.
3. The great rabbi Shammai (d. ca. 20 C.E.) said, "Fix a period for your study" (Avot 1:15). By this, commentators for generations have understood that Jews are not to make their ritual study something casual or occasional. That is why, for example, in the yeshiva there is a seder, or fixed order and time, for all of the sacred study.
4. Chaim Shapiro, "The Kaminetzer Partnership," *Jewish Observer*, October 1980, p. 17.
5. See Jacob Katz, *The Shabbos Goy*, trans. Yoel Lerner (Philadelphia: Jewish Publication Society, 1989).
6. Rabbi Yerachmiel Yisrael Yitzhak Danziger of Alexander, *Yismach Yisrael* (Vienna, 1933), quoted in Mendel Piekarz, *Ideological Trends of Hasidism in Poland During the Interwar Period and the Holocaust* (Jerusalem: Bialik Institute, 1990), p. 66.
7. Piekarz, *Ideological Trends*, p. 90.
8. *Yishray Lev* (Lublin, 1906 [rev., B'nai B'rak, 1969]) 19b.
9. From the yeshiva perspective, the layman abandoned the rarefied and superior environs of the world of study. This naturally limited or perhaps reflected the limit of his intellectual accomplishments in Torah study.
10. These were all rabbis who served or serve today as leaders of the nonhasidic community of haredim.

Chapter 18. Passages: Matchmaking, Betrothal, and Wedding

1. Arnold van Gennep, *The Rites of Passage*, trans. M. K. Vizedom and G. L. Caffee (Chicago: University of Chicago Press, 1960 [1908]).
2. Ibid., pp. 116–165.
3. BT, *Yebamot* 63a.
4. Tosefta *Yebamot* 8.2.
5. BT, Kiddushin 29b.
6. Avot 5.
7. Vayikra Rabbah 21:8.
8. BT, *Yebamot* 65a; Tosefta *Yebamot* 8:3.
9. Amnon Levy, *The Haredim* (Jerusalem: Keter Publishing House, 1989), p. 104.
10. Ibid.

Chapter 19. Passages: Funeral

1. Elizabeth Kübler-Ross, *On Death and Dying* (New York: Macmillan, 1969), p. 13.

Chapter 20. Passing Signs: The Writing on the Wall

1. Menachem Friedman, whose collection of these posters is among the most comprehensive and from whom I have borrowed several of the posters in this chapter, is at present completing a manuscript in which he analyzes the full range of haredi life from these broadsides. The book, as yet unpublished, is to be called *The Poster People*.
2. Lewis Coser, *The Functions of Social Conflict* (New York: Free Press, 1956), p. 34.
3. March 1990, from the collection of Menachem Friedman.
4. Sigmund Freud, "The Resistances to Psychoanalysis," in *Collected Papers*, vol. 5, ed. and trans. James Strachey (New York: Basic Books, 1959), p. 170.

Chapter 21. The Triumph of Sex

1. Georg Simmel, "The Stranger," in Kurt Wolff, ed. and trans., *The Sociology of Georg Simmel* (New York: Free Press, 1950), p. 404.
2. William F. Whyte, *Street Corner Society* (Chicago: University of Chicago Press, 1955), p. 302.
3. Simmel, "The Stranger," pp. 333–334.
4. Ibid., p. 333.
5. Words of a meditation to be recited before retiring at night, from Chaim Vital, *Pri Etz Chaim Sha'ar Kriyat Shema She'al Ha Mita* (Jerusalem: Kol Jehuda Publishers, 1985), ch. 11, p. 343.
6. Code of Jewish Law, *Orach Hayim* 231.
7. *Or la-Shamayim*, 1850, *Parashat Va-Yishlach* 15a, quoted in *Encyclopedia Judaica*, vol. 9, p. 1228.
8. Eliezer Papo, "Eating and Drinking," in *Pele Yo'etz* (Jerusalem: Tushia, 1987], p. 27.
9. Ibid.
10. Ibid.
11. Midrash, *Genesis Rabbah* 17:5, and Papo, "Sleep," in *Pele Yo'etz*, p. 553.
12. Avot 3:10.
13. Papo, "Sleep," in Pele Yo'etz, p. 554, and Shulhan Arukh, *Orach Hayim* 231.
14. Amnon Levy, *The Haredim* (Jerusalem: Keter Publishing House, 1989), pp. 120–121.
15. BT, Yebamot 63b; Shulhan Arukh, *Even Ha Ezer* 1:1.
16. Maimonides, *Hilchot Ishut* 15:16.

17. Kalonymus Kalman Epstein, *Maor Ve'Shemesh* (Jerusalem, 1986), on Exodus 21–22, p. 210.

18. Howard S. Becker, *"Art Worlds* Revisited," in *Sociological Forum,* vol. 5, no. 3 (September 1990), p. 500.

19. Cf. Rhonda Berger-Sofer, *Pious Women, A Study of Women's Roles in a Hasidic and Pious Community: Me'ah She'arim* (unpublished Ph.D. thesis, Rutgers University, 1979), who argues that the common haredi assumption is that while men think forbidden thoughts more easily than women, women are the stimuli that can cause the men to think those thoughts and lose control over their animal instincts.

See also Susan Starr Sered, "Halakha, Modesty, and Women: From a Female Perspective," in *Jewish Folklore and Ethnology Review,* vol. 12, nos. 1 and 2 (1990), pp. 14–16.

20. Levy, *The Haredim,* p. 47.

21. BT, Haggigah 5b.

22. Genesis 4:16, quoted in Daniel Frisch, *Kedusha U'tzinut* [Holiness and Modesty] (Jerusalem, 1988), p. 50b.

23. See chapter 2.

24. Claude Lévi-Strauss, *Tristes Tropiques,* trans. John and Doreen Weightman (New York: Washington Square Press, 1973 [1955]), p. 255.

25. The words come from Jane Gould, "The Virtues of Virtue," *New York Times Magazine,* January 27, 1991, p. 14; the attitude is pure Breindel.

26. Yisrael Eichler, "An Open Eye," in *Ha-Machaneh Ha-Haredi,* May 3, 1990, p. 3; Psalms 40:5.

27. Lévi-Strauss, *Triste Tropiques,* p. 82.

Chapter 22. Scribal Apotheosis

1. Claude Lévi-Strauss, *Tristes Tropiques,* trans. John and Doreen Weightman (New York: Washington Square Press, 1973 [1955]), p. 33.

2. Ibid., p. 440.

3. Ibid., p. 32.

4. Ibid., p. 159.

5. Numbers 23:9.

6. Peter L. Berger, Brigitte Berger, and Hansfried Kellner, *The Homeless Mind: Modernization and Consciousness* (New York: Random House, 1973), p. 165.

7. Lévi-Strauss, p. 10; p. 9.

8. Michael M. J. Fischer, "Ethnicity and the Arts of Memory," in *Writing Culture,* ed. James Clifford and George E. Marcus (Berkeley: University of California Press, 1986), p. 230. See also Michel Serres, *L'Interférence* (Paris: Editions de Minuit, 1972), p. 172 et passim.

Epilogue: Ethnographic Afterwords

1. Claude Lévi-Strauss, *Tristes Tropiques*, trans. John and Doreen Weightman (New York: Washington Square Press, 1973 [1955]), pp. 375–376.
2. James Clifford and George Marcus, eds., *Writing Culture* (Berkeley: University of California Press, 1986), p. 2.
3. James Clifford, *The Predicament of Culture* (Cambridge: Harvard University Press, 1988), p. 121.
4. Clifford Geertz, *The Interpretation of Cultures* (New York: Basic Books, 1973), p. 357.
5. James Clifford, "On Ethnographic Allegory," in *Writing Culture*, p. 99.
6. Ibid., p. 116.
7. Lévi-Strauss, *Tristes Tropiques*, p. 50.
8. Ruth Benedict, *Patterns of Culture* (New York: Houghton Mifflin, 1934 [Mentor, 1946]), p. 42.
9. Eric R. Wolf, *Anthropology* (Englewood Cliffs, N.J.: Prentice-Hall, 1964).
10. Margaret Mead, "How an Anthropologist Writes," introduction to *Male and Female: A Study of Sexes in a Changing World* (New York: Morrow, 1949).

Afterword

1. "Goyim" is Hebrew for "nations," but in connotation has come to be designated those who are not Jews.

Index